V&R

Forschungen zur Religion und Literatur
des Alten und Neuen Testaments

Edited by
Ismo Dunderberg, Jan Christian Gertz,
Hermut Löhr and Joachim Schaper

Volume 276

Writing a Commentary on Leviticus

Hermeneutics—Methodology—Themes

Edited by
Christian A. Eberhart and Thomas Hieke

Vandenhoeck & Ruprecht

Bibliographic information published by the Deutsche Nationalbibliothek:
The Deutsche Nationalbibliothek lists this publication in the Deutsche Nationalbibliografie;
detailed bibliographic data available online: http://dnb.de.

Typesetting by textformart, Göttingen
Printed and bound by ⊕ Hubert & Co GmbH & Co. KG, Göttingen
Printed in the EU

Vandenhoeck & Ruprecht Verlage | www.vandenhoeck-ruprecht-verlage.com

ISSN 2198-1183
ISBN 978-3-525-53471-7

IN MEMORIAM

Hermine Eberhart, January 27, 1935 – October 05, 2018

Hans-Winfried Jüngling SJ, July 12, 1938 – October 04, 2018

Contents

Preface

This volume features presentations delivered at annual conferences of the Society of Biblical Literature. In 2014 and 2015, they were offered for the "Sacrifice, Cult, and Atonement" section, which existed between 2007 and 2015; its objective was the study of the practices, interpretations, and reception history of sacrifice and cult in early Judaism, Christianity, and their larger cultural contexts (ancient Near East and Greco-Roman antiquity). This program unit offered panels under the title "Writing a Commentary on Leviticus" that were intended to provide scholars working on such commentary volumes with a forum of scholarly discussion and exchange. The panel series was proposed by Thomas Hieke, who was then working on a Leviticus commentary for the academic series *Herders Theologischer Kommentar zum Alten Testament* (HThKAT, published by Herder in 2014). It was welcome and adopted by Christian A. Eberhart, founder and former chair of the "Sacrifice, Cult, and Atonement" section. The third and final panel was housed in the "Ritual in the Biblical World" section at the annual conference of the Society of Biblical Literature in 2016.

The present volume makes the presentations by these scholars, and with them an important segment of the work of the "Sacrifice, Cult, and Atonement" section, available to a wider academic audience. It is thus a sequel to the volumes *Ritual and Metaphor: Sacrifice in the Bible* (SBLRBS 68; Atlanta: Society of Biblical Literature, 2011), edited by Christian A. Eberhart, and *Sacrifice, Cult, and Atonement in Early Judaism and Christianity: Constituents and Critique* (SBLRBS 85; Atlanta: SBL Press, 2017), edited by Henrietta L. Wiley and Christian A. Eberhart.

We wish to thank Nicole Duran, Steve Finlan, Bill Gilders, Jason Tatlock, and Henrietta L. Wiley, the members of the steering committee of the "Sacrifice, Cult, and Atonement" section, for their ongoing collaboration. They have pursued the themes of this program section with scholarly rigor and professional engagement for almost a decade. We are also grateful to Ada Taggar-Cohen and Jason Lamoreaux, the chairs of the "Ritual in the Biblical World" section, for hosting the final panel of our project, thus allowing us to complete the three-year cycle. We would also like to express our deep gratitude to all of the scholars who enthusiastically accepted our invitation. They shared their research on Leviticus first through presentations, then in writing, and finally by submitting further samples of their previously published scholarship that were considered to enrich this volume. Thus, some of the contributions are revised or translated versions of essays that were printed roughly within the last decade (Watts, "Unperformed Rituals"; Eberhart, "Sacrifice"; Meshel, "Form and Function"; Hieke, "Prohibition"; Wright, "Law and Creation"). The place of the original publication is indicated at the beginning of each contribution. We owe special thanks to all publishers for granting permission to reuse and update this material.

We are, moreover, very thankful to Elisabeth Hernitscheck of Vandenhoeck & Ruprecht (Göttingen) for her continued interest in the topic of this collection of essays and the pleasant cooperation, and to the editorial board of *Forschungen zur Religion und Literatur des Alten und Neuen Testaments* (FRLANT) for adopting the present volume into their series. We also gratefully acknowledge the competent assistance of Andrea Klug (Johannes Gutenberg-Universität Mainz) who prepared the manuscript for publication and of Clint Boyd (University of Houston), Assistant to Christian A. Eberhart, who helped with the task of proof reading.

Christian A. Eberhart (Houston, USA)
Thomas Hieke (Mainz, Germany)

Christian A. Eberhart/Thomas Hieke

Introduction

Writing a Commentary on Leviticus

Writing a commentary on a biblical book is not limited to the scholar's study and desk. Hence, several experts in the field of Hebrew Bible currently writing a larger commentary on the book of Leviticus followed the invitation of Christian A. Eberhart (University of Houston) and Thomas Hieke (Johannes Gutenberg-Universität Mainz) to meet between 2014 and 2016 at annual conferences of the Society of Biblical Literature. They shared their experiences, discussed a variety of hermeneutical and methodological approaches, probed critical questions, and presented their ideas about particular themes and issues in the third book of the Torah. The results of the three consultative panels had a significant impact on the production of the commentaries.

These discussions and insights, however, are also worth sharing with the broader scholarly community, which is what this volume does. It starts with essays reflecting on the process of writing a Leviticus commentary, including boosts and obstacles, while suggesting innovative insights on particular problems of the book. Further articles identify certain themes of Leviticus, especially sacrifices and rituals ("the cult"), the notion of unintentional and deliberate sins and purity/impurity ("the bad") and how to eliminate them, and the relationship to the sphere of God ("the holy"). The various stances taken here demonstrate three important aspects: (1) commenting on a biblical book highly depends on the perspective that a scholar takes; (2) different commentaries on the same biblical text come to different conclusions relative to their specific methodological and hermeneutical approaches; (3) it is of utmost importance to reflect on these perspectives and approaches and make them transparent. These issues are innate in the subject matter; in the end the variety of approaches bears witness to the complexity, intricacy, and richness of the biblical text. This volume, therefore, offers a fascinating inside view into the studies and onto the desks of several prolific biblical experts who share their reflections and concepts about their commentaries on Leviticus with an interested audience.

The volume opens with a general reflection by Thomas Hieke: He demonstrates that writing a commentary on a biblical book is a research achievement. Society usually associates "research" with other activities (expensive experiments in laboratories etc.). In search for an official definition of "research," Hieke points to the *Frascati Manual* of the Organisation for Economic Co-operation and Development (OECD). In his essay, he argues that writing a commentary on a biblical book increases the stock of knowledge, devises new applications of available knowledge, and is novel, creative, uncertain, systematic, transferable and/or reproducible. Hence, the scholarly endeavor of commenting on a biblical book meets the OECD definition of "research."

James W. Watts, in "Unperformed Rituals in an Unread Book," highlights the unusual challenge posed to commentators by the fact that many of Leviticus's ritual instructions have not been performed for almost 2,000 years and that Christians, at least, tend not to read it at all. Since commentary is supposed to explain the meaning of the text, he asks: What is the significance of an unperformed ritual? What is the meaning of an unread text? His reflections, excerpted and expanded from the Introduction to his commentary, explore the nature of textual rhetoric, of ritual rhetoric, of theological symbolism, and of priestly interpretive authority. He concludes that Leviticus's status as scripture pushes commentators to consider the whole range of the text's uses, not just as an authoritative text but also as a performative text and as religious icon.

The paper "Commentary as Ethnography" by William K. Gilders focuses on the role played in his forthcoming commentary on Leviticus by anthropology and ritual theory, which Gilders believes to be the most important element in that work. In drawing on the work of anthropologists, he takes the risk of characterizing the commentary as a work of ethnography in which he acts as a "professional stranger" (the anthropologist M.H. Agar's designation for the ethnographer). This approach is exemplified through discussion of Leviticus 2, the basic legislation for the קרבן מנחה ("tribute offering"), in order to highlight the desire to disengage treatment of the offerings in Leviticus from the idea that "sacrifice" necessarily involves the killing of animal victims. Gilders explains how his commentary will constitute an ethnography of the ways in which Aaronide priests represent and interpret Israelite cultural practices through the medium of the texts they composed and edited. Gilders intends for the commentary to do justice to what his ancient Israelite informants tell him and to provide a cultural translation for its presumed audience of twenty-first century readers. He sets out a multi-layered interpretation of the cultural data on the basis of the theoretical models he finds most compelling and productive. Specifically, while he largely avoids offering symbolic-communicative explanations of ritual performances, Gilders explicates the indexical force of such practices in terms of Peircian semiotics. His goal is to strike a balance between providing sufficient interpretation and providing too much.

In her contribution "The Role of Second Temple Texts in a Commentary on Leviticus," Hannah K. Harrington takes a Second Temple perspective to Leviticus. She asks how the book was read by Second Temple priests and sages. She finds special value among these sources for: 1) determining the state of the text of Leviticus; 2) clarifying ambiguity in Leviticus; and 3) fixing the chronological development of specific Levitical traditions while bringing into relief Second Temple issues. Her contribution focuses on Ezra-Nehemiah and the Dead Sea Scrolls. Ezra-Nehemiah may have been redacted around the same time as the *textus receptus* of Leviticus and thus the data and issues of both texts are relevant to each other. The earliest witnesses to the actual text of Leviticus, the Dead Sea Scrolls, also supply important textual variants. They also disclose issues in interpretation. Harrington demonstrates how the Scrolls bring into relief ambiguity in the text of Leviticus and provide clarity for complex laws (e.g. purity regulations). Harrington urges commentators to grapple with the development of various Levitical traditions throughout the Second Temple period. With four examples, she illustrates the necessity of examining single traditions in light of Second Temple literature: a) tithing; b) holy days; c) the resident alien; and d) intermarriage.

The title "Writing on Leviticus for the HThKAT Series: Some Key Issues on Sacrificial Rituals" conveys that Thomas Hieke reflects on central problems that emerged during his work on the Leviticus commentary for the series "Herders Theologischer Kommentar zum Alten Testament" (HThKAT). (1) Especially the first chapters of Leviticus use a very stereotypical or standardized language. The sacrifices and the various components of the respective rituals are tagged with a certain technical language and terminology. Hence, he elaborated a glossary explaining this general vocabulary and placed it after the introduction and before the commentary proper. (2) The introductory formulas (e.g., Lev 1:1–2; 4:1; 6:1; 8:1 etc.) are theologically crucial for the way the text wants to be understood: The rituals are—according to the biblical text—not invented by humans but revealed by God. (3) The meaning of the hand-leaning rite (e.g., Lev 1:4) is still a disputed issue. The contribution and the commentary present a new solution for interpreting this necessary part of the ritual. (4) Finally, the essay discusses problems of the nomenclature of the sacrifices, especially the so-called "sin offering".

In his contribution "Sacrifice? Holy Smokes! Reflections on Cult Terminology for Understanding Sacrifice in the Hebrew Bible," Christian A. Eberhart explores interpretive aspects of sacrificial rituals that are manifest in both Hebrew and Greek technical terms for sacrifices and selected ritual aspects or components. The individual profile and common implications of this terminology offer insights into perceptions of early communities, tradents, and translators of the texts, who understood sacrifices as dynamic processes of approaching God and as tokens of reverence and reconciliation. Eberhart concludes that this terminology conveys the importance of the burning rite as a ritual component; such a methodological approach allows the incorporation of both animal sacrifices and sacrifices from vegetal substances into modern scholarly theorizing. This understanding is corroborated by a brief investigation of rituals that do not count as sacrifices in the Hebrew Bible.

Naphtali S. Meshel investigates "The Form and Function of a Biblical Blood Ritual." He scrutinizes the consensus in current exegetical research that Levitical law never requires blood to be tossed upon the upper surface of the altar. He posits that this conception has reinforced—and has been reinforced by—an understanding that YHWH is never to be offered blood. He argues that, according to several priestly texts, the blood of many sacrifices, including wellbeing, whole-burnt and reparation offerings, is to be tossed upon the upper surface of the altar. Based on these observations, the claim that the ritual indicates that YHWH, like the Israelites, refrains from the consumption of blood, is being reassessed.

In his essay "Purification Offerings and Paradoxical Pollution of the Holy," Roy E. Gane answers objections to his proposal regarding a challenging question that any serious commentator on Leviticus must face: How do physical ritual impurities (*ṭumʾôt*) and sins (*ḥaṭṭāʾôt*) pollute the sanctuary so that they must be purged from there on the Day of Atonement (Lev 16:16, 19)? In his book *Cult and Character* (2005), Gane concluded that these evils affect the sanctuary through purification offerings during the course of the year, as indicated by Leviticus 6:20–21. Here blood of a most holy purification offering that spatters on a garment must be washed off in a holy place because it paradoxically carries some pollution, and a vessel in which purification offering flesh is boiled must be broken or scoured and rinsed in water for the same reason. The pollution comes from the offerer when the sacrifice removes the evil from that person. So when a priest applies some of the blood to part of the sanctuary, the sanctuary receives the pollution. Christophe Nihan has countered Gane's interpretation in part of his previously published essay titled "The Templization of Israel in Leviticus: Some Remarks on Blood Disposal and *Kipper* in Leviticus." Nihan finds the idea that purification offerings transfer pollution from offerers to the sanctuary to be problematic because ancient Near Eastern people were afraid of defiling sacred places, and he rejects the inference from Leviticus 6:20–21 that most holy purification offerings carry pollution, preferring the view that verse 20 requires the washing of priestly vestments to remove contagious holiness. In the present essay, Gane responds to these and other objections through exegetical analysis of the relevant biblical passages, reference to ancient Near Eastern texts, and clarification of his interpretation. It is especially significant that the rules in Leviticus 6:20–21 apply only to the purification offering, which removes sins (Lev 4:1–5:13) and physical impurities (e.g., 12:6–8).

Scholarship on the Priestly system of pollution and purification tends to view the diverse sources of ritual pollution as if they were located on a one-dimensional scale, from most severe to least severe—to some extent under the influence of rabbinic literature. With the title "Some New Questions in the Fundamental Science of P," Naphtali S. Meshel's second contribution to this volume offers an alternative model in which each impurity comprises several factors—including duration (how long the impurity lasts), tenacity (how difficult it is to eliminate the impurity), and contagion (how easily it is transmitted from one object to another). There is not always a direct correlation between the various factors, as one type of pollution may last a long time without being highly contagious, and another may be highly contagious but of relatively short duration. This alternative, multidimensional model leads to several new questions, for example: If one becomes defiled by one type of impurity, then later by another, are the waiting periods counted as overlapping periods of time or successive periods of time (does "time served" count)? Does it matter if the impurities are of the same type (e.g., contact with two different corpses) or of different types (e.g., menstruation and contact with a corpse)? While P does not explicitly address these questions, several post-Biblical sources discuss them explicitly, suggesting that a full understanding of the Priestly ritual system entails careful consideration of these scenarios—some of which are outlandish, but others quite commonplace.

In "Constructing Contagion on Yom Kippur: The Scapegoat as *Ḥaṭṭāʾt*," Nicole J. Ruane considers how the writer of Leviticus 16 understood the two goats of the Yom Kippur rites to act together as a single *ḥaṭṭāʾt* offering (16:5). Ruane argues that although this ritual complex with the two goats is quite different from the paradigmatic *ḥaṭṭāʾt* rites in Leviticus 4–5, it nonetheless must be understood as a *ḥaṭṭāʾt* offering. Moreover, taking this designation of the two goats as a *ḥaṭṭāʾt* seriously helps to articulate the fundamental features of all *ḥaṭṭāʾt* rites, namely, the separation of the offering into two distinct parts, one of which becomes portrayed as harmful or unclean, and the elimination of that negative part.

The third essay by Thomas Hieke reflects on "Participation and Abstraction in the Yom Kippur Ritual according to Leviticus 16." Yom Kippur, the Day of Atonement, is widely observed as a Holy Day among Jewish people all over the world. Although it goes back to the description of the ritual in Leviticus 16, the actual celebration of the day differs widely from the biblical text. A long and intensive process of abstraction took place over centuries. The issue of abstraction lies at the roots of the ritual itself; abstraction already occurred at the time when the ritual was actually carried out at the Second Temple in Jerusalem (before 70 C.E.). Yet the inner logic and concern of Yom Kippur was central for the composers of the book of Leviticus and the Torah: They placed the description within the center of the Torah. Hieke demonstrates that the central position of Leviticus 16 (the prescription for the Day of Atonement) is also justified and corroborated by content-related aspects. In Leviticus 16, *all* groups within the people of Israel participate (the High Priest, the priests, the Israelites), *all* sorts of sins and impurities are eliminated, and the ritual itself shows the *highest degree* of abstraction (a minimal amount of blood in an empty room suffices for the efficacy of the ritual). Methodologically, an exegetical commentary has to explore the inner logics of the text and to detect its semantic concepts. In this sense, Leviticus 16 represents a comprehensive reset of cultic and social relationships; the concept includes purification as well as reconciliation (or atonement), in a collective and individual way as well. By means of abstraction, the ritual itself turns into a metaphor, even at the time when it actually still took place in Jerusalem. Jews all over the diaspora abstained from food consumption and thus participated spiritually in the ritual of the Holy Day. These concepts constitute the basis and starting point for multiple transformations and further abstractions as well as metaphorical charging in Judaism (the liturgy in the synagogue, fasting, rest from working) and Christianity (the christological application in Rom 3:25: Christ as *hilasterion*—expiation or place of atonement, etc.).

The second paper by William K. Gilders has the title "Is There an Incense Altar in This Ritual? A Question of Ritual-Textual Interpretive Community." Taking a theoretical start from the work of Stanley Fish on the authority of interpretive communities (presented in his influential 1980 book, *Is There a Text in This Class?*), Gilders explores how interpreters determine that the ritual complex for the "Day of Atonement" set out in Leviticus 16 includes, or does not include, the application of blood to a golden incense altar inside the tent-shrine. The importance of interpretive assumptions about the incense altar and the blood rituals it receives are the focus of his paper. He investigates the activity of two significant ritual-textual interpretive communities that engage with Leviticus 16 and the ritual complex it presents: those who adopt a largely holistic and synthesizing approach to the text and those who attend to what David Carr calls the "fractures" in the textual corpus. Gilders highlights the crucial role played by Exodus 30:10 for interpretive decisions to see an incense altar and blood rites directed at that altar in Leviticus 16. His paper concludes that the answer to its titular question is: It depends on whom you ask!

Commenting on a biblical book sometimes requires the suggestion of new solutions to much disputed problems. During his work on Leviticus 18 and 20, Thomas Hieke identified "the Molech" as a *crux interpretum* and proposed a new understanding of the term *la-molech* (לַמֹּלֶךְ, 18:21 and 20:1–5). He presented the results in an article in the journal *Die Welt des Orients* and in his HThKAT commentary, all of which were written in German. Hence the essay "The Prohibition of Transferring an Offspring to 'the Molech:' No Child Sacrifice in Leviticus 18 and 20" presents the results for the first time in English and is an updated version of these publications. After a brief overview of the pertinent terminology, the article summarizes usual interpretations: *la-molech* as a term for a Canaanite deity; a term for a sacrifice; a dedication rite for children. The context of Leviticus 18 and 20, however, does not fit these interpretations. Hieke therefore argues that the phrase "you shall not give any of your offspring to pass them over to Molech" may be read as a cipher or code. He understands the consonants *l-m-l-k* as a reference to pre-exilic stamp seals in Judaea containing the words "for the king;" the Septuagint translation ἄρχοντι of Leviticus 18:21 points in the same direction. The reality behind the phrase is the priestly prohibition for the Jewish community to hand over any of their children to serve in the Persian army or the households of the Persian authorities. The children given as servants to foreigners were lost for the Jewish cult community. However, the priests could not express their opposition to this kind of collaboration with the Persian authorities directly without raising suspicion; hence, they used the well-known sequence of consonants *lmlk*. This interpretation fits both the context of Leviticus 18 and 20, which features family laws, and the socio-historical reality of Jewish life under Persian domination.

In his essay "Law and Creation in the Priestly-Holiness Writings of the Pentateuch," David P. Wright argues that a chief goal of the Priestly-Holiness (PH) corpus of the Pentateuch is to explain Yahweh's election of Israel and associated obligations of cultic practice. Wright looks specifically at PH's portrayal of the development of various cultic practices and phenomena (sacrifice, use of the divine name, the calendar, purity and holiness practices, the divine glory [*kavod*]), as well as PH's portrayal of the genealogical evolution of Israel and its use of creation language in narrative. The PH corpus tells a story in which the culmination of creation, as described in Gen 1:1–2:4, is the establishment of the nation Israel with accompanying obligations of cultic service. This set the stage for then describing how the nation acquired its land.

Some texts in Leviticus and in many other biblical books explicitly support genocide, indiscriminate capital punishment, patriarchy, and slavery. In "Drawing Lines: A Suggestion for Addressing the Moral Problem of Reproducing Immoral Biblical Texts in Commentaries and Bibles," James W. Watts observes that these verses pose a moral challenge for commentators and Bible publishers because they conflict with the legal and ethical teachings of Jewish and Christian traditions, and also with the laws of modern nations. By publishing Bibles and commentaries that reproduce these texts, translators and commentators continue to promulgate a document that claims divine endorsement for immoral and illegal behavior. Though long-standing traditions of *halakhah*, preaching, canon law and commentary have restrained the social force of these texts, the iconic status of biblical texts has often overridden interpretive traditions. These restraints have become easier to ignore as revolutions in printing and, now, digitization have made biblical texts ever more accessible. Anyone can cite a verse of Leviticus with the accurate preamble, "the Bible says," and can do so to justify harming other people. Interpretations of biblical texts, their social contexts, and their reception history remain essential to countering malevolent uses of the Bible, but they are not enough. Watts suggests that commentaries and mass-market Bible translations should strike through immoral normative texts to indicate typographically that Jewish and Christian traditions have long-standing objections to reading them as representing the divine will.

Thomas Hieke

Writing a Commentary as a Research Achievement

1 Introduction[1]

Writing a commentary on a book of the Old or New Testament is generally met with a certain amount of respect, especially, if the *magnum opus* is quite substantial. Nevertheless, one quickly encounters some difficulties if the author of such a commentary considers his work to be "research." This term is usually associated with other activities, undertaken in the field of natural or life sciences, carried out in laboratories, involving expensive equipment and high effort experiments. Society unfailingly acknowledges that these activities are highly relevant and important. An indicator for that esteem are the high sums of money that state and society invest in these research activities. Quite naturally, the public applies to them the term "research" without hesitation. What "research" means in the first place is however very rarely reflected upon. The following considerations will present a possible definition of "research," and then explore three aspects in which the project of writing a biblical commentary meets this very definition.

2 The Definition of "Research" According to the *Frascati Manual* of the OECD

Since 1963, the Organisation for Economic Co-operation and Development (OECD) has framed internationally acknowledged standards for "research and experimental development statistics" (R&D) in the so called *Frascati Manual.*[2] The Manual is named after the place of the first meeting in Villa Falconieri in Frascati in 1963. It was meant to create the basis for a common language of "research and experimental development" and its outcomes. Therefore, it is instructive how the *Frascati Manual* in its current edition of 2015 defines "research." The Manual uses the acronym "R&D" for "research and experimental development." The short definition in article 1.32 on page 28 reads:

---

1 I would like to thank Franziska Rauh for the English translation of this contribution.

2 OECD (2015), *Frascati Manual 2015: Guidelines for Collecting and Reporting Data on Research and Experimental Development, The Measurement of Scientific, Technological and Innovation Activities*, OECD Publishing, Paris. DOI: http://dx.doi.org/10.1787/9789264239012-en.

> R&D comprise creative and systematic work undertaken in order to increase the stock of knowledge—including knowledge of humankind, culture and society—and to devise new applications of available knowledge.

The list of criteria for calling an activity "research" is of further interest. Article 1.33 states:

> A set of common features identifies R&D activities that aim to achieve either specific or general objectives, even if these are carried out by different performers. For an activity to be an R&D activity, it must satisfy five core criteria. The activity must be: novel, creative, uncertain, systematic, transferable and/or reproducible.

Strikingly, this definition is much broader than the common notion of "research." Is it possible to demonstrate that writing a commentary on a biblical book meets the criteria of this definition?

3 "Systematic, transferable and/or reproducible"— Method-driven and Intersubjective

Writing a commentary on a biblical text is not an adventurous expedition, where you trust your luck and sail off. One does not simply start reading and present some agreeable findings afterwards, associatively grasped, and imaginatively ordered. Nor is writing a commentary intended to bend the text commented on into the shape of any institution's doctrine or mission, not even that of a church or Christian community.

Writing a commentary in accordance with the standards of present-day academic theology is "systematic" as well as "transferable and/or reproducible." As a matter of course, "systematic" does not refer in any way to a dominance of 'Systematic Theology,' but to the core value of scientific work: the application of approved and established, but also innovative methods still to be validated, and the reflection upon these methods' mode of operation.

Writing a commentary on a biblical text demands a clear matrix of methodical textual analysis and an author's reflection upon it. Thus, 'commenting' does not mean 'writing down what comes to your mind,' but 'adopting a thought-out and transparent approach (methodology)' and 'presenting the outcomes.' In an exegetical article on a single verse, a small paragraph (pericope), or a specific subject, the application of the methods can be demonstrated step by step, so that conclusions are reached in an argumentative way. In the course of commenting, this part of the working process runs in the background and is explicitly not included in the commentary. Owing to manageability, space is naturally limited, with the result that the commentary displays the outcomes of proceeding methodically in the end, but not the full argument behind them. Hence, commentaries are often flanked by various single studies on related issues, which show the methodical way towards and the argumentative basis of the outcomes presented in the commentary.[3]

The commentary per se already is a 'publication,' and the flanking single studies support the intersubjective transparency of its findings. Insofar, this procedure meets another core requirement of scientific nature: intersubjectivity. The commentary is intended to not only make the biblical text comprehensible to others; it is also supposed to be plausible in its own line of reasoning. It does not draw its authority from an external institution in such a way that a church authority, e.g. a bishop, or a professor of theology as an unchallenged expert, decrees, as it were, how to understand a certain verse of the Bible. Instead, the commentary is a reading suggestion, developed from scientific methods and criteria, and presented for discussion via publication. As a rule, a scientific discourse precedes the publication. This discourse works on two levels: On the one hand, an author writing a commentary does not only apply a skillful selection of methods, but also considers the suggestions of earlier secondary literature and consequently deals with the reading suggestions of previous researchers. On the other hand, the author presents partial results and puts them up to discussion in the written form of individual publications or the oral form of talks ('papers') at conferences. All these intersubjective processes find their way into the commentary.

Another feature of a method-driven approach is that its methods are "transferable" on various objects of research and the outcomes are "reproducible." A method of textual analysis that cannot be applied to more than one text is none—hence, it is possible (and common practice) that the method applied by one person in commenting on one biblical text is applied in the same way by another person to another text. If new results are achieved this way, the method starts proving itself. The reproducibility of a commentary is verified if someone applies the given method (usually set forth in the foreword or an individual publication) to the same biblical text—and reaches similar, if not the same insights that are presented in the commentary. That is how research results are confirmed. This does not mean in turn that no research was done if this process does not lead to success. But it highlights that the method or its application needs to be improved in some way or another—which is not unusual, but even productive in terms of research.

4 "Creative, novel, uncertain"—Relating Data Reasonably

"Research," the *Frascati Manual* of the OECD continues, is "creative," "novel," "uncertain." Again, these criteria are applicable to commenting on biblical texts. The "uncertainty" of research obviously does not refer to the operation of nuclear

3 The essays gathered in this collection demonstrate this procedure vividly.

research reactors or microbiological laboratories—hopefully, high safety standards apply to these facilities. Rather, "uncertainty" means that, at the beginning of a research process, the outcomes are not certain yet. If somebody comments on a biblical passage and, before his/her first reading of the text, already knows what the result in the commentary will be, then his/her work is unscientific and boring. This is what happens in a bad sermon on a Sunday: After a few sentences, the sermon repeats the same old statements and well-known, hollow phrases every time, regardless of the previous scripture readings. By contrast, whoever comments on a biblical text must be creative and innovative—instead of summing up what was said so far. However, it is not necessary either to desperately state something completely different, just to make one's own work stand out against the mainstream of secondary literature.

Research in STEM (science, technology, engineering, and mathematics) areas is typically based on the collection of billions of data via sophisticated methods of measurement and corresponding technical equipment—and relating them rationally. Insight grows if the amount of data increases or if an innovative idea emerges to interpret these data: New models or theories come to the fore and in turn prove themselves, if they are in the same way able to explain fresh data collected afterwards—if not, the theory must be improved. At this point, commenting on biblical texts starts from a slightly different position, as the database of the object of research seems to have remained the same for thousands of years, at least at first glance. But on closer inspection, a different picture emerges: Indeed, the object of research is not only the stock of the Hebrew and Greek texts which have become biblical, and which are called the Old and New Testament from a Christian point of view. Rather, it includes the texts' environment, which archaeological and historical studies on the Ancient Near East, Ancient Egypt, and the Graeco-Roman world try to illuminate. In addition, scholars have to consider a huge variety of texts from the area in which the biblical texts emerged. Here as well, an abundance of data waits to be analyzed, which occasionally grows. A much-referenced example is the discovery of the Dead Sea Scrolls. The writings found in 1947 and subsequent years cast new light on the body of texts of the Bible and its cultural environment, which one naturally has to take into account when commenting on the biblical books as contemporaries of these texts. Researchers still have not fully caught up with these findings. Furthermore, it is well known that many museums and collections house an abundance of text material from the Ancient Near East, Egypt, and the Graeco-Roman world that has not been edited yet. Theoretically, this material could bring to light insights that are able to broaden, or even punctually change the present view on the history of Israel and the culture that shaped the biblical texts.

5 "Increase the stock of knowledge, devise new applications of available knowledge"—New Insights and Applications

The above already shows that many possibilities remain for scientific research on the Bible and its environment "to increase the stock of knowledge." But "knowledge" does not only include the stock of "facts," because "knowledge" is more than an assemblage of verified facts. "Knowing" includes the ability to relate various facts or data, to connect them and thus create new realizations and applications. All of this happens when a biblical text is commented on. In this process, the uniqueness of the subject has to be considered: Even as an ancient text, the Bible is not dead matter, the constituents and structure of which could be reasoned out once and for all after a certain time of research. Nor must the research of a biblical text confine itself to probable assertions concerning its origin and the intentions of the historical authors. A text is no fossil or mountain crystal, even if biblical stories might sometimes appear as old or as beautiful and shimmering. A text provides various potential meanings that only emerge in an active reading process. Whoever reads a text already interprets the data stored in it and creates a new complex of meaning influenced by the time and the circumstances of the recipient. This influence can be of a negative kind, if, say, the historical and cultural environment of the readers, for example our current modern context, fundamentally differs from the circumstances at the time of the text's origin. This is why the reading process as a process of 'making sense' in the reception of a text is subject to various changing parameters, whereas the underlying text is more or less a constant. What is generally true for all texts is particularly important for biblical texts. The Bible is an extraordinary subject in several ways: In the whole history of its reception, people reading it refer to this ancient text as to a message that is to be of concern for them here and now. These readers of the Bible gather in institutions like church and synagogue communities, or they might be individuals who read the Bible as a matter of faith or for other reasons, e.g. in ways of artistic engagement. At least two religions (Judaism and Christianity) regard the Bible (in different manifestations) a holy and normative text. The Bible was and is considered not only a historical document, but also a text of an immediate concern that has to be dealt with (even if this means refusing it).

Commenting on a biblical text must reckon with these parameters, the constant and the changing ones. Therefore, this activity is never finished, but has to be tackled time and time again. New bridges have to be built constantly to reach the developing society, culture and religion anew, in order to unlock the potential of meaning of the biblical text to a changing readership. This is even more important if communities of believers in Judaism and Christianity adhere to the conviction that these texts are not only their religious, but also their cultural and ethical basis. If one does not accompany the reading process of these basic texts by a method-driven, reflective, intersubjective, and therefore scientific process, then the floodgates are open to ideological abuse and political instrumentalization of these texts and their religious authority. The history of Christianity provides many pertinent examples, while the present time witnesses analogous developments in terms of Christian fundamentalism abusing the Bible for (in fact) political aims or Islamism ideologizing the Quran for a military agenda.

Hence, commenting on biblical texts also meets the requirement "to devise new applications of available knowledge:" It shows how a present-day faith community can gain valuable impetus for its religious life and for the shaping of society and culture out of the old, holy texts—without falling into backward-looking ideologization.

6 Conclusion

Writing a commentary on a biblical text is, according to modern academic standards as manifest in the OECD definitions, a "research activity." This statement is valid at least in principle—the ongoing endeavor of research can differ, which is true not only for religious studies and has more to do with general human limitations. With reference to the definitions provided above, I shall now formulate as a thesis what a commentary on a biblical text ought to be and often is in terms of a research activity:

> Commenting on a biblical text is a creative and systematic, therefore method-driven and intersubjectively comprehensible undertaking that is intended to increase the stock of knowledge about the research object "biblical text," its historical and cultural environment, as well as its impact and current possibilities of understanding. On this basis, it results in innovative suggestions of reading and interpreting these texts and proposes new perspectives of how they shape today's life in religion and society.

Bibliography

OECD (2015), *Frascati Manual 2015: Guidelines for Collecting and Reporting Data on Research and Experimental Development, The Measurement of Scientific, Technological and Innovation Activities, OECD Publishing*, Paris. DOI: http://dx.doi.org/10.1787/9789264239012-en.

James W. Watts

Unperformed Rituals in an Unread Book

I was invited to address the Sacrifice, Cult and Atonement Section of the Society of Biblical Literature meeting in San Diego in 2014 on a panel about "Writing a Commentary on Leviticus: Reflections on Methodology and Sacrificial Rituals." Just the year before, I had published the first volume of my HCOT commentary on Leviticus.[1] The panel organizers asked me (1) to outline my distinct methodology or approach in writing the commentary and (2) to reflect on sacrificial rituals in the book of Leviticus. My paper reproduced parts of the Introduction to my commentary. It appears below with only slight supplementations by kind permission of Peeters Publishers.

1 My Approach to Writing a Commentary on Leviticus

My commentary begins with two questions that have haunted me since I began writing it: What is the significance of an unperformed ritual? What is the meaning of an unread text?

The most basic purpose of commentary is to explain the meaning of a text and the significance of its contents. One of the purposes of the HCOT commentary series is also to describe the history of the text's interpretation, that is, its meaning over time. In a commentary on the book of Leviticus, however, these three goals frequently lead in different directions.

Synagogues since antiquity have read the entire Torah through over the course of one year, or sometimes three years. The sounds of the words of Leviticus and the images they evoke have played a central role in Jewish ritual. In traditional Jewish education, children first learn to read Hebrew by reading Leviticus. The offerings mandated by Leviticus, however, have fallen into abeyance since the destruction of the Jerusalem Temple in 70CE. For the ancient rabbis and their successors, studying Torah along with prayer and acts of charity took the place of offerings that are no longer possible. In Jewish synagogues, the instructions for offerings get read, but do not get performed as written.[2]

---

1 J.W. Watts, *Leviticus 1–10* (HCOT; Leuven: Peeters, 2013).

2 See the summary in Watts, *Leviticus 1–10*, 75–7, 80–2. For more details and examples, see G. Bodendorfer, "Der Horizont einer Exegese des Buches Levitikus in den rabbinischen Midraschim," in H.-J. Fabry/H.-W. Jüngling (ed.), *Levitikus als Buch* (Berlin: Philo, 1999) 343–71;

Christians, by contrast, do not read Leviticus very often, if at all. Churches do not usually include verses from Leviticus in the lectionary readings for public worship, except to read portions of chap. 19 as preface to the love commandment in 19:18 and to ground some major holy days in the festival calendar of chap. 23.[3] They especially avoid the rules for offerings, having inveighed since antiquity against any practice of animal "sacrifice." One frequently hears of attempts to read the Bible through that foundered on the book of Leviticus, or skipped it altogether. Yet key terms and ideas from the book, such as sacrifice, atonement, sin, guilt, priesthood, purity, holiness, love of neighbor, and Jubilee have played central roles in Christian theology and practice from antiquity to the present.[4]

Leviticus is also scripture for a third religious tradition. Samaritan ritual practices and polity differ in crucial respects from those of Jews and Christians.[5] The most famous difference is that Samaritans still perform the Passover sacrifice annually as the rules in Exodus 12 prescribe, though not the temple offerings of Leviticus 1–7. Unlike Jews and Christians, Samaritans continue to be led by a hereditary high priest claiming descent from Aaron, just as Leviticus, Exodus and Numbers mandate.

Despite these differences, all three religious traditions that revere Leviticus as scripture prohibit people from performing many of its ritual instructions. That has stimulated attempts to interpret their meaning in non-literal ways using midrash, typology, allegory, theology, and ideological critique.

I think that biblical commentary should focus on explaining a book's meaning as scripture, because it is its status as scripture that generates most of the interest in commentary in the first place. Now theological interpretation is the approach that most Christian commentators take for addressing questions of scripture.[6]

H.K. Harrington, "The Rabbinic Reception of Leviticus," in R. Rendtorff/R. Kugler (ed.), *The Book of Leviticus: Composition and Reception* (VTSup 93; Leiden: Brill, 2003) 383–402; Z.J. Braiterman, "Martin Buber and the Art of Ritual," in M. Zankl (ed.), *New Perspectives on Martin Buber* (Tübingen: Mohr Siebeck, 2006), 111–24.

3 See F. Just, "Lectionary Statistics" on the Roman Catholic *Lectionary for Mass* (2009), online at http://catholic-resources.org/Lectionary/Statistics.htm (accessed 12/21/2015).

4 See the summary in Watts, *Leviticus 1–10*, 77–80, 83–6. For more details and examples, see E. Clark, *Reading Renunciation: Asceticism and Scripture in Early Christianity* (Princeton: Princeton University Press, 1999), 208–22, 279–81; A. Firey, "The Letter of the Law: Carolingian Exegetes and the Old Testament," in J.D. McAuliffe (ed.), *With Reverence for the Word: Medieval Scriptural Exegesis in Judaism, Christianity, and Islam* (Oxford: Oxford University Press, 2003) 204–24.

5 For Samaritan beliefs and practices, see R.T. Anderson/T. Giles, *The Keepers: An Introduction to the History and Culture of the Samaritans* (Grand Rapids, MI: Baker, 2001), 117–34; for early Samaritan history, see G.N. Knoppers, *Jews and Samaritans: The Origins and History of Their Early Relations* (Oxford: Oxford University Press, 2013).

6 Most influential in recent decades has been the canonical approach of B.S. Childs, *Introduction to the Old Testament as Scripture* (Minneapolis: Fortress, 1979). M. Douglas abandoned her anthropological methods to adopt a theological approach also, in *Leviticus as Literature*

But Leviticus does very little explicit theology compared to many other biblical books, and even less compared to later summaries, *halakhot*, commentaries and harmonies. There is, of course, theology in the book. God appears as both a character and a subject of discourse. The book emphasizes the theological importance of crucial ideas represented by words such as קדש "holy," כפר "mitigate or atone," חטאת "sin, sin offering," אשם "guilt, guilt offering," טמא "pollution," אהב "love," etc. Leviticus does very little, however, to define these terms. It does not expound on their meaning or describe their relationship to one another.[7] Instead, it demands that Israel maintain the positive qualities and avoid or counteract the negative ones by observing its regulations. It asks its hearers and readers to interpret its teachings by their practices, rather than their words. Theological interpretation therefore runs against the grain of the book's plain meaning. Theology turns instructions for ritual, moral and legal practices into symbols of religious doctrines.

A rhetorical approach to Leviticus as a scripture can bridge the gap between the plain meaning of the Hebrew text and its various interpretations in subsequent traditions better than theology can. Rhetorical analysis asks "Who is trying to persuade whom of what with this text?"[8] The persuasive impact of a text depends on who is speaking, who is being addressed, and for what purpose. More accurately, it depends on who the listener or reader thinks is speaking. Similarly, persuasion depends on listeners' or readers' judgment about who is being addressed. They frequently decide that it is someone other than themselves. Many Christians view most of Leviticus as addressed to Jews rather than Christians.[9] Historians read ancient texts, including the Bible, as addressed to ancient audiences rather than themselves. These decisions determine how readers and listeners interpret the purpose of the text, why it has one message and not another, what effect it aims to have on its audience, and how real audiences actually respond. From such a rhetorical perspective on persuasion, the "meaning" of the text derives from its use in a particular relationship, and the text has no meaning apart from such a relationship. Its meaning necessarily changes whenever the parties to the relationship change.

The history of how a text has been used, however, will not explain why its authors wrote it this way. To explain the unique form and contents of a particular

(Oxford: Oxford University Press, 1999). Recent theological treatments of Leviticus have included E. Radner, *Leviticus* (Brazos Theological Commentary to the Bible; Grand Rapids: Brazos, 2008), and M. W. Elliott, *Engaging Leviticus: Reading Leviticus Theologically with its Past Interpreters* (Eugene: Cascade, 2012).

7 For more on this point, see W. K. Gilders, "Commentary as Ethnography," in this volume.

8 J. W. Watts, *Reading Law: the Rhetorical Shaping of the Pentateuch* (Sheffield: Sheffield Academic Press, 1999), 32–60.

9 As I have discovered by questioning many Christian students in my university classes over the years.

text, we must try to reconstruct what rhetorical relationship its authors intended for it. We need to determine who they were, whom they were trying to persuade, and of what, so as to figure out why they shaped the text in this way. Such work is necessarily speculative, and never definitive.[10] Nevertheless, because the text's rhetoric functions only in the context of a relationship between speaker/author and listener/reader, estimating their identities is essential and basic work in order to read any text as a communication between people and as persuasive rhetoric. Since biblical texts contain overt evidence of an intention to communicate and persuade, and since they are commonly read that way within the religious traditions that cherish them as scripture, rhetorical analysis proves very helpful for understanding both their original and later functions.

Finally, ancient authors shaped their works primarily for oral recitation by scribes and aural reception by everyone else.[11] They may also have included features noticeable only to sages who committed the text to memory.[12] Analysis of pre-modern texts must therefore pay particular attention to those features designed to affect aural reception, such as refrains, word plays, and sudden verbal and thematic juxtapositions—of which there are very many in Leviticus.

2 The Instructions for Ritual Offerings in Leviticus

Leviticus distinguishes itself by its emphasis on rituals, and interpreting it requires discussion of the nature of rituals and ritual texts to a greater degree than anywhere else in the Bible. Interpreting Leviticus therefore provides an opportunity to meld the traditions of biblical scholarship with the insights of other disciplinary fields concerned with ritual aspects of religion, such as the history of religions, sociology, and anthropology, and now the separate specialty, ritual studies.

---

10 The problem of authorial intentionality, which is the epistemological challenge of how to determine an author's intentions in writing, played a major role in challenges to biblical historical criticism by formalist literary critics in the 1980s (drawing on the New Criticism of the 1950s and 60s) and by post-modern critics in the 1990s (drawing on the continental philosophy of the 1970s and 80s). The critics pointed out that the intentions of authors can never be reconstructed with any certainty, and that appreciating many kinds of literature (such as poems and hymns) obviously does not require reconstructing a single authorial meaning. Nevertheless, the process of hearing or reading a text always requires the audience to think about who is addressing them so they know how to identify its genre correctly and know how to respond, including the question of whether the author's meaning and intention is relevant to their interpretation or not. A nuanced evaluation of the outcome for biblical studies can be found in J. Barton, "Reading the Bible as Literature: Two Questions for Biblical Scholars," *Journal of Literature & Theology* 1 (1987) 135–53.

11 Watts, *Leviticus 1–10*, 24–8.

12 Watts, *Leviticus 1–10*, 159–65.

There is, however, a deep methodological conflict between ritual and textual approaches, one that has bedeviled many attempts to employ ritual theory in biblical scholarship. The problem, in essence, is that we do not have access to ancient Israel's rituals, only to texts that happen to describe or refer to them. We cannot observe Aaronide priests purifying themselves and then making offerings in Jerusalem's temple, or any of the comparable practices of ancient Jews, Israelites, Egyptians, Babylonians, Hittites, Phoenicians, Greeks and Romans. We have only stories that use rituals to further their plots and ritual instructions that urge hearers and readers to do as they say. The authors of texts describe rituals to further their own goals in writing texts, not to reflect whatever purposes may have lain behind a ritual's performance. The application of ritual theories must always be deferred until those textual interests have been accounted for, or else the latter will undermine the conclusions of the former. Even in the very rare instances when writers try to explain a ritual, the textual medium itself impedes that goal. The problem, as several interpreters of biblical rituals have recently argued, is that texts are not rituals and rituals are not texts.[13]

Written texts usually encode rhetorical purposes different from the goals that motivate ritual performances. Even in modern cultures, most ritual texts exhort their audience to perform a ritual or instruct them in how to perform it rather than explaining what it means. On the other hand, great effort goes into interpreting rituals that we no longer perform or that are performed in cultures other than our own.[14] Symbolic interpretation of ritual is therefore a symptom of ritual strangeness, not a typical feature of ritual performance itself.

The dominance of symbolic theology in Western religions, however, blinds theorists and interpreters to the fact that not all or even most rituals receive symbolic commentary traditions. Many rituals function culturally without requiring verbal explanations of their meaning or purpose. When anthropologists or tourists do inquire about a ritual's meaning, they frequently discover that there are as many interpretations as there are participants and observers. Multivalence is a characteristic feature of rituals and does not impede their social functions.[15]

---

13 See W.K. Gilders, *Blood Ritual in the Hebrew Bible: Meaning and Power* (Baltimore: Johns Hopkins, 2004), 9–11; W.J. Bergen, *Reading Ritual: Leviticus in Postmodern Culture* (JSOTSup 417; London: T&T Clark, 2005), 7–9; J.W. Watts, *Ritual and Rhetoric in Leviticus: From Sacrifice to Scripture* (Cambridge: Cambridge University Press, 2007), 27–32; D.P. Wright, "Ritual Theory, Ritual Texts, and the Priestly-Holiness Writings of the Pentateuch," in S.M. Olyan (ed.), *Social Theory and the Study of Israelite Religion* (Atlanta: SBL, 2012), 197–209. I have recently summarized and reviewed the progress of this discussion in J.W. Watts, "Text Are Not Rituals and Rituals Are Not Texts, with an Example from Leviticus 12," in C. Nihan/J. Rhyder (ed.), *Text and Ritual in the Pentateuch* (Winona Lake, IN: Eisenbrauns, forthcoming).

14 Such as sacrifice: see J.W. Watts, "The Rhetoric of Sacrifice" in Watts, *Ritual and Rhetoric*, 173–92.

15 F. Staal, "The Meaninglessness of Ritual," *Numen* 26/1 (1979) 2–22; J.Z. Smith, *To Take Place: Toward Theory in Ritual* (Chicago: University of Chicago Press, 1987), 108; R.L. Grimes,

Interpreters who choose one interpretation over another risk either taking sides in traditional contests over ritual meaning or else imposing a meaning that does not appear in the ritual's cultural context at all.

The persuasive intent of many of Leviticus' regulations aims rather obviously to motivate people to make offerings in the Tabernacle or its later replacements, the temples of YHWH in Israel and Judah, or Yehud and Samaria. The book aims to convince Judeans and Samaritans to identify with the people of Israel whom the book addresses (1:2, etc.).[16] By doing so, they oblige themselves to bring offerings to the sanctuary and obey the other stipulations of Torah and to accept the ritual and interpretive authority of the Aaronide priests (10:10–11). P's concern for centralizing the cult does not involve its location, as in Deuteronomy, but rather its personnel. P insists that only the descendants of Aaron may exercise priestly duties at the altar. Leviticus therefore seems to reflect the interests of the Aaronide dynasties of the Second Temple period who controlled multiple temples dedicated to the worship of YHWH.[17]

P, however, does not describe offering rituals in stone temples but in the tent sanctuary, the Tabernacle, that accompanied Israel's wilderness wanderings. The problem, then, that confronts Jewish and Christian readers of whether and how to apply the book's instructions in different circumstances was posed by the priestly writers from the beginning. But they did not leave it to every reader or hearer of these instructions to resolve questions of application by themselves, nor did they vest interpretive authority in a class of scholarly scribes or rabbis as post-Second Temple Judaism did, or in a divine prophet-messiah and his apostles as Christianity did. Leviticus 10:10–11 gives only the Aaronide priests the authority to determine how to apply Tabernacle rituals to later circumstances. The interpretive demands deliberately posed by the utopian setting of the wilderness Tabernacle reinforce P's rhetorical goal of empowering Aaronide control over Israel's religion – a goal amply fulfilled in Judea until 70 CE and still effective among Samaritans to this day.

What heightens the significance of these divine grants is the fact that priests receive the only grants of centralized leadership authority in the Pentateuch. The Pentateuch, through P, gives only priests leadership over a centralized hierarchy in Israel and a hereditary right to wield that authority.

For me, that makes Leviticus a particularly fascinating text through which to think about the nature and rhetoric of scripture. The different polities of Samar-

---

Ritual Criticism (Columbia: University of South Carolina, 1990), 16–18; C. Bell, *Ritual Theory/Ritual Practice* (New York: Oxford University Press, 1992), 88–93; and N.J. Ruane, "Constructing Contagion on Yom Kippur," in this volume.

16 H. Nasuti, "Identity, Identification, and Imitation: The Narrative Hermeneutics of Biblical Law," *JLR* 4.1 (1986) 9–23.

17 D.M. Carr, *The Formation of the Hebrew Bible: A New Reconstruction* (Oxford: Oxford University Press, 2011), 212–14; Watts, *Leviticus 1–10*, 107–11.

itans, Jews and Christians represent different political choices made at various points in their histories, and those choices have left their mark on the contents of their canons of scripture.[18] For Samaritans, the Pentateuch alone is scripture, because the Torah's privileging of the Aaronides still matches their community's polity. For Jews and Christians, the Pentateuch has been contextualized not only by a larger Hebrew canon, but also by Talmudic literature in one case and a New Testament in the other. Both Talmud and NT displace Aaronides from their central position as the authoritative interpreters of law and religious practice.

Yet while Jewish and Christian canons and histories of interpretation displaced Aaronide leadership, they retained Leviticus and the Pentateuchal rhetoric that established Aaronide pre-eminence. Political contests for denominational and congregational leadership continue to reflect Leviticus's ideas, even when they do not cite its texts. For example, debates over whether women and openly gay men should be allowed into the ranks of rabbis, Torah scribes, priests and ministers still regularly employ a rhetoric of purity that evokes the menstrual and sexual rules of Leviticus 12, 15, 18, 20 and 21.[19] Since Jewish and Christian congregations do not intend to empower the descendants of Aaron in these roles, this rhetoric occupies an interstitial space between the plain meaning of Leviticus and its completely metaphorical interpretation. The book's designation of priestly authority continues to haunt subsequent re-allocations of it, despite the profound changes in congregational polity, theology, and political culture that have taken place over two millennia.

So what is the significance of an unperformed ritual? And what is the meaning of an unread text?

The intuitive answer, that unperformed rituals and unread texts have no meaning, is clearly wrong in the case of Leviticus. The rituals depicted in its text mean a great deal, because Jews, Samaritans and Christians continue to ritualize Leviticus as part of their scriptures. Leviticus's status as the third book of scripture has remained virtually uncontested throughout the histories of these three religions, despite the fact that people do not observe many of its offering instructions or, among Christians, even read much of its text. It retains its place among the sacred scrolls and books reproduced by each religion.

Therefore if the job of commentary is to explain the meaning of Leviticus, it cannot stop with the book's words, much less their original referents. The mean-

18 J. W. Watts, "The Political and Legal Uses of Scripture," in J. Schaper/J. C. Paget (ed.), *The New Cambridge History of the Bible* (Cambridge: Cambridge University Press, 2013) 1.345–64.

19 For examples, see K. De Troyer, "Blood: A Threat to Holiness or Toward (Another) Holiness?" in K. de Troyer/J. A. Herbert/J. A. Johnson/A.-M. Korte (ed.), *Wholly Woman, Holy Blood: A Feminist Critique of Purity and Impurity* (Harrisburge, PA: Trinity, 2003) 45–64. Some have argued, however, that the Christian marginalization of women in worship on the grounds of their impurity owes less to Leviticus than to ancient medical beliefs: so J. Schultz, "Doctors, Philosophers, and Christian Fathers on Menstrual Blood," in *Wholly Woman, Holy Blood*, 97–116.

ings of Leviticus have been broadcast by the sounds of its words and the sight of the books and scrolls that contain it as much as by semantic interpretations of its contents, which have themselves been manifested in ritual and legal performances as well as in sermons and commentaries. Out of all this emerges the phenomenon of scripture, of which Leviticus is an original and integral part.[20]

Bibliography

Anderson, R. T./Giles, T., *The Keepers: An Introduction to the History and Culture of the Samaritans* (Grand Rapids, MI: Baker, 2001).

Barton, J., "Reading the Bible as Literature: Two Questions for Biblical Scholars," *Journal of Literature & Theology* 1 (1987) 135–53.

Bell, C., *Ritual Theory/Ritual Practice* (New York: Oxford University Press, 1992).

Bergen, W. J., *Reading Ritual: Leviticus in Postmodern Culture* (JSOTSup 417; London: T&T Clark, 2005).

Bodendorfer, G., "Der Horizont einer Exegese des Buches Levitikus in den rabbinischen Midraschim," in H.-J. Fabry/H.-W. Jüngling (ed.), *Levitikus als Buch* (Berlin: Philo, 1999) 343–71.

Braiterman, Z. J., "Martin Buber and the Art of Ritual," in M. Zankl (ed.), *New Perspectives on Martin Buber* (Tübingen: Mohr Siebeck, 2006) 111–24.

Carr, D. M., *The Formation of the Hebrew Bible: A New Reconstruction* (Oxford: Oxford University Press, 2011).

Childs, B. S., *Introduction to the Old Testament as Scripture* (Minneapolis: Fortress, 1979).

Clark, E., *Reading Renunciation: Asceticism and Scripture in Early Christianity* (Princeton: Princeton University Press, 1999).

De Troyer, K., "Blood: A Threat to Holiness or Toward (Another) Holiness?" in K. de Troyer/J. A. Herbert/J. A. Johnson/A.-M. Korte (ed.), *Wholly Woman, Holy Blood: A Feminist Critique of Purity and Impurity* (Harrisburge, PA: Trinity, 2003) 45–64.

Douglas, M., *Leviticus as Literature* (Oxford: Oxford University Press, 1999).

Elliott, M. W., *Engaging Leviticus: Reading Leviticus Theologically with its Past Interpreters* (Eugene: Cascade, 2012).

Firey, A., "The Letter of the Law: Carolingian Exegetes and the Old Testament," in J. D. McAuliffe (ed.), *With Reverence for the Word: Medieval Scriptural Exegesis in Judaism, Christianity, and Islam* (Oxford: Oxford University Press, 2003) 204–24.

Gilders, W. K., *Blood Ritual in the Hebrew Bible: Meaning and Power* (Baltimore: Johns Hopkins, 2004).

Grimes, R. L., *Ritual Criticism* (Columbia: University of South Carolina, 1990).

Harrington, H. K., "The Rabbinic Reception of Leviticus," in R. Rendtorff/R. Kugler (ed.), *The Book of Leviticus: Composition and Reception* (VTSup 93; Leiden: Brill, 2003) 383–402.

Just, F., "Lectionary Statistics" on the Roman Catholic *Lectionary for Mass* (2009), online at http://catholic-resources.org/Lectionary/Statistics.htm (accessed 12/21/2015).

Knoppers, G. N., *Jews and Samaritans: The Origins and History of Their Early Relations* (Oxford: Oxford University Press, 2013).

Nasuti, H., "Identity, Identification, and Imitation: The Narrative Hermeneutics of Biblical Law," *JLR* 4.1 (1986) 9–23.

20 See now J. W. Watts, *Understanding the Pentateuch as a Scripture* (London: Wiley Blackwell, 2017).

Radner, E., *Leviticus* (Brazos Theological Commentary to the Bible; Grand Rapids: Brazos, 2008).
Schultz, J., "Doctors, Philosophers, and Christian Fathers on Menstrual Blood," in K. de Troyer/J. A. Herbert/J. A. Johnson/A.-M. Korte (ed.), *Wholly Woman, Holy Blood: A Feminist Critique of Purity and Impurity* (Harrisburge, PA: Trinity, 2003) 97–116.
Smith, J. Z., *To Take Place: Toward Theory in Ritual* (Chicago: University of Chicago Press, 1987).
Staal, F., "The Meaninglessness of Ritual," *Numen* 26/1 (1979) 2–22.
Watts, J. W., *Reading Law: the Rhetorical Shaping of the Pentateuch* (Sheffield: Sheffield Academic Press, 1999).
–, *Ritual and Rhetoric in Leviticus: From Sacrifice to Scripture* (Cambridge: Cambridge University Press, 2007).
–, *Leviticus 1–10* (HCOT; Leuven: Peeters, 2013).
–, "The Political and Legal Uses of Scripture," in J. Schaper/J. C. Paget (ed.), *The New Cambridge History of the Bible* (Cambridge: Cambridge University Press, 2013) 1.345–64.
–, *Understanding the Pentateuch as a Scripture* (London: Wiley Blackwell, 2017).
–, "Text Are Not Rituals and Rituals Are Not Texts, with an Example from Leviticus 12," in C. Nihan/J. Rhyder (ed.), *Text and Ritual in the Pentateuch* (Winona Lake, IN: Eisenbrauns, forthcoming).
Wright, D. P., "Ritual Theory, Ritual Texts, and the Priestly-Holiness Writings of the Pentateuch," in S. M. Olyan (ed.), *Social Theory and the Study of Israelite Religion* (Atlanta: SBL, 2012) 195–216.

William K. Gilders

Commentary as Ethnography

1 Introduction

I am writing a commentary on Leviticus for the Old Testament Library (OTL) series published by Westminster John Knox Press. My contribution to the series will be its third volume on Leviticus, joining the commentaries by Martin Noth and Erhard Gerstenberger,[1] which were translated from German originals in the Alte Testament Deutsch (ATD) series;[2] my work, therefore, will be the first commentary on Leviticus prepared specifically for the OTL series in English.

Like any monograph, a biblical commentary by a single author should have a clear and distinctive authorial voice; it should be unmistakably the work of a specific interpreter. I have thought very deliberately, therefore, about how my work should express my particular approach to Leviticus. I would describe my commentary, in brief, as follows: It is an historical-critical work, strongly informed by anthropology and ritual theory, and sensitive to the theological concerns of its readers. In this paper, I will focus on the important role played by anthropology and ritual theory in my work with Leviticus, because it represents what I believe to be the most characteristic element of my commentary, that which produces the distinctive tone and pitch of my authorial voice. To provide concrete examples of my engagement with Leviticus I have opted to draw on my work with Leviticus 2, the basic legislation for the קרבן מנחה ("tribute offering"[3]), consisting of cereal products prepared in a variety of ways. I have made this choice in order to highlight my desire to disengage treatment of the offerings in Leviticus from the concept that "sacrifice" necessarily involves the killing of animal victims.[4] Rather, in Leviticus (and elsewhere in the Hebrew Bible) animal offerings are only the

1 M. Noth, *Leviticus: A Commentary* (OTL; Philadelphia: Westminster, 1965); E. Gerstenberger, *Leviticus: A Commentary* (OTL; Louisville, KY: Westminster John Knox, 1996).

2 M. Noth, *Das dritte Buch Mose: Leviticus* (ATD; Göttingen: Vandenhoeck & Ruprecht, 1962); E. Gerstenberger, *Das dritte Buch Mose: Leviticus* (ATD; Göttingen: Vandenhoeck & Ruprecht, 1993).

3 I have elected to use a philologically "literal" rendering of the term מנחה, "tribute," rather than the common rendering, "grain offering," which identifies the material of the offering. My approach to the translation of technical ritual vocabulary in Leviticus aligns with that set out by J. W. Watts, *Leviticus 1–10* (HCOT; Leuven: Peeters, 2013), 4–8.

4 My perspective on decentering killing in the interpretation of sacrificial ritual is very similar to the one articulated by K. McClymond, *Beyond Sacred Violence: A Comparative Study of Sacrifice* (Baltimore: Johns Hopkins University Press, 2008).

most prominent element of a larger complex of offering performances that center on the Israelite shrine's courtyard altar.

2 Writing an Ethnographic Commentary

In the preface to the second edition of her selected essays, *Implicit Meanings*, the anthropologist Mary Douglas wrote: "Anyone interested in belief, religion, and symbols looks to anthropology for insight."[5] My hearty agreement with Douglas's statement will find clear expression in my commentary, as I draw on the work of anthropologists and apply an ethnographic perspective to Leviticus, indeed, taking the risk of characterizing the commentary as a work of ethnography. As defined by the *Dictionary of the Social Sciences*, "ethnography" is:

> The study of the culture and social organization of a particular group or community, as well as the published result of such study (an ethnography). Ethnography refers to both the data-gathering ... and the development of analyses of specific peoples, settings, or ways of life. In both cases, it is generally distinguished from the subsequent comparative and historical analyses of ethnographic data.[6]

My first serious reflections on taking an ethnographic approach to Leviticus took place when I composed the article, "Anthropological Approaches," for the David Petersen Festschrift volume, *Method Matters*, some time after I had engaged in rather piecemeal deployment of anthropological ideas in my book, *Blood Ritual in the Hebrew Bible*.[7] Looking into the ways anthropologists had engaged with the Hebrew Bible, I discovered that the noted British anthropologist Edmund Leach had encouraged readers of his textbook, *Culture and Communication*, to treat biblical ritual texts as if they were ethnographic field notes,[8] an approach I found quite problematic. As I wrote:

---

5 M. Douglas, *Implicit Meanings: Selected Essays in Anthropology* (London: Routledge, ²1999), vii; I first highlighted this statement in my contribution to the Festschrift for David L. Petersen: W.K. Gilders, "Anthropological Approaches: Ritual in Leviticus 8, Real or Rhetorical?," in J.M. LeMon/K.H. Richards (ed.), *Method Matters: Essays on the Interpretation of the Hebrew Bible in Honor of David L. Petersen* (RBS 56; Atlanta: Society of Biblical Literature, 2009) 233–50, on p. 233.

6 "Ethnography," in C. Calhoun (ed.), *Dictionary of the Social Sciences* (Oxford: Oxford University Press, 2002), 149.

7 W.K. Gilders, *Blood Ritual in the Hebrew Bible: Meaning and Power* (Baltimore: Johns Hopkins University Press, 2004).

8 E. Leach, *Culture and Communication: The Logic by which Symbols are Connected: An Introduction to the Use of Structuralist Analysis in Social Anthropology* (Themes in the Social Sciences; Cambridge: Cambridge University Press, 1976), 84–5.

> Biblical texts are not ethnographic writings, that is records of what a "participant-observer" has experienced. Rather, the texts are cultural products, best regarded as equivalent to the information provided by "native informants" whose statements about their society and its culture must be recorded, organized, compared, collated, and interpreted.[9]

My observation pointed to a way of treating biblical texts ethnographically, but also indicated a significant problem, which I noted: "Unlike ethnographers, biblical scholars have no access to lived practice." Unlike the anthropologist, whose work Leach defines as "the analysis and interpretation of ethnographic facts, *customary behaviour as directly observed*,"[10] in dealing with Leviticus, I am encountering particular informant voices in a highly limited textual form; I have no access to "customary behaviour as directly observed." A comparable field situation would involve an ethnographer who is told by one or more ritual experts how rituals are performed and what they mean, but who is forbidden any experience of the actual performance and, moreover, can find no ordinary members of the community willing or able to talk about the rituals from their perspectives. Thus, while I might claim to be conducting ethnography under such limited circumstances, the truth is that I am not in a "field" situation. Still, I am engaging with Leviticus as a "professional stranger"—the anthropologist M.H. Agar's designation for the ethnographer.[11] In this particular sense, my commentary is a work of ethnography, a report on my study of the cultural expressions of a particular human group.

I am not doing ethnography as most anthropologists would, because I cannot engage in direct participant observation, which is commonly identified as a defining feature of ethnography. But it is possible to imagine what it would be like to engage with the authors of Leviticus as native informants in a fieldwork setting, listening to the texts as informant voices. Moreover, there are significant precedents for this kind of text-based ethnography from within the anthropological guild. For example, Valerio Valeri's sophisticated study of Hawaiian religion is based almost entirely on written documents, a feature of the work that Valeri explicitly addresses.[12] Most obviously relevant to my own project is the example of Mary Douglas's large body of work on biblical material, beginning with her seminal essay, "The Abominations of Leviticus," the third chapter of *Purity and*

---

9 Gilders, "Anthropological Approaches," 235.

10 Leach, *Culture and Communication*, 1 (emphasis added).

11 M.H. Agar, *The Professional Stranger: An Informal Introduction to Ethnography* (San Diego: Academia Press, ^{2}1996).

12 V. Valeri, *Kingship and Sacrifice: Ritual and Society in Ancient Hawaii* (Chicago: University of Chicago Press, 1985), xvii–xxviii, especially p. xxviii, where Valeri emphasizes that the textual sources "cannot be treated like the *Ersatz* of a nonexistent ethnography."

Danger,[13] and including especially her book, *Leviticus as Literature*, which she defines as a reading of Leviticus "as an anthropologist."[14]

Much of the standard work of any historical-critical commentary on Leviticus is implicitly ethnographic, making every scholar who prepares such a commentary a "professional stranger." Like an ethnographer, a biblical commentator is describing and interpreting a cultural formation on the basis of engagement with native informants. Like any ethnographer, I must identify and describe those informants. Drawing on a strong consensus of critical scholarship, I identify the author-editors who produced Leviticus (and its underlying sources, insofar as they can be hypothetically reconstructed) as Israelite priests who claimed descent from Aaron: Aaronide priests. To apply a designation I have picked up from Stanley K. Stowers, these priests were *literate cultural producers*. Although Stowers refers specifically to authors of the Hellenistic and Roman periods, his description applies equally to the authors of Leviticus:

> These people were specialists by virtue of the skills, prestige, and legitimacy derived from their belonging to the perhaps 2 percent or less of people who were literate enough to produce and authoritatively interpret complex, written texts.[15]

Leviticus is a document that is expressive of the values and convictions of these specialist informants. This crucial ethnographic limitation must always be kept in view. A commentary on Leviticus does not record and interpret ancient Israelite culture as a whole, but only a very limited part of it, as presented by a distinctive group of literate cultural producers.

3 Towards an Ethnographic Commentary on Leviticus 2

Like an ethnographer, the commentator on a biblical ritual text engages in various acts of cultural translation, conveying and explaining information obtained from engagement with native informants to recipients in a different cultural context. This activity includes, fundamentally, the translation of indigenous technical vocabulary into another language, such as English. In the very first verse of Lev 2 we are confronted with several technical terms, which require such translation:

13 M. Douglas, *Purity and Danger: An Analysis of Concepts of Pollution and Taboo* (New York: Praeger, 1966).

14 M. Douglas, *Leviticus as Literature* (Oxford: Oxford University Press, 1999), v.

15 S. Stowers, "The Religion of Plant and Animal Offerings Versus the Religion of Meanings, Essences, and Textual Mysteries," in J. W. Knust/Z. Várhelyi (ed.), *Ancient Mediterranean Sacrifice* (Oxford: Oxford University Press, 2011) 35–56, on p. 41.

> And when a person would offer [תקריב] a tribute offering [קרבן מנחה] to Yahweh, their offering [קרבן] must be fine flour, and they must pour olive oil upon it and must place frankincense upon it.

Here I will briefly discuss two terms. First, we have קרבן ("offering"), a noun based on the root קרב, which has the basic sense of "come forward." In a sequential reading of Leviticus, this term first appears in the book's first chapter, and naturally enough, my initial elucidation of it is in my treatment of Lev 1. However, in Lev 2 we learn more from our Aaronide informants about what is included in this category and thus of its cultural semantic range. While Lev 1 might have left the impression that a קרבן consists only of living creatures (designated quadruped livestock or birds), Lev 2 indicates that there can also be a קרבן of cereal products. Such a קרבן is specified as a מנחה, for which I offer the etymological rendering, "tribute." This translation will need to be explained to present-day readers with reference to the concept of reciprocal exchange (in distinction from market exchange), which is well-elucidated by Stowers as involving gift-giving (often between unequal parties), which creates and sustains an ongoing relationship.[16] While the מנחה always involves the burning of some portion in the altar fire, which precludes the inclusion of leaven or fruit syrup (דבשׁ, conventionally, "honey"; Lev 2:11, which I will discuss below), we also learn that the larger category of קרבן can include cereal items not burned on the altar, the קרבן ראשׁית, "first-processed offering" (Lev 2:12).

Leviticus 2 is clearly a text about activity commonly identified by anthropologists and biblical scholars as "ritual." Therefore, I turn now to questions about the interpretation of ritual. "Ritual theory" is an interdisciplinary field of inquiry. While it draws heavily on the work of anthropologists, many ritual theorists are not guild anthropologists, for example, Catherine Bell, Nancy Jay, Ronald Grimes, and Frits Staal. These non-anthropologists often draw on theoretical resources that have been neglected by anthropologists, while anthropologists frequently appeal to the work of these non-anthropologists.

A biblical scholar who decides to draw on the work of anthropologists and other ritual theorists inevitably becomes involved in the ongoing debates within those fields and must take a position within those debates. Theoretical neutrality is impossible. My own stance, which will be elaborated in my commentary, is most fully articulated in a 2013 publication in which I affirmed my agreement with ritual theorists who variously challenge the widely-held identification of ritual behavior as inherently and necessarily symbolic-communicative activity.[17] I looked particularly to the work of four anthropologists whose critiques of symbolic-

16 Stowers, "Religion of Plant and Animal Offerings," 39–40.

17 W.K. Gilders, "Ancient Israelite Sacrifice as Symbolic Action: Theoretical Reflections," *SEÅ* 78 (2013) 1–22.

communicative theories of ritual are rooted in their ethnographic experiences: Dan Sperber,[18] Gilbert Lewis,[19] and Caroline Humphrey and James Laidlaw.[20]

Keeping in view the theoretical work of these anthropologists and of numerous other anthropologists and ritual theorists who have challenged the hegemony of what can be termed "representational" understandings of ritual,[21] I ask questions about how the authors of Leviticus, as indigenous literate cultural producers, present ritual activity. In my commentary I will emphasize a key fact: the author-editors of Leviticus *never* use the language of symbolic meaning with reference to ritual practices. Within Leviticus, we never find statements of the type, "this represents," "this means" or "this signifies."[22] This fact has not stopped biblical scholars from treating biblical rituals as essentially symbolic behavior in need of decoding interpretation. The most forceful and thoroughgoing attempt in this direction has come recently from Jonathan Klawans, who draws explicitly on the work of many anthropologists, particularly Mary Douglas and Victor Turner.[23]

---

18 D. Sperber, *Rethinking Symbolism* (Cambridge: Cambridge University Press, 1975); this work reflects Sperber's experience with the Ethiopian Dorze people.

19 G. Lewis, *Day of Shining Red: An Essay on Understanding Ritual* (CSSA; Cambridge: Cambridge University Press, 1980); this work is based on Lewis's fieldwork with the Gnau people of New Guinea.

20 C. Humphrey/J. Laidlaw, *The Archetypal Actions of Ritual: A Theory of Ritual Illustrated by the Jain Rite of Worship* (Oxford Studies in Social and Cultural Anthropology; New York: Oxford University Press, 1994); this study is inspired by their work with Jains in western India.

21 See, e.g., J. Skorupski, *Symbol and Theory: A Philosophical Study of Theories of Religion in Social Anthropology* (Cambridge: Cambridge University Press, 1976); J. Fabian, *Time and the Other: How Anthropology Makes Its Object* (New York: Columbia University Press, 1983); S. W. Foster, "Symbolism and the Problematics of Postmodern Representation," in K. M. Ashley (ed.), *Victor Turner and the Construction of Cultural Criticism: Between Literature and Anthropology* (Bloomington: Indiana University Press, 1990) 117–37; T. Asad, *Genealogies of Religion: Discipline and Reasons of Power in Christianity and Islam* (Baltimore: Johns Hopkins University Press, 1993); P. Buc, *The Danger of Ritual: Between Early Medieval Texts and Social Scientific Theory* (Princeton, N. J.: Princeton University Press, 2001); B. Kapferer, "Ritual Dynamics and Virtual Practice: Beyond Representation and Meaning," *Social Analysis* 48.2 (2004) 35–54; W. S. Sax, "Ritual and the Problem of Efficacy," in W. S. Sax/J. Quack/J. Weinhold (ed.), *The Problem of Ritual Efficacy* (New York: Oxford University Press, 2010) 3–16.

22 "Sign" (אות) language about ritual performance does occur outside of Leviticus in a few Aaronide texts (see, e.g., Gen 17:11, with reference to circumcision; Exod 31:17, with reference to the sabbath); see also Num 15:39–40, which states that Israelites who look at the tassels on four-cornered garments will remember and observe the commandments. However, these limited examples provide a weak basis for asserting that the Aaronides understood all ritual behavior as symbolic-communicative. Gilders, "Ancient Israelite Sacrifice," 10–12.

23 J. Klawans, *Purity, Sacrifice, and the Temple: Symbolism and Supersessionism in the Study of Ancient Judaism* (New York: Oxford University Press, 2006); idem, "Methodology and Ideology in the Study of Priestly Ritual," in B. J. Schwartz et al. (ed.), *Perspectives on Purity and Purification in the Bible* (LHBOTS [JSOTSup] 474; New York: T&T Clark, 2008) 84–95; idem, "Symbol, Function, Theology, and Morality in the Study of Priestly Ritual," in J. W. Knust/Z. Várhelyi (ed.), *Ancient Mediterranean Sacrifice* (New York: Oxford University Press, 2011) 106–22.

This is not surprising. As Humphrey and Laidlaw comment: "The idea that ritual is essentially communicative and expressive is almost a social compact in anthropology …"[24]

To illustrate the difference between the approach that Klawans approvingly refers to as "ubiquitous symbolism"[25] and my own, I will briefly discuss the prohibition against the inclusion of leaven (שׂאר) and fruit syrup (דבשׁ) in the מנחה and the requirement for the inclusion of salt with the מנחה (and, apparently, *all* offerings). Leviticus 2:11–13 reads:

11 כל־המנחה אשר תקריבו לה׳ לא תעשׂה חמץ כי כל־שׂאר וכל־דבשׁ לא תקטירו ממנו אשה לה׳: 12
קרבן ראשית תקריבו אתם לה׳ ואל־המזבח לא־יעלו לריח ניחח: 13 וכל־קרבן מנחתך במלח תמלח ולא
תשבית מלח ברית אלהיך מעל מנחתך על כל־קרבנך תקריב מלח

> 11. No tribute that you offer to Yahweh may be made[26] of leavened dough, for you must not turn any leavening agent[27] or any fruit syrup[28] to smoke[29] as a fire-gift[30] for Yahweh. 12. You may offer them as a first-processed[31] offering to Yahweh, but they must not go up to the altar for a soothing scent. 13. And your[32] every tribute offering you must season with salt and you must not let the salt of your deity's covenant cease from being with your tribute. With your every offering you must offer salt!

Reflecting the anthropological "social compact" to which Humphrey and Laidlaw refer, Mary Douglas writes that ritual is "pre-eminently a form of communication."[33] This view of ritual is on full display in her treatment of the rules about leaven, fruit syrup, and salt in Lev 2:11–13 in *Leviticus as Literature*.[34] Douglas poses the question why leaven and fruit syrup are prohibited from being offered on the altar while salt is required, and offers a clear answer:

24 Humphrey and Laidlaw, *Archetypal Actions*, 73.

25 Klawans, "Methodology and Ideology," 85–6.

26 While the Septuagint reflects the reading תעשׂו ("you may make"), I have followed the MT reading.

27 As Milgrom notes, the term חמץ here refers to the leavened product, while שׂאר is the leavening agent itself (*Leviticus 1–16*, 188).

28 As Milgrom argues, the term דבשׁ here probably refers to a syrup made from fruit (especially dates), rather than to the product of bees (*Leviticus 1–16*, 189–90).

29 While some MT manuscripts and the Samaritan text read, תקריבו, which is reflected in the Septuagint and Targum Pseudo-Jonathan (BHS textual note), I have followed the reading of the standard MT text, תקטירו, which makes sense in the context, which is referring to what may be offered by burning on the altar.

30 I follow J. W. Watts, *Leviticus 1–10*, 209–11, in employing this translation of אשׁה.

31 See Milgrom, *Leviticus 1–16*, 190–1.

32 While the Septuagint reflects a second masculine plural possessive suffix throughout this verse (in line with the second masculine plural verbs of the previous verses), I have retained the MT reading of a second masculine singular.

33 M. Douglas, *Natural Symbols: Explorations in Cosmology* (New York: Random House, 1970), 20.

34 Douglas, *Leviticus as Literature*, 163–6.

> The answer invokes the major division of the biblical world-view: on the one hand, natural generation, including sexual reproduction of humans, and on the other, divine generation by the covenant, symbolized by circumcision of the people of Israel. Honey and leaven work in the natural mode of generation, sacrifice works in the divine mode, and to teach the lesson they are kept apart.[35]

Note Douglas's assertion that the *purpose* of the specific exclusions and inclusions is to "teach the lesson" about the larger conceptual system she describes. This "lesson," however, is not given in Lev 2 itself, but must be brought to bear upon the ritual rules it presents. That is, the rules do not themselves teach the "lesson"; they must be interpreted in view of information applied to decode them.

Jacob Milgrom offers an explanation from the same basic theoretical perspective as Douglas, but with a radically different identification of the symbolic communication taking place: "Fermentation is equivalent to decay and corruption and for this reason is prohibited on the altar."[36] Milgrom cites a variety of sources from late antiquity that appear to reflect a negative conceptualization of leaven, asserting that, although from a period much later than the composition of Leviticus, these sources

> undoubtedly reflect an older and universal regard of leaven as the arch-symbol of fermentation, deterioration, and death and, hence, taboo on the altar of blessing and life.[37]

It is not surprising to find such a dramatic interpretive difference given that the symbolic meanings of leaven, fruit syrup, and salt brought to bear on Lev 2 are not clearly expressed anywhere in the Hebrew Bible.[38] In other words, these meanings are not given by native informants; they are creations of the "professional stranger," who is convinced that they must exist within the culture. To the interpretations of both Douglas and Milgrom, the critical observation from Gilbert Lewis aptly applies:

> Strange customs tempt an anthropologist more strongly to interpret them when he [or "she"!] feels the people have not given him a good enough reason for following them.[39]

---

35 Douglas, *Leviticus as Literature*, 165.

36 Milgrom, *Leviticus 1–16*, 188.

37 Milgrom, *Leviticus 1–16*, 189.

38 This fact is noted by a number of commentators (especially with regard to leaven and fruit syrup or honey); see, e.g., G.J. Wenham, *The Book of Leviticus* (NICOT; Grand Rapids, Mich.: Eerdmans, 1979), 71; Watts, *Leviticus 1–10*, 262; T. Hieke, *Levitikus 1–15* (HThKAT; Freiburg: Herder, 2014), 207. Notably, while both Wenham and Hieke emphasize that the text does not specify the reason for the prohibition of leaven and fruit syrup or honey, they do develop detailed symbolic explanations for the salt (see Wenham, *Leviticus*, 207; Hieke, *Levitikus 1–15*, 211).

39 Lewis, *Day of Shining Red*, xv.

I agree with the critical judgment offered by Humphrey and Laidlaw against such scholarly meaning-making:

> It is a short but utterly fallacious step to suppose that the purpose of the ritual is to communicate or express these ideas to the people, who already know them (and from whom, rather than from the ritual itself, the anthropologist in practice learns them). Even when a ritual can validly be cited as *evidence* that people hold this or that belief, it does not follow that the purpose of performing the ritual is to *communicate* the belief.[40]

In contrast to the symbolic-communicative explanations offered by Douglas and Milgrom, Baruch J. Schwartz suggests more down-to-earth reasons for the prohibition of leaven and fruit syrup and for the inclusion of salt. According to Schwartz, leavening is prohibited

> most likely for practical reasons, so that the preparation, offering, and eating of food gifts would all take place within a short period of time and in proximity to the altar. The preparation of leavened cakes would take much longer ... The requirement to salt the grain offering is a corollary of the prohibition of leaven: Salt is an anti-fermentation agent and would impede natural leavening.[41]

Jeffrey Stackert offers a very similar explanation of the text, but adds the suggestion that salt was also included to function "as a flavor enhancer for the deity's food, as it does in Mesopotamian food offerings ..."[42] Schwartz also asserts that ברית in the formula "the salt of your deity's covenant" (NJPS: "the salt of your covenant with God") "is used here in the sense of imposed obligation, and simply means that the salting of offerings is to be observed perpetually,"[43] in sharp contrast to Douglas's affirmation that the term invokes the special bond between God and the Israelites. I cite these alternative explanations not because I necessarily agree with them, but to illustrate the diverse range of interpretations that can be given by those in the role of "professional stranger" in response to cultural phenomena that native informants fail to explain.

In my commentary, I will avoid offering the kinds of explanations offered by Douglas and Milgrom, because I believe they are rooted in a problematic theoretical model of ritual as communicating symbolic meanings from a coherent cultural system. Rather than imposing symbolic-communicative interpretations

---

40 Humphrey and Laidlaw, *Archetypal Actions*, 73–4.

41 B.J. Schwartz, "Leviticus," in A. Berlin/M.Z. Brettler (ed.), *The Jewish Study Bible* (Oxford: Oxford University Press, [2]2014) 193–266, on p. 199.

42 J. Stackert, "Leviticus," in M.D. Coogan (ed.), *The New Oxford Annotated Bible* (Oxford: Oxford University Press, [4]2010) 141–83, on p. 145.

43 Schwartz, "Leviticus," 199. Stackert, similarly, explains ברית as referring to "a statutory requirement" or "a due or allotment," and asserts that the text is best translated as, "You shall not omit from your grain offering the salt required by your God" ("Leviticus," 145).

on texts that lack them, I will focus on elucidating what the textual informants actually assert, what Victor Turner termed "indigenous interpretation (or, briefly, the exegetical meaning)" of ritual.[44] In Lev 2, the few explanatory comments refer to instrumental effects of a relational character: the burning of the אזכרה ("representative portion") in the altar fire produces a "soothing scent for Yahweh" (Lev 2:2, 9); the emphasis of the author-editors of Lev 2 is on what the offering achieves for the offerer's relationship with Yahweh, an emphasis marked through repetition.

While my primary focus will be on what the texts explicitly state about the significance of ritual actions and elements, I will not neglect trying to identify larger cultural significances, which might not be so clearly expressed but which appear to be a factor in the shaping of the rituals. For this level of interpretation, my thinking about how ritual actions can signify is strongly informed by the semiotic theories of Charles Sanders Peirce, who emphasized the conventionality of symbols, and therefore sought to distinguish symbols from other types of signs.[45] I have found Peirce's distinction between *symbols, icons* and *indices* (*indexes*) as three types of signs extremely helpful to my work with ancient Israelite ritual, in particular, Peirce's identification of indexical signs. A symbol, Peirce emphasizes,

> is a sign which refers to the Object that it denotes by virtue of a law, usually an association of general ideas, which operates to cause the Symbol to be interpreted as referring to that object.[46]

To put it more simply, as Nancy Jay does, a symbol "is related to its object by convention."[47] The meaning of a symbol, then, is assigned to it, and is not inherent in the thing itself. An index, however, "is a sign which refers to the Object that it denotes by virtue of being really affected by that Object."[48] An indexical sign

---

44 V. Turner, *The Forest of Symbols: Aspects of Ndembu Ritual* (Ithaca: Cornell University Press, 1967), 50.

45 The material in this section is drawn from my treatment of Peircian semiotics in "Anthropological Approaches," 244–5, and "Ancient Israelite Sacrifice," 14–16; see also, idem, "Why Does Eleazar Sprinkle the Red Cow Blood? Making Sense of a Biblical Ritual," *JHS* 6 (2006) (online: online: http://jhsonline.org/Articles/article_59.pdf). For helpful entry to Peirce's theory of signs, see J. Buchler (ed.), *Philosophical Writings of Peirce* (New York: Dover, 1955), 98–119; on the value of Peirce's ideas for the understanding of sacrificial ritual, see N. Jay, *Throughout Your Generations Forever: Sacrifice, Religion, and Paternity* (Chicago: University of Chicago Press, 1992), 6–7; see also R. Rappaport's elucidation and critique of Peirce's theory in *Ritual and Religion in the Making of Humanity* (Cambridge Studies in Social and Cultural Anthropology 110; Cambridge: Cambridge University Press, 1999), 54–68.

46 Peirce in Buchler, *Philosophical Writings*, 102.

47 Jay, *Throughout Your Generations Forever*, 6.

48 Peirce in Buchler, *Philosophical Writings*, 102.

> is in dynamical (including spatial) connection both with the individual object, on the one hand, and with the senses or memory of the person for whom it serves as a sign, on the other hand.[49]

While discussing examples of indices, Peirce provides perhaps his simplest definition of an index:

> A rap on the door is an index. Anything which focusses the attention is an index. Anything which startles us is an index, in so far as it marks the junction between two portions of experience.[50]

This explanation clarifies that Peirce's category of the index integrally includes deliberate human actions that indicate something. Thus, in his refinement of Peirce's theory, Roy Rappaport refers to "Constructed Indices" which "are deliberately constructed and employed by humans to indicate whatever they do indicate."[51] Such constructed indices, while dependent on human action, and thus conventional, do not depend on convention for their significance. Rather, as Jay helpfully explains,

> Because the relation of sign to signified is not conventional, indices can be understood across cultural and linguistic boundaries. They *indicate* their object rather than represent it.[52]

In Leviticus 2, I believe we can identify several constructed indices at work. Distinctions between lay Israelites and Aaronide priests are indicated (*indexed*) by the handling of offering materials and by access to the altar. Another index of priestly identity and status is the fact that priests receive the remainder of every "tribute," which is explicitly interpreted as "a most holy thing from the fire-gifts of Yahweh" (vv. 3 and 10). The priests receive the same substance, in its quality as a sacred gift to Yahweh, as the altar, which establishes an existential relationship between the priesthood and Yahweh, centered at the altar. This ritually-indexed relationship clearly distinguishes priests from non-priests in the world envisaged by the text.

4 Conclusion

My engagement with Leviticus as a "professional stranger" is still in process. Thus, the final product is very much in formation, malleable and changeable. My goal for the commentary is do justice to what my informants tell me, to

49 Peirce in Buchler, *Philosophical Writings*, 107.
50 Peirce in Buchler, *Philosophical Writings*, 108–9.
51 Rappaport, *Ritual and Religion*, 63.
52 Jay, *Throughout Your Generations Forever*, 6.

achieve a cultural translation so that present-day readers can engage with the world behind and within Leviticus, and to strike a balance between providing sufficient interpretation and providing too much.

My commentary will constitute an ethnography of the ways in which Israelite Aaronide priests, a small group of literate cultural producers, represent and interpret Israelite cultural practices through the medium of the texts they composed and edited. As an ethnographic work, it will provide cultural translation for its presumed audience of twenty-first century readers. It will also present a multi-layered interpretation of the cultural data on the basis of the theoretical models I find most compelling and productive. Specifically, while I will largely avoid offering symbolic-communicative explanations of ritual performances, I will explicate the indexical force of such practices in Peircian terms. This approach to ritual will represent a major element in my distinctive authorial self-presentation, the voice with which my work will speak.

Bibliography

Agar, M. H., *The Professional Stranger: An Informal Introduction to Ethnography* (San Diego: Academia Press, ^{2}1996).

Asad, T., *Genealogies of Religion: Discipline and Reasons of Power in Christianity and Islam* (Baltimore: Johns Hopkins University Press, 1993).

Buc, P., *The Danger of Ritual: Between Early Medieval Texts and Social Scientific Theory* (Princeton, N. J.: Princeton University Press, 2001).

Buchler, J. (ed.), *Philosophical Writings of Peirce* (New York: Dover, 1955).

Douglas, M., *Purity and Danger: An Analysis of Concepts of Pollution and Taboo* (New York: Praeger, 1966).

–, *Natural Symbols: Explorations in Cosmology* (New York: Random House, 1970).

–, *Implicit Meanings: Selected Essays in Anthropology* (London: Routledge, ^{2}1999).

–, *Leviticus as Literature* (Oxford: Oxford University Press, 1999).

Fabian, J., *Time and the Other: How Anthropology Makes Its Object* (New York: Columbia University Press, 1983).

Foster, S. W., "Symbolism and the Problematics of Postmodern Representation," in K. M. Ashley (ed.), *Victor Turner and the Construction of Cultural Criticism: Between Literature and Anthropology* (Bloomington: Indiana University Press, 1990) 117–37.

Gerstenberger, E., *Das dritte Buch Mose: Leviticus* (ATD; Göttingen: Vandenhoeck & Ruprecht, 1993).

–, *Leviticus: A Commentary* (OTL; Louisville, KY: Westminster John Knox, 1996).

Gilders, W. K., *Blood Ritual in the Hebrew Bible: Meaning and Power* (Baltimore: Johns Hopkins University Press, 2004).

–, "Why Does Eleazar Sprinkle the Red Cow Blood? Making Sense of a Biblical Ritual," *JHS* 6 (2006) (http://www.jhsonline.org/Articles/article_59.pdf doi:10.5508/jhs.2009.v6.a9).

–, "Anthropological Approaches: Ritual in Leviticus 8, Real or Rhetorical?," in J. M. LeMon/ K. H. Richards (ed.), *Method Matters: Essays on the Interpretation of the Hebrew Bible in Honor of David L. Petersen* (RBS 56; Atlanta: Society of Biblical Literature, 2009) 233–50.

–, "Ancient Israelite Sacrifice as Symbolic Action: Theoretical Reflections," *SEÅ* 78 (2013) 1–22.

Hieke, T., *Levitikus 1–15* (HThKAT; Freiburg: Herder, 2014).
Humphrey, C./Laidlaw, J., *The Archetypal Actions of Ritual: A Theory of Ritual Illustrated by the Jain Rite of Worship* (Oxford Studies in Social and Cultural Anthropology; New York: Oxford University Press, 1994).
Jay, N., *Throughout Your Generations Forever: Sacrifice, Religion, and Paternity* (Chicago: University of Chicago Press, 1992).
Kapferer, B., "Ritual Dynamics and Virtual Practice: Beyond Representation and Meaning," *Social Analysis* 48.2 (2004) 35–54.
Klawans, J., *Purity, Sacrifice, and the Temple: Symbolism and Supersessionism in the Study of Ancient Judaism* (New York: Oxford University Press, 2006).
–, "Methodology and Ideology in the Study of Priestly Ritual," in B.J. Schwartz et al. (ed.), *Perspectives on Purity and Purification in the Bible* (LHBOTS [JSOTSup] 474; New York: T&T Clark, 2008) 84–95.
–, "Symbol, Function, Theology, and Morality in the Study of Priestly Ritual," in J.W. Knust/Z. Várhelyi (ed.), *Ancient Mediterranean Sacrifice* (New York: Oxford University Press, 2011) 106–22.
Leach, E., *Culture and Communication: The Logic by which Symbols are Connected: An Introduction to the Use of Structuralist Analysis in Social Anthropology* (Themes in the Social Sciences; Cambridge: Cambridge University Press, 1976).
Lewis, G., *Day of Shining Red: An Essay on Understanding Ritual* (CSSA; Cambridge: Cambridge University Press, 1980).
McClymond, K., *Beyond Sacred Violence: A Comparative Study of Sacrifice* (Baltimore: Johns Hopkins University Press, 2008).
Noth, M., *Das dritte Buch Mose: Leviticus* (ATD; Göttingen: Vandenhoeck & Ruprecht, 1962).
–, *Leviticus: A Commentary* (OTL; Philadelphia: Westminster, 1965).
Rappaport, R., *Ritual and Religion in the Making of Humanity* (Cambridge Studies in Social and Cultural Anthropology 110; Cambridge: Cambridge University Press, 1999).
Sax, W.S., "Ritual and the Problem of Efficacy," in W.S. Sax/J. Quack/J. Weinhold (ed.), *The Problem of Ritual Efficacy* (New York: Oxford University Press, 2010) 3–16.
Schwartz, B.J., "Leviticus," in A. Berlin/M.Z. Brettler (ed.), *The Jewish Study Bible* (Oxford: Oxford University Press, [2]2014) 193–266.
Skorupski, J., *Symbol and Theory: A Philosophical Study of Theories of Religion in Social Anthropology* (Cambridge: Cambridge University Press, 1976).
Sperber, D., *Rethinking Symbolism* (Cambridge: Cambridge University Press, 1975).
Stackert, J., "Leviticus," in M.D. Coogan (ed.), *The New Oxford Annotated Bible* (Oxford: Oxford University Press, [4]2010) 141–83.
Stowers, S., "The Religion of Plant and Animal Offerings Versus the Religion of Meanings, Essences, and Textual Mysteries," in J.W. Knust/Z. Várhelyi (ed.), *Ancient Mediterranean Sacrifice* (Oxford: Oxford University Press, 2011) 35–56.
Turner, V., *The Forest of Symbols: Aspects of Ndembu Ritual* (Ithaca: Cornell University Press, 1967).
Valeri, V., *Kingship and Sacrifice: Ritual and Society in Ancient Hawaii* (Chicago: University of Chicago Press, 1985).
Watts, J.W., *Leviticus 1–10* (HCOT; Leuven: Peeters, 2013).
Wenham, G.J., *The Book of Leviticus* (NICOT; Grand Rapids, Mich.: Eerdmans, 1979).
"Ethnography," in C. Calhoun (ed.), *Dictionary of the Social Sciences* (Oxford: Oxford University Press, 2002), 149.

Hannah K. Harrington

The Role of Second Temple Texts in a Commentary on Leviticus

1 Introduction

There are many components to consider when writing a commentary on Leviticus. These include, but are not limited to, the use of ancient near eastern sources for studies of cultic traditions and philology, tradition history, source criticism, literary and rhetorical analyses, theology, anthropology, ritual studies, women's studies and canonical criticism. Alongside all of these worthy pursuits, I want to endorse and discuss the inclusion of Second Temple Jewish texts within any commentary effort on Leviticus. Indeed most scholars today regard Leviticus itself as a product of Second Temple Judaism.

1.1 Date and Audience

Consideration of the book's date and audience is at the heart of contemporary scholarship on Leviticus and must be dealt with in a good commentary. However, there is no agreement among scholars on the date of Leviticus' sources: pre-exilic, exilic, post-exilic. Personally, I agree with those who regard what is commonly called H (the Holiness Code; Leviticus 17–27) as coming after the priestly traditions (P). The writer of H is building on the earlier material.[1] The book clearly

1 Many scholars are now placing H after P (I. Knohl, *The Sanctuary of Silence: The Priestly Torah and the Holiness School* [Minneapolis: Fortress Press, 1995], 152–7; 220–1; J. Milgrom, *Leviticus 1–16* [AB 3; New York, NY: Doubleday, 1991], 13 notes that H builds on P's purity laws and abbreviates the prescriptions for the well-being offering, 7:18 vs. 19:7–8); holiness is extended from the priests to all Israel (e.g., 19:2; 20:7–8, 26; 21:8, 23; 22:9, 16, 33). H alters vocabulary of P by using other synonyms (Milgrom, *Leviticus 1–16*, 36), e.g. *maʿal* is replaced with *ḥillel* which can refer not only to sancta desecration (21:12) but pollution (22:9) and abstract rebellion against God (26:40); Niddah is a technical term for menstrual discharge in P but in H and in derivative literature (e.g. Ezek 7:19,20; Lam 1:9, 18; Ezra 9:11) it becomes a metaphor for impurity, indecency or disgrace that stems from moral rather than physical causes (Milgrom, *Leviticus 1–16*, 38). C. Nihan, *From Priestly Torah to Pentateuch: A Study in the Composition of the Book of Leviticus* (FAT.2 25; Tübingen: Mohr Siebeck, 2007), agrees with Milgrom and Knohl that H never stood as an independent document outside of Leviticus but revises P, p. 546. According to Nihan, H originates "in a first edition of the Torah in the Persian period, as argued by Otto, probably in the second half of the fifth century BCE," p. 548.

exhibits levels of redaction over a long period of time. Most scholars place the final redaction of the book in the late Persian period with some extending it into the Hellenistic period.[2] To be sure, the Dead Sea Scrolls (DSS) reveal variants of the Pentateuch well into the Hellenistic era, but even with these, the Torah was considered authoritative for practice. Most, but not all, scholars would agree that Leviticus does reflect the practice, to a large extent, of the Second Temple cult, and that its compilation as we have it is a Second Temple document although its separate traditions reach back into antiquity.[3]

A good commentary on Leviticus then should be interested in how the book was read by Second Temple priests and sages. Taking the book as a reflection of practice, to some extent, how does it align with other Second Temple cultic sources? The question is not only what Leviticus can tell us about later second temple sources but what can other second temple sources tell us about Leviticus. Indeed Leviticus cannot be understood as a coherent system of laws let alone be implemented without considerable interpretation as well as oral tradition.[4] I want to discuss here three major areas of benefit for a commentary on Leviticus to include later Second Temple sources related to the cult: 1) determining the state of the text; 2) clarifying ambiguity in Leviticus; and 3) fixing the chronological development of specific traditions while bringing into relief Second Temple issues.

---

2 Cf. the collected essays in T. Römer/K. Schmid (ed.), *Les dernières rédactions du Pentateuque, de l'Hexateuque et de l'Ennéateuque* (BETL 203; Leuven: Peeters, 2007), and T. Römer (ed.), *The Books of Leviticus and Numbers* (Leuven: University Press, 2007). Cf. also L. L. Grabbe (ed.), *Did Moses Speak Attic? Jewish Historiography and Scripture in the Hellenistic Period* (JSOTSup 317; Sheffield: Sheffield Academic Press, 2001), esp. the article by R. Albertz against N. P. Lemche on Hellenistic background, "An End to the Confusion? Why the Old Testament Cannot Be a Hellenistic Book!" 30–46, and in the same volume, B. Becking, "The Hellenistic Period and Ancient Israel: Three Preliminary Statements," 86, notes that there are no references to the struggles of the Hellenistic period or the notion of divine providence. The final redaction of Leviticus, in any case, cannot be later than the mid-third century BCE, because of the book's appearance among early Dead Sea Scrolls.

3 L. L. Grabbe summarizes a broad consensus with caution: "One is that the present form of the book was not reached until the Persian period; another is that the text as it now stands incorporates some material of considerable antiquity. Finally, the book probably says a good deal about the temple cult in the Second Temple period, but one should be cautious in assuming it is an actual description of what went on at that time," *An Introduction to Second Temple Judaism: History and Religion of the Jews in the Time of Nehemiah, the Maccabees, Hillel, and Jesus* (London: T&T Clark, 2010), 128.

4 E. Ben Zvi, "Inclusion and Exclusion from Israel," in S. W. Holloway (ed.), *The Pitcher is Broken* (Sheffield: Sheffield Academic Press, 1995), 127; M. Fishbane, *Biblical Interpretation in Ancient Israel* (Oxford: Clarendon Press, 1985), 91–5.

1.2 Texts

What comparative texts from Second Temple times would be of most benefit to a commentary on Leviticus? Although not an exhaustive list, by any means, it is essential that Ezra-Nehemiah and at least some of the Dead Sea Scrolls are taken into consideration.

Ezra-Nehemiah is the most extensive second temple work of a cultic nature. Scholars are arguing for later and later dates for the redaction of the final work, based on perceived Hellenistic components, e.g. modes of rhetoric.[5] Indeed the last referenced ruler is Darius III placing the *textus receptus* near the end of the 4th century BCE at the earliest. Thus, the question arises: which book, Ezra-Nehemiah or Leviticus, is first? A current trend is to opt for the intertwining of the dates of composition of the sources of both books. Christophe Nihan, for example, argues for three stages of composition in Leviticus parallel to the time of Ezra-Nehemiah, during the Persian Period, with closure effected in the late Persian or early Hellenistic period.[6] In any case, it is clear that a commentator needs to examine these two texts in tandem.

The Dead Sea Scrolls, although written later than Leviticus, should be included in a commentary on Leviticus because they provide an early reception history of Leviticus well within the Second Temple period. They may reflect older forms of the text. They may also clarify ambiguity in Leviticus, whether on a scribal level only or in actual practice, filling cracks in the rock and giving rise to intellectual vegetation. It is often possible to identify contemporary issues in Second Temple Judaism by the way in which the authors interpret Leviticus.

The most fertile DSS for a commentary on Leviticus will be cultic texts from the second-first century BCE: The Temple Scroll is stylized as a direct divine revelation of a new type but careful analysis reveals that the author knew and paraphrased sections of Leviticus as well as other books of the Pentateuch. Miqṣaṭ Maʿaseh ha-Torah and the Damascus Document disclose issues in interpretation and bring into relief ambiguity in the text of Leviticus itself. The Tohorot texts

5 Cf. also the collected essays of M.J. Boda/P.L. Redditt (ed.), *Unity and Disunity in Ezra-Nehemiah: Redaction, Rhetoric, and Reader* (Sheffield: Sheffield Phoenix Press, 2008). For the notion of a textual core centered in Nehemiah with accretions into the Hellenistic period, cf. J.L. Wright, "A New Model for the Composition of Ezra-Nehemiah," in O. Lipschits/R. Albertz/G. Knoppers (ed.), *Judah and the Judeans in the 4th Century BCE* (Winona Lake, IN: Eisenbrauns, 2007), 333–48.

6 Nihan, *From Priestly Torah to Pentateuch*, 19. See also M. Leuchter, "The Politics of Ritual Rhetoric: A Proposed Sociopolitical Context for the Redaction of Leviticus 1–16," *VT* 60 (2010) 345–65, who regards the priestly (but not the Holiness) traditions of Leviticus as a reaction to Nehemiah's usurpation of authority. Leviticus 1–16 supports Aaronide authority and combats Nehemiah's support of the Levites. Leviticus 1–16 supports the temple where Nehemiah extends prestige to the entire city of Jerusalem.

reveal the complexity of reading the purity laws of Leviticus and provide an early interpretation. This essay focuses on the benefits of using Ezra-Nehemiah and the Dead Sea Scrolls in a commentary on Leviticus.

2 State of the Text

The Dead Sea Scrolls include fragments of Leviticus that reveal slight variants but little substantial difference from the MT. More fruitful perhaps are the many paraphrases or quotations from Leviticus scattered throughout Second Temple literature. As an example, some form of Leviticus provides the basis for Nehemiah's wood collection decree which, according to Neh 10:35 [Heb], is "written in the law." At first glance, Nehemiah's insistence that the wood command is written in the Torah seems erroneous and authority-seeking since there is no reference to such a wood offering in the Pentateuch.[7] One could argue that the prescription does not refer to the collection process but to the immediately preceding words, "to burn on the altar of the Lord our God," an order recorded in Lev 6:1–6 [Heb]. But, burning wood on the altar seems self-evident, and a well-accepted cultic convention hardly in need of argument and reference to the law. Rather, Nehemiah is more likely arguing that an organized community wood collection is based on the law. But where is this law?

Recently, a possible solution has come to light. A heretofore unknown section of Leviticus may be reflected among the Dead Sea Scrolls and may be the base text for Nehemiah's wood collection: 4Q365, fragment 23 (see Figure 1). Scholars are presently developing criteria for determining if a Qumran text following a biblical book is an interpretation or an actual version of that book, for example, the extent and manner of reworking, voice, scope, and coverage.[8] The original assessment

7 But cf. Josephus, who refers to "the festival of wood-offering" on the 15th day of the 5th month (Ab) when all the people were accustomed to bring wood for the altar (War 2.425), and the Mishnah (m. Taʿan 4:5), which lists nine times during the year when certain families brought wood, one of which was a public collection on the 15th of Ab from the entire people. Preferred manuscripts attest a public collection also on the 9th of Ab (Milgrom, *Leviticus 1–16*, 387). Milgrom, *Leviticus 1–16*, 388, explains: "The wood was brought to the Temple with great ceremony. Bearers of the wood were forbidden to work on that day and were required to spend the night in Jerusalem, returning to their homes the following morning. ʾAggadic tradition tells of the courage and perseverance of those bringing the wood even in the face of danger to their lives (t. Taʿan 4:7–8)."

8 M. Segal, "4QReworked Pentateuch or 4QPentateuch?," in L.H. Schiffman et al. (ed.), *The Dead Sea Scrolls: Fifty Years After Their Discovery* (Jerusalem: Israel Museum, 2000), 394–5; id., "Between Bible and Rewritten Bible," in M. Henze (ed.), *Biblical Interpretation at Qumran* (Grand Rapids: Eerdmans, 2005), 15–16; M.M. Zahn, "The Problem of Characterizing the 4QReworked Pentateuch Manuscripts: Bible, Rewritten Bible, or None of the Above?," *DSD* 15 (2008), 316.

of 4Q365, fragment 23, by Tov and White was that the text was non-scriptural, but this conclusion has been challenged separately by several scholars because of the known variation among versions of the biblical text in the early Second Temple period, and recently Tov has changed his position to the Scripture camp as well.[9] Indeed the text speaks in the same voice of the Leviticus material without interruption. In fact 4Q365 23 introduces the legislation on the wood offering, "And the Lord spoke to Moses, saying." This is an introductory formula, which occurs throughout Leviticus, and is especially prominent in the Festival Calendar (Lev 23:1, 9, 23, 26, 33; 24:1).[10] Thus, in 4Q365 we have possible evidence of a version of Leviticus that did have a wood festival. The tradition of a wood festival in the Second Temple is corroborated by the Temple Scroll, Josephus and the Mishna (cf. 11Q19; War 2.425; m. Taʿan. 4:5).[11] Perhaps a version of Leviticus was circulating in Second Temple times which contained a prescription for wood collection. This would explain why Nehemiah states that he found the regulation in the law. A good commentary on Leviticus would check the Dead Sea Scrolls for textual variants.

Translation of the additional text (line 4 until line 11):

4 And Yahweh spoke to Moses, saying, command the children of Israel, [Lev 24:1–2a] saying, when you come to the land which

5 I am giving to you for an inheritance, and you dwell upon it securely, you will bring calves for a burnt offering and for all the wo[r]k of

6 [the H]ouse which you will build for me in the land, to arrange them upon the altar of burnt offering, and the calv[es] …

7 … for Passover sacrifices and for whole burnt offerings and for thank offerings and for free-will offerings and for burnt-offerings, daily …

9 E. Tov/S. White, "Reworked Pentateuch," in H. Attridge et al. (ed.), *Discoveries in the Judaean Desert XIII* (Clarendon Press: Oxford 1994), 191; E. Tov, "Biblical Texts as Reworked in Some Qumran Manuscripts with Special Attention to 4QRP and 4QParaGen-Exod," in E. Ulrich/J. C. VanderKam (ed.), *The Community of the Renewed Covenant: The Notre Dame Symposium on the Dead Sea Scrolls* (Notre Dame, IN: University of Notre Dame Press, 1994), 113–14. See further citations and discussion in Zahn, "Problem," 316–17.

10 Zahn, "Problem," 331.

11 On the basis of 4Q365 23, Y. Yadin identified the festival of Columns 23–25 in the Temple Scroll as a wood offering festival to be celebrated exactly 50 days after the New Oil festival (last week of Elul, the 6th month). The author describes the festival continuing for 6 days, with two different tribes bringing wood per day (11Q19; 4Q365). The equality of the tribes is reflected in both the Temple Scroll and 4Q365. Unlike the later Rabbis, neither of these authors nor Nehemiah gives privilege to any group of Israel concerning the wood collection. The order of days too is the same in the Temple Scroll as in 4Q365, Y. Yadin, *The Temple Scroll*, I (Jerusalem: Israel Exploration Society, 1983), 125; J. Milgrom, *Leviticus 23–27* (AB 3B; New York, NY: Doubleday, 2001), 2073–4.

8 ... and for the doors and for all the work of the House the[y] (or: he) will br[ing] ...

9 ... *the [fe]stival (or: appointed time) of fresh oil they will bring wood two [by two] ...*

10 ... *the ones who bring on the fir[st] day, Levi ...*

11 ... *[Reu]ben and Simeon and [on t]he fou[rth] day ... ix*

Figure 1: 4Q*365* Frag. 23—Lev 23:42–24:2 + add

3 Identification and Clarification of Ambiguity in the Text

The cultic texts of the DSS bring into relief ambiguities in Leviticus and provide early interpretations of them from Second Temple times. Some would argue that the overall point of Leviticus is to establish the authority of the Torah and the Aaronide priests, but there is a noticeable lack of clear polemics in the case of particular laws.[12] Focus on the early reception of Leviticus in the DSS shifts the focus from context of Leviticus, which is limited and quite speculative, to the meaning of the text. Here are some examples from the cult:

3.1 Cultic Procedures

(1) According to Leviticus 5:5, sinners must first confess the sin they have committed before presenting a sacrifice. However, the text does not state to whom they should confess—the priest? God? Themselves? The Damascus Document explains that they first confess to the priest (CD IX, 13). Some may argue that the Damascus Document is being polemical because the later rabbis state that confession could be private and inaudible (b. Sot 32b; y. Yeb 8:3 = private and inaudible). However, the Damascus Document is much closer to the time of Leviticus.

(2) Leviticus also requires persons healed of scale-disease to bring accompanying cereal offerings and libations for purification (Lev 14:10). Does this mean that all sinners are to bring these offerings? This is indeed the position of the Temple Scroll. (11Q19 XVIII, 5–6; XXV, 6,14; opp. m. Menaḥ. 9:6). It is possible that the Temple Scroll is a witness here to early practice; the Rabbis later reject this view but have difficulty in doing so (b. Menaḥ. 90b–91b).[13]

12 Cf. e.g. J.W. Watts, "Ritual Rhetoric in the Pentateuch: The Case of Leviticus 1–16," in T. Römer (ed.), *The Books of Leviticus and Numbers* (BETL; Leuven: Peeters, 2008), 314.

13 Cf. Milgrom, *Leviticus 1–16*, 845–6, for the difficulty of the Rabbis in arguing that the adjunct cereal offering and libation for scale disease treat only that type of impurity and are not required for all sinners.

3.2 Food

(1) *Sacrificial food.* The power of Leviticus and its priestly interpreters in Second Temple times comes into view by the prohibition of slaughter by local butchers of all animals of sacrificial types, e.g. lamb, goat, bull. Lev 17:3–4 requires Israel to offer all meat of these animals first as sacrifices at the sanctuary, with choice portions given to the priests. Deuteronomy 12, by contrast, allows for secular slaughter away from the sanctuary in the villages of Israel once Israel settles throughout the land and the journey is simply too far to travel to Jerusalem for every meat occasion. What is interesting is that Second Temple exegetes prefer the Leviticus version. The priests behind the Temple Scroll required sacral slaughter of animal meat within three days journey of Jerusalem, in effect encompassing all the cities of Israel (11Q19 LII, 13–15; opp. Sifre Deut 71[134]). This interpretation could be relegated to the visionary category except that a non-eschatological, legal Scroll, *Miqtsat Maʿaseh ha-Torah* (MMT), regards sacrifice as legitimate only at the Jerusalem sanctuary (MMT B 27–35). MMT is clearly of sectarian provenance, and preserved by the settlers at Qumran, who apparently did not attend the Jerusalem Temple and may not have offered sacrifices at all.[14] Nevertheless, in a perfect world, the author regards slaughter of these kinds of animals for meat as legitimate only at the Jerusalem sanctuary (MMT B 27–35). It appears that Leviticus was taken very seriously in Second Temple times to the benefit of powerful priests in Jerusalem.

An offshoot of this attitude that meat should be sacrificed before eating, is the tendency among many Second Temple Jews to eat ordinary food in a state of purity. Both Essenes and Pharisees require eating ordinary food in a state of purity (Josephus; see also Mark 7). It has been said that these Jews were trying to mimic the holy activity of the priests, following the Exodus 19:6 mandate of the nation to be a royal priesthood (Jubilees).[15] However, these pious Jews were not trying to function as priests by eating in a cultic state of purity, but they believed they were honoring the Torah's intent. Leviticus 17 provides fertile soil for the practice of eating in purity (see also Lev 11:2, which directs pure food laws to all Israel). If all Jews must eat their meat first as sacrifices, they would all have to be in a state of ritual purity before eating meat.

(2) *Holy fruit.* Leviticus 19:24 states that a fruit tree's first yield in the fourth year is holy. Also, Leviticus 27:30 is clear that firstborn animals and, in fact, all

---

14 But see J. Magness, "Were Sacrifices Offered at Qumran? The Animal Bone Deposits Reconsidered," *JAJ* 7 (2016), 5–34.

15 See discussion in T. Kazen, *Issues of Impurity in Early Judaism* (CBNTS 45; Winona Lake, IN: Eisenbrauns, 2010), 115–23.

tithes are holy as well and belong, by definition, to the Lord.[16] What does this mean? Does the offerer give it to the priest? Eat it in the sanctuary courts? Give it to a Levite? The Dead Sea Scrolls clarify this ambiguity. The Temple Scroll and MMT assign these items to the priest (11Q19 LX 2–3; MMT B 62). Apparently, this was not without controversy. Some interpreters, like the later Rabbis, did not assign these items to the priests but, following Deuteronomy's tithing laws, allowed Jewish owners to eat their own tithes joyfully in the temple environs (Deut 14:23; cf. also 11Q19 L 7–12).[17] Do the Rabbis represent a later alleviation of the law while the Scrolls attest to early practice? In any case, the ambiguity resident in Leviticus comes into relief when reading these early interpretations, and the modern commentator must deal with it.

3.3 Sexuality

The sexual laws of Lev 18–20 form a significant part of the writer's call to holiness, but gaps in the description of the law cause ambiguity, which must be settled for actual practice. Second Temple Jews read these laws conservatively and decided ambiguity with a strong degree of caution even for these non-priestly laws incumbent on all Jews. Take incest for example:

(1) Leviticus 18:13 prohibits a man to marry his aunt. But, this raises the question whether or not he is allowed to marry his niece? Is this not the same type of relationship? The Temple Scroll and the Damascus Document both point this out (11Q19 LXVI, 14–17; CD V, 7–11); both writers explicitly forbid uncle-niece marriages. This is not the view of the later Rabbis who read Leviticus more literally in this case and forbid only nephew-aunt marriages.[18]

(2) In the same vein, Leviticus 18:18 rules, “You shall not take a woman as a rival wife to her sister, having sexual relations with her while her sister is alive.” Does this only refer to marriage with two sisters or is it a prohibition against polygamy, which causes rivalry between wives? The Temple Scroll rules decidedly against both polygamy and divorce even for the king, interpreting that a man is under obligation to his wife as long as she lives (11Q19 LVII, 17f).

Reading Leviticus with Second Temple exegetes brings the ambiguities of the text and their early interpretations into relief. The list continues beyond the

16 Technically speaking, the holy part of the tithe is the tenth of it which the Levites set aside for the priests (Num 18:25–32).

17 One of the reforms Nehemiah is especially proud of is the re-assignment of the holy portions of crops to the Levites and priests (Neh 12:47; cf. 13:10–14), since Jews were not “setting aside as holy” agricultural gifts. Furthermore, priests who were not qualified were barred from receiving the sacred perquisites (Ezra 2:63; Neh 7:65).

18 Also, non-legal texts from Qumran report that Amram married his aunt Jochebed and Miriam married her uncle Uzziel; 4QVisions of Amram; cf. Aramaic Levi Document 11:10–11.

examples provided here with clarifications of which kinds of creatures may/may not be eaten, which kinds of vessels are impure, or not, and the extent of contamination among impure persons. Clearly, the text was considered authoritative by Jews of the time, many of whom were careful to observe its rules regarding food and sex in an effort to maintain holiness. A thorough commentary on Leviticus should treat it within the full context of the Second Temple: its interpretation, application, and surrounding issues.[19]

4 Chronology of the Text

In a strong commentary on Leviticus the reader should find some understanding of how Second Temple authors interacted with the traditions found in the text and some early development of interpretation. To this end, the commentator should be attuned to the evolution of terminology and examine particular traditions for a logical sequence of thought.

4.1 Terminology

Ezra-Nehemiah is a good place to begin a comparison of terms and traditions with Leviticus. In my view, Leviticus informs all sources of Ezra-Nehemiah.[20] Prescriptions for the offerings are understood in detail, e.g. the guilt offering which is brought for *maʿal*, "sacrilege" (Ezra 10:19) and the various needs of the temple cult (cf. Ezra 6:9–10; Neh 10:31–39). Moreover, in addition to general cultic traditions, Ezra-Nehemiah utilizes specific text and terminology from Leviticus sometimes in a different way.[21] The cultic terms, *maʿal* and *ʾasham*,

19 J. Sawyer, "A Critical Review of Recent Projects and Publications," *Hebrew Bible and Ancient Israel* 1.3 (2012) (special issue on Reception History, edited by C. Newsom), 319, reminds the would-be commentator, "As biblical experts, are we not primarily concerned with the text and its interpretations? The historical, contextual data are essential, but ancillary to our main task which is interpreting the Bible." For publications on the DSS and Leviticus, see his compendium, *Reading Leviticus: Responses to Mary Douglas* (LHB/OTS; Sheffield: Sheffield Academic Press, 1996); for more recent works on the rereading of the Bible at Qumran, see A. Feldman/L. Goldman, *Scripture and Interpretation: Qumran Texts that Rework the Bible* (BZAW 449; Berlin: De Gruyter, 2014).

20 In fact, the author of Ezra-Nehemiah refers several times to practices that are "written in the law" (Ezra 3:2; Neh 8:17; 10:34, 36; cf. Neh 13:1, "The Book of Moses").

21 Milgrom, *Leviticus 23–27*, 2277 finds a correlation between Leviticus and 26:1–2 and Nehemiah 10:31–40, although he argues that they both use the same earlier source. When pledging themselves to the covenant, the community moves from fidelity to Yahweh (Neh 10:30–31//Lev 26:1) to Sabbath observance (Neh 10:32//Lev 26:2a) to sanctuary veneration (Neh 10:33–40//Lev 26:2b).

"reparation," have moved from their moorings in the sanctuary where they label sacrilege and its reparation of holy items to the desecration of Jewish bodies.

Purity terms in Ezra-Nehemiah reflect some development from an older usage in Leviticus. *Tum'ah*, a technical term for ritual impurity in Leviticus, is applied to outsiders in Ezra-Nehemiah.[22] The root *badal*, "to separate, distinguish," is used as a general mantra in the priestly traditions for the priests who must separate sacred from profane items (Lev 10:10) and distinguish pure foods from impure ones (Lev 11:47). But in the holiness traditions a rationale for this imperative is given: just as pure animals must be distinguished from impure ones, so Israel herself is to be separated from other nations (Lev 20:24–26). Ezra-Nehemiah goes one step further in labeling those other nations impure and identifying Israel as only those of the returnees group. Whereas Leviticus uses *badal* to emphasize separation between purity and impurity (cf. Lev 11:47; 20:25), Ezra-Nehemiah uses the term to separate people of different origins.[23]

Leviticus 18, especially, informs Ezra 9–10 with its emphasis on *tame'*, "impure," *niddah*, "menstrual impurity," and *toevah*, "abomination." The writer of Ezra-Nehemiah, like Leviticus, applies these terms to the threat of illicit sexual relations, but he increases the emphasis on pollution (Ezra 9:10–11; cf. Lev 18:24–27). While *niddah* refers only to menstrual impurity in Leviticus with one exception for incest (Lev 20:21), Ezra-Nehemiah uses the term more broadly in the phrases "impure land" and "impurity of the peoples of the land" (Ezra 9:11). Ezra-Nehemiah follows exilic and post-exilic usage (Ezek 7:19–20; Lam 1:17; 2 Chron 29:5) in using *niddah* as a metaphor for sin. Furthermore, Leviticus 18 does not extend this abomination to intermarriage. This is an innovation of Ezra-Nehemiah (cf. Ezra 9–10). Additionally, the root גאל *ga'al*, "defile, pollute, stain," with *'alef* is introduced to describe the defilement of the priesthood by intermarriage (Neh 13:29). This root is a later form of געל, *ga'al*, a pollution term found in Leviticus (e.g. Lev 26:11, 43).[24]

22 Also, *ḥaram* has moved from a wartime destruction commanded by Yahweh to a peace-time dedication of goods to the sanctuary in accord with Leviticus 27. Another term, *'am ha'aretz* (Lev 4:7, 20:2), refers to a resident alien living among the people of Israel who supports their traditions and law in Leviticus and Deuteronomy, but in Ezra-Nehemiah the term refers to foreigners, Milgrom, *Leviticus 17–22* (AB 3A; New York, NY: Doubleday, 2000), 1362.

23 Fishbane, *Biblical Interpretation*, 117–23.

24 F. Brown et al., *The New Brown, Driver, Briggs, Gesenius Hebrew-English Lexicon* (Peabody: Hendrickson Publishers, 1979), 146. Cf. also later usage of this root, spelled with *'ayin* only, in rabbinic literature, e.g. m. 'Abod.Zar. 5:12; b. 'Abod.Zar. 76a; b. Zebaḥ. 88a, M. Jastrow, *Sefer Milim: Dictionary of the Targumim, Talmud Babli, Yerushalmi, and Midrashic Literature* (New York: The Judaic Press, 1982), 261.

4.2 Logical Sequence of Traditions

Terminology alone will not decide chronology issues. Commentators must also analyze chronology of the sources and traditions of Leviticus and Ezra-Nehemiah based on the most logical sequence of development of the law. Four examples illustrate the necessity of examining single traditions: a) tithing; b) holy days; c) the resident alien; d) intermarriage.

Tithing. The priestly tithing laws (Lev 27:32; cf. Num 18:21), which assume a 1–10 ratio of priests to Levites, are assumed to be binding in Ezra-Nehemiah (Neh 11). But the reality of the text in Ezra-Nehemiah is that the Levites comprise a very small percentage of temple personnel, with the ratio of priests to Levites being closer to 12 priests to 1 Levite. Thus, Ezra-Nehemiah did not innovate tithing but the priestly regulations must precede it.[25]

Holy Days. While my position is that Leviticus in some form influences Ezra-Nehemiah, some scholars disagree, and the commentator on Leviticus will need to sort these views out.[26] One major contention is that the fast of Yom Kippur is not mentioned in Ezra-Nehemiah although there is a strong emphasis on the other sacred assemblies of the seventh month. Is it possible that the writer did not know about Yom Kippur? Also, Ezra-Nehemiah seems unaware of the Leviticus tradition on Sukkot, with its mention of different trees and fruit.[27] In my view, Ezra-Nehemiah facilitates the text of Leviticus 23 by specifying what materials and fruit are to be included in the observance of the festival (Neh 8:13–18; cf. Lev 23:40), but others would place Leviticus 23 after Nehemiah 8.

Resident Alien. Leviticus regards the *ger*, "resident alien," as part of the Israelite community; he is not a stranger like the Canaanites of Deuteronomy who must be destroyed. Milgrom regards the *ger* as a "protected stranger" explaining that "he has uprooted himself (or has been uprooted) from his homeland and has taken permanent resident in the land of Israel."[28] He is a free person with the same civil rights as the Israelite except that he may not own land; he is not a slave but a hired hand. According to Leviticus 19, Israel must love this stranger who lives among them as themselves (19:34).[29] In fact, Leviticus17 enjoins the *ger* to observe the laws of purity and sacrifice alongside native-born Israelites (Lev 17:8–15).

---

25 Milgrom, *Leviticus 1–16*, 12.

26 See, for example, L.L. Grabbe, "The Law of Moses in the Ezra Tradition: More Virtual Than Real," in J.W. Watts (ed.), *Persia and Torah: The Theory of Imperial Authorization of the Pentateuch* (Atlanta: SBL Press, 2001), 91–114.

27 See discussion in H.G.M. Williamson, *Studies in Persian Period History and Historiography* (Tübingen: Mohr Siebeck, 2004), 238.

28 Milgrom, *Leviticus 17–22*, 1416.

29 Based on vocabulary of Near Eastern treaties, this is not intimate affection or familiarity but practical obligation to be loyal to the *ger* and provide him with essentials, if needed, Milgrom, *Leviticus 17–22*, 1418.

Still, the *ger* is always distinguished from Israel. There is no sense of conversion of his status, but he remains in a separate category and some obligations as well as benefits do not apply to him.[30] Milgrom points out, "Conversion as such was unknown in the ancient world. Ethnicity was the only criterion for membership in a group."[31] Against Gerstenberger (1996), he argues that while the *ger* may not worship other gods (Lev 17:8–9), he is still not a member of Israel's "faith community."[32]

Championing the binary opposition of pure/impure and holy/profane, second Temple cultic sources often try to exclude the *ger* from Israel in spite of the generous attitude of Leviticus (cf. 11Q19 XL, 5–7; 4QFlor I, 4).[33] The idea of separation and distinction in the context of holiness in Ezra-Nehemiah no doubt comes from the priestly traditions of Leviticus, but the author ostracizes the "people of the land" who live among them and labeled them "impure" (cf. Ezra 6:19–21; 9:11; cf. Neh 13:9). The Aramaic Targum of Leviticus goes so far as to drop the term "*ger*" from the text on occasion (cf. Targum Ps.-Jonathan on Lev 20:2–3, which omits the *ger* from the prohibition against child sacrifice and reinterprets the law as a ban on intermarriage. Giving one's offspring to Molek is reinterpreted as giving a child in marriage to a non-Israelite; see below.)[34]

A question for the Leviticus commentator is: Do the expansive statements of Leviticus toward the *ger* precede or follow Ezra-Nehemiah? Mary Douglas argues that Leviticus is a response to the harsh decrees of Ezra-Nehemiah toward outsiders. Douglas claims that Leviticus' progressive notions about impurity follow Ezra-Nehemiah rather than precede them.[35] However, if this were the case, why is there no overt polemic in Leviticus and instead a neutral sense of

30 According to Milgrom, *Leviticus 23–27*, 2022, the *ger* is not included in H's Yom Kippur rites; his advertent sins do not pollute the sanctuary. He may also slaughter meat profanely, Milgrom, *Leviticus 17–22*, 1357 on Lev 17:3–4.

31 Milgrom, *Leviticus 17–22*, 1499.

32 Cf. Milgrom, *Leviticus 17–22*, 1495, 1499; E.S. Gerstenberger, *Leviticus*, tr. D.W. Stott [Das dritte Buch Mose: Leviticus (Göttingen; Vandenhoeck & Ruprecht, 1993)] (Louisville, KY: Westminster John Knox, 1996), 279, 326.

33 See H.K. Harrington, "Intermarriage in the Temple Scroll: Strategies of Neutralization," in R.E. Gane/A. Taggar-Cohen (ed.), *Current Issues in Priestly and Related Literature: The Legacy of Jacob Milgrom and Beyond* (Atlanta: SBL Press, 2015), 474–8.

34 Targum Ps.-Jonathan on Lev 18:21 makes the matter explicit:

וּמִן זַרְעָךְ לָא תִתֵּן בְּתַשְׁמִישְׁתָּה לְצֵיד בַּת עַמְמִין לְמֶעְבְּרָא לְפוּלְחָנָא אוֹחְרָא וְלָא תָפִיס יַת שְׁמָא דֶאֱלָהָךְ אֲנָא יְיָ:

"And do not give up any of your seed to sexual relations with a daughter of the Gentiles, passing them to foreign worship; you shall not profane the name of your God. I am Yhwh." Nevertheless, Targum Onqelos keeps the original meaning of giving a child to Molek:

וּמִזַּרְעָךְ לָא תִתֵּין לְאַעְבָרָא לְמוֹלֵךְ וְלָא תַחֵיל יָת שְׁמָא דַאֱלָהָךְ אֲנָא יוי:

"And do not give up any of your seed to pass through (fire) to Molek and do not profane the name of your God. I am Yhwh."

35 M. Douglas, "Responding to Ezra: The Priests and the Foreign Wives," *BibInt* 10 (2002), 16–23.

teaching the particulars of the laws of purity and pollution? (cf. Lev 11:1–2; 12:1–2; 14:1–2; 15:1–2).

To my mind, the narrow attitude toward the resident alien fits an Israel lacking in political autonomy, which is suspicious of and even paranoid of a foreign element, however sympathetic, within the community. Leviticus, on the other hand, regards the *ger* as part of the community, not one of the idolatrous Canaanites which Israel must keep separate from (Lev 20:23–26). The *ger* observes the law along with native-born Israelites—even to offering sacrifices (Lev 17:18) and cleansing from ritual impurity (Lev 17:15). It makes more sense to see Leviticus' generous attitude to the *ger* as having roots in an Israel which is in charge of her own destiny and land from pre-exilic times, no matter when its final redaction. Ezra-Nehemiah, on the other hand, reveals the constraints of invasion, deportation and return as a threatened minority. In any case, a good commentary on Leviticus needs to deal with its relationship to Ezra-Nehemiah.

Intermarriage. Related to the exclusion of the *ger*, many Second Temple texts starting with Ezra-Nehemiah also share a prohibition on intermarriage. While Leviticus warns Israel to keep separate from her neighbors and their idolatrous practices, it gives no explicit bans on marriage with a resident alien, except in the case of the high priest (Lev 21:14). By contrast, Ezra-Nehemiah not only prohibits intermarriage with any non-Israelite but Ezra forces the dissolution of existing unions (Ezra 10:5–12). Furthermore, other Second Temple texts interpret Leviticus to mean that such intermarriage is forbidden.

The judgment against one who "has given of his seed unto Molek, to pollute my sanctuary, and to profane my holy name" (Lev 20:3; cf. 18:21), is probably rooted in ancient forms of child sacrifice, but is interpreted in Second Temple times as the desecration of giving one's child in marriage to a foreigner (Targum Ps.-Jonathan on Lev 18:21; Jub 30:13–15; cf. m. Meg. 4:9). Jubilees adds that the father who gives his daughter in marriage to a foreigner becomes defiled as well (Jub 30:10). Some might regard Ezra-Nehemiah as an anomaly in its harsh marriage attitude without much influence on later times, but the Scrolls reveal that opposition to intermarriage formed a strong trajectory in Second Temple Judaism.[36]

36 M. Himmelfarb, "Levi, Phinehas, and the Problem of Intermarriage at the Time of the Maccabean Revolt," *JSQ* 6 (1999), 1–24, on pp. 17–23 argues that intermarriage between Jews and Gentiles was not an issue for MMT, and in fact not in Second Temple times. Himmelfarb agrees with the editors of MMT that the problem is between priests marrying women from non-priestly families. However, C. Hayes, *Gentile Impurities and Jewish Identities* (Oxford: Oxford University Press, 2002), points out that the intermarriage at issue here is marriage between an Israelite and a resident alien, not with an outright foreigner: "Intermarriage with unconverted Gentiles was not a widespread social problem, as Himmelfarb demonstrates, nor was it broadly tolerated as an acceptable practice in theory," 83. Hayes sees the problem as marriage between Jews and converted Gentiles, "those persons of profane seed who are assimilated through circumcision and intermarriage." So also is the problem in Jubilees 30.

The cultic material available, largely Jubilees, Aramaic Levi, and several of the Dead Sea Scrolls, never endorses intermarriage.[37] Rather many of these texts are pointedly against it following in the same vein as Ezra-Nehemiah.[38] It seems that there is a tightening of the ranks here that places Leviticus earlier rather than later than Hellenistic times. If the Holiness traditions are to be dated after Ezra-Nehemiah, one would expect some argument against alienating the stranger and forcing divorce in the case of intermarriage. Rather, the author seems to be grappling with Leviticus, rather than the other way around. The commentator of Leviticus should take into account the whole field of Second Temple cultic data when attempting to develop a chronology of its traditions.

In the cases of the resident alien and intermarriage, later interpreters have placed a spin on Leviticus that coheres with their agenda. However, sometimes a "spin" may actually reflect the original understanding of the text. Leviticus 19:19 reads:

אֶת־חֻקֹּתַי תִּשְׁמֹרוּ בְּהֶמְתְּךָ לֹא־תַרְבִּיעַ כִּלְאַיִם שָׂדְךָ לֹא־תִזְרַע כִּלְאָיִם וּבֶגֶד כִּלְאַיִם שַׁעַטְנֵז לֹא יַעֲלֶה עָלֶיךָ׃

> You shall heed my statutes: You shall not let your cattle mate with a different kind (*kilʾaim*); you shall not sow your field with two kinds (*kilʾaim*) of seed; and clothing made of two kinds (*kilʾaim*) of yarn you shall not put on yourself.

The text continues immediately with the law of a man who has had sexual intercourse with a slave girl assigned to another man who has not been ransomed or released. Thus, the text starts with unlawful mixtures of crops, animal mating, and fabric weaving and proceeds to an illicit sexual union among humans.[39]

The most striking exegesis of Lev 19:19 among Second Temple interpreters is found in MMT:

---

37 I.C. Werrett, *Ritual Purity and the Dead Sea Scrolls* (Leiden: Brill, 2007) lists all passages in the Qumran Scrolls on intermarriage (CD 19:15–21; 4Q251 17 7; 4Q394 8 iii 9b–19a; 4Q396 1–2 iv 4–11a; 4Q513 2 ii 2–5; 11Q19 57:15b–17a) and finds that only 11Q19 57:15b–17a, which appears to endorse the captive foreign bride, permits it, 287; but cf. Harrington, "Intermarriage," for the argument that this "endorsement" is really a strategy of neutralization, 478–81.

38 There is a strain in early Second Temple times, which maintains a more open attitude toward intermarriage, at least for laity, which eventually gives rise to the notion of formal conversion, cf. Hayes, *Gentile Impurities*, 78; Milgrom, *Leviticus 17–22*, 1501. However, I would argue, that this strain is not the dominant one, especially in priestly-legal circles. Although some would point to Ruth as inclusive, a second glance shows that it is not. Ruth remains a Moabite throughout the text, even after her marriage to Boaz (Milgrom, *Leviticus 1–16*, 1417); only her progeny become Israelite. Isaiah and Ezekiel envision a time when the *ger* can fully participate in the cult (Isa 14:1) and own land in Israel (Ezek 47:22–23), but that time is not the present under the oppression of foreign empires.

39 Many scholars have conjectured that the agricultural cases given are metaphors for illicit sexual union (e.g. G.J. Wenham, *The Book of Leviticus* [NICOT; Grand Rapids: Eerdmans, 1979]; C.M. Carmichael, "Forbidden Mixtures," *VT* 32 [1982], 392–415; H. Eilberg-Schwartz, *The Savage in Judaism* [Bloomington: Indiana University Press, 1990]). However, Milgrom

it is written that one must not let it mate with another species; and concerning his clothes [it is written that they should not] be of mixed stuff; and he must not sow his field and vine[yard with mixed specie]s. Because they (Israel) are holy, and the sons of Aaron are [most holy.] (tr. Qimron/Strugnell, *Qumran Cave 4*, 57).

The citation of Leviticus 19:19 here is unmistakable, although, like the Aramaic Targum, the author uses the root *eirev* instead of *kil'aim* for forbidden mixtures.[40]
Furthermore, the text compares intermarriage to these amixia:

And you know that some of the priests and the people intermarry and mix and defile the holy seed and also [even] their own [i. e., the priests' most holy] seed, with (female outsiders [i. e. Gentile women] (tr. Hayes, *Gentile Impurities*, 84).[41]

One can see from the analogy provided by Lev 19:19, that is, fabrics, animals, crops, that the contention is physical amixia. For the author, intermarriage is simply improper hybridism. Assimilated or not, a gentile is still a gentile.

The fact is that throughout late biblical literature, *eirev* is used to describe illicit sexual unions (cf. Ps 106:34–35; Dan 2:43). Ezra-Nehemiah utilizes the term, *eirev*, "mixture," to ban intermarriage (Ezra 9:2; Neh 13:3). The writer explains that by eradicating intermarriage, Israel removed all of the *eirev* within it (Neh 13:3).[42] Ezra-Nehemiah also seems to take its cue on impure mixtures from Lev 19:19 with its prohibition on mixing seeds. The elders are flabbergasted that the people are mixing *zera' qadosh*, "holy seed" (Ezra 9:2). Only the unadulterated remnant, i. e. the returnees, is "holy seed."[43] The "seed" text (forgive the pun) for improper

---

rightly questions why the author would not simply issue a law against intermarriage, if that were his intention (Milgrom, *Leviticus 17–22*, 1659). But the intention of the mixed agriculture laws is difficult to ascertain. The fact that they are presented in Leviticus immediately preceding the prohibition on sexual relations between a Jew and a slave girl (Lev 19:20) may give further credence to a sexual intention and interpretation. As J. Burnside, *God, Justice, and Society: Aspects of Law and Legality in the Bible* (Oxford: Oxford University Press, 2010), 396, points out, "However, although Leviticus 19:20 only prohibits this sexual relationship, Qumran law uses Leviticus 19 as a springboard to prohibit sexual relations between *all* Israelites and non-Israelites." Burnside notes that while this seems like a manipulation of the text, the Qumran author does not see a difference between his text and Leviticus itself.

40 Instead of the Hebrew term *kil'aim* for improper mixtures, the Aramaic Targum prefers cognates *erubin* (Onkelos) and *irbubin* (Ps-Jon), although *kil'aim* is retained in the Neofiti, cf. Milgrom, *Leviticus 17–22*, 1659.

41 Qimron and Strugnell see the problem as sexual relations between priestly and non-priestly families (*Qumran Cave 4*, 57), but I agree with Hayes that the issue is more likely between Israelites and Gentiles who reside among them; cf. Hayes, *Gentile Identities*, 82.

42 G. Hepner, "The Relationship between Biblical Narrative and Biblical Law," *JBQ* (2001), 263–8. This harks back as well to the exodus situation in which an *eirev rav*, a "mixed multitude," came up out of Egypt, i. e. Israelites and Egyptians, and caused contention later.

43 H. G. M. Williamson, *Ezra, Nehemiah* (WBC 16; Waco, TX: Word, 1985), 132, grapples with this strange phrase and suggests that it was "coined by a mental combination of the frequent use of the phrase 'the seed of Abraham,' the use of the cognate verb, '(sow) seed,' in Lev 19.19,

mixtures is Lev 19:19. One has to ask, was the levitical writer using these mixtures symbolically to make a statement against intermarriage with idolaters? Perhaps the symbolic point of the forbidden mixtures is to discourage intermarriage.

5 Conclusion

A few decades ago, the idea that one should examine late Second Temple texts when writing a commentary on Leviticus may have seemed like a methodologically faulty enterprise but no longer. The later dates of the redaction of Leviticus in recent scholarship require scholars to take the entire second temple collection of cultic texts seriously. Ezra-Nehemiah especially may have been redacted around the same time as the *textus receptus* of Leviticus and thus the data and issues of both texts are relevant to each other. The Dead Sea Scroll authors, who viewed Leviticus as authoritative text, are especially important to a commentary on Leviticus and place a limit on the time of its redaction. They also represent our earliest witnesses to the actual text. The gaps which they fill in the text of Leviticus represent an early reception of the text, one much closer to the original than heretofore available.

The interpretations of Leviticus and polemics found in the Scrolls would be of interest to readers of a Leviticus commentary. Commentators should grapple with the chronology of cultic traditions reflected throughout the Second Temple period when making decisions regarding the date of particular traditions. Issues related to the cult and sexuality remain high on the agenda of many Second Temple authors, especially the priestly sect responsible for many of the Dead Sea Scrolls. The way to holiness is decidedly physical and genealogical for many second temple authors in the aftermath of Leviticus, and issues regarding intermarriage and gentiles, for example, could only be properly solved by taking the authoritative data of Leviticus (as well as the rest of the Torah) into account. The modern commentator of Leviticus too would do well to take into account the fruition, which develops in Second Temple Judaism from the seedbed of Leviticus.

Bibliography

Albertz, R., "An End to the Confusion? Why the Old Testament Cannot Be a Hellenistic Book!," in L.L. Grabbe (ed.), *Did Moses Speak Attic? Jewish Historiography and Scripture in the Hellenistic Period* (JSOTSup 317; Sheffield: Sheffield Academic Press, 2001), 30–46.

---

and the term 'holy people.' If so, the phrase is likely first to have been used in the present historical setting." The identity of "seed" becomes an issue also for some of the priests who were unable to verify their descent, "their seed" (Neh 7:61; Ezra 2:59).

Becking, B., "The Hellenistic Period and Ancient Israel: Three Preliminary Statements," in L. L. Grabbe (ed.), *Did Moses Speak Attic? Jewish Historiography and Scripture in the Hellenistic Period* (JSOTSup 317; Sheffield: Sheffield Academic Press, 2001), 78–90.

Ben Zvi, E., "Inclusion and Exclusion from Israel," in S. W. Holloway (ed.), *The Pitcher is Broken* (Sheffield: Sheffield Academic Press, 1995), 95–149.

Boda, M. J./Redditt, P. L. (ed.), *Unity and Disunity in Ezra-Nehemiah: Redaction, Rhetoric, and Reader* (Sheffield: Sheffield Phoenix Press, 2008).

Brown, F. et. al., *The New Brown, Driver, Briggs, Gesenius Hebrew-English Lexicon* (Peabody: Hendrickson Publishers, 1979).

Burnside, J., *God, Justice, and Society: Aspects of Law and Legality in the Bible* (Oxford: Oxford University Press, 2010).

Carmichael, C. M., "Forbidden Mixtures," *VT* 32 (1982), 392–415.

Douglas, M., "Responding to Ezra: The Priests and the Foreign Wives," *BibInt* 10 (2002), 16–23.

Eilberg-Schwartz, H., *The Savage in Judaism* (Bloomington: Indiana University Press, 1990).

Feldman, A./Goldman, L., *Scripture and Interpretation: Qumran Texts that Rework the Bible* (BZAW 449; Berlin: De Gruyter, 2014).

Fishbane, M., *Biblical Interpretation in Ancient Israel* (Oxford: Clarendon Press, 1985).

Gerstenberger, E. S., *Leviticus*, tr. D. W. Stott [*Das dritte Buch Mose: Leviticus* (Göttingen; Vandenhoeck & Ruprecht, 1993)] (OTL; Louisville, KY: Westminster John Knox, 1996).

Grabbe, L. L. (ed.), *Did Moses Speak Attic? Jewish Historiography and Scripture in the Hellenistic Period* (JSOTSup 317; Sheffield: Sheffield Academic Press, 2001).

Grabbe, L. L., "The Law of Moses in the Ezra Tradition: More Virtual Than Real," in J. W. Watts (ed.), *Persia and Torah: The Theory of Imperial Authorization of the Pentateuch* (Atlanta: SBL Press, 2001), 91–114.

–, *An Introduction to Second Temple Judaism: History and Religion of the Jews in the Time of Nehemiah, the Maccabees, Hillel, and Jesus* (London: T&T Clark, 2010).

Harrington, H. K., "Intermarriage in the Temple Scroll: Strategies of Neutralization," in R. E. Gane/A. Taggar-Cohen (ed.), *Current Issues in Priestly and Related Literature: The Legacy of Jacob Milgrom and Beyond* (Atlanta: SBL Press, 2015), 463–82.

Hayes, C., *Gentile Impurities and Jewish Identities* (Oxford: Oxford University Press, 2002).

Hepner, F. G., "The Relationship between Biblical Narrative and Biblical Law," *JBQ* (2001), 263–8.

Himmelfarb, M., "Levi, Phinehas, and the Problem of Intermarriage at the Time of the Maccabean Revolt," *JSQ* 6 (1999), 1–24.

Jastrow, M., *Sefer Milim: Dictionary of the Targumim, Talmud Babli, Yerushalmi, and Midrashic Literature* (New York: The Judaic Press, 1982).

Kazen, T., *Issues of Impurity in Early Judaism* (CBNTS 45; Winona Lake, IN: Eisenbrauns, 2010).

Knohl, I., *The Sanctuary of Silence: The Priestly Torah and the Holiness School* (Minneapolis: Fortress Press, 1995).

Leuchter, M., "The Politics of Ritual Rhetoric: A Proposed Sociopolitical Context for the Redaction of Leviticus 1–16," *VT* 60 (2010), 345–65.

Magness, J., "Were Sacrifices Offered at Qumran? The Animal Bone Deposits Reconsidered," *JAJ* 7 (2016), 5–34.

Milgrom, J., *Leviticus 1–16* (AB 3; New York, NY: Doubleday, 1991).

–, *Leviticus 17–22* (AB 3A; New York, NY: Doubleday, 2000).

–, *Leviticus 23–27* (AB 3B; New York, NY: Doubleday, 2001).

Nihan, C., *From Priestly Torah to Pentateuch: A Study in the Composition of the Book of Leviticus* (FAT.2 25; Tübingen: Mohr Siebeck, 2007).

Qimron, E./Strugnell, J., *Qumran Cave 4: Miqṣat Maʿaśe Ha-Torah* (DJD 10; Oxford: Clarendon, 1994).

Römer, T. (ed.), *The Books of Leviticus and Numbers* (Leuven: University Press, 2007).

–, /Schmid, K. (ed.), *Les dernières rédactions du Pentateuque, de l'Hexateuque et de l'Ennéateuque* (BETL 203; Leuven: Peeters, 2007).
Sawyer, J. (ed.), *Reading Leviticus: Responses to Mary Douglas* (LHB/OTS; Sheffield: Sheffield Academic Press, 1996).
–, "A Critical Review of Recent Projects and Publications," *Hebrew Bible and Ancient Israel* 1,3 (2012), 298–326.
Segal, M., "4QReworked Pentateuch or 4QPentateuch?," in L. H. Schiffman et al. (ed.), *The Dead Sea Scrolls: Fifty Years After Their Discovery* (Jerusalem: Israel Museum, 2000), 391–9.
–, "Between Bible and Rewritten Bible," in M. Henze (ed.), *Biblical Interpretation at Qumran* (Grand Rapids: Eerdmans, 2005), 10–28.
Tov, E., "Biblical Texts as Reworked in Some Qumran Manuscripts with Special Attention to 4QRP and 4QParaGen-Exod," in E. Ulrich/J. C. VanderKam (ed.), *The Community of the Renewed Covenant: The Notre Dame Symposium on the Dead Sea Scrolls* (Notre Dame, IN: University of Notre Dame Press, 1994), 111–34.
–, /White, S., "4QReworked Pentateuch," in H. Attridge et al. (ed.), *Qumran Cave 4. VIII Parabiblical Texts, Part 1* (DJD 13; Oxford: Clarendon Press, 1994), 187–351, pl. XIII–XXXVI.
–, /White, S., "4QReworked Pentateuch," in H. Attridge et al. (ed.), *Discoveries in the Judaean Desert XIII*, Clarendon Press: Oxford 1994).
Watts, J. W., "Ritual Rhetoric in the Pentateuch: The Case of Leviticus 1–16," in T. Römer (ed.), *The Books of Leviticus and Numbers* (BETL; Leuven: Peeters, 2008), 305–18.
Wenham, G. J., *The Book of Leviticus* (NICOT; Grand Rapids: Eerdmans, 1979).
Werrett, I. C., *Ritual Purity and the Dead Sea Scrolls* (Leiden: Brill, 2007).
Williamson, H. G. M., *Ezra, Nehemiah* (WBC 16; Waco, TX: Word, 1985).
–, *Studies in Persian Period History and Historiography* (Tübingen: Mohr Siebeck, 2004).
Wright, J. L., "A New Model for the Composition of Ezra-Nehemiah," in O. Lipschits/R. Albertz/G. Knoppers (ed.), *Judah and the Judeans in the 4th Century BCE* (Winona Lake, IN: Eisenbrauns, 2007), 333–48.
Yadin, Y., *The Temple Scroll*, I (Jerusalem: Israel Exploration Society, 1983).
Zahn, M. M., "The Problem of Characterizing the 4QReworked Pentateuch Manuscripts: Bible, Rewritten Bible, or None of the Above?," *DSD* 15 (2008), 315–39.

Thomas Hieke

Writing on Leviticus for the HThKAT Series

Some Key Issues on Sacrificial Rituals

1 Introduction

The following considerations reflect on several key issues that occurred during my work on the commentary on the Book of Leviticus, which was published in the series "Herders Theologischer Kommentar zum Alten Testament" (HThKAT, German). (1) Especially the first chapters of Leviticus use a very stereotyped or standardized language. The sacrifices and the various components of the respective rituals are tagged with a certain technical language and terminology. A glossary as the second part of the introduction explains this general vocabulary. (2) The introductory formulas (e.g., Lev 1:1–2; 4:1; 6:1; 8:1 etc.) are theologically crucial for the way the text wants to be understood: The rituals are—according to the presentation in the biblical text—not invented by humans but revealed by God. (3) The meaning of the hand-leaning rite (e.g., Lev 1:4) is still a disputed issue. This essay as well as the commentary will present a new solution for interpreting this necessary part of the ritual. (4) Finally, the paper will discuss problems of the nomenclature of the sacrifices, especially the so-called "sin-offering."

In 2005, I began work on my commentary on the Book of Leviticus for the "Herders Theologischer Kommentar zum Alten Testament" series by producing my own working translation. When I tried to render the Hebrew original of the Masoretic text into my vernacular language, I very soon started a list called "Übersetzungskonventionen." The stereotyped language urged me to make sure that I translate every recurring term with the same German equivalent—as far as possible, though. The recurring terms then led me to the understanding that there are a few basic key concepts behind the numerous prescriptions about sacrifices, purity, atonement, and other cultic and ethical matters. Hence, I extracted and systematized these concepts in a longer glossary before the commentary proper. Secondly, regarding the "theology" of the Book of Leviticus, I found it crucial to pay special attention to the introductory formulas that subdivide the book into smaller units (see, e.g., Lev 1:1–2; 4:1–2; etc.). The priestly theologians who wrote that book as part of the "Torah of Moses" repeatedly insisted on the ideological framework that God revealed the divine will to Moses who should pass it on to the Israelites and/or Aaron and the priests. This literary device bears much on the understanding and the interpretation of the commandments. In the third part of this essay, I will demonstrate the results of my research with the help of a new solution for the interpretation of the gesture of "hand-leaning," which is the first step of the sacrifice of an animal. Lastly, I will discuss the so-called "sin offering" as an example for misleading translations and for the problems of the nomenclature of sacrifices.

2 The Stereotyped Language: The Glossary in the Introduction to the Commentary

The Book of Leviticus uses—especially in the first chapters – a very standardized language. Several terms and phrases occur repeatedly; they are not defined or explained, but obviously have a special technical meaning. The writers presuppose that the envisioned audience is acquainted with this stereotyped technical language. A commentary must try to explain the presupposed meaning and concept behind the terms and phrases even when the text itself does not support that. Hence, one has to involve other texts using the same term, be it in Leviticus or elsewhere. The standardized language allows it to locate the explanation of the technical terms before the commentary proper. Therefore, the second part of the introduction of my commentary consists of a glossary, which explains repeatedly occurring technical terms (such as the names of the sacrifices) and phrases characteristic for the language of Leviticus. The order in the three parts of the glossary (sacrificial terms, other technical terms, coined phrases and formulas) follows the alphabetical order of the German translation. The English translations stem from the commentaries by Milgrom (M) and Watts (W).[1]

German translation	*Hebrew*	*Transcription*	*English translation(s)*
Brandopfer	עלה	*ʿolā*	burnt offering (M) rising offering (W)
Darbringung	קרבן	*qorbān*	offering (M) present (W)
Entschuldigungs-opfer	אשם	*ʾāšām*	reparation offering (M) guilt offering (W)
Entsündigungsopfer	חטאת	*ḥaṭṭāʾt*	purification offering (M) sin offering (W)
Feueropfer	אשה	*ʾiššæh*	food gift (M) fire (offering) (W)

1 J. Milgrom, *Leviticus 1–16* (AB 3; New York et al.: Doubleday, 1991); J. W. Watts, *Leviticus 1–10* (HCOT; Leuven: Peeters, 2013).

German translation	*Hebrew*	*Transcription*	*English translation(s)*
Heilsgemeinschafts-opfer	זבח (ה)שלמים	*zæbaḥ (ha-)šᵉlāmīm*	well-being offering (M) amity slaughter offering (W)
Speiseopfergabe	מנחה	*minḥā*	cereal offering (M) commodity offering (W) tribute (Gilders)[2]
		Coined phrases	
Duft der Beruhigung	ריח ניחח	*rēaḥ nīḥoaḥ*	pleasing aroma (M) soothing scent (W)
Emporhebungsgabe	תנופה	*tᵉnūpā*	elevation offering (M) raised (offering) (W)
Erhebungsgabe	תרומה	*tᵉrūmā*	contribution (M) withholding (W)
Gedächtnisanteil	אזכרה	*ʾazkārā*	token portion (M) memorial (portion) (W)
Hochheiliges	קדש קדשים	*qodæš qodāšīm*	most sacred portion (M) most holy (W)
Priester	כהן	*kohēn*	priest
rein/unrein heilig/profan	טמא/טהור חל/קדש	*ṭāhōr/ṭāmēʾ* *qōdæš/ḥol*	pure/impure (M) clean (pure)/polluted (W) sacred/common (M) holy/secular (W)
Versöhnung erwirken	כפר	*kippær*	to expiate (M) to mitigate (W)
		Formulas	
Anredeformel	וידבר יהוה אל משה לאמר	*wa-yiddabēr Yhwh ʾæl Mošǣ lē-ʾmor*	address formula
Gebotsformel	כאשר צוה יהוה את משה	*kaʾašær ṣiwwā Yhwh ʾæt Mošǣ*	commandment formula
Generationenformel	חקת עולם לדרתיכם לדרתם	*ḥuqqat ʿōlām lᵉ-dōrōtē-kæm/ lᵉ-dōrōt-ām*	generations formula
Herausführungs-formel	המוציא אתכם מארץ מצרים להיות לכם	*ha-mōṣīʾ ʾæt-kæm mē-ʾæræṣ miṣrayim li-hyōt lā-kæm lē-ʾlohīm*	"Out of Egypt" formula
Klassifikationsformel	עלה הוא	*ʿolā hūʾ*	classification formula

2 See the contribution by W.K. Gilders, "Commentary as Ethnography," in this volume, pp. 35–47.

German translation	*Hebrew*	*Transcription*	*English translation(s)*
Reinheitsformel	וטהר וטהרה	*w^e-ṭāhēr* *w^e-ṭāharā*	purity formula
Toraformel	זאת תורת ...	*zō᾽t tōrat …*	Torah formula
Versöhnungs- und Vergebungsformel	וכפר עלהם הכהן ונסלח להם	*w^e-kippær ʿalē-hæm ha-kohēn w^e-nislaḥ lā-hæm*	atonement and forgiveness formula
Weitergabeformel	דבר אל בני ישראל לאמר	*dabbēr ᾽æl benē Yiśrā᾽ēl lē-᾽mor*	transmission formula

3 The Introductory Formulas: Rituals not Invented by Humans but Established by God

One characteristic feature of the standardized language of the Book of Leviticus consists of the introductory formulas that structure the text in larger sections on different topics. The structuring function of these formulas has attracted much attention.[3] However, the formulas slightly differ in shape and content, and they are obviously not all on the same level regarding the outline of Leviticus.[4] Usually, the divine speech formulas contain two parts: (1) The first part consists of the narrative remark that Yahweh addresses Moses (וידבר יהוה אל משה לאמר, *wa-yiddabēr Yhwh ᾽æl Mošæ lē-᾽mor*). I recommend the term "address formula" (German: "Anredeformel"). There are 35 occurrences in Leviticus; in 30 cases Moses is the addressee, in four cases Moses and Aaron are addressed (Lev 11:1; 13:1; 14:33; 15:1—remarkably in the passage about "pure" and "impure"), in one case (Lev 10:8) Aaron alone is addressed. (2) The second part of the introductory formula and usually the continuation of the address formula is already part of the divine speech. It is Yahweh's command to tell someone (usually the Israelites) the following commandments, i.e., to transmit the contents of the divine speech to a certain audience (דבר אל בני ישראל לאמר, *dabbēr ᾽æl b^enē Yiśrā᾽ēl lē-᾽mor*). I call this part the "transmission formula" (German: "Weitergabeformel"). In 23 cases the address formula is followed by a transmission formula (usually with an imperative of *DBR*: *dabbēr* or *dabrū*; in Lev 6:2 and 24:2 one finds צַו, *ṣaw*, "command"; in Lev 20:2 *᾽MR* replaces *DBR*). Hence, we have a two-tiered introductory formula that embeds the commandments in a narrative framework ("Yahweh spoke to

3 See, e.g., the monograph by D. Luciani, *Sainteté et pardon. Tome 1: Structure littéraire du Lévitique. Tome 2: Guide technique* (BEThL 185; Leuven: Peeters, 2005); see further E. Zenger, "Das Buch Levitikus als Teiltext der Tora/des Pentateuch. Eine synchrone Lektüre mit kanonischer Perspektive," in H.-J. Fabry/H.-W. Jüngling (ed.), *Levitikus als Buch* (BBB 119; Berlin et al.: Philo, 1999) 47–83.

4 See, e.g., Watts, *Leviticus 1–10*, 329.

Moses") and stresses the two main persons in the process of the revelation of the divine commands: Yahweh and Moses. It is *Yahweh* who addresses Moses and who is the source of all the detailed instructions for the cult and everyday life; it is *Moses* who hears them and who is commanded to pass them on to the Israelites (or the priests).

With this literary device, the two tiered introductory formula, the priestly authors of the Book of Leviticus achieved several goals. (1) They placed their instructions and directives in an ideal and unquestionable past, in the situation of the revelation of the divine Torah at Mount Sinai. (2) Moreover, they disguised the human author of the commandments: While the priests of Jerusalem were the real authors in the history of the origin of the book, the ideal human source of the commandment bears the name "Moses." (3) Moses, however, only passed on what he heard directly from Yahweh. Thus, the priestly texts insinuate that the commandments are of immediate divine origin without saying that straightforwardly. The priests imply that the described and hence stipulated rituals are not inventions by humans but established and enacted by Yahweh himself (via Moses, the mediator of revelation or *Offenbarungsmittler*). This process makes the text as well as the praxis that follows the text and hence the priests' position indisputable and unassailable. On the other hand, the text that is regarded as of divine origin itself binds those who propagate it: The priests themselves are obliged to follow these rules, especially since these rules are not limited to their own knowledge but are disseminated to all Israelites. The transmission formula underscores that the divine commandments are not an arcane knowledge limited to an elite, but are made known and hence normative to everybody. Thus, the literary device of the two-tiered structuring introductory formula has far-reaching theological implications.

4 The Meaning of the Hand-Leaning Ritual

The first part of the burnt offering (and all other sacrifices of animals)[5] consists of the much-disputed hand-leaning ritual. The Hebrew phrase (סמך יד, *sāmak yād*)[6] insinuates a pressing of the hand with some force on the forehead

5 See Watts, *Leviticus 1–10*, 189.

6 See, e.g., B. Janowski, *Sühne als Heilsgeschehen* (WMANT 55; Neukirchen-Vluyn: Neukirchener, 1982; ^{2}2000), 199–221.430–1; C. Eberhart, *Studien zur Bedeutung der Opfer im Alten Testament. Die Signifikanz von Blut- und Verbrennungsriten im kultischen Rahmen* (WMANT 94; Neukirchen-Vluyn: Neukirchener, 2002), 25–6; D. Calabro, "A Reexamination of the Ancient Israelite Gesture of Hand Placement," in H. L. Wiley/C. A. Eberhart (ed.), *Sacrifice, Cult, and Atonement in Early Judaism and Christianity: Constituents and Critique* (Resources for Biblical Study 85; Atlanta: SBL Press, 2017) 99–124. Calabro tries to demonstrate that in biblical times there was only one gesture, carried out with both hands. Later on, the gesture and its function

of the animal. The rabbinic interpretation points to the core of the meaning of this ritual action when the Talmud (b. Menaḥ. 93b) insists that this is the only part of the entire sacrificial ritual, in which no substitute or representative can replace the offering person. The commentaries by Rendtorff, Milgrom, Hartley, and others summarize the various suggestions for the interpretation of this gesture.[7] The biblical text does not offer an explicit explanation. Hence, the following speculations about the meaning of the pressing of the hand emerge: (1) delegation or transmission, (2) identification between offering person and offered animal, (3) indication of ownership, (4) assigning the recipient to a particular "position in an organizational order," (5) juridical act of handing over the animal to a legal killing for sacrifice. However, these explanations do not fit the contents and situation of the sacrifices. The hand-leaning ritual must not be confused with the delegation or transmission of an office like the priesthood (see, e.g., Lev 8, the ordination of the priests) or with the transmission of sins on the scapegoat in Lev 16:21 by Aaron the high priest. The idea of identification between offering person and offered animal proffers a too high theology of substitution: The killing of the offered animal does not stand for the death of the offering person, because this person does not always deserve death for a sinful act.[8] The indication of ownership, however, sounds a little bit too banal for such an important gesture. To understand this as a gesture effecting the assignment of the recipient to a particular "position in an organizational order," according to the semantics of the verb פקד,[9] surely fits all occurrences of this action. However, this understanding is too general and unspecific, so that it does not satisfactorily explain the ritual. And finally, the idea of a "legal killing" of the animal makes too much of the act of killing or slaughtering which is definitely not the core of the ritual[10] but rather a subplot that can be carried out by anybody, usually by the offering person herself/himself.

Looking for a new explanation of the hand-leaning action, one has to consider the effect of the sacrifice that is indicated in Lev 1:4 by the phrase לְכַפֵּר עָלָיו, "as atonement for you" (NRSV), "in expiation for him" (JPS-TNK), "to mitigate for them" (Watts). One can describe the intended (or promised) impact of the sacrifice as the re-establishment of the relationship between the offering person and God. The concept of the Hebrew term *kipper*, usually translated with "to atone" or "to expiate," denotes the removal of everything that separates the human

---

fell into oblivion so that later sources, including the vocalized Masoretic text, misunderstood the consonantal text and assumed two gestures, with one hand or two hands respectively. Although Calabro mentions some interesting observations and extra-biblical sources, his reasoning rests on too many implications and appears to be over-sophisticated.

7 See also Calabro, "Reexamination," 116–21.

8 See especially Eberhart, "Opfer," 54–5.

9 This is the recent suggestion by Calabro, "Reexamination," 124.

10 See, e.g., Eberhart, "Opfer," 49.

being from God. In other words, the human being experiences that there is something—whatever it might be—that stands like a separating wall between her or him and God, something that disturbs the contact with and the relationship to God substantially. Then God commands and the humans carry out an act called *kipper* that implies the divine promise to remove this "disturbing something" and to re-establish a life-giving relationship. One can observe the basic idea of *kipper* at its first occurrence in the Hebrew Bible in Gen 32:21: the reconciliation of Jacob and Esau. Jacob tries to obtain reconciliation (אֲכַפְּרָה) with his brother Esau by sending a present (מִנְחָה), and Esau receives Jacob favourably (Gen 33:10: וַתִּרְצֵנִי, see the same root *RṢY* in Lev 1:4, וְנִרְצָה: the offering will count in his/her favour, it shall be accepted). Hence, the effect of the offering or sacrifice results in a personal encounter. Reconciliation happens between persons, between the personal God Yahweh and the individual offering person. In order to indicate the exact person on whose behalf the offering takes place and who will find favour in the eyes of Yahweh, this person has to press her or his hand (singular!) on the offered animal's forehead. As the animal goes up on the altar and in the smoke up to Yahweh, a visible connection between the offering person and Yahweh emerges. The hand-leaning ritual underscores this line, or, as William K. Gilders puts it: "The hand-pressing indexes a relationship between offerer and animal."[11] This dedication *ad personam* of the offering's impact is the internal reason for the rabbinic prescription that the hand leaning is the only act in the ritual that a substitute or a representative cannot take over. It has to be performed personally, or, as the German language conveys more vividly, "eigenhändig," with one's own hand.

5 What is "Sin" in the "Sin-Offering"? Problems of the Nomenclature of Sacrifices

Within the Hebrew language, the nomenclature of the sacrifices in Leviticus 1–7 shows a coherent and sophisticated system. The dilemma, however, occurs as soon as one tries to translate this system into a modern language, say, English or German. One of the most misleading terms is the classical "sin offering" for the Hebrew חַטָּאת (the term "guilt offering" for Hebrew אָשָׁם causes almost the same problems). A "sin offering" is not suitable to deal with "sins" in the usual sense, i. e., with intentionally committed moral wrongdoings and trespasses against God's

11 W. K. Gilders, *Blood Ritual in the Hebrew Bible. Meaning and Power* (Baltimore/London: Johns Hopkins University Press, 2004), 81; see also R. E. Gane, *Cult and Character: Purification Offerings, Day of Atonement, and Theodicy* (Winona Lake, IN: Eisenbrauns, 2005), 56; C. Körting, *Der Schall des Schofar. Israels Feste im Herbst* (BZAW 285; Berlin/New York: De Gruyter, 1999), 182–3; Watts, *Leviticus 1–10*, 192.

commandments. A "sin offering" rather must be offered if someone notices that he or she violated *unintentionally* (בִּשְׁגָגָה) one of Yahweh's commandments (see Leviticus 4:1–5:13). Even in cases that happen by nature and cannot be avoided by human beings at any rate, see, e.g., the birth of a child, a "sin offering" has to be offered (Lev 12:6–8). Especially this last passage caused Jacob Milgrom to suggest the translation "purification offering." According to Milgrom, the occurrences that require a "purification offering" have nothing to do with moral behavior of people but rather render the sanctuary "impure" (even over longer periods). The חַטָּאת purifies the sanctuary and the altar.[12] R. E. Gane argued against this concept and concluded that in most cases the "purification offering" purifies the offering person, not the sanctuary.[13] Hence, one has to ask about the meaning of "sin" in the term "sin offering" which, by the way, in Hebrew is identical with the term for "sin" itself. "Sin" in this very broad sense denotes everything that separates a human being from God, everything that disturbs, endangers or terminates the human relationship with God. This wide category suits for intentionally committed trespasses against God's commandments (see, e.g., Isa 59:2[14]) as well as for events occurring by nature that frighten human beings and make them feel close to death (like the blood flowing from the mother's womb during the birth process or the various skin diseases mentioned in Leviticus 13). In short, "something" happened that makes a person feel alienated from God, the source of life, and close to death. God himself now offers a way to restore the relationship and to remove the separating issue (whatever it might be). The ritual of the חַטָּאת accomplishes the process of *kipper*. The priest "makes atonement" (or, as Watts translates Lev 4:26, "mitigates his sin for him"[15]), and, if the intentions and the material of the sacrifice are valid, God promises to grant favor: "he/she [the offering person] shall be forgiven," or, in the case of acquired uncleanness, "he/she shall be clean."

Hence, for the translation, we need a term that expresses the "removal" of "something," the removal of "sin," now broadly understood as a kind of substance that estranges the human being from God. In German, we have the privative prefix "ent-" ("away from") that enables me to translate the Hebrew חַטָּאת with "Entsündigungsopfer."[16] The term "purification offering" hence has much to

12 See, e.g., Milgrom, *Leviticus 1–16*, 254–6.

13 See Gane, *Cult and Character*, 106–43.—On the discussion see, e.g., J.M. Vis, "The Purgation of Persons through the Purification Offering," in H.L. Wiley/C.A. Eberhart (ed.), *Sacrifice, Cult, and Atonement in Early Judaism and Christianity. Constituents and Critique* (Resources for Biblical Study 85; Atlanta: SBL Press, 2017) 33–57, on pp. 48–57.

14 "Rather, your iniquities have been barriers between you and your God, and your sins (חַטּוֹאתֵיכֶם) have hidden his face from you so that he does not hear" (NRSV).

15 Watts, *Leviticus 1–10*, 351.

16 The German term "Entsündigungsopfer" has the advantage that it still contains the stem "sünd" (= sin) and thus imitates a little bit the Hebrew phenomenon that "sin" and "sin offering," i.e., the offering that removes the "sin," are the same term חַטָּאת.

commend, as long as one understands it as "purification" from every "substance" that intrudes disturbingly between God and human beings.[17]

6 Issues for Further Discussion

Understanding the concepts of the Hebrew Bible on sacrifices and purity is one thing, translating the crucial terms in a modern language in a way that the translations mirror the concepts is another, much more difficult issue. Writing a scholarly commentary with a fresh German translation, I tried to avoid the classical, misleading standard translations whenever I found a new possibility. I did not avoid rather technical expressions like "Entsündigungsopfer" and "Heilsgemeinschaftsopfer" (for זֶבַח שְׁלָמִים), because I have the impression that the priestly authors themselves applied a rather technical language using abbreviations (or shorthand technique) and coining new phrases and terms. However, what remains indispensable is the correct understanding of the concepts behind the Hebrew terms. Further research should look for a consensus about the contents and meanings of the ritual descriptions; perhaps we find new and apt modern translations for the terms. Moreover, scholars need to discuss the implications of our understanding of the terms and concepts of the sacrifices in Leviticus 1–7 for Jewish and Christian theology today.

Bibliography

Calabro, D., "A Reexamination of the Ancient Israelite Gesture of Hand Placement," in H. L. Wiley/C. A. Eberhart (ed.), *Sacrifice, Cult, and Atonement in Early Judaism and Christianity. Constituents and Critique* (Resources for Biblical Study 85; Atlanta: SBL Press, 2017) 99–124.

Eberhart, C., *Studien zur Bedeutung der Opfer im Alten Testament. Die Signifikanz von Blut- und Verbrennungsriten im kultischen Rahmen* (WMANT 94; Neukirchen-Vluyn: Neukirchener, 2002).

–, "Opfer, Sühne und Stellvertretung im Alten Testament," in M. Hüttenhoff/W. Kraus/K. Meyer (ed.), *"... mein Blut für Euch." Theologische Perspektiven zum Verständnis des Todes Jesu heute* (Biblisch-theologische Schwerpunkte 38; Göttingen: Vandenhoeck & Ruprecht, 2018) 40–55.

Gane, R. E., *Cult and Character: Purification Offerings, Day of Atonement, and Theodicy* (Winona Lake, IN: Eisenbrauns, 2005).

Gilders, W. K., *Blood Ritual in the Hebrew Bible. Meaning and Power* (Baltimore/London: Johns Hopkins University Press, 2004).

Hartley, J. E., *Leviticus* (WBC 4; Dallas, TX: Word Books, 1992).

Hieke, T., *Levitikus 1–15; Levitikus 16–27* (HThKAT; Freiburg i. Br.: Herder, 2014).

17 See also Eberhart, "Opfer," 47–8.

Janowski, B., *Sühne als Heilsgeschehen* (WMANT 55; Neukirchen-Vluyn: Neukirchener, 1982; ²2000).
Körting, C., *Der Schall des Schofar. Israels Feste im Herbst* (BZAW 285; Berlin/New York: De Gruyter, 1999).
Luciani, D., *Sainteté et pardon. Tome 1: Structure littéraire du Lévitique. Tome 2: Guide technique* (BEThL 185; Leuven: Peeters, 2005).
Milgrom, J., *Leviticus 1–16* (AB 3; New York et al.: Doubleday, 1991; pp. 1–1163).
–, *Leviticus 17–22* (AB 3A; New York et al.: Doubleday, 2000; pp. 1267–1892).
–, *Leviticus 23–27* (AB 3B; New York et al.: Doubleday, 2001; pp. 1895–2714).
Rendtorff, R., *Leviticus 1,1–10,20* (BKAT 3/1; Neukirchen-Vluyn: Neukirchener, 2004).
Vis, J. M., "The Purgation of Persons through the Purification Offering," in H. L. Wiley/C. A. Eberhart (ed.), *Sacrifice, Cult, and Atonement in Early Judaism and Christianity. Constituents and Critique* (Resources for Biblical Study 85; Atlanta: SBL Press, 2017) 33–57.
Watts, J. W., *Leviticus 1–10* (HCOT; Leuven: Peeters, 2013).
Zenger, E., "Das Buch Levitikus als Teiltext der Tora/des Pentateuch. Eine synchrone Lektüre mit kanonischer Perspektive," in H.-J. Fabry/H.-W. Jüngling (ed.), *Levitikus als Buch* (BBB 119; Berlin et al.: Philo, 1999) 47–83.

Christian A. Eberhart

Sacrifice? Holy Smokes!

Reflections on Cult Terminology for Understanding Sacrifice in the Hebrew Bible*

In honor of Rudolf Leopold Eberhart,
on the occasion of his 88th birthday.

Cultic sacrifices are mentioned and described throughout the Hebrew Bible, they are central to the worship of ancient Israel and Judah, and they are a true treasury for metaphorical language. Yet their interpretation is the subject of much debate among modern scholars. In this essay I intend to make a contribution to this debate by studying 'native' interpretations of cultic sacrifices as they are manifest in comprehensive technical terms employed in the priestly texts of both the Hebrew Bible and the Septuagint, especially in the book of Leviticus. I will thus focus on Hebrew words such as קרבן, מנחה, זבח, אשה, and ריח ניחוח and on the Greek words θυσία, κάρπωμα, and ὀσμὴ εὐωδίας. In these reflections, I shall describe specific meanings of these technical terms while being attentive to their common implications. I argue that the modern endeavor of interpreting sacrificial rituals or of developing theories of sacrifice can benefit from paying attention to aspects of such 'native' interpretation of sacrificial rituals. In particular, these early interpretive layers broaden the modern perceptions of sacrifice through their focus on the burning rite. Ritual sacrifices then emerge, for example, as dynamic processes of approaching the altar or as tokens of reverence to God. These reflections are corroborated by the application of such cultic terminology in the Dead Sea Scrolls and rabbinic literature, as well as by its metaphorical usage in the Hebrew Bible and the New Testament.

1 Introduction: Terminology and Ambivalence

What is a sacrifice? This term refers to universal phenomena in human cultures throughout history. When the term 'sacrifice' references religious rituals, it is recognized by scholars in anthropology, history, and religion alike as a crucial factor

* This essay was originally published in the volume *Ritual and Metaphor: Sacrifice in the Bible* (SBLRBS 68; ed. C. A. Eberhart, Atlanta: Society of Biblical Literature, 2011) 17–32. I am grateful to SBL Press for granting permission to reprint it. This version has been corrected, updated, and expanded for the present volume.

that helps to decode basic principles of interaction and exchange within these cultures. Of course, it helps in particular to comprehend the religious dimension of these cultures. At the heart of Second Temple Judaism, for example, a well-developed cult featured sacrificial rituals that conveyed early Jewish core beliefs about God. Through its suggestive potential, this cult became a terminological and conceptual resource for diverse groups in early Judaism to frame practical mandates for commoners. The fact that the sacrificial cult was drawn on for these purposes suggests that it was not only a well-known, but also a widely accepted and authoritative institution. Thus metaphors derived from the sacrificial cult gradually permeated the religious and secular rhetoric of Judaism and, later, also of Christianity.

Yet while modern scholars generally acknowledge that ritual sacrifice is important for the decoding of human culture and religion, they also face the situation that this concept has eluded attempts of arriving at an interpretive agreement regarding its purpose and nature. Sacrifice was indeed defined in a variety of different ways, for example as the setting for totemistic meals that were understood to sustain communal life in the ancient Semitic world,[1] as a process of identification of the offerer with the sacrificial animal that leads to consecration or to an approach of the divine,[2] or as a scenario that allows a society to domesticate or redirect the violence that naturally develops among humans and thus provides positive group-dynamic effects,[3] to name but a few hypotheses. The multitude of different theories on the symbolism and meaning of sacrifice appears to some as proliferation.[4] In her recent essay "Mise à mort rituelle," Catherine Bouanich concisely states that there are as many definitions of the term 'sacrifice' as there are specialists of ancient religions: "Autant d'auteurs spécialistes des religions anciennes, autant de définitions du mot 'sacrifice'."[5] In a critical

1 Cf. W. R. Smith, *Lectures on the Religion of the Semites: The Fundamental Institutions: First Series* (London: Adam & Charles Black, 1889; 2nd ed. by J. S. Black, 1894).

2 Cf. H. Hubert/M. Mauss, "Essai sur la nature et la fonction du sacrifice," *ASoc* 2 (1899) 29–138; H. Gese, "The Atonement," in idem, *Essays on Biblical Theology* (Minneapolis: Augsburg Publishing House, 1981), 93–116.

3 Cf. R. Girard, *Violence and the Sacred* (Baltimore: Johns Hopkins University Press, 1977); idem, *Des choses cachées depuis la fondation du monde* (Paris: Grasset, 1979); W. Burkert, *Homo Necans: The Anthropology of Ancient Greek Sacrificial Ritual and Myth* (Berkeley: University of California Press, 1983).

4 Cf. J. Drexler, *Die Illusion des Opfers: Ein wissenschaftlicher Überblick über die wichtigsten Opfertheorien ausgehend vom deleuzianischen Polyperspektivismusmodell* (Münchener Ethnologische Abhandlungen 12; München, Anacon-Verlag, 1993).

5 C. Bouanich, "Mise à mort rituelle," in S. Georgoudi/R. Koch Piettre/F. Schmidt (ed.), *La cuisine et l'autel: Les sacrifices en questions dans les sociétés de la Méditerranée ancienne* (BEHE.R 124, Turnhout: Brepols, 2006), 149–62, on p. 149. The variety of theories of sacrifice, however, should not be considered as entirely incompatible. Divergences can in part be attributed to different approaches and objectives of inquiry. Some theories, for example, approach sacrifice in the Hebrew Bible in relation to comparative data from surrounding cultures. Phenomena in one

response, therefore, some scholars have more recently affirmed the multivalence of ritual sacrifices and rejected the fundamental assumption that sacrifice must necessarily be understood symbolically. Based on anthropology, ritual studies, and other disciplines, these scholars pay specific attention to the immediate meaning of ritual activity and its socio-cultural implications.[6]

This brief survey of the scholarly interpretation of sacrifice clearly shows that it is not easy to answer the question of what is a sacrifice. The variety of interpretations outlined above is in part due to the fact that terms that are commonly used may change their meaning over time. Eventually they refer to an entire spectrum of phenomena; their original meaning then becomes difficult to determine or to define. The term 'inferno' is such an example. It is widely regarded as a classical term for 'hell' and a modern term for a large uncontrolled fire (see, e.g., the 1974 disaster movie 'Towering Inferno'). Yet it is interesting to note that the term 'inferno' is actually derived from the Latin adjective '*infernus*' meaning 'below' or 'under.' In ancient three-story worldviews, this term came to be used as a standard designation of hell, located 'under' the earth. And only due to the idea that an eternal fire of punishment burns there did the term 'inferno' gradually assume its modern meaning. It is apparent, however, that such an understanding of the term constitutes a considerable change of meaning when compared to the original adjective '*infernus*.'

After these reflections I would like to return to the term 'sacrifice,' which is also of Latin origins. What do we mean in everyday speech when we use this term? And why is there such a variety of different interpretations among scholars regarding its meaning? Apart from the possibility that it might also have undergone some change in meaning, another reason for this diversity of opinions is the fact that the Hebrew Bible does not feature any explicit theories of sacrifice.[7] Occasional rationales such as the statement that animal blood, life,

culture are then a priori not studied exclusively on their own terms, but are used to illuminate similar phenomena in the other culture. Some theories, on the other hand, focus on different aspects of ritual activities that are mentioned or described in the Hebrew Bible. For instance, some scholars venture into conjecturing previous developments of such rituals, others are principally concerned with symbolic meanings, while again others prefer to study latent layers of meaning that are accessible below the surface of explicit interpretations in the Hebrew Bible. Therefore, the variety of theories of sacrifice can to some extent be understood as a corollary of multiple perspectives on the subject matter.

6 Cf. I. Gruenwald, *Rituals and Ritual Theory in Ancient Israel* (Brill Reference Library of Judaism 10; Atlanta: Society of Biblical Literature, 2003); W.K. Gilders, *Blood Ritual in the Hebrew Bible: Meaning and Power* (Baltimore: Johns Hopkins, 2004); M. Modéus, *Sacrifice and Symbol: Biblical* Šělāmîm *in a Ritual Perspective* (CB.OT 52; Stockholm: Almqvist & Wiksell International, 2005).

7 Cf. A. Marx, "The Theology of the Sacrifice According to Leviticus 1–7," in R.A. Kugler/R. Rendtorff (ed.), *The Book of Leviticus: Composition and Reception* (VT.S 93; Leiden/Boston: Brill, 2003), 103–20, on p. 103; J.W. Watts, *Ritual and Rhetoric in Leviticus: From Sacrifice to Scripture* (Cambridge: Cambridge University Press, 2007), 30, 180–1. According to Watts, the

and atonement are connected (Lev 17:11) remain an exception. Yet this does not mean that traces of interpretation do not exist at all or that the communities and original tradents of the texts did not have any opinion on sacrifice. Every process of human speech or writing is ultimately an act of interpretation through the selection of elements that are deemed worthy of being mentioned and through the choice of appropriate terminology. At this point, it should be noted that the term 'sacrifice' designates multiple referents: First, it describes an *actual ritual*, customarily carried out at a sanctuary and/or on an altar, in the course of which special material is being 'sacrificed.' Second, the term 'sacrifice' designates this very *material*, typically understood today as an animal *victim* that is being sacrificed. Due to this terminological ambivalence we could say that a sacrifice (namely the victim) is offered during sacrifice (namely during a sacrificial ritual).[8] However, attributing the term 'sacrifice' to a certain sequence of ritual activity and the material offered there is in itself an act of interpretation.

Within the Hebrew Bible, this is best illustrated through the Passover ritual. The earliest Passover regulations describe an archaic ritual that is conducted at the homes of the Israelites and not at any sanctuary; the Passover lamb is, furthermore, roasted and then eaten in its entirety by the family so that no piece of it is actually offered to God on any altar; finally, its blood is used for apotropaic purposes (Exod 12:1–13).[9] It might be due to these features that the priestly texts do not include the Passover ritual in their catalogue of cultic sacrifices featured in Lev 1–7. A later redactor nevertheless labels this ritual 'Passover sacrifice (זבח־פסח) for YHWH' (Exod 12:27; see also Num 9:7, 13). This observation hints

reluctance of explaining sacrifice is also characteristic of other cultures and religions: '… animal offerings were central rites for ancient Roman society, yet this highly literate culture produced little speculation about their meaning. When explanations were offered for traditional Greek rites they seem to be rationalizations of existing practice, usually in the face of criticisms, or rationalizations for changing the tradition' (ibid. 181).

8 For the purposes of this essay, the distinction between sacrificial ritual and sacrificial material may suffice. A further distinction is that between ritual and text, that is, between the very action of performing a sacrificial ritual according to the parameters of a particular socio-religious tradition and, on the other hand, the production of oral and literary statements for the purpose of regulating or reflecting on such rituals (cf. Watts, *Ritual*, 27–32). Since this essay deals with sacrificial rituals as they are mentioned or described in the Hebrew Bible and the Septuagint, it is not concerned with the past reality of their actual performance.

9 The chapter of Exod 12 is probably composed of three sources: The oldest layer commonly attributed to Y/E consists of vv. 21–23 and 27b; the layer attributed to P consists of vv. 1–20 and 43–47; a layer of dtr. redaction is contained in vv. 24–27a. For a comprehensive overview of the recent scholarly discussion see C. Houtman, *Exodus, vol. 2: Chapters 7:14–19:25* (HCOT; Kampen: Kok Publishing House, 1996), 147–8. See also W. H. Schmidt, *Exodus* (BKAT 2/2$_3$; Neukirchen-Vluyn: Neukirchener Verlag, 2016), 493–542; F. H. Polak, "Storytelling and Redaction: Varieties of Language Usage in the Exodus Narrative," in J. C. Geertz et al. (ed.), *The Formation of the Pentateuch: Bridging the Academic Cultures of Europe, Israel, and North America* (FAT 111; Tübingen: Mohr Siebeck, 2016), 443–75, on pp. 454–9. On the interpretation of the Passover blood rite as an apotropaic ritual, see below.

at the fact that, already at the time of ancient Israel and Judah, there was some debate regarding the question of which ritual could be considered a sacrifice, and perhaps also regarding the corollary of how to define a sacrifice.

These two meanings of the term 'sacrifice' refer to sacrificial rituals. Apart from them, the term 'sacrifice' is used for an even broader spectrum of phenomena. It is important to mention that, third, this term occurs already in the Hebrew Bible, the Septuagint, and the New Testament in a *metaphorical sense*. Key expressions from the sacrificial cult were especially transferred into other areas of worship. This is manifest in the following phrase about an appropriate pious attitude: 'The sacrifices of God (זבחי אלהים) are a broken spirit' (Ps 51:17 [51:19MT]; see also Ps 119:108; Heb 13:16). Fourth, the term can also be applied *metaphorically within the secular realm*. Thus Paul expressed his gratitude for material support which he received on behalf of the congregation in Philippi with the words:

> I have received everything and more; I have abundantly, having received from Epaphroditus the things you sent, a pleasing odor (ὀσμὴν εὐωδίας), an acceptable sacrifice (θυσίαν δεκτήν), pleasant to God (Phil 4:18).

Today a somewhat comparable usage occurs when the term 'sacrifice' designates something that is given or deployed for a particular cause or for the sake of a greater good. Thus parents 'make sacrifices' when they put aside financial resources for the future college education of their children. Here, the term has an impersonal referent as it refers to money while such action is supposed to benefit persons. Fifth and finally, the term 'sacrifice' is used today to directly *designate a personal referent*, namely somebody who (voluntarily) gives him- or herself for a particular cause or for the sake of a greater good. This usage has become increasingly common in modern patriotic discourse. In this case, 'sacrifice' particularly designates people who agree to pursue dangerous missions, while it is an abstract or larger entity such as a nation or 'the free world' (however it may be defined) that is thought to benefit from such action.[10]

10 For modern, secular notions of sacrifice, see, e.g., G. De Vos/M. Suarez-Orozco, "Sacrifice and the experience of power," *Journal of Psychoanalytic Anthropology* 10 (1987), 309–40; K. L. Florczak, "An Exploration of the Concept of Sacrifice," *Nursing Science Quarterly* 17 (2004), 195–200; K. McClymond, *Beyond Sacred Violence: A Comparative Study of Sacrifice* (Baltimore: Johns Hopkins University Press, 2008), 160–3 (McClymond notes how, in the events of September 11, 2001 and the pursuant responses, sacrificial language was employed by Al Qaeda terrorists and the U.S. political administration to validate the loss of lives). For summaries of the history of research on the theory of sacrifice from various perspectives, see J. Milbank, "Stories of Sacrifice: From Wellhausen to Girard," *Theory Culture Society* 12 (1995), 15–46; C. A. Eberhart, "Introduction: Constituents and Critique of Sacrifice, Cult, and Atonement in Early Judaism and Christianity," in H. L. Wiley/C. A. Eberhart (ed.), *Sacrifice, Cult, and Atonement in Early Judaism and Christianity: Constituents and Critique* (SBLRBS 85; Atlanta: SBL Press, 2017), 1–29, on pp. 2–12).

These three examples of metaphorical usage share a common aspect: Sacrificial language serves the purpose of assigning importance to gestures or actions along widely accepted categories of a religious value system. Whether in religious contexts or not, this terminology is implicitly recognized as rhetorically authoritative.

Hence the term 'sacrifice' can be used for a number of different phenomena: it denotes sacrificial rituals as such and the materials ('victims') to be offered; it can also designate acts of worship not directly associated with such sacrificial rituals, and in everyday speech it can designate things that are given, or persons who are deployed, for the sake of a greater good.[11] With such a large spectrum of meanings, the term 'sacrifice' is a polyvalent category. On the one hand it refers to actual sacrificial rituals; on the other hand it is used as a metaphor. The usage of this term in antiquity usually occurs in religious contexts while the modern metaphorical usage does not; it has been secularized.[12] For the sake of terminological precision, I shall therefore distinguish between '*cultic*'/'*ritual* sacrifice' or 'sacrificial rituals' and 'sacrificial *metaphors*' in this essay.

It should be noted that the usage of the term 'sacrifice' in ancient religious contexts and in the Bible can have joyous and festive connotations; by contrast, the modern secularized usage has predominantly negative connotations as it associates loss and misfortune. This corresponds to the observation that biblical texts usually do not apply the term 'sacrifice' to martyrs and cases that we today would label 'self-sacrifice.' It should, moreover, be noted that modern scholarly theories of sacrifice usually deal with cultic sacrifices. It is nevertheless a concern that many modern theories of cultic sacrifice in antiquity are influenced by modern secularized concepts of sacrifice with rather negative connotations. In theological, anthropological, and historical scholarship, therefore, ritual sacrifice is often associated with violence or death.[13] Such opinions are also manifest where sacrifice is depicted as being inseparably connected to blood rituals.[14] This has led to common assumptions that the temple as the very center of ancient Israelite/early Jewish worship was an institution bent on the annihilation of life. The legitimacy of such scholarly views has recently been questioned by, for example, K. McClymond who observes a tendency to 'exaggerate the importance of killing.'[15]

---

11 Similar categories for the distinction of the term 'sacrifice' are proposed in W. Stegemann, "Zur Metaphorik des Opfers," in B. Janowski/M. Welker (ed.), *Opfer: Theologische und kulturelle Kontexte* (Stw 1454; Frankfurt am Main: Suhrkamp, 2000), 191–216, on pp. 191–5.

12 Cf. Stegemann, "Metaphorik," 195; C. A. Eberhart, "The Term 'Sacrifice' and the Problem of Theological Abstraction: A Study of the Reception History of Genesis 22:1–19," in C. Helmer (ed.), *The Multivalence of Biblical Texts and Theological Meanings* (Symposium Series 37, Atlanta: Society of Biblical Literature, 2006), 47–66, on pp. 47–50.

13 Cf. Hubert/Mauss, "Essai," 67, 71–75; Burkert, *Homo Necans*, 5, 12–48.

14 Cf. G.W. Ashby, "The Bloody Bridegroom: The Interpretation of Exodus 4:24–26," *ExpTim* 106 (Jan 1995), 203–5, on p. 204.

15 McClymond, *Beyond Sacred Violence*, 17.

2 Ritual Sacrifice in the Hebrew Bible/Septuagint

The present contribution to the ongoing scholarly discussion on the nature of cultic sacrifices attempts to orient itself along traces of 'native' or original interpretations. It is interested in the question: How did the ancient Israelite/early Jewish communities that produced and passed on the texts of the Hebrew Bible as well as the diaspora groups that translated them into Greek understand sacrificial rituals? As stated above, explicit theories of sacrifice are featured nowhere in the Hebrew Bible; yet the choice of mentioning certain ritual activity in various texts on sacrificial rituals and the choice of terminology can be understood as rudimentary traces of such native interpretation. Hence I shall investigate aspects of meaning of key terms that are frequently used for cultic sacrifices in the Hebrew Bible and the Septuagint.

Through this combination of several elements of original interpretation in the texts on cultic sacrifices, I aim at avoiding problems that might occur if terminology is considered without further attention to its semantic context. In this regard, the classic caveat of James Barr still needs to be taken seriously that sometimes generalizations are made on fairly narrow evidence, particularly when broad arguments are based on the modern interpretation of individual words or their etymology. Barr therefore advises to support such arguments by consulting the context in each case.[16] My approach to determining meaning, therefore, shall be guided by the consideration of the sense of individual words within their larger discourse units. This approach thus rests on the assumption that the process of choosing or coining technical terms was part of a conscious procedure in the development of a larger cultic system.[17]

The most detailed information on ritual sacrifices in the Hebrew Bible is featured in the priestly texts of Lev 1–7.[18] These texts distinguish between five different types of sacrifice, namely the burnt offering, the cereal offering, the sacrifice of well-being, the sin offering, and the guilt offering. Even though the

16 Cf. J. Barr, *The Semantics of Biblical Language* (Oxford: Oxford University Press, 1962) 155–6. In its own historical context, some of Barr's argument was specifically directed against what he called "the root fallacy" (ibid. 100–6) in lexicographical studies and the exegesis of Hebrew Bible texts. A similar position is that of Moisés Silva who emphasizes that "linguists … would assign a *determinative* function to context; that is, the context does not merely help us understand meaning—it virtually *makes* meaning" (*Biblical Words and Their Meaning: An Introduction to Lexical Semantics* [Grand Rapids: Zondervan, 1983], 139; italics original).

17 In this regard, see the words of Ithamar Gruenwald: "… the cultic environment of the sanctuary leaves nothing to chance or to non-systematic performance. Indeed, it activates a more sophisticated systematization of rituals, in which clearly specified names and functions play a major role …" (*Rituals*, 208).

18 Alfred Marx considers the section of Lev 1–7 as an independent unit that he calls "the Holy of Holies in the book of Leviticus" due to its "prominent position" ("Theology," 106).

rituals and individual instructions for all of these types of sacrifice are different, the priestly texts employ one comprehensive term for all of them: קרבן (Lev 1:2, 3, 10, 14; 2:1, 4, 7, 12; 3:1; 4:23, 28, 32; 5:11; 7:38; etc., see also 17:4; Num 15:4).[19] For example, the regulations in Lev 1–7 conclude with the following recapitulatory statement:

> This is the law (זאת התורה) of the burnt offering (עלה), the cereal offering (מנחה), the sin offering (חטאת), the guilt offering (אשם), the offering of ordination (מלואים), and the sacrifice of well-being (זבח שלמים), which YHWH commanded Moses on Mount Sinai, when he commanded the people of Israel to bring their offerings to YHWH (להקריב את־קרבניהם ליהוה), in the wilderness of Sinai (Lev 7:37–38).[20]

The term קרבן is a nominal derivative from the root קרב—'to draw near, to bring near.' Its literal meaning, therefore, is 'that which is brought near.'[21] The standard English translation of קרבן—'offering'[22] is perhaps based on its Septuagint rendering δῶρον—'offering, present.'[23] Such a קרבן is always a קרבן ליהוה—an 'offering for YHWH.' It captures the dynamic movement of sacrificial material towards the sanctuary and ultimately towards God who, according to the priestly concepts, resides there. These ritual dynamics are also conveyed through multiple occurrences of the verb קרב *hiphil*—'to bring near' (Lev 1:2, 3, 5, 10; 2:2, 4; 3:1; 4:3, 14; 5:8; 7:9) alongside the nominal derivative קרבן, accompanied by equivalents such as בוא *hiphil* (Lev 2:2, 8; 4:23, 28; 5:6, 11) and נגשׁ *hiphil* (Lev 2:8), which both mean 'to bring near.'[24]

These observations show that nouns and verbs conveying the approach of the sanctuary permeate the regulations on ritual sacrifice in Lev 1–7. Such an approach was actualized, for example, during regular pilgrimages to regional

---

19 The following reflections are based on C. Eberhart, "Qorban," *Wissenschaftliches Bibellexikon im Internet* (Stuttgart: Deutsche Bibelgesellschaft, http://www.wibilex.de; 2010).

20 It is surprising that this list contains the 'offering of ordination' (מלואים) that is not featured in Lev 1–7. Instead this type of sacrifice is prescribed in Exod 29:19–28; a description follows in Lev 8:22–28. J. Milgrom explains that the 'offering of ordination' is inserted here because of "its rank in the order of holiness" (*Leviticus 1–16: A New Translation with Introduction and Commentary* [AncB 3; New York/London: Doubleday, 1991], 436).

21 Cf. J. Milgrom, *Leviticus 1–16*, 145; H.-J. Fabry, "קָרְבָּן *qōrbān* קֻרְבָּן *qurbān*," in *TDOT* 13; Grand Rapids/Cambridge [U.K.]: Eerdmans, 2004), 152–8: 152; R. Rendtorff, *Leviticus vol. 1: Leviticus 1,1–10,20* (BKAT 3; Neukirchen-Vluyn: Neukirchener Verlag, 2004), 24; T. Hieke, *Levitikus 1–15* (HThKAT; Freiburg/Basel/Wien: Herder, 2014), 84–5, 159.

22 Cf. KJV, RSV, NRSV, NIV; B. A. Levine, *Leviticus* ויקרא*: The Traditional Hebrew Text with the New JPS Translation* (JPSTC; Philadelphia/New York/Jerusalem: Jewish Publication Society, 1989), 5. See also the French translation 'présent' (*Traduction Œcuménique de la Bible, Nouvelle Bible Segond*).

23 Cf. P. Harlé/D. Pralon, *La Bible d'Alexandrie: Le Lévitique* (Paris: Éditions du Cerf, 1988), 35.

24 Cf. A. Marx, *Les systèmes sacrificiels de l'Ancien Testament: Formes et fonctions du culte sacrificiel à Yhwh* (VT.S 105; Leiden/Boston: Brill, 2005), 109.

cult sites or to the central sanctuary (Exod 23:14–17; 34:18–26; Lev 23:1–44; Deut 16:1–17). With regard to earlier observations on modern theorizing, it may be mentioned that such terminological choices of the priestly communities and the ancient tradents of the Hebrew Bible texts do not convey any negative connotations. Instead, further Hebrew Bible texts indicate that specifically the burnt offering, the cereal offering, and the sacrifice of well-being are often associated with a cheerful, merry, and celebratory atmosphere (1 Sam 1:13–14; 2 Chr 29:20–36).

Furthermore, these terminological choices do not point to the act of slaughter at all. In animal sacrifice, slaughter occurs towards the beginning of the ritual; however, the ritual continues after this activity, leading towards the act of burning all or a portion of the sacrificial material on the so-called altar of burnt offering (Lev 1:9, 13; 2:2, 11; 3:5, 11; 4:10, 31). The connection between the latter and the designation of sacrifices as קרבן ליהוה—'offering for YHWH' is manifest in the interpretive comment that the priestly community usually attached to the burning rite, namely ריח ניחוח ליהוה—'a pleasing odor for YHWH' (Lev 1:9, 13, 17; 2:2, 3:5, 16; 4:31). The ritual dynamics of the cultic sacrifice thus conclude when the sacrificial material is being transformed by the altar fire and its odor is perceived by God.

Finally, this terminology that conveys the dynamics of cultic sacrifices occurs also in the context of the ritual of the cereal offering (Lev 2). As this type of sacrifice consists of vegetal substances accompanied by oil, frankincense (v. 1), and salt (v. 13), it is clear that its ritual does not feature any act of slaughter. The movement indicated in Lev 2 by the noun קרבן and the verbs קרב *hiphil*, בוא *hiphil*, and נגש *hiphil* also concludes with the burning rite, which is further accentuated because all of the frankincense is to be added.

Beyond the Hebrew Bible, the term קרבן occurs frequently in later literature such as the Dead Sea Scrolls and rabbinic texts. In the latter, קרבן also designates referents that are not sacrificial rituals, for instance the wood offering (m.Taʿan. 4:5) or the hair of the Nazir (m. Naz. 2:5–6).

The cereal offering leads us to consider the word מנחה, a second term for cultic sacrifice in the Hebrew Bible. This term occurs in the priestly texts as the very designation of the cereal offering (also called 'grain offering' or 'meal offering'). It is to be prepared from raw or unprepared grains of cereal that are to be baked, toasted, or fried.[25] It occurs 213 times in the Hebrew Bible of which 150 refer to this specific type of sacrifice. In another thirty instances, however, מנחה has a broader meaning.[26] It refers, for example, to both Cain's sacrifice from 'the fruits

25 Cf. Levine, *Leviticus*, 11–14; McClymond, *Beyond Sacred Violence*, 72–3; Hieke, *Levitikus 1–15*, 196, 198–9, 205–7.

26 For the numbers here and in the following see A. Marx, *Les offrandes végétales dans l'Ancien Testament: Du tribut d'hommage au repas eschatologique* (VT.S 57; Leiden/New York/Köln:

of the soil' and to the suet portions that Abel offers of the firstlings of his flock (Gen 4:3–5). In yet another context, the term מנחה refers exclusively to animal sacrifices that are offered at the sanctuary of Shiloh (1 Sam 2:17; see also Num 16:15; etc.).[27] Rainer Kessler notes that the term occurs very frequently in the book of Malachi, which therefore features a 'theology of the gift.'[28] In each of these instances, the term has the broader meaning of 'offering.'

For a closer investigation of its further connotations, it is instructive that the term מנחה occurs another thirty-three times in entirely secular contexts where it designates a gift or present of reverence or reconciliation, for instance in the scene of Jacob's encounter with Esau (Gen 32:13 [14MT], 18 [19MT], 21 [22MT]; 33:10). At their meeting, Jacob's gift was accompanied by various expressions of respect (Jacob bowed to the ground seven times, 33:3; also the women and children bowed down, vv. 6–7; Jacob addressed Esau repeatedly as אדני—'my lord,' vv. 8, 13, 14; Jacob expressed his hope to find favor with Esau, v. 10; etc.). In addition, the term מנחה is parallel to ברכה—'gift/present of blessing' (v. 11). The term occurs with a similar meaning in the story of King Ben-Hadad of Aram who asked Hazael to bring presents to the prophet Elisha so that the latter would predict whether the king would recover from his illness or not (2 Kgs 8:7–9). Its meaning is somewhat different, for instance, in the narrative of Israel's defeat and subsequent oppression through King Eglon of Moab. Here it designates the 'tribute' that Ehud, who would later deliver Israel, initially had to pay to Eglon (Judg 3:15–18; for a similar usage of מנחה, see also 2 Sam 8:2 / 1 Chr 18:2; 1 Kings 4:21 [1 Kings 5:1MT]). In all of these texts, מנחה signifies a present or payment that corresponds to a power differential in the private or political realm. The act of giving a present or tribute constitutes a required and due gesture of submission.[29]

The connotations and functions of the term in secular contexts provide parameters for its meaning in cultic contexts: מנחה indicates that a ritual sacrifice is a gift of reverence or reconciliation for God. It conveys both the submission of the offerer and his or her acknowledgement of the superior status of God.[30] This is the

Brill, 1994), 1; R. Kessler, "Die Theologie der Gabe bei Maleachi," in F.-L. Hossfeld/L. Schwienhorst-Schönberger (ed.), *Das Manna fällt auch heute noch: Beiträge zur Geschichte und Theologie des Alten, Ersten Testaments* (FS E. Zenger; HBS 44; Freiburg et al.: Herder, 2004), 392–407, on p. 394. See also N. H. Snaith, "Sacrifices in the Old Testament," *VT* 7 (1957), 308–17, on pp. 309, 314–16; Hieke, *Levitikus 1–15*, 100–1.

27 Cf. A. Marx, *Offrandes*, 6–15; Rendtorff, *Leviticus*, 87–8.

28 "Theologie der Gabe;" Kessler, "Theologie," 392, 394, 401, etc.

29 Cf. G. A. Anderson, *Sacrifices and Offerings in Ancient Israel: Studies in their Social and Political Importance* (HSM 41; Atlanta: Scholars Press, 1987), 27–34, 53–4; Milgrom, *Leviticus 1–16*, 196.

30 Cf. I. Willi-Plein, *Opfer und Kult im alttestamentlichen Israel: Textbefragungen und Zwischenergebnisse* (SBS 153; Stuttgart: Katholisches Bibelwerk, 1993), 82; C. Eberhart, *Studien zur Bedeutung der Opfer im Alten Testament: Die Signifikanz von Blut- und Verbrennungsriten im kultischen Rahmen* (WMANT 94; Neukirchen-Vluyn: Neukirchener Verlag, 2002), 184.

ultimate reason why sacrifices must be of high quality—only a precious gift truly displays human respect (Lev 21:17–25; Deut 17:1). Consequently the prophet Malachi criticizes the practice of offering blind, lame, or sick animals for God; such sacrifices send the opposite message because they indicate that the offerer despises God (Mal 1:6–14). With these specific connotations and functions, the meaning of מנחה is in some measure comparable to that of the term קרבן, which is customarily translated as 'offering' (see above). It focuses, however, more strongly on "the relationship between the individual worshiper and God and between the Israelite community and the God of Israel."[31]

A third group of terms for cultic sacrifice in the Hebrew Bible are the verbal and nominal derivates of the root זבח. A common opinion on the meaning of the noun זבח was articulated by Norman H. Snaith:

> What then was the זבח? Gray ... said the word 'means simply what is slain', and no one will quarrel with that. If therefore we want an English word for זבח, ... it ought to be 'slain-offering'...[32]

In addition, Snaith follows the classical argument of William Robertson Smith according to which sacrificial meals affirmed the unity of primitive clans through the consumption of consecrated meat.

> The זבח is therefore a common meal in that all the people together eat of the Holy Food; they 'eat the god', and so find vigour and new life for body and soul. It is therefore a shared meal, a communion meal, not because God eats some of it, but rather because they 'eat God'.[33]

Is it possible to substantiate either aspect of this interpretation?

The verb זבח can mean 'to slaughter' (Deut 12:15, 21; 1 Sam 28:24); in these cases it is equivalent to טבח—'to slaughter, massacre' (1 Sam 25:11; Jer 12:3) and to שׁחט—'to slaughter.'[34] The regulations on cultic sacrifices in Lev 1–7, however, never feature the verb זבח to articulate animal slaughter; instead they always use שׁחט. Yet the spectrum of meaning of the root זבח is not limited to just animal slaughter; it also comprises at least the following two aspects. First, the type of

---

According to T. H. Gaster, another expression of submission is the gesture of removing one's shoes before approaching the sanctuary; iconographic evidence even attests to the ancient Near Eastern custom of ritual nudity (cf. T. H. Gaster, "Sacrifices and Offerings, OT," in *IDB* 4 [Nashville/New York: Abingdon, 1962] 147–59, on pp. 156–7). Gaster also mentions that the association of מנחה to tribute has parallels in several Akkadian texts (ibid. 148).

31 Levine, *Leviticus*, xxiii.

32 Snaith, "Sacrifices," 309 (with reference to G. B. Gray, *Sacrifice in the Old Testament: Its Theory and Practice* [Oxford: Clarendon Press, 1925], 6). The term 'slain-offering' is equivalent to the customary German rendering of זבח as '*Schlachtopfer*.'

33 Ibid. 313.

34 Cf. C. Eberhart, "Schlachtung/Schächtung," *Wissenschaftliches Bibellexikon im Internet* (Stuttgart: Deutsche Bibelgesellschaft, http://www.wibilex.de; 2006), § 1.

sacrifice called זבח in the Hebrew Bible encompasses a festive meal during which the offerer, together with family and friends, had the privilege of eating sacrificial meat (Gen 31:54; Exod 18:12; 24:5; Deut 27:7; 1 Sam 1:3–4; 2:13–16; 9:12–13; 1 Kings 8:62–66; 19:21; Hos 8:13; 1 Chr 29:21–22). Such a meal is an integral part of this sacrifice and implied in the term זבח. However, in response to Snaith's argument that a meal following a זבח could be interpreted as a communion meal that consists of the consumption of something holy, and therefore of God, it must be emphasized that no Hebrew Bible text supports such an idea. To the contrary, the prohibition against eating suet because it belongs to God (Lev 3:17; 7:25) indicates a strict separation between that which is for God and that which is for humans. It is impossible, then, to claim that the God of Israel would be identified with the sacrificial animal.[35] Rather the fact that sacrificial rituals are performed 'before YHWH' (לפני יהוה, Lev 1:5; see also 3:2 etc.) and that sacrifices are eaten 'before YHWH, your God' (לפני יהוה אלהיך, Deut 27:7) suggests both proximity to God while simultaneously maintaining a clear sense of separation.

Second, it is of interest to note that the Akkadian equivalent *zebû* is used for fumigation. Burning is also a component of the type of sacrifice called זבח שלמים in the Hebrew Bible; its ritual in Lev 3 features lengthy regulations on exactly which suet portions and organs of the sacrificial animal are to be burnt as a 'pleasing odor for YHWH' (ריח ניחוח ליהוה) on the altar of burnt offering (Lev 3:3–5; 9–11, etc.). The ritual of this type of sacrifice progresses towards, and attains its purpose in, the burning rite and the festive meal. These two aspects belong to the 'apportionment' of the sacrificial animal; in the end, God, the offerer, and even the priests receive their portions.[36] It is therefore likely that the term זבח used by the ancient Israelite communities and early tradents of the texts for this type of sacrifice comprised both the burning rite and the subsequent sacrificial meal.[37] Hence a more appropriate translation of the verb זבח is 'to sacrifice;' the noun should respectively be rendered as 'sacrifice.'

A final consideration concerns the Hebrew term for 'altar,' the noun מזבח. Derived from זבח, this noun is often considered to convey that an altar is the locus of ritual animal slaughter. However, this does not match the ritual reality as it emerges from the priestly texts in the Hebrew Bible. Animals are not slaughtered on the altar of burnt offering but north of it near the entrance of the courtyard (Lev 1:5, 11; see also later traditions like m. Zebaḥ. 5:1). Ezekiel mentions eight tables in the vestibule of the gate that are reserved for animal slaughter (Ezek 40:39–41).[38] By contrast, this altar is the location where substances from

35 Cf. Milgrom, *Leviticus 1–16*, 221.

36 Apportionment of sacrificial substances means its division and distribution, usually for consumption; cf. McClymond, *Beyond Sacred Violence*, 56–9, 131–51.

37 Cf. Eberhart, *Studien*, 89–90.

38 Cf. Milgrom, *Leviticus 1–16*, 154–5; Eberhart, *Studien*, 180.

all types of cultic sacrifices—including the cereal offering—are offered to God through the burning rite.[39] An altar, then, is more appropriately understood as a place of sacrifice in general that is conveyed by the Hebrew noun מזבח.[40] This specific function is captured in the characteristic designation of the altar in the courtyard of the tabernacle, which is known as the 'altar of burnt offering' (מזבח העלה, Exod 30:28; 31:9; 35:16; 38:1; 40:6; Lev 4:7, 10, 18, 25; etc.).

At this point an investigation of Greek terminology is instructive. Both the Greek verb θύω and the related noun θυσία can refer to the act of slaughter (Exod 12:21; Deut 12:15, 21; 1 Sam 25:11; 28:24). Yet both have a broader meaning as well. This is manifest when considering the usage of these terms in pagan Greek texts such as the *Leges Sacrae*, which were widely spread throughout the Mediterranean between the fifth century BCE and the third century CE.[41] They contained detailed instructions for the offering of ritual sacrifices at specific sanctuaries. For example, Xenophon (ca. 430–354 BCE) gave directives for tithes (τὴν μὲν δεκάτην καταθύειν) from agricultural yields during annual festivals in honor of the goddess Artemis (Xen. Anab. 5:3:13).[42] According to Fred S. Naiden, the Greeks employed the term θυσία for both animal sacrifice and vegetal offerings; Plato coined the adage 'sacrificing is gift-giving to the gods' (τὸ θύειν δωρεῖσθαί ἐστι τοῖς θεοῖς, Euthyphro 14C).[43] The translators of the Septuagint adopted this terminology and deployed it in similar ways.[44] Here, the noun θυσία occurs not only 138 times as translation of the term זבח, but also 134 times as the equivalent of the term מנחה in both its meaning of 'cereal offering' (e.g., Lev 2:1, 3, 4, 5, 6, 7, 8, 9, 10, 11, 13, 14, 15; 9:4, 17, 18; Num 15:4) and as a general term for 'sacrifice'

39 Cf. K. Galling, "Altar," in *IDB* 1 (Nashville/New York: Abingdon, 1962), 96–100, on p. 96.

40 Even the English term 'altar' is derived from Latin *altare*—'altar' which is probably related to the verb *adolere*—'to burn.'

41 Cf. M. Vahrenhorst, *Kultische Sprache in den Paulusbriefen* (WUNT 230; Tübingen: Mohr Siebeck, 2008), 75–86.

42 For a detailed archeological study of ancient Greek plant offerings, mostly fruits and nuts, see, e.g., F. Megaloudi, "Burnt Sacrificial Plant Offerings in Hellenistic Times: An Archaeological Case Study from Messene, Peloponese, Greece," *Veget. Hist. Archaeobot* 14 (2005), 329–40.

43 Cf. F. S. Naiden, *Smoke Signals for the Gods: Ancient Greek Sacrifice from the Archaic Through Roman Periods* (Oxford: Oxford University Press, 2013), 36, 280–2. See also the comments on the meaning of θυσία in Harlé/Pralon, *Le Lévitique*, 35: "En principe, dans l'usage classique, *thusía* ne vise que l'action de consumer (*thúein*: offrir par le moyen du feu, en faisant fumer) …"

44 Both Exod^{LXX} and Lev^{LXX}, the books containing a large amount of cultic terminology that set the standard for the use in other books of the Septuagint, were most likely translated in the third century BCE for Jews in a non-Jewish, Hellenistic environment of Egypt. Cf. P. Schwagmeier, "1.2 Exodos/Exodos/Das zweite Buch Mose," in S. Kreuzer (ed.), *Einleitung in die Septuaginta, LXX.H vol. 1* (Gütersloh: Gütersloher Verlagshaus, 2016), 120–36, on pp. 132, 134; M. Vahrenhorst, "1.3 Levitikon/Levitikus/Das dritte Buch Mose," in S. Kreuzer (ed.), *Einleitung in die Septuaginta, LXX.H vol. 1* (Gütersloh: Gütersloher Verlagshaus, 2016), 137–45, on pp. 141–2.

(e.g., Gen 4:3, 5).[45] Consisting of vegetal substances, the cereal offering naturally features no act of slaughter. Instead the only ritual step to be carried out at the sanctuary is the burning rite on the central altar.

How can this spectrum of meaning of θύω and the related noun θυσία be explained? According to an article in *Theologisches Wörterbuch zum Neuen Testament*, the verb θύω originally denotes a forceful motion of the air, water, etc. with the meaning of 'to well up, to boil up' from which the meaning of 'to smoke,' and 'to cause to go up in smoke' as well as 'to sacrifice' developed.[46] These clarifications are an invitation to broaden the common perception of what the Greek terms θύω and θυσία mean; they evidently are not limited to acts of slaughter or killing. It can be interpreted, in line with Plato's adage, as 'gift-giving,' which is effected through the burning rite. This has important ramifications for the understanding of the term θυσία. In addition, there are instances where θύω or θυσία is equivalent to the verb or noun derived from the root זבח and implies the participation in a sacrificial meal (Exod 18:12; 24:5; Deut 27:7; 1 Sam 1:3–4; 2:13–16; 1 Kings 8:62–66; 19:21; Hos 8:13; 1 Chr 29:21–22).

Only such a broader meaning allows one to comprehend why later the apostle Paul could use the term θυσία as a metaphor for, on the one hand, gifts that Epaphroditus had delivered on behalf of the congregation in Philippi (Phil 4:18; see above)[47] and, on the other hand, the behavior of members of the congregation in Rome, whom he urges 'to present your bodies as a sacrifice, living, holy [and] acceptable to God' (παραστῆσαι τὰ σώματα ὑμῶν θυσίαν ζῶσαν ἁγίαν εὐάρεστον

45 Due to its limited scope, the present essay can only explore selected aspects of Septuagint terminology. It is worth mentioning that, as one of the most important documents of early Hellenistic Judaism, the Septuagint deserves more scholarly attention than that. It is "an interpretation of the Hebrew Scriptures on an unprecedented scale: one of the oldest and most important witnesses of the history of Biblical exegesis" (J. Joosten, "Exegesis in the Septuagint Version of Hosea," in idem, *Collected Studies on the Septuagint: From Language to Interpretation and Beyond* [Tübingen: Mohr Siebeck, 2012], 123–45, on p. 123). See also J. W. Wevers, "The Interpretative Character and Significance of the Septuagint Version," in M. Sæbø (ed.), *Hebrew Bible/Old Testament: The History of Its Interpretation, vol. 1. From the Beginnings to the Middle Ages (Until 1300): Part 1* (Göttingen: Vandenhoeck & Ruprecht, 1996), 84–107.

46 F. Büchsel, "θυμός," in *ThWNT* 3 (Stuttgart/Berlin/Köln: Kohlhammer, 1938), 167–73, on p. 167. Cf. J. Behm, "θύω," ibid. 180–90, on pp. 180–1; Harlé/Pralon, *Le Lévitique*, 39.

47 Jane L. Patterson explains the association between sacrificial metaphors and the burning rite: "Thus, the material gifts provided by the Philippians to Paul during his imprisonment are described as ὀσμὴ εὐωδίας (sic), then as θυσία δεκτή, and then finally εὐάρεστος (sic) τῷ θεῷ (Phil 4:18). The sequence almost seems to describe the ascent of the smoke of the sacrifices, as the reader moves from what can be experienced of them physically (their fragrance), to their ritual acceptability (a human abstraction), and finally to their effect on God (something that cannot be seen at all, but is attested here by Paul)" (*Keeping the Feast: Metaphors of Sacrifice in 1 Corinthians and Philippians* [Early Christianity and its Literature 16; Atlanta: SBL Press, 2015], 106).

τῷ θεῷ, Rom 12:1).[48] Regarding the latter, if the point of an actual ritual of a θυσία was killing or death, then the metaphor of a 'living sacrifice' would be an oxymoron. Paul's usage of this term in both passages demonstrates that it carries a different meaning.[49] It focuses on the aspect of giving, which is highlighted by the attributes εὐάρεστος—'acceptable' and δεκτός—'pleasant.' Both words articulate the intended effect of the procedure of offering sacrifices on God. Clearly, these terms belong to the socio-cultural background of gift-giving and are well-attested in the context of sacrificial rituals, for example in those of the book of Leviticus.[50]

To sum up these terminological reflections, all comprehensive words for cultic sacrifices in the Hebrew Bible have individual profiles: the word קרבן conveys an approach or a dynamic movement through sacred space that concludes in the burning rite on the altar and the smoke ascending to heaven; מנחה expresses a relationship between humans and God while pointing at a status difference that necessitates appropriate gifts of reverence. The noun זבח and its Greek equivalent θυσία, found also in the Septuagint, reference the entire activity of ritual sacrifice that can comprise animal slaughter, burning, and meat consumption. Greek θυσία can be understood as gift-giving. This means that none of these comprehensive terms focus exclusively on slaughter; instead all of them include the final act of burning.

It should be mentioned that yet another two comprehensive terms for cultic sacrifices are attested in the Hebrew Bible. The first one is אשה—'fire offering.' In the priestly texts, it usually alludes to the process of transforming the material offering into a new, ethereal essence through the burning rite. Against proposals

---

48 Translation by R. Jewett, *Romans: A Commentary* (Hermeneia; Minneapolis, MN: Fortress, 2007), 724–5. See the equivalent rendering in W. Schmithals, *Der Römerbrief: Ein Kommentar* (Gütersloh: Gütersloher Verlagshaus, 1988), 425, 428.

49 Walter Schmithals observes that the majority of interpreters understands Paul's reference to a 'living … sacrifice' as an allusion to the resurrection of Christians from death. He finally concludes that the metaphor conveys receiving life out of death (*Römerbrief*, 428). The problem with all of these interpretations is that they see death as a fundamental aspect of the spectrum of meaning of θυσία. I have shown above that this is not the case.

50 The correct execution of the ritual of, for instance, a burnt offering is 'for acceptance in your behalf before YHWH' (לרצנו לפני יהוה, Lev 1:3; see also 22:17–30 with a broader focus). Thomas Hieke explains that this phrase is typical of the priestly cult terminology and that it imagines a successful communication between humans and God (*Levitikus 1–15*, 164). The importance of the concept of acceptability is evident in a variety of prophetic texts that deny this expected outcome of sacrificial rituals; God is said to find sacrifices 'not acceptable' (Hos 6:6; Amos 5:21–27). These statements should, however, not be understood as categorical rejections of the temple cult (cf. A. Glaim, "'I Will Not Accept Them': Sacrifice and Reciprocity in the Prophetic Literature," in H. L. Wiley/C. A. Eberhart [ed.], *Sacrifice, Cult, and Atonement in Early Judaism and Christianity: Constituents and Critique* [SBLRBS 85; Atlanta: SBL Press, 2017], 125–49, on pp. 135–49). The Septuagint features the equivalent δεκτός—'acceptable,' which is also attested in pagan Greek texts (Homer, Il. 2:420; Hymn. Ap. 274; Hymn. Cer. 29; Corp. Herm. 1:31). However, Lev 1:3 LXX and 22:17–30 LXX modify the MT; acceptability is now an attribute of the sacrificial material, no longer of the offerer.

that אשה would have no connotations to 'fire,'[51] it is instructive to explore once more the translation practice of the Septuagint. Here, a total of eight equivalent is attested, which can be taken as evidence of some controversial debate about the precise meaning of this term in antiquity.[52] Among these equivalents, however, the most frequent ones are κάρπωμα (34 times) and θυσία (9 times); attested are also ὁλοκαύτωμα, θυσίασμα, θυμίαμα, πῦρ, and the verbs καρπόω and θυσιάζω. Notable about these equivalents is the fact that three among them are also used to render the term עלה—'burnt offering.' Almost all of them have connotations to the act of burning or to fire, especially the terms κάρπωμα[53] and -καύτωμα; the latter comes from the verb καίω—'to burn' (Dan 3:23; compare to Test.Naph. 7:4: ἐκαιόμην τοῖς σπλάγχνοις—'my heart burned within myself'). Thus the composite ὁλοκαύτωμα denotes that which is totally burned. These observations should be taken as an indication that the ancient tradents and translators did associate the term אשה with 'fire.' Choosing the translation 'fire offering,' I follow a suggestion by Suzanne Daniel that אשה denotes the sacrificial material under the aspect of what is consumed by the altar fire.[54]

The second term is ריח ניחוח—'pleasing odor' or 'appeasing odor.' It typically refers to the ascent of the sacrificial smoke from the earthly to the heavenly sphere.[55] More specifically, it denotes the 'effect' of a sacrificial offering on the God of Israel.[56] The Septuagint typically renders this formula as ὀσμὴ εὐωδίας—'pleasing odor.' With this terminological choice, the Alexandrian translators decided to convey the positive aspect of ריח ניחוח but to drop its negative aspect of appeasement, thus reducing the spectrum of anthropomorphic descriptors of God.[57]

---

51 Cf. Milgrom, *Leviticus 1–16*, 161–2, 394; Rendtorff, *Leviticus*, 63–5; C. Houtman, *Exodus, vol. 3: Chapters 20–40* (HCOT; Leuven: Peeters, 2000), 538.

52 See also the comments in Harlé/Pralon, *Le Lévitique*, 39.

53 Cf. M. Vahrenhorst, "Exkurs 'Hinweise zur Opferterminologie im LXX-Pentateuch,'" in M. Karrer/W. Kraus (ed.), *Septuaginta Deutsch: Erklärungen und Kommentare zum griechischen Alten Testament, vol. 1: Genesis bis Makkabäer* (Stuttgart: Deutsche Bibelgesellschaft, 2011), 335–46, on p. 338.

54 S. Daniel, *Recherches sur le vocabulaire du culte dans la Septante* (EeC 61; Paris: Librairie C. Klincksieck, 1966), 155: "… *'iššèh* désigne le sacrifice en tant qu'il est destiné à être consumé sur l'autel."

55 Cf. Eberhart, *Studien*, 40–50, 361–81; idem, "A Neglected Feature of Sacrifice in the Hebrew Bible: Remarks on the Burning Rite on the Altar," *HTR* 97 (2004) 485–93, on pp. 489–90. See also Houtman, *Exodus*, 538; Marx, *Systèmes sacrificiels*, 138–9; Hieke, *Levitikus 1–15*, 105–7.

56 Cf. Rendtorff, *Leviticus*, 68: "Diese Belege zeigen, daß bei dem Ausdruck ריח ניחח der Gedanke eine Rolle spielt, wie das Opfer bei der Gottheit 'ankommt' …" See also Hieke, *Levitikus 1–15*, 106.

57 Cf. Daniel, *Recherches*, 176, 188; Vahrenhorst, "Exkurs," 343; C. Eberhart, "Beobachtungen zu Opfer, Kult und Sühne in der Septuaginta," in W. Kraus/S. Kreutzer (ed.), *Die Septuaginta—Text, Wirkung, Rezeption: 4. Internationale Fachtagung veranstaltet von Septuaginta Deutsch (LXX.D), Wuppertal 19.–22.7.2012* (unter Mitarbeit von Martin Meiser und Marcus Sigismund; WUNT 325, Tübingen: Mohr Siebeck, 2014), 297–314, on pp. 302–6.

With these meanings, both אשה and ריח ניחוח are frequently featured as interpretive terms in, for example, the sacrificial rituals Lev 1–7. They also occur in later Jewish texts such as m. Menaḥ. 13:11:

נאמר בעולת הבהמה אשה ריח ניחוח ובעולת העוף אשה ריח ניחוח ובמנחה אשה ריח ניחוח ללמד שאחד המרבה ואחד הממעיט ובלבד שיכון אדם את דעתו לשמים

> It is said of the burnt offering of the herd, a fire offering, a pleasing odor, and of the bird offering, a fire offering, a pleasing odor, and of the cereal offering, a fire offering, a pleasing odor to teach that all the same are the one who offers much and the one who offers little, provided that a person will direct his intention to Heaven.

The importance of these interpretive terms is manifest as well in other rabbinic guidelines specifying that a ritual sacrifice is to be sacrificed for the sake of six things, among them 'for the sake of the [altar] fires (לשם אשים), for the sake of the odor (לשם ריח), for the sake of the pleasing smell (לשם ניחוח)' (m. Zebaḥ. 4:6).

Yet beyond these specific functions, both terms also occur repeatedly as comprehensive references for the entire sacrificial cult. According to a calendar of appointed festivals, the feast of unleavened bread is celebrated for seven days during which the 'fire offering for YHWH' (אשה ליהוה) is to be offered daily (Lev 23:8; see also Exod 30:20; Lev 6:10, 11; 21:6, 21; 22:22, 27; Num 15:25; 28:3, 19; 1 Sam 2:28; etc.). And a pronouncement of judgment because of Israel's disobedience mentions three areas that God will affect through divine punishment: 'I will lay your cities waste, I will make your sanctuaries desolate, and I will no longer smell your pleasing odor (ולא אריח בריח ניחחכם)' (Lev 26:31). In this passage, a corollary of the desolation of human dwelling places is the abandonment of local worship sites; the latter, in turn, leads to the termination of the sacrificial cult that is customarily performed there. The phrase ריח ניחוח is used with similar purposes in Num 15:17; Ezek 6:13; 16:19; 20:28; and so on. It is still known in later literature of early Judaism, for instance in 1QS 8:9; 4Q179 Frag. 1:6 and in m. Zebaḥ. 14:10:

רבי יהודה אומר אין מנחה בבמה וכהון ובגדי שרת וכלי שרת וריח ניחוח

> Rabbi Judah says, 'There is no cereal offering on a high place nor the priestly service, nor the wearing of garments of ministry, nor the use of utensils of ministry, nor the pleasing odor'.

Both אשה and ריח ניחוח also occur together as comprehensive references to the sacrificial cult (Lev 23:13, 18; Num 15:3, 14; 28:2; 29:6; etc.). In addition, a general term for 'sacrifice' in biblical Aramaic is ניחחין (Dan 2:46; Ezra 6:8–10), which is derived from ריח ניחוח. Hence comprehensive terminology that references the sacrificial cult in the Hebrew Bible strongly relies on the burning rite, suggesting that it is an important element.[58] The title of this contribution suggests that

58 Cf. Eberhart, *Studien*, 40–50, 303–8.

through fire and smoke, materials offered by humans, be they animals or vegetal substances, are transformed and transported to God.

These reflections on the terminology of ritual sacrifice also yield the result that, in the Hebrew Bible and the Septuagint, comprehensive terminology for sacrificial rituals does not exclusively focus on the act of animal slaughter. This corresponds to the observation that statements attributing any specific value or effect to the act of animal slaughter in the context of sacrificial rituals are not attested.[59] In some concluding thoughts, I shall verify these observations by briefly investigating rituals that do not count as 'sacrifice' in the Hebrew Bible.

3 Which Rituals are Not Considered as Sacrifice in the Hebrew Bible?

Due to the burning rite, the burnt offering, cereal offering, sacrifice of well-being, sin offering, and guilt offering are each in their own right called קרבן ליהוה—'offering for YHWH' in Lev 1–7. By contrast, other rituals usually do not count as קרבן ליהוה in the Hebrew Bible. I shall now examine four of them.[60]

a) The Passover ritual was already discussed above: According to Exod 12, the Israelites were supposed to slaughter a lamb that had to be consumed in its entirety. Any remainder had to be destroyed by fire; the Hebrew verb for this action is שׂרף (v. 10). It is thus terminologically distinguished from the burning rite on the altar of the sanctuary that is always designated through the verb קטר *hiphil*. Then the apotropaic blood rite had to be performed that would protect the Israelites from the fatal strike directed at Egypt's firstborn (vv. 7, 22–23).[61]

This ritual is not counted as קרבן in the sacrificial regulations of Lev 1–7. The reason might be that it is performed at the residence of laypeople; at least the directives in Exod 12 lack any provisions of 'approaching' the sanctuary (this is different in, for example, the dtr. version in Deut 16:1–8). Furthermore, since no portion of the lamb is offered for God, the Passover lacks any aspect of giving a token of reverence or reconciliation that would correspond to the status

59 See also the remark of J.-C. Margueron: "Mais il convient de souligner que même si l'immolation était ressentie ainsi par les anciens, c'est nous qui en faisons un élément particulier du culte, car dans l'antiquité orientale, la notion de *sacrifice* recouvre l'ensemble de l'offrande et non pas seulement sa partie sanglante: tout ce qui est offert au dieu devient sacré et donc objet du sacrifice" ("L'espace sacrificiel dans le Proche-Orient ancien," in R. Étienne/M.-Th. Le Dinahet [ed.], *L'espace sacrificiel dans les civilisations méditerranéennes de l'antiquité: Actes du colloque tenu à la Maison de l'Orient, Lyon, 4–7 juin 1988* [Publications de la Bibliothèque Salomon-Reinach 5; Paris: De Boccard, 1991], 235–42, on p. 236 [italics original]).

60 Cf. Eberhart, *Studien*, 319–20.

61 On the apotropaic character of the Passover blood rite see, for example, B. S. Childs, *The Book of Exodus: A Commentary* (OTL; Philadelphia: Westminster John Knox, 1974), 192, 200; Gilders, *Blood Ritual*, 44; Hieke, *Levitikus 1–15*, 257–8.

difference between humans and God, thus allowing the Passover ritual to be recognized as a מנחה.

b) Animal blood is used in the purification ritual for what is called a 'leprous person' (מצרע) and a 'leprous house' (Lev 14). In both cases a ritual with two birds is performed: after one bird is slaughtered, the second one is dipped into the blood of the first and becomes the medium for sprinkling the blood seven times upon the person (v. 7) or house (v. 51). This blood application rite 'cleanses' (v. 7) the person or 'removes sin' from the house and 'atones' for it (v. 52). Then the second, living bird is released to fly into the field. This is an elimination ritual in which the live bird carries the disease away.[62] The ritual then concludes with the offering of sacrifices at the sanctuary (vv. 10–20).

It is evident that the elimination ritual as such features dynamics contrary to those of cultic sacrifices. While in the latter humans offer their best animals and choice products to God who dwells in the sanctuary at the center of human civilization, in elimination rituals human defilement, perceived of in a quasi-material quality, is transported away from civilization into uncultivated territory.[63] Once more, therefore, no approach of the sanctuary occurs that would warrant this ritual to be labeled קרבן, and no portion is offered for God as a gesture of reverence due to which the ritual could be called a מנחה.

c) The best-known elimination ritual in the Hebrew Bible is the scapegoat (Lev 16:10, 20–22). On the Day of Atonement, Aaron the high priest transfers all of the sins and impurities of Israel onto a live goat 'for Azazel' (לעזאזל). This goat then carries Israel's guilt and sin away into the wilderness. The structural similarities with the previous bird ritual are evident; therefore its logic is also diametrically opposed to that of cultic sacrifice. Hence the scapegoat ritual is not considered a קרבן or מנחה in the Hebrew Bible.

d) As a consequence of bloodshed, the land is generally considered to be defiled by the victim's blood (Gen 4:11–12; Num 35:33; Ezek 7:23). If no culprit can be determined and the punishment of the perpetrator is impossible, a unique ritual is intended to provide substitution for the death of the murderer (Deut 21:1–9). During this ritual, the elders of the community where the bloodshed has occurred bring a heifer and break its neck. This procedure is not a sacrifice but a killing ritual; it atones for the bloodguilt (v. 8) and purges 'the guilt of innocent blood from your midst' (v. 9). It is, therefore, not called קרבן or מנחה.

This brief examination of several rituals in the Hebrew Bible shows that consistent 'standards' for cultic sacrifices seem to have existed to some degree.

---

62 Cf. Milgrom, *Leviticus 1–16*, 853, 855; see also ibid. 864.

63 Cf. B. Jürgens, *Heiligkeit und Versöhnung: Levitikus 16 in seinem literarischen Kontext* (HBS 28; Freiburg et al.: Herder, 2001), 75; F. Hartenstein, "Zur symbolischen Bedeutung des Blutes im Alten Testament," in J. Frey/J. Schröter (ed.), *Deutungen des Todes Jesu im Neuen Testament* (WUNT 181; Tübingen: Mohr Siebeck, 2005), 119–37, on p. 128.

Aspects of these 'standards' are conveyed through, among other things, the comprehensive terminology for sacrifice and show that sacrifices belong primarily to the context of worship and the domain of sacredness. The latter aspect is appropriately communicated by the modern English term 'sacrifice' that goes back to Latin. The literal meaning of the Latin term *sacrificium* is 'to make holy' and 'to dedicate.' Even this Latin term, therefore, features no explicit connotations to killing or slaughter.

4 Conclusions: Sacrifice? Holy Smokes!

I hope that my contribution helps to use the word 'sacrifice' in a more reflective manner. This term has a spectrum of different meanings; it is polyvalent. The modern use of the term as a secularized metaphor with rather negative connotations of loss and destruction belongs to this spectrum. This meaning is by no means original, yet it is a natural linguistic development that language and especially technical terms change their import over time. The modern secularized meaning should, however, not be applied to sacrificial rituals in the Hebrew Bible (or the Septuagint) from which such metaphors were derived. To recover layers of how the original communities, tradents, and translators of the texts understood cultic sacrifices, I investigated comprehensive terminology for sacrifice in the Hebrew Bible and the Septuagint. The study demonstrates that this terminology does not focus on aspects of killing but includes a variety of ritual activities. The burning rite especially emerges as an essential element of cultic sacrifice. This ritual component is the conclusion of a dynamic process of approaching God. It manifests that humans offer tokens of reverence, thus affirming a relationship despite and through the acknowledgement of the status difference between them and God. Such a perspective allows the incorporation of more than just animal sacrifices or blood application rites into modern scholarly theorizing; it opens the door for the inclusion of ritual sacrifices from vegetal substances.

Bibliography

Anderson, G. A., *Sacrifices and Offerings in Ancient Israel: Studies in their Social and Political Importance* (HSM 41; Atlanta: Scholars Press, 1987).

Ashby, G. W., "The Bloody Bridegroom: The Interpretation of Exodus 4:24–26," *ExpTim* 106 (Jan 1995) 203–5.

Barr, J., *The Semantics of Biblical Language* (Oxford: Oxford University Press, 1962).

Behm, J., "θύω," in *ThWNT* 3 (Stuttgart/Berlin/Köln: Kohlhammer, 1938) 180–90.

Bouanich, C., "Mise à mort rituelle," in S. Georgoudi/R. Koch Piettre/F. Schmidt (ed.), *La cuisine et l'autel: Les sacrifices en questions dans les sociétés de la Méditerranée ancienne* (BEHE.R 124; Turnhout: Brepols, 2006) 149–62.

Büchsel, F., "θυμός," in *ThWNT* 3 (Stuttgart/Berlin/Köln: Kohlhammer, 1938) 167–73.

Burkert, W., *Homo Necans: The Anthropology of Ancient Greek Sacrificial Ritual and Myth* (Berkeley: University of California Press, 1983).
Childs, B.S., *The Book of Exodus: A Commentary* (OTL; Philadelphia: Westerminster John Knox, 1974).
Daniel, S., *Recherches sur le vocabulaire du culte dans la Septante* (EeC 61; Paris: Librairie C. Klincksieck, 1966).
De Vos, G./Suarez-Orozco, M., "Sacrifice and the experience of power," *Journal of Psychoanalytic Anthropology* 10 (1987) 309–40.
Drexler, J., *Die Illusion des Opfers: Ein wissenschaftlicher Überblick über die wichtigsten Opfertheorien ausgehend vom deleuzianischen Polyperspektivismusmodell* (Münchener Ethnologische Abhandlungen 12; München, Anacon-Verlag, 1993).
Eberhart, C., *Studien zur Bedeutung der Opfer im Alten Testament: Die Signifikanz von Blut- und Verbrennungsriten im kultischen Rahmen* (WMANT 94; Neukirchen-Vluyn: Neukirchener Verlag, 2002).
–, "A Neglected Feature of Sacrifice in the Hebrew Bible: Remarks on the Burning Rite on the Altar," *HTR* 97 (2004) 485–93.
–, "Schlachtung/Schächtung," *Wissenschaftliches Bibellexikon im Internet* (Stuttgart: Deutsche Bibelgesellschaft, http://www.wibilex.de; 2006).
–, "The Term 'Sacrifice' and the Problem of Theological Abstraction: A Study of the Reception History of Genesis 22:1–19," in C. Helmer (ed.), *The Multivalence of Biblical Texts and Theological Meanings* (Symposium Series 37, Atlanta: Society of Biblical Literature, 2006) 47–66.
–, "Qorban," *Wissenschaftliches Bibellexikon im Internet* (Stuttgart: Deutsche Bibelgesellschaft, http://www.wibilex.de; 2010).
–, "Beobachtungen zu Opfer, Kult und Sühne in der Septuaginta," in W. Kraus/S. Kreutzer (ed.), *Die Septuaginta—Text, Wirkung, Rezeption: 4. Internationale Fachtagung veranstaltet von Septuaginta Deutsch (LXX.D), Wuppertal 19.–22.7.2012* (unter Mitarbeit von Martin Meiser und Marcus Sigismund; WUNT 325, Tübingen: Mohr Siebeck, 2014) 297–314.
–, "Introduction: Constituents and Critique of Sacrifice, Cult, and Atonement in Early Judaism and Christianity," in H.L. Wiley/C.A. Eberhart (ed.), *Sacrifice, Cult, and Atonement in Early Judaism and Christianity: Constituents and Critique* (SBLRBS 85; Atlanta: SBL Press, 2017) 1–29.
Fabry, H.-J., "קָרְבָּן *qōrbān* קֻרְבָּן *qurbān*," in *TDOT* 13 (Grand Rapids/Cambridge [U.K.]: Eerdmans, 2004) 152–8.
Florczak, K.L., "An Exploration of the Concept of Sacrifice," *Nursing Science Quarterly* 17 (2004) 195–200.
Galling, K., "Altar," in *IDB* 1 (Nashville/New York: Abingdon, 1962) 96–100.
Gaster, T.H., "Sacrifices and Offerings, OT," in *IDB* 4 (Nashville/New York: Abingdon, 1962).
Gese, H., "The Atonement," in idem, *Essays on Biblical Theology* (Minneapolis: Augsburg Publishing House, 1981) 93–116.
Gilders, W.K., *Blood Ritual in the Hebrew Bible: Meaning and Power* (Baltimore: Johns Hopkins, 2004).
Girard, R., *Violence and the Sacred* (Baltimore: Johns Hopkins University Press, 1977).
–, *Des choses cachées depuis la fondation du monde* (Paris: Grasset, 1979).
Glaim, A. "'I Will Not Accept Them': Sacrifice and Reciprocity in the Prophetic Literature," in H.L. Wiley/C.A. Eberhart (ed.), *Sacrifice, Cult, and Atonement in Early Judaism and Christianity: Constituents and Critique* (SBLRBS 85; Atlanta: SBL Press, 2017) 125–49.
Gray, G.B., *Sacrifice in the Old Testament: Its Theory and Practice* (Oxford: Clarendon Press, 1925).
Gruenwald, I., *Rituals and Ritual Theory in Ancient Israel* (Brill Reference Library of Judaism 10; Atlanta: Society of Biblical Literature, 2003).

Harlé, P./Pralon, D., *La Bible d'Alexandrie: Le Lévitique* (Paris: Éditions du Cerf, 1988).
Hartenstein, F., "Zur symbolischen Bedeutung des Blutes im Alten Testament," in J. Frey/ J. Schröter (ed.), *Deutungen des Todes Jesu im Neuen Testament* (WUNT 181; Tübingen: Mohr Siebeck, 2005) 119–37.
Hieke, T., *Levitikus 1–15* (HThKAT; Freiburg/Basel/Wien: Herder, 2014).
Houtman, C., *Exodus, vol. 2: Chapters 7:14–19:25* (HCOT; Kampen: Kok Publishing House, 1996).
–, *Exodus, vol. 3: Chapters 20–40* (HCOT; Leuven: Peeters, 2000).
Hubert, H./Mauss, M., " Essai sur la nature et la fonction du sacrifice," *ASoc* 2 (1899) 29–138.
Jewett, R., *Romans: A Commentary* (Hermeneia; Minneapolis, MN: Fortress, 2007).
Joosten, J., "Exegesis in the Septuagint Version of Hosea," in idem, *Collected Studies on the Septuagint: From Language to Interpretation and Beyond* (Tübingen: Mohr Siebeck, 2012) 123–45.
Jürgens, B., *Heiligkeit und Versöhnung: Levitikus 16 in seinem literarischen Kontext* (HBS 28; Freiburg et al.: Herder, 2001).
Kessler, R., "Die Theologie der Gabe bei Maleachi," in F.-L. Hossfeld/L. Schwienhorst-Schönberger (ed.), *Das Manna fällt auch heute noch: Beiträge zur Geschichte und Theologie des Alten, Ersten Testaments* (FS E. Zenger; HBS 44; Freiburg et al.: Herder, 2004) 392–407.
Levine, B. A., *Leviticus ויקרא: The Traditional Hebrew Text with the New JPS Translation* (JPSTC; Philadelphia/New York/Jerusalem: Jewish Publication Society, 1989).
Margueron, J.-C., "L'espace sacrificiel dans le Proche-Orient ancien," in R. Étienne/M.-Th. Le Dinahet (ed.), *L'espace sacrificiel dans les civilisations méditerranéennes de l'antiquité: Actes du colloque tenu à la Maison de l'Orient, Lyon, 4–7 juin 1988* (Publications de la Bibliothèque Salomon-Reinach 5; Paris: De Boccard, 1991) 235–42.
Marx, A., *Les offrandes végétales dans l'Ancien Testament: Du tribut d'hommage au repas eschatologique* (VT.S 57; Leiden/New York/Köln: Brill, 1994).
–, "The Theology of the Sacrifice According to Leviticus 1–7," in R. A. Kugler/R. Rendtorff (ed.), *The Book of Leviticus: Composition and Reception* (VT.S 93; Leiden/Boston: Brill, 2003) 103–120.
–, *Les systèmes sacrificiels de l'Ancien Testament: Formes et fonctions du culte sacrificiel à Yhwh* (VT.S 105; Leiden/Boston: Brill, 2005).
McClymond, K., *Beyond Sacred Violence: A Comparative Study of Sacrifice* (Baltimore: Johns Hopkins University Press, 2008).
Megaloudi, F., "Burnt Sacrificial Plant Offerings in Hellenistic Times: An Archaeological Case Study from Messene, Peloponese, Greece," *Veget. Hist. Archaeobot* 14 (2005) 329–40.
Milbank, J., "Stories of Sacrifice: From Wellhausen to Girard," *Theory Culture Society* 12 (1995) 15–46.
Milgrom, J., *Leviticus 1–16: A New Translation with Introduction and Commentary* (AncB 3; New York/London: Doubleday, 1991).
Modéus, M., *Sacrifice and Symbol: Biblical* Šĕlāmîm *in a Ritual Perspective* (CB.OT 52; Stockholm: Almqvist & Wiksell International, 2005).
Naiden, F. S., *Smoke Signals for the Gods: Ancient Greek Sacrifice from the Archaic Through Roman Periods* (Oxford: Oxford University Press, 2013).
Patterson, J. L., *Keeping the Feast: Metaphors of Sacrifice in 1 Corinthians and Philippians* (Early Christianity and its Literature 16, Atlanta: SBL Press, 2015).
Polak, F. H., "Storytelling and Redaction: Varieties of Language Usage in the Exodus Narrative," in J. C. Geertz et al. (ed.), *The Formation of the Pentateuch: Bridging the Academic Cultures of Europe, Israel, and North America* (FAT 111; Tübingen: Mohr Siebeck, 2016) 443–75.
Rendtorff, R., *Leviticus vol. 1: Leviticus 1,1–10,20* (BKAT 3; Neukirchen-Vluyn: Neukirchener Verlag, 2004).
Schmidt, W. H., *Exodus* (BKAT 2/2$_3$; Neukirchen-Vluyn: Neukirchener Verlag, 2016).

Schmithals, W., *Der Römerbrief: Ein Kommentar* (Gütersloh: Gütersloher Verlagshaus, 1988).
Schwagmeier, P., "1.2 Exodos/Exodos/Das zweite Buch Mose," in S. Kreuzer (ed.), *Einleitung in die Septuaginta, LXX.H vol. 1* (Gütersloh: Gütersloher Verlagshaus, 2016) 120–36.
Silva, M., *Biblical Words and Their Meaning: An Introduction to Lexical Semantics* (Grand Rapids: Zondervan, 1983).
Smith, W. R., *Lectures on the Religion of the Semites: The Fundamental Institutions: First Series* (London: Adam & Charles Black, 1889; 2nd ed. by J. S. Black, 1894).
Snaith, N. H., "Sacrifices in the Old Testament," *VT* 7 (1957) 308–17.
Stegemann, W., "Zur Metaphorik des Opfers," in B. Janowski/M. Welker (ed.), *Opfer: Theologische und kulturelle Kontexte* (Stw 1454; Frankfurt am Main: Suhrkamp, 2000) 191–216.
Vahrenhorst, M., *Kultische Sprache in den Paulusbriefen* (WUNT 230; Tübingen: Mohr Siebeck, 2008).
–, "Exkurs 'Hinweise zur Opferterminologie im LXX-Pentateuch,'" in M. Karrer/W. Kraus (ed.), *Septuaginta Deutsch: Erklärungen und Kommentare zum griechischen Alten Testament, vol. 1: Genesis bis Makkabäer* (Stuttgart: Deutsche Bibelgesellschaft, 2011) 335–46.
–, "1.3 Levitikon/Levitikus/Das dritte Buch Mose," in S. Kreuzer (ed.), *Einleitung in die Septuaginta, LXX.H vol. 1* (Gütersloh: Gütersloher Verlagshaus, 2016) 137–45.
Watts, J. W., *Ritual and Rhetoric in Leviticus: From Sacrifice to Scripture* (Cambridge: Cambridge University Press, 2007).
Wevers, J. W., "The Interpretative Character and Significance of the Septuagint Version," in M. Sæbø (ed.), *Hebrew Bible/Old Testament: The History of Its Interpretation, vol. 1. From the Beginnings to the Middle Ages (Until 1300): Part 1* (Göttingen: Vandenhoeck & Ruprecht, 1996) 84–107.
Willi-Plein, I., *Opfer und Kult im alttestamentlichen Israel: Textbefragungen und Zwischenergebnisse* (SBS 153; Stuttgart: Katholisches Bibelwerk, 1993).

Naphtali S. Meshel

The Form and Function of a Biblical Blood Ritual*

1 Introduction

The ritual manipulation of blood is a recurrent theme in Biblical and other ancient Near Eastern ritual texts, as well as in several post-Biblical texts foundational to Christianity and Judaism. As a result, the ritual application of blood has received special attention in works dedicated to the study of Priestly Biblical traditions and in theoretical works on sacrifice.[1]

Despite great advances in the endeavor to understand the technicalities and possible "meanings" of these rituals in the Israelite context in the last few decades, primarily following the works of Rendtorff and of Milgrom,[2] several aspects of blood-application remain obscure or misunderstood.

The present study examines one particular act central to the ritual texts in P, namely the act commonly denoted by זָרַק דָּם ... עַל הַמִּזְבֵּחַ (סָבִיב). This is a recurrent ritual act, pertaining (at least) to wholeburnt (עֹולָה), wellbeing (שְׁלָמִים), reparation (אָשָׁם) and ordination (מִלּוּאִים) offerings. In fact, the blood manipulation of the vast majority of private and public sacrificial animal offerings (of quadrupeds) made by Israelites, as envisioned in P, consists primarily of this act.

There is a wide consensus in modern literature that the formula under discussion refers to an act at the conclusion of which the blood lands on the sides ("walls") of the bronze altar. With this understanding in mind, scholars have ventured to suggest several interpretations of the meaning of the blood rite involved in wholeburnt, wellbeing and reparation offerings in P – assuming that the phrase זרק דם על המזבח סביב designates the application of blood to the walls of

* This contribution was originally published as: Naphtali S. Meshel, "The Form and Function of a Biblical Blood Ritual," *VT* 63 (2013) 276–289. The author and editors wish to thank Brill Publishers for the kindness of granting permissions to reprint this essay.

1 See for example W. K. Gilders, *Blood Ritual in the Hebrew Bible: Meaning and Power* (London: The Johns Hopkins University Press, 2004); and Y. Feder, *Blood Expiation in Hittite and Biblical Ritual: Origins, Context, and Meaning* (Writings from the Ancient World Supplements; Atlanta: Society of Biblical Literature, 2011), and the bibliography cited there.

2 See in particular J. Milgrom, *Leviticus: A New Translation with Introduction and Commentary* (3 vols.; AB 3, 3A, 3B; New York: Doubleday, 1991–2001); R. Rendtorff, *Studien zur Ge-schichte des Opfers im alten Israel* (WMANT 24; Neukirchen-Vluyn: Neukirchener, 1967); idem, *Leviticus* (BKAT III.1–4; Neukirchen-Vluyn: Neukirchener, 1985); see also A. Marx, *Les systèmes sacrificiels de l'Ancien Testament: Formes et fonctions du culte sacrificiel à Yhwh* (VTSup 105; Leiden: Brill, 2005).

the altar. It has been suggested, for example, that the blood is placed on the walls to withhold it from human consumption; similarly, that it is merely a means of disposal of the blood; and that it serves a function of purgation.[3] As noted in the past, these explanations are inadequate, as they fail to explain the *specific* choice of the walls rather than the ground, the upper surface, or the horns.[4] Alternatively, it has been suggested that the blood is placed on the walls rather than atop the altar where it would have been consumed by fire because the blood belongs to YHWH *a priori*, and therefore cannot be part of the offerer's sacrificial gift burnt upon the altar; or in order to indicate that YHWH, like the Israelites, refrains from the consumption of blood. According to this last explanation, it demonstrates YHWH's respect for life and sets an example for human beings.[5]

I will argue that these explanations are unsatisfactory because they fail to recognize that, in P, the formula זרק דם על המזבח סביב, which is linguistically ambiguous, actually implies the tossing of blood onto the upper surface of this altar, that is, atop the altar. It is only in texts from the Hellenistic period onwards that this formula was understood to imply the dashing of blood against parts of the altar other than its upper surface.

2 Linguistic Evidence—Formal Ambiguity

The formula זָרַק ... עַל הַמִּזְבֵּחַ סָבִיב occurs twelve times in the Hebrew Bible, all in P (including H) and always with blood (דָּם) as the direct object of the verb and with one or more priests as the subject (including Moses when he performs priestly rituals during the seven days of ordination): Exod 29:16, 20, Lev 1:5, 11; 3:2, 8, 13; 7:2; 8:19, 24; 9:12, 18.[6]

In Biblical Hebrew, זָרַק denotes the throwing of liquid, powdery or grainy substances horizontally or vertically.[7] Thus, despite some unclearness as to the

3 For a brief summary of several views, see R. P. Knierim, *Text and Concept in Leviticus 1:1–9: A Case in Exegetical Method* (FAT 2; Tübingen: J. C. B. Mohr, 1992), 56–7; see also A. Schenker, "Das Zeichen des Blutes und die Gewissheit der Vergebung im Alten Testament," *MTZ* 34 (1983) 195–213, who links form and function on p. 200, and the bibliography cited there.

4 *Pace* Knierim, *Text and Concept*, 56–7. The last explanation (no. 3) is insufficient, since the same act pertains to wellbeing offerings, where—at least in P—no purgation is implied (see B. Schwartz, *The Holiness Legislation: Studies in the Holiness Code* (Jerusalem: Magnes, 1999 [in Hebrew]), 102–20; see also R. E. Gane, *Ritual Dynamic Structure* (Gorgias Dissertations 14.2; Piscataway: Gorgias, 2004), 87–8).

5 Gane, *Ritual Dynamic*, 86–7.

6 See also 7:14, which reads plainly: לַכֹּהֵן הַזֹּרֵק אֶת־דַּם הַשְּׁלָמִים, with no specified indirect object. Related to these passages is Leviticus 17:11, on which see Gane, *Ritual Dynamic*, 86–7 (following Schwartz).

7 See *BDB* 284b; *HALOT* 1.283 s.v. I זרק. For non-sacrificial contexts, see Exod 9:8, 10 (powdery substance, upwards), Isa 28:25 (grains, sideways), Ezek 36:25 (liquids, direction

precise technicalities of the act denoted by זָרַק in the present ritual contexts—for example, the exact amount of blood involved, and the (unmentioned) vessel with which it was probably carried out[8]—it is uncontested that in these contexts, the verb זָרַק denotes an act that includes imparting momentum to a relatively large quantity of blood, which consequently passes through the air and onto a target. Thus, it differs in a sacrificial context from other acts like הִזָּה, which denotes imparting momentum to a much smaller quantity of liquid;[9] and שָׁפַךְ, which denotes applying a similarly large quantity of blood, but imparting little or no momentum to it, so that it is primarily the force of gravity that acts on the liquid.[10] This consensus is justified.

However, there is also a wide consensus in modern literature that the formula under discussion refers to an act at the conclusion of which the blood lands on the sides ("walls") of the bronze altar.[11] This, on the other hand, is far from certain.

---

unspecified), 2 Chron 34:4 (powdery substance, sideways and downwards), Job 2:12 (powdery substance, upwards).

8 This tossing is supposedly achieved with the use of a vessel named מִזְרָק. Though P does not mention this vessel in the context of blood applications, it does mention it in other contexts (Num 7:13, 19, etc.), and with particular reference to the bronze altar (e.g., Exod 27:3, 38:3, Num 4:14). In any case, some kind of vessel is clearly necessary for the tossing of the blood of quadrupeds, for practical reasons. See Gilders, *Blood Ritual*, 113, 216 n. 17. It is noteworthy that in Biblical Hebrew, the verb זָרַק is associated not with single solid bodies (e.g., a stone), but with powdery and liquid substances.

9 See, however, the use of the passive *qal* of זר"ק in Num 19:14–20, implying that in this (non-sacrificial) text, זָרַק and הִזָּה may be interchangeable.

10 This view, which gained wide acceptance following N. H. Snaith, *Leviticus and Numbers* (The Century Bible; London: Nelson, 1967), 30 and N. Snaith, "The Sprinkling of Blood," *The Expository Times* 82 (1970) 23–4 (Snaith translates זָרַק as "throw"), and is reflected in P. J. Budd, *Numbers* (WBC; Waco: Word, 1984) 206, and in Milgrom's standard translation of the term as "dash"; see already W. M. Rodwell, *The Mosaic Sacrifices in Leviticus I–VIII* (London: Griffith, Farran, Okeden and Welsh, 1889) 14–15; G. B. Gray, *Numbers* (ICC; Edinburgh, T&T Clark, 1903), 230. For "sprinkle," see J. G. Murphy, *A Critical and Exegetical Commentary on the Book of Leviticus* (Andover: Draper, 1874), 40; R. K. Harrison, *Leviticus: An Introduction and Commentary* (Tyndale Old Testament Commentaries; Downers Grove, Illinois: Inter-Varsity, 1980), 45; K. Elliger, *Leviticus* (HAT 4; Tübingen: J. C. B. Mohr, 1966), 35. The quantity of blood involved in each separate act of "tossing/sprinkling" would depend, among other considerations, on the aperture of the vessel presumably used for performing this act. Since P never mentions the possibility of disposing the rest of the blood after performing the act designated by זָרַק (contrast Exod 29:10; Lev 4:7; 17–18; 25, 30, 34; following נָתַן and הִזָּה; see also 5:9), it stands to reason that a few tosses would suffice for the entire amount of blood—even of the largest bull—to be emptied out (but cf. *b Zeb* 37a).

11 This is reflected in various translations (JPS: "dash… against all sides of the altar"; JB: "pour out … on the borders of the altar"; NEB: "fling against the altar all round"; RSV "throw … round about against the altar"); see also Rendtorff, *Geschichte des Opfers*, 146; idem, *Leviticus*, 52; J. E. Hartley, *Leviticus* (WBC; Dallas: Word, 1992), 21; W. Kornfeld, *Levitikus* (Die Neue Echter Bibel 6; Würzburg: Echter, 1983), 14–15; Knierim, *Text and Concept*, 56–7; Milgrom, *Leviticus*, 1.155–6; T. Staubli, *Die Bücher Levitikus, Numeri* (Neuer Stuttgarter Kommentar Altes Testament 3; Stuttgart: Katholisches Bibelwerk, 1996), 50; Gilders, *Blood Ritual*, 66 and 210 n. 26;

2.1 זָרַק ... עַל הַמִּזְבֵּחַ (Without סָבִיב)

For the sake of clarity, let us first consider the formula זָרַק ... עַל הַמִּזְבֵּחַ without the adverb סָבִיב. This formula is found in Ezekiel and in the Deuteronomistic history, as well as twice in the Priestly literature in the Pentateuch[12]—in Lev 17:6, concerning the wellbeing offering; and in Num 18:17, concerning the offering of firstborn cattle.

From a purely formal linguistic point of view, the phrase זָרַק ... עַל הַמִּזְבֵּחַ is ambiguous. In Biblical Hebrew, it could denote dashing (the blood) against one or more of the sides of the altar, tossing it onto the upper surface of the altar, or both. Simple lexical analysis of these three words does not enable one to ascertain which of the meanings is implied.[13] Note that this ambiguity is retained even one assumes that the priest performing the act is located on the ground, near the altar, since, as noted above, זרק may imply tossing a substance horizontally and/or vertically.[14] Moreover, as we shall see below, it is not even certain that such relative positioning is to be imagined.

2.2 Non-Priestly Texts

Evidence that זָרַק דָּם עַל הַמִּזְבֵּחַ in Biblical Hebrew *can* denote the application of blood to the upper surface of the altar rather than to its sides is found, for example, in Ezekiel 43:18, which refers to the ritual activity related to the altar as לְהַעֲלוֹת עָלָיו עוֹלָה וְלִזְרֹק עָלָיו דָּם ("to offer wholeburnt offerings upon it and to toss blood upon it"). That application of blood atop the altar is implied is evident not only from the coupling of the two acts in this verse (note the identical use of עָלָיו in both cases), but also from Ezekiel's reference to the suet and blood as YHWH's food (בְּהַקְרִיבְכֶם אֶת לַחְמִי חֵלֶב וָדָם, 44:7), offered upon YHWH's table (שֻׁלְחָנִי, with reference to the altar, 44:16). The explicit analogy to a table in Ezekiel suggests

M. Noth, *Leviticus: A Commentary* (trans. J.E. Anderson; Philadelphia: SCM, 1965), 22; Murphy, *Leviticus*, 40; Snaith, *Leviticus and Numbers*, 30–1; Marx, *Systèmes sacrificiels*, 123; G. Maier, *Das dritte Buch Mose* (Wuppertaler Studienbibel; Wuppertal: Brockhaus, 1994), 52; Elliger, *Leviticus*, 35; N. Kiuchi, *Leviticus* (Apollos Old Testament Commentary; Nottingham: Apollos, 2007), 93; G.J. Wenham, *The Book of Leviticus* (NICOT 3; Grand Rapids: Eerdmans, 1979), 54; E.S. Gerstenberger, *Das dritte Buch Mose: Leviticus* (ATD 6; Göttingen: Vandenhoeck & Ruprecht, 1993), 29 notes that the blood is poured "ringsum an den Altarsockel" (perhaps under the influence of LXX on Lev 7:2).

12 Both are in H; see I. Knohl, *Sanctuary of Silence: The Priestly Torah and the Holiness School* (Minneapolis: Fortress, 1995), 105.

13 The formal ambiguity of עַל הַמִּזְבֵּחַ in these contexts pertains also to the term הַמִּזְבֵּחָה in similar contexts, see 2 Chron 29:22, 24 and Lev 1:9.

14 Above, n. 7.

almost unequivocally that the *materia sacra* should be placed where food would normally be placed on a table—not on its legs, or beneath the table, but upon its upper surface.[15]

The assertion that, in BH, זרק דם על המזבח *can* denote the application of blood to the upper surface of the altar rather than to its sides is supported by two other non-priestly texts. 2 Kings 16:12–13 depicts King Ahaz ascending atop the altar and there causing the flesh to turn into smoke by placing it on the fire, as well as tossing the blood upon the altar (וַיִּזְרֹק את דם השלמים אשר לו על המזבח). If ... זרק על המזבח denoted tossing the blood against the walls of the altar in this case, one would have to imagine the unlikely scenario of King Ahaz leaning over the edge of the altar and somehow managing to toss the blood onto the altar's side(s). Since this is hardly likely, one must admit that at least in this narrative, זרק את דם השלמים ... על המזבח denotes tossing the blood onto the upper surface of the altar—in this case, by a person who is himself standing atop the altar.

One other non-priestly Biblical text that ought to be considered in this context is MT of Deut 12:27:[16]

וְעָשִׂ֤יתָ עֹלֹתֶ֙יךָ֙ הַבָּשָׂ֣ר וְהַדָּ֔ם עַל־מִזְבַּ֖ח יְהוָ֣ה אֱלֹהֶ֑יךָ וְדַם־זְבָחֶ֗יךָ יִשָּׁפֵךְ֙ עַל־מִזְבַּח֙ יְהוָ֣ה אֱלֹהֶ֔יךָ וְהַבָּשָׂ֖ר תֹּאכֵֽל׃

By coupling הבשר והדם in 27a, MT suggests that the blood of wholeburnt offerings is placed in the same area as the flesh, i.e., atop the altar.[17] By using the phrase שפך על in 27b, the author quite clearly implies that the blood of wellbeing offerings is applied atop the altar: since שפך, in contrast to זרק, denotes the application of a liquid without imparting momentum to it, it is highly unlikely that the blood thus manipulated would be applied to the walls of the altar.[18]

Thus, in its present form, the verse implies that the following three types of *materia sacra* are placed atop the altar (על מזבח יהוה אלהיך): (a) the flesh of one's wholeburnt offerings; (b) the blood of one's wholeburnt offerings; and (c) the

15 The immediate context implies that in this verse, the "table" denotes the outer altar rather than the other, smaller "table" referred to in 41:22. In the context of purification offerings, Ezekiel twice mentions the daubing of blood on the four corners of one of the ledges of the outer altar (עזרה; see 43:13–17), and, in one case, the daubing (נָתַן) of blood on its horns (43:20, 45:19). These act clearly differ from the act denoted in Ezekiel by לזרק עליו דם, since they appear to involve daubing, i.e., applying small amounts of blood directly to specific points on the altar—not the tossing of large quantities of blood through the air.

16 For the LXX see the discussion J. W. Wevers, *Notes on the Greek Text of Deuteronomy* (SBL Septuagint and Cognate Studies Series 39; Atlanta: Scholars, 1995), n. 33.

17 Only a forced reading might separate the two, rendering the verse to mean "the flesh upon the altar; the blood upon its walls."

18 Such activity would include pressing the rim of a vessel against the wall of the altar and tilting it—an act that is theoretically possible (in fact, it is imagined in a late rabbinic text, in a different context, *b Pes* 121a), but it is a result of midrash halacha, not a natural rendering of the words שפך על המזבח in BH.

blood of one's *zebaḥ*-type offerings (the flesh of which offerings one is permitted to consume).

While it is unjustified to assume that the ritual details concerning blood-application envisioned by these non-Priestly authors are identical to those assumed by the Priestly authors, this verse may serve as further evidence of the practice of applying the blood of wholeburnt and *zebaḥ*-type offerings in ancient Israel to the upper surface of the altar, apparently where the flesh is placed.[19] More importantly, these examples demonstrate that in BH the phrase על המזבח (including זרק על המזבח, not to mention שפך דם על המזבח) *can* be used in the context of the application of blood to the upper surface of the altar, for in fact the phrase *is* undeniably used thus at least twice.

2.3 With the Adverb סביב

In the past, it has been argued that the presence of the adverb סָבִיב, which follows the phrase זרק דם ... על המזבח in ten out of the twelve occurrences listed above, disambiguates the (otherwise ambiguous) phrase זרק דם על המזבח, clarifying that the target is not the upper surface of the altar, but rather its walls.[20] However, there is little reason to believe that this is the import of the adverb סביב in these verses.

First, in the priestly literature, the application of the blood of wellbeing offerings is sometimes referred to as על המזבח (without סביב: Lev 17:6, see Num 18:17 concerning firstborn offerings). Though the matter is not certain, it is doubtful that two different types of ritual activity are implied by זרק על המזבח and זרק על המזבח סביב.[21] Note, for example, that the phrases על קרנות המזבח and על קרנות המזבח סביב, which are also found in P (see, for example, Lev 4:25, 16:18, respectively)

19 Some commentators, reluctant to admit the blood is offered on top of the altar, translate even here "poured out against." See for example S. R. Driver, *Deuteronomy* [ICC; Edinburgh: T&T Clark, 1902], 149).

20 See, for example, Rendtorff, *Leviticus*, 52; Gilders, *Blood Ritual*, 66, who states—without adducing any proof—that "[b]lood that is tossed round about could not be tossed onto the top of the altar. 'Round about' implies the sides." This is logically false, and, as demonstrated below, also linguistically untrue. Rendtorff does not explain why it must be that סביב indicates that the blood is splashed "nicht 'auf' sondern 'gegen' den Altar."

21 Many scholars, once again, perhaps under the influence of the (much more common) על המזבח סביב, render these as "against the altar." See Gray, *Numbers*, 231. Since these two verses are attributed to H, whereas the other Priestly verses discussed here are ascribed to P, it is possible that the difference between the phrase preferred by H and the phrase preferred by P reflects: (a) stylistic preferences of different authors; (b) abbreviation due to the nature of the texts: Lev 17:6 and Num 18:17 do not describe the sequential ordering of ritual activity and are thus not comparable to the other attestations. See also the use of the abbreviated form, לכהן הזרק את דם השלמים, in P (Lev 7:14); or, finally (c) a legal disagreement between P and H as to the precise nature of blood-tossing: the former envisioned it as consisting of several acts of tossing; whereas the latter envisioned it as one act. See also m. Zebaḥ. 5:8.

and are certainly related to the phrase under discussion, are demonstrably interchangeable in Exod 29:12 || Lev 8:15.

In fact, the phrase על המזבח סביב is formally no less ambiguous than על המזבח. Consider for example the two distinct nuances of עַל ... סָבִיב in Ezekiel 27:11: In the phrase שלטיהם תלו על חומותיך סביב (Ezek 27:11b), the objects are presumably envisioned as being mounted on the vertical surface of the fortification wall, whereas in the phrase בני ארוד וחילך על חומותיך סביב (Ezek 27:11a), the soldiers are envisioned as standing atop the fortification wall.[22]

By analogy, it appears that the phrase זרק דם על המזבח סביב can denote either (a) "on(to) the walls of the altar, round about," i.e., by implication, "on all four sides of the altar;" or (b) "on(to) the upper surface of the altar, round about," i.e., by implication, upon the perimeter of the upper surface.[23]

A third possibility should be suggested with some caution. Due to the occasional use of the term סביב in BH, perhaps by extension, to mean "all around," or "around" in the sense of "at various locations" (rather than "on the perimeter"), it is unnecessary to rule out the possibility that the adverb סביב in this context carries the force of "upon several locations (on the upper surface of the altar)" rather than, strictly speaking, "on the perimeter (thereof)." Such a usage would be analogous to (c) וישלחו בארץ פלשתים סביב (1 Sam 31:9), which is often rendered "they sent them [or: they sent messengers] throughout the land of the Philistines" [NRSV, JPS]), where no circumambulation, strictly speaking, is implied.[24]

All of the examples adduced thus far do not prove that זרק על המזבח (סביב) in Leviticus *must* denote "toss upon the upper surface of the altar (round about)."

22 Num 3:26, Jer 1:15, and similar passages are irrelevant here, since in these passages על denotes "by" not "on." Note that the fact that the verbs תָּלָה and זָרַק denote activity performed *onto* a target (regardless of whether the agent is located upon it), whereas the nominal construction in 11a denotes location *on* a target, has no bearing on the conclusions reached here.

23 This act would have the additional advantage of not dampening the fire. P nowhere indicates the thickness of wood used in the construction of the bronze altar, or how much of the altar's upper surface is covered with firewood. Presumably, some safety margin would be required, if only for the practical purpose of preventing embers from falling onto the ground. Contrast the structure of the Herodian altar as described in *m Mid* 3:1.

24 The reason that this suggestion is made with great caution is that in the vast majority of its attestations, סביב (including the phrase סביב סביב) *does* in fact denote "along the circumference," including in P (e.g., Exod 25:10 [note, moreover לו || עליו, *not* in the sense of "atop"], 25; 30:3; 37:2, 11, 26). However, for comparable examples see Gen 23:17 וכל העץ אשר בשדה אשר בכל גבלו סביב, often translated "all the trees that were in the field, throughout its whole area" (e.g., NRSV); Num 11:31–32, where סביבות המחנה is commonly rendered "all around the camp" (NRSV, JPS) in the sense of "in various places in the camp," since the quails are strewn not in a ring but over the entire camp and beyond, a day's journey in every direction (thus, JPS translates על המחנה in v. 31 "over the camp"); and והעבירני עליהם סביב סביב (Ezek. 37:2)—since Ezekiel is in the midst of the field, there is little reason to assume that he was led in circles, or along the perimeter of the field. The prophet is "led around," probably literally *on* a huge pile of bones, or—as Zimmerli suggests hesitantly—climbing over individual piles of bones. See W. Zimmerli, *Ezekiel 2* (transl. J. D. Martin; Hermeneia; Philadelphia: Fortress, 1983), 260.

They only demonstrate that the phrase *may* denote *either* "toss upon the walls of the altar (round about)" *or* "toss upon the upper surface of the altar (round about)". Let us now determine which of these two denotations of זרק ... על המזבח (סביב) is more likely to be the case in the passages under discussion.

3 Argument on the Basis of the Style of P

It has now been established that זרק דם על המזבח (סביב) is linguistically ambiguous. However, a consideration of P's unique style and its imagined *realia* may disambiguate this formula.

P names several parts of the bronze altar, including (one of) its sides (קיר המזבח, e.g., Lev 1:14), its horns (קרנֹת מזבח העֹלה, e.g., 4:25), and its base (e.g., יסוד המזבח, 4:30).[25] P never refers to its upper surface by name, but the texts imply that it had an upper surface.[26] Similarly, P names several parts of the golden altar, including its horns (e.g., קרנות מזבח קטרת הסמים, 4:7), its upper surface (גגו, e.g., Exod 30:3) and its walls (קירֹתיו, e.g., 37:26).

Elsewhere in the ritual texts, when wishing to indicate that blood is applied to the wall, horns, or base of the bronze altar, P says so explicitly (e.g., על קיר המזבח, אל יסוד המזבח, and על קרנות המזבח in Lev 5:9, 4:25, 4:30, respectively). By contrast, in the sacrificial ritual texts, when P wishes to express the placement of materials—e.g., flesh, suet, or even coal—atop the upper surface of the bronze altar, the objects in question are consistently said to be placed simply "on the altar" (על המזבח).[27] Similarly, when P wishes to refer to the application of blood to the horns of the golden altar, it says so specifically (על קרנת המזבח, 4:18), whereas the placement of materials such as incense or even (prohibited) liquid libations upon

25 See also Exod 27:1–8; 38:1–7. It is unnecessary to imagine that in P the "base" (יסוד) is anything more than the area near the foot of the altar, though in later texts, the יסוד is conceived as a ledge. See Milgrom, *Leviticus*, 1.238–9.

26 Lev 1:7 and 6:3 refers to a fire that is placed on the altar (עַל הַמִּזְבֵּחַ rather than בַּמִּזְבֵּחַ). This implies that the altar was not a hollow cavity covered with a grill, but that it in fact had a solid upper surface. Concerning the precise form of this upper surface, see M. Haran, "מזבח," *Encyclopedia Biblica*, 4 (1962) 770–5 (in Hebrew). The argument made here is valid also if one presumes that the altar is envisioned as a bronze frame filled with dirt; see Z. Zevit, *The Religions of Ancient Israel: A Synthesis of Parallactic Approaches* (New York: Continuum, 2001) 276–314. Presumably, this upper surface would have been considered גג המזבח, like the upper surface of the incense altar (Exod 30:3; 37:26).

27 See Lev 1:7 (coals); 4:10 (suet); 9:13 (flesh); 9:17 (grain offering) *et passim*. See also Num 4:13–14 (various vessels). One apparent exception to the observation made here is the use of ועשית עליו with reference to the ark in Exod 25:11 (analogous to ועשית לו, compare Exod 37:2); but this phrase pertains not to materials placed on a piece of furniture but to ornaments that form part of it.

the upper surface (גג, 'roof') of the golden altar is referred to simply as עליו ("upon it," Exod 30:7, 9), never as על גגו ("upon its 'roof'").

Thus, it appears that על המזבח, never על גג המזבח, is P's way of stating "atop the altar." Note in particular that in the two cases where P clearly wishes to express that the blood of an animal be applied to the wall of the bronze altar, it says so explicitly: והזה מדם החטאת על קיר המזבח ("he shall flick some of the blood of the purification offering *upon the wall of the altar*," Lev 5:9), in the context of a bird purification offering; and ונמצה דמו על קיר המזבח ("its blood shall be squeezed out *onto the wall of the altar*," Lev 1:15), in the context of a bird wholeburnt offering. The latter phrase immediately follows—and contrasts with—the phrase וזרקו ... את דמו על המזבח סביב (1:11), in the context of an ovine wholeburnt offering. Had the authors wished to imply that the blood of wholeburnt, wellbeing, reparation, or ordination offerings was to be applied to the walls of the altar as well, they might have said so explicitly, just as in the other cases in which they believe that the blood is to be applied to the wall of the altar. The use of P's standard phrase for placement of *materia sacra* atop the altar, על המזבח, rather than the phrase P uses to denote the application of blood to the walls[28] suggests, in fact, that the blood of these types of offerings is to be placed on the upper surface of the altar, not on its walls.[29]

---

28 Either על קיר המזבח or על קירות המזבח (סביב); perhaps even על קיר המזבח סביב would be grammatical. For the *pl* קירות with reference to an altar (but not the bronze altar), see Exod 30:3; 37:26, and compare the phrase על קרנות המזבח סביב (Lev 16:18). Note that the Samaritan version reads אל קיר המזבח in both Lev 1:15 and 5:9.

29 Thus, far from serving as evidence that על המזבח in P denotes "upon the walls of the altar," as Elliger argues (*Leviticus*, 35), Lev 1:15, actually serves as strong evidence against this understanding. Since Lev 1:14–17 may be an interpolation (see Milgrom, *Leviticus*, 1.166), one might argue that by using על קיר המזבח (15b) instead of על המזבח, the author of this passage offers the earliest evidence of the shift from tossing the blood of wholeburnt offerings upon the upper surface of the altar to the application of the blood of such offerings to its wall(s). However, even if this passage is secondary, there is no evidence that the interpolators presumed that blood of birds offered as whole burnt offerings is applied at the same precise location as that of quadrupeds, and hence no evidence that the interpolator interpreted זרק ... על המזבח סביב as "dash against the walls of the altar." First, על קיר המזבח (1:15) might not be identical with על המזבח סביב (1:5 etc.) even if על המזבח סביב denoted the walls—since על קיר המזבח probably refers to one wall only, rather than all four (see P's use of the *pl* קירותיו in Exod 30:3, where all four sides are implied; but cf. Ezek 41:12). Moreover, note that a comparison of 5:9 and 4:30, 34 demonstrates that at least in the case of the purification offering (חטאת), the blood of these two groups of animals is applied to different parts of the altar.

4 Further Considerations, Pertaining to the Imagined "Realia"

In P, applying the blood to the upper surface of the altar does not necessarily imply ascending the altar. In fact, it is unclear whether the altar was usually ascended in the sanctuary envisioned in P, as P's altar was low enough—its height was three cubits according to Exod 27:1 (שָׁלֹשׁ אַמּוֹת קֹמָתוֹ)—to obviate ascending it in order to perform ritual actions upon its upper surface; moreover, no stairs (or ramp) are mentioned in the context of P's altar, despite the fact that its architectural plan is described in great detail.[30]

However, a fortunate slip of the pen in Leviticus 9:22 suggests that P was acquainted with essentially the same *realia* as the authors of 2 Kings 16 (discussed above), namely, the manipulation of (at least some of) the *materia sacra* from atop the altar. If understood literally,[31] the verb וַיֵּרֶד contradicts P's (the narrative's) imaginary setting—in which priests are depicted as ascending the (small) altar, and discloses P's (the author's) historical setting, in which priests were required to ascend a large altar.[32] Note that 2 Chr 1:6, too, imagines Solomon ascending "the bronze altar fashioned by Bezal'el" in order to offer "one thousand wholeburnt offerings."

In sum, the priests in P are to toss the blood of wholeburnt, wellbeing, and reparation offerings on the upper surface of the altar rather than dash it against the walls. Concerning the precise location of the priests there is some dispute: since P never mentions a staircase or a ramp, they should probably be imagined as tossing the blood in a low arc onto the altar while standing beside it; but if Lev 9:22 is indicative of P's intention, they might be imagined to ascend it and—assuming that there is room enough for a priest to stand on the edge of the bronze altar

30 P mentions neither a staircase nor a ramp in Exod 27:1–8; 38:1–7. Cf. Ezekiel's visionary altar (43:17), which has a staircase, and the altar in the Herodian temple (*m Mid* 3:1–4), which was ascended by a ramp. See Haran, "מזבח," 770–5.

31 See Milgrom, Leviticus, 1.587–8; Staubli, *Levitikus, Numeri*, 83.

32 This is perhaps reaffirmed by another slip, namely, the wording of Num 4:14: ונתנו עליו את כל כליו אשר ישרתו עליו בהם (literally, "Upon [the altar] they shall place all its vessels by means of which they officiate upon it"). The formula שָׁרֵת על המזבח cannot refer to a situation in which the vessels are upon the altar but the officiating priests are not, since ישרתו does not refer to the vessels (these are indicated by בהם). The persons of whom it is said ישרתו עליו (even if the subject is indefinite, forming a phrase that may be translated in the passive voice) cannot "officiate" upon an altar without standing on it, though they can throw blood on the altar without standing on it. Previous translators and commentators may have missed this clear reference to שרת על המזבח, or purposely avoided the implication that priests officiate while standing upon the altar, e.g., RSV: "all the utensils of the altar, which are used for the service there"; NEB: "all the equipment used in its service." It appears that P has a different way of denoting a situation in which the utensils are used on a large vessel, while the officiating priest stands beside it: אשר ישרתו לה בהם (see, Num 4:9).

(P never mentions the breadth of this area)—toss the blood from atop the altar onto a number of points on the (perimeter of its) upper surface.

5 The Shift from "Toss Upon" to "Dash Against"

It has now been established that in P the blood of wholeburnt, wellbeing, reparation, and ordination offerings is envisioned as tossed upon the upper surface of the altar. However, several Jewish texts from the Hellenistic period onwards suggest that the blood of at least some of these types of offerings is to be tossed onto an area other than the upper surface of the altar—either the wall(s) of the altar (Aramaic Document of Levi, Philo), or more specifically two of its vertices (rabbinic literature),[33] or onto its base (LXX, Temple Scroll, Genesis Apocryphon).[34] It appears that in this case the later texts do not reflect the original intent of the Biblical text.

While a detailed analysis of these and other sources will be reserved for a future study, it should be noted that since several of these sources are apparently independent, their evidence concerning the application of the blood on an area other than the upper surface of the altar is believed to reflect actual practice in the Jerusalem Temple.[35] However, since these texts are not in perfect agreement with one another it is likely that one should not imagine a single shift, but a series of changes.

Thus, it would appear that at a certain point, no later than the third century BCE, a shift began to take place in the ritual procedures in the Jerusalem Temple: blood of offerings previously applied to the upper surface of the altar began to be applied elsewhere—on its walls, more specifically on its vertices, or on its base.

---

33 See m Zebaḥ. 5:4–7 *et passim*. This type of blood-manipulation is to be performed in the most economical manner in which the blood can be applied to all four walls, namely by tossing the blood twice onto two diagonally opposite vertices of the altar, the diagonal vertices selected being the northeastern and southwestern vertices.

34 For a brief evaluation of the evidence from the Septuagint, the Temple Scroll and early rabbinic literature, see P.E. Dion, "Early Evidence for the Ritual Significance of the 'Base of the Altar'," *JBL* 106 (1987) 487–92; J.W. Wevers, *Notes on the Greek Text of Leviticus* (SCS 44; Atlanta: Scholars, 1997), 80; idem, *Greek Text of Deuteronomy*, 221–2. See also 1Q20 10:15 (*Genesis Apocryphon*); Philo, *De Specialibus Legibus*, 1.205. The evidence from Jubilees is less clear and somewhat anomalous (see for example 7:4, with reference to a purification offering). The earliest unequivocal evidence of the custom of tossing the blood of wholeburnt offerings onto the wall(s) of the altar is apparently found in Aramaic Document of Levi, 8:1.

35 See Dion, "Early Evidence"; Wevers, *Notes*, 221–2: "What this shows is that the translator here reflects an old Halachic tradition, which he has formulated in his own way." As Dion notes, by pairing the standard equivalent of זָרַק, προσχέω, with the base of the altar (יסוד המזבח), LXX appears to envision ritual activity that is never attested in MT.

6 Conclusions

As noted at the outset, the study of the technicalities of Levitical blood-manipulation is often bound up with an examination of their meanings. Thus, in accordance with the accepted (mis)reading of P, it has been suggested in the past that the placement of blood on an area other than the upper surface of the altar is to be understood as indicative of a process of purgation or merely disposal, that it serves to withhold blood from human consumption, and that it implies that the blood belongs to YHWH *a priori*, and therefore cannot be part of the offerer's sacrificial gift.

Once it is acknowledged that זרק דם על המזבח סביב in P actually denotes the application of blood on the upper surface of the altar, the abovementioned interpretations must be reevaluated. In particular, suggestions stressing the importance of refraining from placing the blood atop the altar, such as the claim that the ritual indicates that YHWH, like the Israelites, refrains from the consumption of blood, must be reconsidered.

However, these scholarly interpretations need not be rejected entirely, as they may prove useful in interpreting the ritual at later stages, as reflected in post-Biblical sources. With this *caveat* in mind, I would like to venture to suggest one of the reasons for the continued misreading of P.

It is likely that for some authors in antiquity a direct correlation existed between form and function: the placement of *materia sacra* upon the upper surface of the altar (not only on its hearth, but even on the perimeter thereof) would have implied that it is offered as part of the deity's meal, served alongside the animal's flesh. This correlation is not mere conjecture, since, as noted above, Ezekiel contains evidence of such an understanding.[36] The shift from placing sacrificial blood upon the altar's upper surface to placing it upon the walls or base of the altar may therefore indicate an aversion, in the first few centuries BCE, to the conception that the deity's meal includes servings of blood. Finally, the accepted (mis)reading of P in modern scholarship may be attributed to the influence of the widespread ancient Jewish readings of this phrase, reinforced by a similar reluctance to admit that P would enjoin offerings of blood to YHWH.

While the textual evidence of a shift in the form of the ritual in early Jewish Hellenistic literature appears to be unequivocal, the reconstruction of the *reasons* for this shift is offered here with some hesitation, since it would be unfair to presume that in all circles in antiquity, a straightforward correlation between form and function of sacrificial procedures was assumed.[37]

---

36 Above, p. 104.

37 See Sirach 50:15, which suggests that wine offered at the *base* of the altar may still serve as an ὀσμὴν εὐωδίας ὑψίστῳ παμβασιλεῖ ("a sweet-smelling odor to the Most High, the King

Concerning P itself, matters are even more complex. Due to the noteworthy reticence of P regarding the "meanings" of the rituals it envisions,[38] it is difficult to ascertain whether P envisioned YHWH's meal as consisting of servings of blood.[39] While the present study suggests that P, like Ezekiel, would have had no qualms about such an interpretation of the ritual,[40] it should be kept in mind that P never makes this claim explicit.

P remains silent regarding the precise meaning of this particular ritual, as it does with regard to the meanings of so many other rituals. Its interpreters are thus left with the tasks of bleeding the text for its meaning and tossing hypotheses round about, only to be dashed against the wall of P's reticence.

Bibliography

Budd, P. J., *Numbers* (WBC; Waco: Word, 1984).

Dion, P. E., "Early Evidence for the Ritual Significance of the 'Base of the Altar,'" *JBL* 106 (1987) 487–92.

Driver, S. R., *Deuteronomy* (ICC; Edinburgh: T&T Clark, 1902).

Elliger, K., *Leviticus* (HAT 4; Tübingen: J. C. B. Mohr, 1966).

Feder, Y., *Blood Expiation in Hittite and Biblical Ritual: Origins, Context, and Meaning* (Writings from the Ancient World Supplements; Atlanta: Society of Biblical Literature, 2011).

Gane, R. E., *Ritual Dynamic Structure* (Gorgias Dissertations 14.2; Piscataway: Gorgias, 2004).

Gerstenberger, E. S., *Das dritte Buch Mose: Leviticus* (ATD 6; Göttingen: Vandenhoeck & Ruprecht, 1993).

Gilders, W. K., *Blood Ritual in the Hebrew Bible: Meaning and Power* (London: The John Hopkins University Press, 2004).

Gray, G. B., *Numbers* (ICC; Edinburgh, T&T Clark, 1903).

Greenfield, J. C./Stone, M. E./Eshel, E. (ed.), *The Aramaic Levi Document: Edition, Translation, Commentary* (Studia in Veteris Testamenti pseudepigrapha 19; Leiden: Brill, 2004).

Haran, M., "מזבח," *Encyclopedia Biblica* 4 (1962) 770–5 (in Hebrew).

Harrison, R. K., *Leviticus: An Introduction and Commentary* (Tyndale Old Testament Commentaries; Downers Grove, Illinois: Inter-Varsity, 1980).

Hartley, J. E., *Leviticus* (WBC; Dallas: Word, 1992).

---

of all"). Conversely, not everything placed atop the altar should automatically be considered an offering (e.g., the wood, which in P is not considered an offering). For the data in P, see Milgrom, *Leviticus*, 1.161–2.

38 See A. Marx, "The Theology of Sacrifice according to Leviticus 1–7," in R. Rendtorff/R. Kugler (ed.), *The Book of Leviticus: Composition and Reception* (Vetus Testamentum, Supplements 93; Leiden et al.: Brill 2003) 103–20; D. A. Kurek-Chomycz, "Spreading the Sweet Scent of the Gospel as the Cult of the Wise: On the Backdrop of the Olfactory Metaphor in 2 Corinthians 2:14–16," in C. A. Eberhart (ed.), *Ritual and Metaphor: Sacrifice in the Bible* (SBLRBS 68, Atlanta: Society of Biblical Literature, 2011) 115–33, on p. 119.

39 Marx, *Systèmes sacrificiels*, 123, notes that in Leviticus 1:5–7, coals are to be placed upon the altar only after the tossing of the blood.

40 For a possible distinction between P and H, at least in terms of the authors' need to resort to "buffer language" (contrast the 1st-person pronominal suffix in לחמי, אשי, ריח ניחחי), see Knohl, *Sanctuary of Silence*, 30, 109, and particularly 126 n. 7.

Kiuchi, N., *Leviticus* (Apollos Old Testament Commentary; Nottingham: Apollos, 2007).
Knierim, R. P., *Text and Concept in Leviticus 1:1–9: A Case in Exegetical Method* (FAT 2; Tübingen: J. C. B. Mohr, 1992).
Knohl, I., *Sanctuary of Silence: The Priestly Torah and the Holiness School* (Minneapolis: Fortress, 1995).
Kornfeld, W., *Levitikus* (Die Neue Echter Bibel 6; Würzburg: Echter, 1983).
Kurek-Chomycz, D. A., "Spreading the Sweet Scent of the Gospel as the Cult of the Wise: On the Backdrop of the Olfactory Metaphor in 2 Corinthians 2:14–16," in C. A. Eberhart (ed.), *Ritual and Metaphor: Sacrifice in the Bible* (SBLRBS 68, Atlanta: Society of Biblical Literature, 2011) 115–33.
Maier, G., *Das dritte Buch Mose* (Wuppertaler Studienbibel; Wuppertal: Brockhaus, 1994).
Marx, A., "The Theology of Sacrifice according to Leviticus 1–7," in R. Rendtorff/R. Kugler (ed.), *The Book of Leviticus: Composition and Reception* (Vetus Testamentum, Supplements 93; Leiden et al.: Brill 2003) 103–20.
–, *Les systèmes sacrificiels de l'Ancien Testament: Formes et fonctions du culte sacrificiel à Yhwh* (VTSup 105; Leiden: Brill, 2005).
Milgrom, J., *Leviticus: A New Translation with Introduction and Commentary* (3 vols.; AB 3, 3A, 3B; New York: Doubleday, 1991–2001).
Murphy, J. G., *A Critical and Exegetical Commentary on the Book of Leviticus* (Andover: Draper, 1874).
Noth, M., *Leviticus: A Commentary* (trans. J. E. Anderson; Philadelphia: SCM, 1965).
Rendtorff, R., *Studien zur Geschichte des Opfers im alten Israel* (WMANT 24; Neukirchen-Vluyn: Neukirchener, 1967).
–, *Leviticus* (BKAT III.1–4; Neukirchen-Vluyn: Neukirchener, 1985).
Rodwell, W. M., *The Mosaic Sacrifices in Leviticus I–VIII* (London: Griffith, Farran, Okeden and Welsh, 1889).
Schenker, A., "Das Zeichen des Blutes und die Gewissheit der Vergebung im Alten Testament," *MTZ* 34 (1983) 195–213.
Schwartz, B., *The Holiness Legislation: Studies in the Holiness Code* (Jerusalem: Magnes, 1999) (in Hebrew).
Snaith, N. H., *Leviticus and Numbers* (The Century Bible; London: Nelson, 1967).
Snaith, N., "The Sprinkling of Blood," *The Expository Times* 82 (1970) 23–4.
Staubli, T., *Die Bücher Levitikus, Numeri* (Neuer Stuttgarter Kommentar Altes Testament 3; Stuttgart: Katholisches Bibelwerk, 1996).
Wenham, G. J., *The Book of Leviticus* (NICOT 3; Grand Rapids: Eerdmans, 1979).
Wevers, J. W., *Notes on the Greek Text of Deuteronomy* (SBL Septuagint and Cognate Studies Series 39; Atlanta: Scholars, 1995).
–, *Notes on the Greek Text of Leviticus* (SCS 44; Atlanta: Scholars, 1997).
Zevit, Z., *The Religions of Ancient Israel: A Synthesis of Parallactic Approaches* (New York: Continuum, 2001) 276–314.
Zimmerli, W., *Ezekiel 2* (transl. J. D. Martin; Hermeneia; Philadelphia: Fortress, 1983).

Roy E. Gane

Purification Offerings and Paradoxical Pollution of the Holy

1 Introduction

Leviticus 16:16a lists three kinds of evils that are removed (*kipper min*) from the Israelite sanctuary through special purification offerings performed by the high priest annually on the Day of Atonement:

> Thus he shall effect removal for the (inner) holy area from the physical ritual impurities (*ṭum'ôt*) of the Israelites and from their rebellious sins (*pᵉšā'îm*), as well as all their (non-rebellious) sins (*ḥaṭṭā'ôt*) (my translation).[1]

This verse indicates two concepts. First, ritual pollution borne by the sanctuary constitutes an exception to the rule that holiness and impurity must be kept apart (e.g., Lev 7:20–21; 15:31). Second, the sanctuary has limited immunity to the defilement that it bears: It does not cease to be most holy and to function as such, but it must be purified once per year.[2]

How do physical impurities and sins come to pollute the sanctuary? According to Lev 20:3 and Num 19:13, 20, some egregious sins automatically defile the sanctuary when they are committed, but the sinners are condemned to be "cut off" (verbs from the root *k-r-t*), a terminal divinely administered penalty, with no opportunity for expiation and forgiveness through subsequent sacrifice. Automatic defilement in such cases can account for the way in which rebellious sins (*pᵉšā'îm*) reach the sanctuary so that they must be purged from it through the special purification offerings on the Day of Atonement (Lev 16:16).[3] But what about the physical impurities (*ṭum'ôt*) and non-rebellious sins (*ḥaṭṭā'ôt*)?

---

1 On "effect removal" as the meaning of the verb *kipper* (*piel* of *k-p-r*), see W. K. Gilders, *Blood Ritual in the Hebrew Bible: Meaning and Power* (Baltimore: Johns Hopkins University Press, 2004), 28–29. Lev 16:16b prescribes similar purgation of the outer sanctum, i. e., from the same evils. Verse 19 abbreviates, only referring to the first of the three evils: the physical ritual impurities (*ṭum'ôt*).

2 In Lev 16:19 the outer altar is (re)consecrated (*piel* of *q-d-š*) on the Day of Atonement, but this does not mean that it has lost its holiness; it is always most holy, so that whatever touches it becomes holy (Exod 29:37; 30:28–29).

3 R. E. Gane, *Cult and Character: Purification Offerings, Day of Atonement, and Theodicy* (Winona Lake, IN: Eisenbrauns, 2005), 296.

2 Movement of Physical Impurities and Non-Rebellious Sins into the Sanctuary

In my book *Cult and Character*, I suggested a way in which physical ritual impurities and non-rebellious sins could enter the sanctuary throughout the year in a first phase of *kippur* (removal of evil) so that they would need to be removed from there in a second phase of *kippur* on the Day of Atonement.[4] I agreed with Milgrom that in Lev 6:20–21 (Eng. vv. 27–28), blood of a most holy purification offering that spatters on a garment must be washed off[5] in a holy place because it paradoxically carries impurity, and a vessel in which purification offering flesh is boiled must be broken (if it is earthenware) or scoured (if it is bronze) for the same reason: because it carries pollution.[6]

According to Milgrom, the defilement as a kind of "aerial miasma" has already contaminated the altar from a distance[7] and the sacrifice subsequently contracts the impurity by contacting the altar.[8] However, as I have shown, such defilement, which I simply call "automatic" because I find it to be nonmaterial, does not apply in such cases, which concern purification offering remedies for non-rebellious sins and serious physical ritual impurities.[9] Moreover, it is hard to imagine how blood applied to the horns of the altar by the priest's finger would then spatter off onto his garment.[10]

Therefore, I concluded that the pollution carried by the purification offering must come from the offerer when the sacrifice removes the evil from that person at the sanctuary. When the priest daubs purification offering blood, carrying defilement from non-rebellious sin or physical ritual impurity, on the horns of the altar, the whole altar and the sanctuary receive the pollution, *pars pro toto* ("part for all").[11]

Some of my esteemed friends have done me the honor of critiquing the interpretation of Lev 6:20–21 just described, and they have not been convinced.[12]

---

4 Ibid., 164–81; on the two phases, see further 267–84.

5 *Pars pro toto* ("part for all") does not apply in this case: Only the bespattered part must be washed, so the offerer is not required to strip off the garment in order to have it laundered in the sanctuary courtyard.

6 J. Milgrom, *Leviticus 1–16: A New Translation with Introduction and Commentary* (AB 3; New York: Doubleday, 1991), 403–7.

7 Ibid., 257.

8 Ibid., 403 regarding the blood, which, "having absorbed the impurity of the sanctum upon which it is sprinkled, now contaminates everything it touches."

9 Gane, *Cult and Character*, 154–60.

10 Ibid., 167–8.

11 Ibid., 172–81. Similarly, if the flesh of the sacrifice carries impurity from the offerer, presumably the suet burned on the altar would also take pollution to the altar.

12 C. Eberhart, "Review of Roy E. Gane, *Cult and Character: Purification Offerings, Day of Atonement, and Theodicy*," *RBL* 7 (2006) 5 [https://www.bookreviews.org/pdf/5068_5341.pdf];

Recently, Christophe Nihan has developed the argument against my theory in part of an essay titled "The Templization of Israel in Leviticus: Some Remarks on Blood Disposal and *Kipper* in Leviticus 4."[13] The essay as a whole is a thorough, penetrating, and logical study that skillfully navigates through the complex array of exegetical problems and scholarly views to settle on convincing interpretations on many issues.

I agree with most of Nihan's minor points and also his major ones that (1) the purification offering in Lev 4 removes evil from the offerer, not from the sanctuary, (2) it is the whole sacrifice, not only the blood application, that effects expiation, and (3) a key point (he proposes *the* key point) of Lev 4 is

> to index the sanctuary as the very place where relations between the community and its patron deity are established and renegotiated; where not only ritual roles, but also social hierarchies and ethical categories, are defined; and where the ritual, moral and even legal dimensions of the community referred to as 'Israel' are articulated and merged into a coherent whole.[14]

Earlier I concluded the same regarding the first two points,[15] but the third is new to me as such. It is profound and seems to be promising for yielding further insights.

In the process of critiquing existing interpretations, Nihan finds several problems with my explication of purification offering blood as a carrier of impurity and the two-phase theory of *kippur* to which it contributes, but which can stand without it. The remainder of the present essay will be devoted to dialogue with his objections.

3 Ancient Near Eastern Fear of Defiling Sacred Places

Nihan observes:

> To begin with, the very notion that the function of the *ḥaṭṭāʾt* ritual in the course of the year—outside of the Day of Atonement—would be to transfer the pollution resulting from severe physical impurities or inadvertent moral transgressions from the offerer to the sanctuary (more precisely, the inner sanctum) is problematic from an ancient Near Eastern (or West Asian) perspective, where the fear of defiling sacred

J. Sklar, "Review of Roy E. Gane, *Cult and Character: Purification Offerings, Day of Atonement, and Theodicy*," *RBL* 4 (2007) 5 [https://www.bookreviews.org/pdf/5068_6109.pdf].

13 In F. Landy/L. M. Trevaskis/B. D. Bibb (ed.), *Text, Time, and Temple: Literary, Historical and Ritual Studies in Leviticus* (HBM 64; Sheffield: Sheffield Phoenix Press, 2015) 94–130.

14 Ibid., 127; cf. 96, where Nihan finds Gilders's interpretation of *ḥaṭṭāʾt* blood manipulations, which emphasizes the indexing of priestly status and prerogatives (*Blood Ritual*, 109–41) to be too restrictive.

15 Gane, *Cult and Character*, 56, 112–43.

> places and thereby forcing the resident deities to depart is a well-established literary *topos*. Surely, as Milgrom and others have surmised, there are reasons to consider that the same concern applied in ancient Israel, especially within priestly circles, as is suggested by the vision in chaps. 8–10 of Ezekiel describing the 'abominations' committed in the sanctuary (Ezek 8) and the resulting abandonment of the city by its patron deity (Ezek 9–10).[16]

In response, first of all I do not believe that it is the function of the purification offering throughout the year to transfer pollution to the sanctuary. The function is to remove evil from the offerer. If transfer of pollution to the sanctuary occurs, it is an unavoidable side-effect of removing the evil from the offerer at the sanctuary.

Second, reference to Ezek 8–10 is off target because those abominations are egregious rebellious sins causing major defilement, which are not the concern of pentateuchal prescriptions for *ḥaṭṭāʾt* sacrifices performed throughout the year. In Leviticus, the purification offering is for minor moral faults[17] and for physical impurities. If the sanctuary receives some pollution through such a sacrifice, the pollution is small because the source is weaker than rebellious sin and the contamination is further weakened by the indirectness of the transfer: from the offerer to the animal and only then through the animal's blood and suet to part of the sanctuary. The offerer does not directly defile the sanctuary; there is only a residual effect from the action of the priest. Therefore, the offerer does not violate the regulation exemplified in Lev 7:20–21 (cf. 22:1–7 regarding priests) that he/she must never bring impurity into direct contact with something holy, such as by eating well-being offering meat while in a state of physical impurity.

Third, while it would be unusual for deliberate transfer of pollution to sacred space to be permitted in the ANE conceptual environment, it would be methodologically invalid to rule out this possibility in Israelite cult on that basis. It is well known that there are features of the Israelite ritual system that are unique, including application of sacrificial blood to sacred objects and spaces in order to remedy moral faults, prerequisite to divine forgiveness.

In the Israelite ritual system, the high priest deliberately pollutes most holy purification offering animals[18] by using them to purge the sanctuary on the Day of Atonement, so that an assistant who contacts them to dispose of their carcasses contracts impurity (Lev 16:28). The main goal is not to pollute something holy.

---

16 Nihan, "The Templization of Israel," 116–17.

17 Inadvertent sins in Lev 4; other minor sins (including neglect from forgetting) in Lev 5:1–13.

18 If the purification offerings in Lev 6 are most holy (vv. 18, 22 [Eng. vv. 25, 29]), *a fortiori* the special purification offerings in Lev 16, the blood of which is brought into the inner sanctum (vv. 14–15), must be most holy, as indicated by the need for the high priest to wash his whole body (rather than just hands and feet, as in Exod 30:19, 21) before burning their suet on the altar (Lev 16:24).

Rather, this is necessary to achieve the goal of purging the sanctuary, just as leaving some residual defilement at the sanctuary has been necessary for removal of evil from an offerer.

The fact that purification offerings carry defilement is demonstrated by the red cow ritual in Num 19, which is a purification offering that provides ashes to remedy corpse contamination (v. 9).[19] Through the burning of the cow the officiating priest and his garments become impure so that he must launder his clothes and bathe before entering the camp, but he remains impure until evening (v. 7). According to Lev 22:1–7, it is forbidden for a priest to contact holy things, including to eat from a sacrifice, while he is in a state of physical impurity, including that which comes from a corpse. But in Num 19 a consecrated priest must deliberately make himself impure through a purification offering. Contracting this permitted impurity is not the reason for the sacrifice, but it is an unavoidable consequence that explains why the ritual must be performed outside the camp.

The fact that purification offerings performed at the sanctuary do not pollute officiating priests to the degree that they need ablutions, even when they eat meat by which they bear culpability (*ʿāwōn*) from the offerers (Lev 10:17), indicates that they are immune to the trace levels of residual pollution from non-rebellious sins and physical impurities in this context. But such low-level impurity accumulates in the sanctuary to the point that it must be removed once a year on the Day of Atonement (Lev 16:16; cf. v. 19).

How does this impurity affect the sanctuary and its sancta? Through the purification offerings. When do they contact the consecrated areas and objects? When their blood is applied there and their suet is placed on the altar. Why should such blood be washed off a garment? In the case of a priest, this could be to preserve his immunity by keeping impurity from building up on him. In the case of a layperson, it could be because purification offering blood is not applied to an offerer: The blood carries impurity away from the offerer to remove it from him/her, so it makes no sense to put it back on the offerer.[20] Why should vessels in which purification offering meat is boiled be broken or scoured? To keep the impurity eaten by the priests to a minimum, again to preserve their immunity.

Elsewhere in the ANE, the idea that sacred objects or spaces could bear ritual defilement was well known. For example, on the fourth day of the Anatolian festival of the god Telipinu, Hittites conveyed idols of this and other deities, along

19 J. Milgrom, "The Paradox of the Red Cow (Num. XIX)," *VT* 31 (1981) 62–72; idem, *Numbers: The Traditional Hebrew Text with the New JPS Translation* (JPSTC; Philadelphia: Jewish Publication Society, 1990), 438–43; Gane, *Cult and Character*, 182–91; cf. Milgrom, *Leviticus 1–16*, 403.

20 Gane, *Cult and Character*, 175.

with a cult pedestal, to a river in order to purify them.[21] Their contamination did not nullify their sanctity, but periodically they had to be cleansed, just as the Israelite sanctuary and its sancta bore pollution that was to be removed on the Day of Atonement.

Likewise, the Ezida cella of the god Nabû required annual purgation from demonic impurity on the fifth day of the Babylonian New Year Festival of Spring (Akītu Festival).[22] The slaughterer who decapitated a ram and the exorcist who wiped (*kuppuru*, cognate to Hebrew *kipper*) the shrine with its carcass threw the carcass and head of the animal "into the river," which must be the Euphrates River. Then these ritual functionaries were required to go out to the open country for the duration of the festival, no doubt because they had contracted impurity from contact with the ram that absorbed impurity from the shrine.

Scholars have pointed out several similarities and differences between the Babylonian procedures and elements of the Israelite Day of Atonement.[23] Additionally, we should remember that the Euphrates River was sacred to the Babylonians.[24] So it appears that the ritual for purging the Ezida deliberately disposed of demonic impurity in something sacred, with the intention that the divine would overcome the demonic. The intention was not to defile something holy, which in this case was apparently immune to pollution, but to get rid of the impurity. Analogously in the Israelite cult, some of the weaker impurities (from minor sins and physical impurities) were consigned to the deity so that he would overcome them, although his sanctuary temporarily bore them in some sense until the Day of Atonement.

4 Interpretation of Leviticus 6:20–21 (Eng. vv. 27–28)

Nihan states that my inference that purification offering blood carries impurity in Lev 6:20 so that this pollution must be removed, as in Lev 11:32–33, "is largely based on the assumption that so-called contagious holiness cannot be removed."[25] He finds the idea of impurity in 6:20–21 to be problematic for several reasons:

21 R.E. Gane, *Ritual Dynamic Structure* (Gorgias Dissertations 14, Religion 2; Piscataway, NJ: Gorgias, 2004), 261–76, 358–60, esp. 265–6.

22 *ANET*, 333.

23 D.P. Wright, *The Disposal of Impurity: Elimination Rites in the Bible and in Hittite and Mesopotamian Literature* (SBLDS 101; Atlanta: Scholars Press, 1987), 64–5; Milgrom, *Leviticus 1–16*, 1068–9; Gane, *Ritual Dynamic Structure*, 231–2; idem, *Cult and Character*, 365–7, 372.

24 See, e.g., the Laws of Hammurabi § 2, where the divine determinative precedes the sign for the river (ID) so that Martha T. Roth renders "the divine River Ordeal" (*Law Collections from Mesopotamia and Asia Minor* [SBLWAW 6; Atlanta: Scholars Press, 1995], 81).

25 Nihan, "The Templization of Israel," 117.

> To begin with, in order to maintain the parallel between washing blood from a garment and washing or destroying a vessel in which the flesh of the *ḥaṭṭāʾt* has boiled, Gane is forced to surmise that the flesh of the *ḥaṭṭāʾt* "imparts impurity to vessels." However, not only is that notion absent from the text but it seems to contradict the statement found immediately before 6:21, in 6:20a, which says exactly the opposite, namely, "all that touches the flesh is sanctified."[26]

Second, Nihan finds that the parallel between 6:21 and 11:32–33 shows the difference between the two cases, rather than supporting my argument, because 11:32–33 explicitly refers to the impurity of objects and their purification, but there is no such reference to impurity or purification in 6:21. At this point Nihan rightly holds me to consistency with an important aspect of my own methodology: It is not legitimate to import the meaning attached to a ritual activity in one context into another context because, as I have emphasized, the same ritual activities can carry different meanings in different contexts.[27]

Third, if purification offering blood carries impurity, why must it be washed from a garment "in a holy place" (6:20)? Elsewhere in Leviticus, priests must eat sacrificial meat in a holy place because it is "most holy" (6:9, 19; 7:6; 10:17), with no indication that it is impure.

Nihan concludes that the inference from Lev 6:20 that the purification offering blood carries impurity "cannot be viewed as compelling and should be rejected. Presumably the most obvious reading of this passage is that it refers to the washing of the priestly vestments when the latter have been sanctified by contact with the blood of the *ḥaṭṭāʾt*, as is usually assumed by commentators."[28]

In response, Jacob Milgrom and David P. Wright already answered Nihan's objections decades ago. Most importantly, the requirements regarding garments and vessels in 6:20–21 are restricted to the purification offering. If the issue were sancta contagion, these rules would also apply to other sacrifices that are designated as most holy,[29] but there is no evidence that they do. Therefore, they must be necessitated by the unique dynamics of the *ḥaṭṭāʾt* sacrifice, which removes minor moral faults and serious physical impurities that can pollute the sanctuary.[30]

It is Milgrom who raised the parallels with Lev 11 and other passages, first with regard to the garment spattered with purification offering blood:

---

26 Ibid., 117–18.

27 Ibid., 118, incl. n. 73, referring to Gane, *Cult and Character*, 21–4, and cf. 4–9, 273.

28 Nihan, "The Templization of Israel," 118.

29 These are grain and reparation offerings (2:3, 10; 6:10 [Eng. v. 17]; 7:1, 6), which make things holy by direct contact like the purification offering (6:20 [v. 27]). See the summary in 6:11 (Eng. v. 18): "Anything that touches these (i. e., the grain, purification, and reparation offerings mentioned in this and the previous verse) shall become holy" (NJPS; parenthetical explanation supplied), as noted by Milgrom, *Leviticus 1–16*, 444.

30 Milgrom, *Leviticus 1–16*, 405; Wright, *The Disposal of Impurity*, 96 n. 8; 130–1.

> Instead of being confiscated by the sanctuary, as would any object that is rendered holy, it is restored to its former status by having its so-called holiness effaced through washing. Thus the garment is actually treated as if it were impure, for it is impure clothing that always requires laundering (e.g., 11:25, 28, 40; 15:5–8, 10–11).[31]

Milgrom observes regarding vessels in which purification offering meat is boiled: "Only impure earthenware needs to be broken (see 11:33, 35; 15:12) because its porous nature so totally absorbs the impurity that it can never again be purified."[32]

Nihan is certainly correct that we should not import meaning from one context to another, and in fact I did not intend to do this when I wrote on Lev 6:

> Like the blood in relation to a garment, the edible flesh is implicitly treated as impure because it imparts impurity to vessels (v. 21[28]; cf. 11:31–33), even though it is most holy.[33]

My note to compare with 11:31–33 simply meant that I saw a similarity in that passage. It is true that there is no explicit statement in 6:20–21 that the blood and flesh of the sacrifice carry impurity. There does not need to be such a statement because this passage explicitly concerns the purification offering (v. 18 [Eng. v. 25]), which serves the function of removing sin or physical impurity (cf. Lev 4:1–5:13; 12:6–8, etc.). Lest anyone suppose that the pollution carried by the sacrifice lessens its sanctity, the passage repeats the affirmation that it is most holy (vv. 18, 22 [Eng. vv. 25, 29]).[34]

Sancta contagion does not make good sense in Lev 6:20–21. Aside from the points already mentioned, if purification offering blood spatters on a priest's garment or he boils the meat in a vessel, why would sancta contagion matter? The priest's garment is already holy and belongs to the sanctuary, and presumably so do the vessels used to boil such meat there. If the concern of verse 20 is restricted to clothes of laypersons, which could be confiscated if holiness were not removed from them, and does not also apply to priests' garments, why doesn't the text say so? On the other hand, impurity from the offerer makes sense because it would be a problem for both lay and priestly garments.

31 Milgrom, *Leviticus 1–16*, 403.

32 Ibid., 405.

33 Gane, *Cult and Character*, 172.

34 Therefore, anything that touches its flesh becomes holy (v. 20 [Eng. v. 27]) and it must be eaten in a holy place (v. 19 [Eng. v. 26]), i.e., the sanctuary courtyard (v. 9 [Eng. v. 16]).

5 Additional Objections to Two Phases of Sin Removal

Nihan concludes his review of my two-phase theory of sin removal—first from the offerer throughout the year and then from the sanctuary on the Day of Atonement—by citing examples of additional difficulties that he regards as significant. First, he suggests that if the physical impurities (*ṭumʾôt*) and non-rebellious sins (*ḥaṭṭāʾôt*) referred to in Lev 16:16 were those that were transferred to the sanctuary from the offerers, these would likely be listed together instead of being separated by the rebellious sins (*pᵉšāʿîm*). "The fact that *ḥaṭṭāʾôt* occurs at the end of this enumeration and is preceded by *lᵉkol* makes better sense if this construct is interpreted as a summarizing category."[35]

As I pointed out in *Cult and Character*, the summarizing interpretation of *lᵉkol* fails because *ḥaṭṭāʾôt* are moral faults, and this category certainly cannot include *ṭumʾôt*, "physical ritual impurities."[36] The rebellious sins may be listed before the non-rebellious sins because the former constitute the more serious category, just as Lev 4 treats the more serious cases of inadvertent sins by the high priest and the whole community (vv. 3–21) before instances that involve individual lay Israelites (vv. 22–35).

Second, Nihan finds that

> in Gane's model it is somewhat difficult to make sense of the statement in 16.30a, according to which the purpose of the annual purification of the sanctuary is to 'purify' (*lᵉṭāhēr*) the community, since according to this model such purification should already have occurred in phase 1.[37]

It is true that purification (*ṭ-h-r*) of offerers from physical impurities does already occur in phase 1.[38] However, Lev 16:30 only concerns *kippur* for non-rebellious sins (*ḥaṭṭāʾôt*) that is effected for the Israelites uniquely "on this day," i. e., the Day of Atonement. That is, the *kippur* that purges the sanctuary secondarily results in their moral purification, as Milgrom has interpreted this verse.[39] This dynamic with use of the *piel* of *ṭ-h-r* for purification from moral faults only appears here. Whereas phase 1 removes non-rebellious sins from the sinners so that they can be forgiven (verb *s-l-ḥ*; 4:20, 26, 31, etc.), the removal of (trace levels of) these sins from the sanctuary provides a second stage of *kippur* for the people in that

35 Nihan, "The Templization of Israel," 119–20.
36 Gane, *Cult and Character*, 289–90.
37 Nihan, "The Templization of Israel," 120.
38 Gane, *Cult and Character*, 275–6.
39 Milgrom, *Leviticus 1–16*, 1056: "The purgation rites in the sanctuary purify the sanctuary, not the people. Yet, as the sanctuary is polluted by the people's impurities, their elimination, in effect, also purifies the people."

not even a vestigial remnant of their sins remains with them at the sanctuary, and therefore there is no remaining impediment to the divine-human relationship.[40]

Third, Nihan claims that I am "forced to interpret the hand-leaning rite, in the case of the *ḥaṭṭāʾt* (see Lev 4.4, 15, 24, 29, 33), as involving the transfer of the moral guilt of the offerer (as well as the pollution attaching to that guilt) on the animal itself, a problematic assumption that is open to criticism."[41] I have agreed that this assumption is problematic and adopted the identification of ownership view.[42] In terms of the way a purification offering becomes contaminated by the offerer, I wrote:

> Apparently it is because the offerer has a connection with his offering as its owner and transfers ownership to YHWH, as affirmed by the hand-leaning gesture when this is required ... However, I argue that it is the departing ownership connection rather than the physical contact itself that is the point ... the fact that hand-leaning is not required in every case shows that this gesture is not indispensable for transferring evil from the offerer to his/her offering.[43]

6 Conclusion

I am grateful for this opportunity to clarify some points that may not have been sufficiently clear in my *Cult and Character*. I am delighted to learn from critiques of my work and ready to accept better ways of interpreting the data if such should present themselves. In the present case, after re-evaluating the evidence, looking for some further data, and testing alternatives, I am forced to conclude that the two-phase theory of *kippur* holds firm with regard to the material covered in this essay.

In light of implications of these phases for relationships between YHWH and members of his covenant community, which I probed in *Cult and Character*,[44] it appears that my theory is compatible with Christophe Nihan's profound insight that the purification offering indexes "the sanctuary as the very place where relations between the community and its patron deity are established and renegotiated."[45] May the exploration and invigorating dialogue continue as we work together to understand Leviticus. I think we are making progress.

---

40 See further on the function of phase two: Gane, *Cult and Character*, 300–23. For the idea that forgiveness (*s-l-ḥ*) can be provisional, see Milgrom, *Numbers*, 112 on Num 14:19.

41 Nihan, "The Templization of Israel," 120.

42 Gane, *Cult and Character*, 53–9.

43 Ibid., 176. Hand-leaning is not performed on a purification offering bird or grain item (Lev 5:8, 12).

44 Ibid., esp. 305–33.

45 Nihan, "The Templization of Israel," 127.

Bibliography

Eberhart, C., "Review of Roy E. Gane, Cult and Character: Purification Offerings, Day of Atonement, and Theodicy," *RBL* 7 (2006) [https://www.bookreviews.org/pdf/5068_5341.pdf].

Gane, R. E., *Ritual Dynamic Structure* (Gorgias Dissertations 14, Religion 2; Piscataway, NJ: Gorgias, 2004).

–, *Cult and Character: Purification Offerings, Day of Atonement, and Theodicy* (Winona Lake, IN: Eisenbrauns, 2005).

Gilders, W. K., *Blood Ritual in the Hebrew Bible: Meaning and Power* (Baltimore: Johns Hopkins University Press, 2004).

Milgrom, J., "The Paradox of the Red Cow (Num. XIX)," *VT* 31 (1981) 62–72.

–, *Numbers: The Traditional Hebrew Text with the New JPS Translation* (JPSTC; Philadelphia: Jewish Publication Society, 1990).

–, *Leviticus 1–16: A New Translation with Introduction and Commentary* (AB 3; New York: Doubleday, 1991).

Nihan, C., "The Templization of Israel in Leviticus: Some Remarks on Blood Disposal and *Kipper* in Leviticus 4," in F. Landy/L. M. Trevaskis/B. D. Bibb (ed.), *Text, Time, and Temple: Literary, Historical and Ritual Studies in Leviticus* (HBM 64; Sheffield: Sheffield Phoenix Press, 2015) 94–130.

Roth, M. T., *Law Collections from Mesopotamia and Asia Minor* (SBLWAW 6; Atlanta: Scholars Press, 1995).

Sklar, J., "Review of Roy E. Gane, Cult and Character: Purification Offerings, Day of Atonement, and Theodicy," *RBL* 4 (2007) [https://www.bookreviews.org/pdf/5068_6109.pdf].

Wright, D. P., *The Disposal of Impurity: Elimination Rites in the Bible and in Hittite and Mesopotamian Literature* (SBLDS 101; Atlanta: Scholars Press, 1987).

Naphtali S. Meshel

Some New Questions in the Fundamental Science of P

to Jacob Milgrom

1 Misreadings[1]

There are two main reasons to write a new commentary on Leviticus. The first is that despite major progress over the course of the last half-century, primarily thanks to the works of Rolf Rendtorff, Jacob Milgrom, Menahem Haran and their followers, Leviticus is still one of the most misread books in the Hebrew Bible.

The misreading of Leviticus usually involves reading P through the eyes of Jewish Hellenistic, early Christian and/or rabbinic authors. Thus, modern misreadings often combine two types of interrelated errors. First, error with regard to ostensibly minute philological detail—such as the misinterpretation of שֶׂה as "lamb" or as a specifically young member of the flock (rather than a sheep or goat of any age), a surprisingly persistent mistranslation—enhanced by (but not originating from) the perception of Jesus as *agnus dei*.[2] Another such case is the widespread interpretation of זרק דם על המזבח as denoting the dashing of blood upon the altar's vertical walls, following early Jewish sources, rather than its actual denotation in P—tossing blood upon its horizontal upper surface—sometimes based on the assumption that blood could not possibly be offered alongside the deity's "meals" on his "table."[3]

The second form of modern misreading, more fundamental than the first—and in a way, more problematic and more difficult to uproot—is apologetics. Apologetics permeate Jacob Milgrom's commentary, which is the most detailed, erudite and insightful work on Leviticus available. For example, Milgrom writes:

---

1 I am thankful to the editors for the license to adhere, to a great extent, to the oral style of the paper read in Atlanta at SBL 2015. The following speculations are best considered a preface to a more thorough study, in which I intend to offer a systematic treatment of the material presented below. – I wish to thank Baruch J. Schwartz and Hillel Mali for their comments on previous versions of this article.

2 N. S. Meshel, *The "Grammar" of Sacrifice: A Generativist Study of the Ancient Israelite Sacrificial System in the Priestly Writings, with: A "Grammar" of Σ* (Oxford: Oxford University Press, 2014), 51–2.

3 As argued in the article "The Form and Function of a Biblical Blood Ritual" (N. S. Meshel, "The Form and Function of a Biblical Blood Ritual," *VT* 63 [2013] 276–89), reprinted in this volume, see pp. 101–14.

> All religions urge reverence for life though few adherents live by it. Albert Schweitzer, who made this principle the core of his life and work, wrote, "The universal effort of Reverence for Life shows the sympathy with animals … to be a duty which no thinking man can escape." But Schweitzer's influence on humanity is a result of his life commitments, not his preachments. In fact, the latter can be conveniently subverted by tendentious reasoning … The Bible, to the contrary, takes no chances with the variables of human nature and insists on being rudely pragmatic. It allows the slaughtering of animals only for human food.[4]

A similar form of apologetics leads Milgrom to juxtapose rabbinic and Priestly theology, on the one hand, with Qumran and "the pagans" or "the polytheistic world," on the other hand. Discussing these various groups' conception of defilement—the main topic of this paper—Milgrom writes:

> In essence, this Priestly theology of sanctuary contamination is structured on the lines of pagan analogues. Indeed, all three laws controlling Israel's system operate with equal validity in the polytheistic world, but with one crucial distinction. The pagans, who gave highest priority to protecting their sanctuary from impurity, believed the latter to be personified demonic forces intent on driving out their patron god from his sanctuary, and they sought magical apotropaic rituals, mediated by the priesthood, to enhance the life force of the deity and shield the sanctuary from invasion. In Israel, these universal laws are recast in terms of its monotheism.[5]

In interpreting Leviticus, it sometimes seems almost as if Milgrom may have created—and I write this out of immense personal and professional respect for the late Professor Milgrom—something of a Priestly author in his own image: a monotheistic, humanitarian, liberal, pro-vegetarian, ritually conservative intellectual. These were all attributes admirably combined in the late Professor Milgrom, but tacitly attributing them to P is, I think, misleading.

A new commentary on Leviticus would be called for were it only for the reasons laid out above. However, a new, systematic analysis of Leviticus is necessary for a second reason: to raise a series of questions that have not been asked before, at any rate not systematically, prompted by new discoveries in the study of ritual and by recent comparative work. These questions are bound to shed light on the two most important ritual systems reflected in P—the ancient Israelite sacrificial system (which I designate Σ) and the ancient Israelite system of purity and contamination (designated Π). It is rarely superfluous to stress—even when preaching to the choir—the centrality of Σ and Π in the study of ancient Israel. Σ and Π, which are inextricably intertwined, together constitute the most elaborate, complex and intricate intellectual construct produced in ancient Israelite and early

---

4 J. Milgrom, *Leviticus 1–16: A New Translation with Introduction and Commentary* (AB 3; New York: Doubleday, 1991), 736.

5 Ibid., 981–2.

Jewish literature. From a quantitative point of view alone, these systems constitute nearly half of the Pentateuch and half of the Mishna. Further, qualitatively, the inner complexity and mechanical intricacy of the sacrificial and purity systems is unparalleled by any other system of ancient Jewish thought, such as philosophy, mathematics, linguistics, astronomy or extispicy—to mention but a few other branches of knowledge that were highly developed elsewhere in antiquity.

In this paper, I would like to focus on the second of these two systems, the purity laws,[6] sketching out a series of questions about Π.

2 *Miasma*

We will begin by following Milgrom's work on *miasma* (pl. *miasmata*, from Greek μίασμα, "pollution"),[7] a term that has become commonplace in the scholarly literature on Leviticus. Forgiving the anachronism for a moment, let us imagine ourselves as fifth-century BCE alchemists attempting to define the precise natural properties of a substance named *miasma*. While Milgrom justifiably strives to distinguish between the dangerous pollution affecting the sanctuary and the usually innocuous pollution affecting ordinary individuals and vessels, let us define *miasma* in a very broad sense that encompasses both. In this definition, *miasma* includes (1) any invisible substance (termed טֻמְאָה, e.g., Lev 5:3) arising from physical situations such as childbirth and touching a dead rat, that affects humans and household vessels, and that is ordinarily removable by means of water and the passing of time; as well as (2) any invisible substance (also termed טֻמְאָה, e.g., Lev 16:19) arising either from the Israelites' transgressions or from many of the physical conditions mentioned in no. (1) above, that accrues in particular parts of the sanctuary (e.g., the horns of the bronze altar), and that must be removed therefrom by means of blood derived from particular sacrificial offerings.

Though modern science does not suggest that *miasma* may exist as an as-yet-undiscovered element in the Periodic Table or as an as-yet-unpatented chemical compound, this does not exempt us from studying it as one would study the physical nature of ether. Even if from the point of view of twenty-first-century physics we know that ether does not exist, one may still want to know precisely how ether, *as perceived by previous physicists*, functioned: was it uniform, or was it thinner in some places and denser in others? Did it consist of tiny particles, and if so—how tiny? Is there only one kind of ether, or are there E_1, E_2, E_3, etc., differing

6 For a treatment of Σ see Meshel, *"Grammar" of Sacrifice*.

7 On the term and its original usage, see R. Parker, *Miasma: Pollution and Purification in Early Greek Religion* (Oxford: Clarendon Press, 1983).

in their chemical, magnetic or gravitational properties?[8] The present discussion focuses primarily on category (1) above, but the reader should keep in mind that many of the questions asked here pertain to the second category as well.

According to the prevalent conception that derives to a great extent from the first chapter of Mishna Kelim, the variety of impurities enumerated in Pentateuchal law—for example, a dead mouse or a person suffering from *bāheret* (e.g., Lev 13:2), as well as people or vessels that have been in some form of contact with such sources of impurity—can be described accurately as located on a spectrum ranging from the most severe to the least severe.

However, the characterization "more severe" and "less severe"—still used by even the most insightful studies—inaccurately describes the data. This is because there are, in fact, seemingly weak impurities of very long duration, just as a common cold can last for many weeks (Lev 12:4, 5b—the second stage of a parturient's waiting period before she can come in contact with sancta). On the other hand, there are short-term, one-day impurities that require seclusion from the camp, just as some severe and highly contagious diseases can be of brief duration (Lev 16:26; Num 19:7).

The lack of correlation between the duration of impurity from a particular source and the degree to which it is contagious can be seen in *Figure 1*. Had there been strict positive correlation between the two factors, all dots on the graph would have appeared on a single, roughly straight line, such as the black arrow in Figure 1.

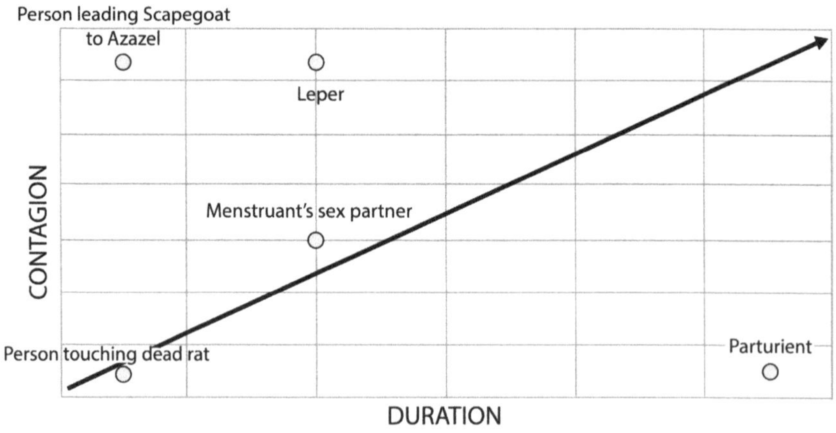

Figure 1: Lack of correlation between contagion and duration in P

8 E. T. Whittaker, *A History of the Theories of Aether and Electricity* (London et al.: Nelson, 1951). Regarding ether's identification as wave/particle, its elasticity, density, magnetic properties etc. in Einstein's writings, see L. Kostro, *Einstein and the Ether* (Montreal: Apeiron, 2000), 14.

Thus, each impurity may be characterized by at least three different variables, in such a way that it can be traced on a three-dimensional grid indicating its (1) duration, (2) tenacity—the complexity of the rites of removal, (3) contagion (see Figure 2). In addition to these, there are other variables that may or may not be present, such as whether the act is permitted or prohibited (e.g., consumption of a dead cow by a priest according to Lev 22:8 is prohibited but apparently requires only laundering one's clothes, bathing one's body and waiting until sunset in order to be rid of the pollution).

Once one locates each impurity on this grid, one may begin asking a set of questions that have only recently begun to be asked in the literature.

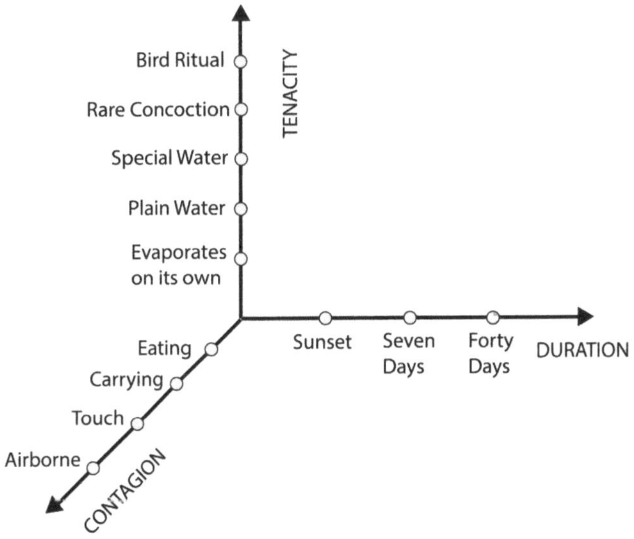

Figure 2: Three-dimensional grid

3 The Cases of Impurity—New Questions

Let us therefore consider a set of cases where the two reasons for writing a commentary on Leviticus overlap: a degree of apologetics in previous literature and the necessity to revisit the fundamentals of the "science of ritual" in the context of Leviticus, and particularly with regard to the system of purity and impurity, Π. The following set of interrelated questions, as we shall see, is never explicitly addressed in the biblical text and is not systematically addressed in rabbinic literature, but these questions are addressed occasionally in Qumranic literature[9] and, more systematically, in Karaite literature. All questions deal with an ostensibly arcane aspect of Π, which, however, has far-reaching ramifications for a basic understanding of the Priestly system of purity and impurity, namely the problem of *compoundment*. The term *compoundment* is used to denote a situation that may arise when a person or an object is simultaneously susceptible to impurity from more than one source—specifically, situations in which the person or object become defiled in more than one way.

Question 1: Are impurities arising from different sources substantially identical—varying only in degree (an imperfect modern metaphor would be voltage, which can be greater or lesser), or are they substantially different (an imperfect modern metaphor would be disease)?

A first caveat: even two ontologically distinct substances may appear identical from a functional point of view. For example,[10] an earthen vessel is treated in the same manner if it is touched by a *pathological suppurant* (here used as a technical term denoting a person with irregular genital discharge, Lev 15:12a), if a dead rat falls into it (11:33), or even if a *ḥaṭṭāʾt* offering is cooked in it (6:21a, though this is not, in P's understanding, a matter of impurity at all).[11] In all three cases, it is to be broken. However, one must not hasten to conclude that suppurants, dead rats, and *ḥaṭṭāʾt* offerings all spread ontologically identical *miasmata*.

A second caveat: Even in our pathological metaphor, different diseases may have similar symptoms. Likewise, different diseases may require similar treatment, or a cluster of treatments may be required, some of which may be shared by different diseases. Similarly, two distinct *miasmata* may require identical purification rites.

Question 2: Even assuming that impurities arising from different human and animal bodily sources are substantially identical, differing only in degree, what happens if a person contracts one impurity immediately followed by another?

a. What happens when the two are of unequal severity—e.g., if a woman, having touched a dead cat, then gives birth, or (in the reverse order) if a parturient touches a dead cat? (One is tempted to assume that the "weaker" impurity has no effect, but such an understanding is neither obvious nor inevitable.)

b. What happens when the two are of equal severity—e.g., a person carries a dead cat, then eats a dead cow (both impurities require laundering and waiting until evening, and presumably bathing as well, according to Lev 11:28, 40a); or a person eats a dead cow, then touches something a *zāb* (a male suppurant) has sat

9 I use the term to include all literature known to us from Qumran, whether composed at Qumran or elsewhere.

10 Milgrom, *Leviticus 1–16*, 254–61.

11 See E. Regev, "Priestly Dynamic Holiness and Deuteronomic Static Holiness," *VT* 51 (2001) 243–61, contra D.P. Wright, "The Spectrum of Priestly Impurity," in G. Anderson/S.M. Olyan (ed.), *Priesthood and Cult in Ancient Israel* (Sheffield: JSOT Press, 1991) 150–81.

upon? In such a case, would the ritual need to be changed because two impurities have been contracted, or can the same ritual remove the impurity for both actions?

Question 3: Assuming, however, that impurities map onto a grid, rather than merely onto a scale from least to most severe, we need to ask our question differently. Since a woman may be both a parturient and also contaminated by touching a corpse—would she need to wait 40 days before entering the Sanctuary (or 80 days, if the baby is a girl; Lev 12) and also undergo aspersions with מי נדה ("water of aspersion" Num 19:13)? Since these are two distinct rituals, rather than possibly redundant performances of the same one, the answer, in all likelihood, is affirmative. However, we must ask: does the time she is required to wait accumulate, or can any given day of impurity count both towards her waiting period as a parturient and also towards her waiting period following corpse impurity? More generally: if one becomes defiled by one type of impurity, then later by another, are the waiting periods counted as overlapping periods of time or successive periods of time (Does "time served" count)?

If the answer is successive periods of time, should we assume that these time periods accumulate even when a seemingly brief impurity follows a longer impurity? For example, would a woman who gives birth to a baby girl and then touches a dead cat have to wait 81 instead of 80 days before entering the sanctuary?

Question 4: One must grant that normally in P, if a person touches one dead man and then another, one need not count more than seven days (Num 31:19 suggests one week of impurity for soldiers returning from battle, where presumably one may have come into contact with more than one human corpse over several days—though this is not stated explicitly). Thus, one may generalize that the duration of impurity following exposure to several sources of "same-type" impurity does not compound in P. But then one must inquire what counts as "same-type impurity," and what counts as "different-type."

A clue may be found in Numbers 5:2–3, which reads:

2 צַו אֶת־בְּנֵי יִשְׂרָאֵל וִישַׁלְּחוּ מִן־הַמַּחֲנֶה כָּל־צָרוּעַ וְכָל־זָב וְכֹל טָמֵא לָנָפֶשׁ׃
3 מִזָּכָר עַד־נְקֵבָה תְּשַׁלֵּחוּ אֶל־מִחוּץ לַמַּחֲנֶה תְּשַׁלְּחוּם וְלֹא יְטַמְּאוּ אֶת־מַחֲנֵיהֶם אֲשֶׁר אֲנִי שֹׁכֵן בְּתוֹכָם׃

[2] Command the Israelites to put out of the camp everyone who is leprous, or has a discharge, and everyone who is unclean through contact with a corpse;

[3] you shall put out both male and female, putting them outside the camp; they must not defile their camp, where I dwell among them (NRSV).

These verses leave many questions open, e.g., with regard to their appearance outside the rest of the purification laws, and with regard to the possibility that they refer to special needs envisaged by the Priestly writer for this point in the narrative. However, one thing seems certain—persons having scale-disease, people with a genital flow (כל זב), and corpse-contaminated people seem to constitute three distinct categories—enough to merit different names (though the law in P seems to place them all together as a single group outside camp). On the other hand, no differentiation is made here between different types of "leprosy-impurities" (e.g., one resulting from *bāheret* and one resulting from *śəʾēt*; Lev 13:2). Furthermore, while the phrasing "any person with a genital flow … male and female" (כל זב ... מזכר עד נקבה) in vv. 2–3 clearly includes both male and female pathological suppurants (i. e., males and females with an irregular genital flow), does their designation by a single name imply that male and female pathological suppurants are segregated *as one group* outside camp? And is a menstruant (also termed זבה in P, but unlike pathological suppurants—her flow is not "irregular") also included in this group?

Question 5: Finally, a question arises regarding the prohibited impurities in P, e.g., the consumption of the flesh of certain animals (Lev 11:4–8, 26–27, 29), and specifically regarding impurities prohibited for priests. Lev 21:1 requires priests to refrain from contracting corpse-impurity (אמר אל הכהנים בני אהרן ואמרת אלהם לנפש לא יטמא בעמיו), unless the deceased is one of the close relatives listed in vv. 2–3. A reasonable reading of this verse in context is that a priest ought to avoid contact with corpses lest he defile the sancta, but that contact with corpses in and of itself is not the problem—only the impurity that it entails. The logic is stated explicitly in verse 6: "for they offer … the food of their God; therefore, they shall be holy" (כי את ... לחם אלהיהם הם מקריבים והיו קדש). Thus, one may reasonably conclude that if the priest needs to become defiled due to the death of a close relative—for example, in order to bury his father in the family plot,[12] contamination by other corpses when he has already contracted impurity from the first corpse poses no particular additional problem. In short, if a priest is going to bury his father, he might as well, to use a modern analogue, go and recite a psalm at his uncle's grave while he is in the family plot.

Now the analogous question arises regarding the injunction to priests in Leviticus 22:8, "That which died or was torn by wild animals he shall not eat, becoming unclean by it" (נבלה וטרפה לא יאכל לטמאה בה). Recall that in priestly literature (contrary to Deut 14:21 and Exod 22:30) non-priests are permitted to eat such flesh, though it is defiling, and, in all appearances, the only reason priests are to avoid eating such flesh is—as in the case of corpse-defilement—the impurity it entails, as the verse just quoted states explicitly, לטמאה בה ("becoming unclean by it"). So a priest might reasonably ask himself—if I have just touched a dead man, might I not just as well eat a dead cow while I am anyway impure? This reasoning

12 Consider P's narrative *realia* of family plots reflected in P's narrative in Genesis 49:31, where Jacob relates that he buried his wife in the same plot in which his parents and paternal grandparents were buried.

may appear counterintuitive in light of our knowledge of Deuteronomy 14 and Exodus 22 and postbiblical law, but it is formally valid within Priestly literature.

I raise these questions not because I am convinced that the authors of P contemplated each and every one of these thoughts. In fact, there is good reason to assume that several of these scholastic, hairsplitting scenarios were not of particular interest to the Priestly authors. However, there are at least three good reasons for inquiring about P's unstated premises with regard to these questions:

First, it is difficult to imagine that the question of compounded impurities never occurred to the legislators—since exposure to several impurities would be quite common. For example, a woman may give birth to a boy and a girl on the same day (Lev 12:2–4, 5), a menstruant (Lev 15:19–24) may touch a dead rat (Lev 11:31), and soldiers in a war against Midian (Num 31:19–20) are likely to touch more than one corpse in battle.

Second, comparative evidence demonstrates that scenarios involving compoundment are discussed in certain texts historically unrelated to P. Specifically, medieval legal Sanskrit texts—commentaries on the Laws of Manu—offer a nuanced discussion of the problem of compoundment, opening a window to the potential theoretical possibilities that one might expect to find in a ritual system where several sources of *miasma* operate side by side. These texts may serve as checks and balances to our intuitions as to what might be "reasonable" or "entirely unlikely" within P.[13]

Finally, many of the scenarios raised above are explicitly addressed in postbiblical texts responding directly to Leviticus, including the Temple Scroll and 4Q274 (4QTohorot A)—the latter making initial steps towards systematization of the problem of compoundment.[14] Of particular interest are Samaritan texts and

13 *Manusmṛti* ("Laws of Manu") 5.79 (trans. P. Olivelle, *The Law Code of Manu: A New Translation* [Oxford: University Press 2004], 90); *Dharmasūtra of Gautama* 14.1 (P. Olivelle [ed.], *Dharmasūtras: The Law Codes of Āpastamba, Gautama, Baudhāyana, and Vasiṣṭha* [Oxford: University Press, 1999], 101); and in particular the medieval commentaries printed in J. H. Dave, *Manu-Smṛti: With Nine Commentaries by Medhātithi, Sarvajñanārāyaṇa, Kullūka, Rāghavānanda, Nandana, Rāmacandra, Maṇirāma, Govindarāja and Bhāruci, Volume III (Adhyāyas 5–6)* (Bombay: Bharatiya Vidya Bhavan, 1978).

14 See, for example, J. M. Baumgarten, "The Laws about Fluxes in 4QTohora[a] (4Q274)," in D. Dimant/L. Schiffman (ed.), *Time to Prepare the Way in the Wilderness: Papers on the Qumran Scrolls by Fellows of the Institute for Advanced Studies of the Hebrew University, Jerusalem, 1989–1990* (Leiden: Brill, 1995) 1–8; J. Milgrom, "4QTohora[a]: An Unpublished Qumran Text on Purities," in D. Dimant/L. H. Schiffman (ed.), *Time to Prepare the Way in the Wilderness: Papers on Qumran Scrolls* (Leiden: Brill, 1995) 59–68; T. Kazen, "4Q274 Fragment 1 Revisited—or Who Touched Whom? Further Evidence for Ideas of Graded Impurity and Graded Purifications," *Dead Sea Discoveries* 17 (2010) 53–87; H. Birenboim, "Expelling the Unclean from the Cities of Israel and the Uncleanness of Lepers and Men with a Discharge according to 4Q274 1 i," *Dead Sea Discoveries* 19 (2012) 28–54; Y. Furstenberg, *Purity and Community in Antiquity: Traditions of the Law from Second Temple Judaism to the Mishnah* (Jerusalem: Magnes, 2016

Karaite texts that explicitly address the topic of comopundment,[15] and especially the 10th century *Kitāb al-Anwār wal-Marāqib* by Qirqīsānī, which dedicates an entire chapter (10.48) to a systematic exposition of the problem of "one who has already become defiled with severe or light impurity—whether or not it is possible for that person to become defiled with another impurity."[16] A careful examination of these texts may teach us something substantive about P's perception—or possibly a spectrum of conflicting perceptions—of the forces of impurity. Additionally, despite Milgrom's claim that rabbinic literature is resoundingly silent on the matter of compoundment,[17] a careful analysis of early and medieval rabbinic texts reveals that the rabbis often tacitly assumed that compoundment takes place in many cases.

4 Conclusion

This final statement brings us back to our opening point: the need for a new commentary on Leviticus, which takes into account new questions regarding the "science of ritual" underlying to the Priestly writings. In Milgrom's preliminary publication of the Qumranic scroll 4Q274, he noted that not a single one of the cases of compoundment discussed in this Qumranic scroll is addressed in rabbinic literature. Contrasting this scroll's interest in the compoundment of ritual impurity with rabbinic literature' silence in this regard, Milgrom reached a clear verdict about ancient Jewish literature:

> Clearly, at work here is a conception of impurity that is vital and active. Moreover, since Qumran espouses a cosmogonic doctrine akin to dualism—ascribing impurity to the forces of Belial—its concept of impurity is more than dynamic; it is demonic. Perhaps it was mainly this reason that accounts for the absence in rabbinic writings of any consideration of the case of impure persons touching each other. For the rabbis, impurity was solely an inert and powerless state. Qumran's concept, on the other hand, held impurity to be autonomous and dangerous, a concept that for the rabbis bordered on heresy.[18]

[in Hebrew],166–70; and M. Shpiegelman, *Removal of Impure People from the Encampments of the Tabernacle* (M. A. Thesis, Department of Talmud, Bar-Ilan University, Ramat Gan, 2016 [in Hebrew]).

15 See I. R. M. M. Bóid, *Principles of Samaritan Halachah* (Studies in Judaism in Late Antiquity 38; Leiden: Brill, 1989), 287; A. ben Elijah Nikomodeo, *Sefer ha-mitsyot ha-gadol: Gan ʿeden* (Eupatoriya, 1866 [in Hebrew]), 111a col. a infra.

16 L. Nemoy (ed.), *Yaʿqūb ibn Isḥāq Qirqisānī, Kitāb al-Anwār wal-marāqib: Code of Karaite Law* (New York: Alexander Kohut Memorial Foundation, 1939–43), 1058.

17 See Milgrom, "4QTohora[a]" 59, 65–66.

18 Ibid., 66.

Milgrom's observation is correct—rabbinic sources are surprisingly silent about the compoundment of impurity. I hope to treat the problem of this case of rabbinic reticence in detail in the future; but at present, I wish only to draw attention to two correctives to Milgrom's argument. First, rabbinic literature is not as silent as Milgrom suggests. A thorough study will need to take into consideration scores of rabbinic texts that discuss situations in which several different impurities are simultaneously present. The majority of these texts (but not all of them) could actually be used to bolster Milgrom's argument, since even these cases, widely varying rabbinic sources—early and late, Babylonian and Palestinian—are often concerned not with compoundment itself but with *another* aspect of the situation at hand.[19]

Second, and more important, the evidence suggests that rabbinic literature is silent about compoundment *not*, as Milgrom assumed, because of a worldview in which impurities have no real existence and therefore do *not* compound but rather because it is taken for granted that a single person *can* be defiled with two different impurities at the same time.[20]

In other words, if we were to follow Milgrom's logic *ad absurdum*, equating pro-compoundment with "paganism" and anti-compoundment with "anti-paganism" (umbrella terms that need to be avoided or carefully defined), it would turn out that many rabbinic texts are "pagan," whereas Qirqīsānī and the "Laws of Manu" are "anti-pagan." In order to avoid such faulty generalizations, it will be necessary to offer a commentary that reconsiders some of the fundamentals of the "science of ritual" in the Pentateuch, and is at the same time attuned to Second Temple literature, to rabbinic and non-rabbinic medieval commentaries, and to comparative data from more distant contexts, following a path that Milgrom has so brilliantly illuminated for us.

19 See for example m. Nid. 10, 4 (corpse impurity + leprosy); m. Neg. 6:5 and 10:6 (concentric and adjacent leprous affections, respectively); t. Šabb. 1, 7 (male and female pathological suppurants, noted already by Baumgarten, "Laws about Fluxes"); b. Nid. 29b (a parturient who is also a pathological suppuration); b. Nid. 68b (male pathological suppuration + ejaculation) and 69a; b. Ker. 7b–8a (five births and five cases of pathological suppuration, cf. several passages in m. Ker., such as 1:6,7, 2:3, 6:5; and several parallel passages in Chapters 3–4 in Sifra Tazria'); b. Ḥul. 126a (a dead dog in whose bowels is flesh of a human corpse that has not yet decomposed); b. Naz. 64a (*śereṣ* and cadaver, *śereṣ* and semen); b. Menaḥ. 24a,b on becoming "saturated" with impurity); and Sifra Tazria' 12:9 (noted, together with b. Pes. 67a in Baumgarten, ibid., 4–5; J. Baumgarten et al., *Qumran Cave 4. XXV: Halakhic Texts* [DJD 35; Oxford: Clarendon, 1999], 101–2).

20 See, for example, *Sifre Zuta* to Numbers, Ḥuqqat, on Ch. 19 v. 19: והזה הטהור על הטמא: כל הטמאין מקבלין הזייה כגון זבין וזבות נדות ויולדות. b. Zeb. 93a even more laconically states נידה—מזין עליה ("One asperses upon a menstruant").

Bibliography

Baumgarten, J. M., "The Laws about Fluxes in 4QTohora[a] (4Q274)," in D. Dimant/L. Schiffman (ed.), *Time to Prepare the Way in the Wilderness: Papers on the Qumran Scrolls by Fellows of the Institute for Advanced Studies of the Hebrew University, Jerusalem, 1989–1990* (Leiden: Brill, 1995) 1–8.

– et al., *Qumran Cave 4. XXV: Halakhic Texts* (DJD 35; Oxford: Clarendon, 1999).

Birenboim, H., "Expelling the Unclean from the Cities of Israel and the Uncleanness of Lepers and Men with a Discharge according to 4Q274 1 i," *Dead Sea Discoveries* 19 (2012) 28–54.

Bóid, I. R. M. M., *Principles of Samaritan Halachah* (Studies in Judaism in Late Antiquity 38; Leiden: Brill, 1989).

Dave, J. H., *Manu-Smṛti: With Nine Commentaries by Medhātithi, Sarvajñanārāyaṇa, Kullūka, Rāghavānanda, Nandana, Rāmacandra, Maṇirāma, Govindarāja and Bhāruci, Volume III (Adhyāyas 5–6)* (Bombay: Bharatiya Vidya Bhavan, 1978).

Furstenberg, Y., *Purity and Community in Antiquity: Traditions of the Law from Second Temple Judaism to the Mishnah* (Jerusalem: Magnes, 2016 [in Hebrew]).

Harrington, H., *The Impurity Systems of Qumran and the Rabbis: Biblical Foundations* (SBL Dissertation Series 143; Atlanta: Scholars, 1993).

Kazen, T., "4Q274 Fragment 1 Revisited—or Who Touched Whom? Further Evidence for Ideas of Graded Impurity and Graded Purifications," *Dead Sea Discoveries* 17 (2010) 53–87.

Klawans, J., *Impurity and Sin in Ancient Judaism* (Oxford: University Press, 2000).

Kostro, L., *Einstein and the Ether* (Montreal: Apeiron, 2000).

Meshel, N. S., "The Form and Function of a Biblical Blood Ritual," *VT* 63 (2013) 276–89 [reprinted in this volume, pp. 101–114].

–, *The "Grammar" of Sacrifice: A Generativist Study of the Ancient Israelite Sacrificial System in the Priestly Writings, with: A "Grammar" of Σ* (Oxford: Oxford University Press, 2014).

Milgrom, J., *Leviticus 1–16: A New Translation with Introduction and Commentary* (AB 3; New York: Doubleday, 1991).

–, "4QTohora[a]: An Unpublished Qumran Text on Purities," in D. Dimant/L. H. Schiffman (ed.), *Time to Prepare the Way in the Wilderness: Papers on Qumran Scrolls* (Leiden: Brill, 1995) 59–68.

Nemoy, L. (ed.), *Ya'qūb ibn Isḥāq Qirqisānī, Kitāb al-Anwār wal-marāqib: Code of Karaite Law* (New York: Alexander Kohut Memorial Foundation, 1939–43).

Nikomodeo, A. ben Elijah, *Sefer ha-mitsyot ha-gadol: Gan 'eden* (Eupatoriya, 1866 [in Hebrew]).

Olivelle, P. (ed.), *Dharmasūtras: The Law Codes of Āpastamba, Gautama, Baudhāyana, and Vasiṣṭha* (Oxford: University Press, 1999).

–, *The Law Code of Manu: A New Translation* (Oxford: University Press, 2004).

Parker, R., *Miasma: Pollution and Purification in Early Greek Religion* (Oxford: Clarendon Press, 1983).

Regev, E., "Priestly Dynamic Holiness and Deuteronomic Static Holiness," *VT* 51 (2001) 243–61.

Shpiegelman, M., *Removal of Impure People from the Encampments of the Tabernacle* (M. A. Thesis, Department of Talmud, Bar-Ilan University, Ramat Gan, 2016 [in Hebrew]).

Whittaker, E. T., *A History of the Theories of Aether and Electricity* (London et al.: Nelson, 1951).

Wright, D. P., *The Disposal of Impurity, Elimination Rites in the Bible and in Hittite and Mesopotamian Literature* (Atlanta: Scholars Press, 1987).

–, "The Spectrum of Priestly Impurity," in G. Anderson/S. M. Olyan (ed.), *Priesthood and Cult in Ancient Israel* (Sheffield: JSOT Press, 1991) 150–81.

Nicole J. Ruane

Constructing Contagion on Yom Kippur

The Scapegoat as *Ḥaṭṭāʾt*

One of the many enigmatic aspects of the complex of rituals described in Leviticus 16 is that the scapegoat is characterized as a *ḥaṭṭāʾt* offering. In Lev 16:5, among the beginning instructions for the rituals, Aaron is to "take from the congregation of the children of Israel two he-goats for a *ḥaṭṭāʾt*" (שני שעירי עזים לחטאת) and these are "along with one ram for an עלה." The two goats will then have lots cast over them. One will be chosen ליהוה "for the LORD," and will be slaughtered in the usual way of the "burnt" *ḥaṭṭāʾt* rite as described in Lev 4:1–21 (though a goat is not the usual species for this form of offering). The other goat will be לעזאזל, often translated "for Azazel." The priest will confess over this second goat all of the Israelites' wrongdoings (עונת) and their transgressions (פשעיהם) and all of their sins (חטאתם) (16:21). He will put these adverse items on the goat, and send the goat out into the wilderness with a man appointed for the task. Yet it is unclear how these acts with the two goats and, especially the scapegoat, are a *ḥaṭṭāʾt*. Is the scapegoat itself a *ḥaṭṭāʾt* offering? Or does the term apply only to the goat clearly offered in the normal way of the "burnt" *ḥaṭṭāʾt*? Or are the two animals together a *ḥaṭṭāʾt*? If the two goats together are the *ḥaṭṭāʾt*, what makes them so, and how does the term relate to their function and the form of the ritual? Most importantly, is it possible that understanding this aspect of the Yom Kippur ritual can help to explain the general priestly concept of *ḥaṭṭāʾt* offerings and their function overall?[1] In this essay I will argue that the term *ḥaṭṭāʾt* refers to the two

1 For studies of *ḥaṭṭāʾt* offerings, see for example, N. Kiuchi, *The Purification Offering in the Priestly Literature: Its Meaning and Function* (JSOTSup 56; Sheffield: JSOT Press, 1987); J. Milgrom, "The Modus Operandi of the *Hattaʾt*: A Rejoinder," *JBL* 109 (1990) 112–13; J. Milgrom, "Sin Offering or Purification Offering?," *VT* 21 (1971) 237–9; J. Milgrom, "Israel's Sanctuary: The Priestly 'Picture of Dorian Gray,'" *RB* 83 (1976) 390–9; A. I. Baumgarten, "HATTAʾT Sacrifices," *RB* 103 (1996) 337–42; J. Dennis, "The Function of the *ḥaṭṭāʾt* Sacrifice in the Priestly Literature: An Evaluation of the View of Jacob Milgrom," *ETL* 78 (2002) 108–29; A. Marx, "Sacrifice pour les péchés ou rites de passages?: Quelques réflexions sur la fonction du hattaʾt," *RB* 96 (1989) 27–48; A. Schenker, "Interprétations récentes et dimensions spécifique du sacrifice *ḥaṭṭāʾt*," *Biblica* 75 (1994) 59–70; N. H. Snaith, "The Sin Offering and the Guilt Offering," *VT* 15 (1965) 73–80; N. Zohar, "Repentance and Purification: The Significance and Semantics of *ḥaṭṭāʾt* in the Pentateuch," *JBL* 107 (1988) 609–18; J. W. Watts, *Ritual and Rhetoric in Leviticus: From Sacrifice to Scripture* (New York: Cambridge University Press, 2007) 79–96, 130–41; R. Gane, *Cult and Character: Purification Offerings, Day of Atonement, and Theodicy* (Winona Lake: Eisenbrauns,

goats together, and that together they display a fundamental element of all *ḥaṭṭā't* rites: the separation of the offering into two distinct parts, one of which becomes portrayed as sinful or unclean, and the elimination of that negative part.

This question of why the two goats are called a *ḥaṭṭā't* has been answered in different ways. For example, Levine (as well as others), suggests that the reason both are given this term of *ḥaṭṭā't* is simply because it is not yet clear which goat will become the slaughtered *ḥaṭṭā't* offering.[2] In contrast, Jacob Milgrom, in his commentary on Leviticus, gives another possible explanation, which is that the scapegoat ritual is like the rite of the red cow in Numbers 19 (which is also called a *ḥaṭṭā't* 19:9, 17), and both of them are non-Israelite, pagan, pre-existing rituals that are not genuine to the priestly schema of offerings.[3] According to Milgrom, these rituals were popular among the people and so, wanting to retain them in some way, the priests termed these unusual rites "*ḥaṭṭā'ôt*" in order to incorporate them into the priestly ritual system. I find the concept that unusual rituals are not genuinely or originally "Israelite" to be highly problematic for several reasons, the most important of which is that this explanation does not respect P's own terminology. Moreover, it assumes that Leviticus includes some "genuine" rituals and some that are not "genuine," and that we can decide which is which.[4] Yet the text clearly applies this label of *ḥaṭṭā't* to these unusual rites just as it does to the more usual rites in Lev 4–6, and it treats them all as important rituals. If we take this designation seriously, and use it to understand the nature of both regular and unusual *ḥaṭṭā'ôt* it may be that the rite of the scapegoat (as well as the red cow) are most instructive about the purpose and nature of *ḥaṭṭā't* offerings. Considering the similarities of form and function among all of these rituals may make clearer what the priestly writers meant by the term *ḥaṭṭā't*.

1 The Scapegoat as *Ḥaṭṭā't*?

In what sense, then, do the scapegoat, or the scapegoat and the other goat together, have the form and function of a *ḥaṭṭā't*? It seems possible that the scapegoat on its own has the function, but not the form, of a *ḥaṭṭā't*. Naphtali Meshel has recently

---

2005); J. Sklar, *Sin, Impurity, Sacrifice, Atonement: The Priestly Conceptions* (Sheffield: Sheffield Phoenix, 2005); Gilders, *Blood Ritual in the Hebrew Bible* (Baltimore: Johns Hopkins University Press, 2004) 109–41.

2 B.A. Levine, *Leviticus* (JPSTC; Philadelphia: Jewish Publication Society, 1989) 101.

3 J. Milgrom, "The Paradox of the Red Cow (Num XIX)," *VT* 31 (1981) 62–72; J. Milgrom, *Leviticus 1-16* (AB 3; New York: Doubleday, 1991), 1018.

4 In "The Paradox of the Red Cow," and his commentary (*Leviticus 1-16*, 1018, 121) Milgrom makes a similar argument when he states definitively that the scapegoat, like the red cow, is not a sacrifice or offering. This position similarly imposes an external label and a foreign schema—"sacrifice"—onto the ritual, in an attempt to make it conform to his own concept of what a "sacrifice" should be.

argued that terms for sacrificial rituals can work on two different levels: one is the "praxemic" level, which addresses the formal ways in which a specifically labelled ritual is actually practiced.[5] For example, on the "praxemic" level, an עלה offering is a male animal, which is almost completely burned on the altar, with specific blood rites, whose meat would not be eaten, and so on, as described in Lev 1 and 6:1–6 [Eng 6:8–13]. Or it can be a bird whose blood undergoes particular rites and is not eaten (Lev 1:14–17). The second level is that of function, which is harder to define, but which implies that offerings of one practical type can work with the purpose and function of a different type. For example, an עלה in practice can be a part of a *ḥaṭṭāʾt* offering in purpose, as in Lev 5:7–10. There, a person who needs to bring a sheep or goat as a *ḥaṭṭāʾt* offering to remedy impurity or sin can instead offer two birds, one as an עלה and one as a *ḥaṭṭāʾt*, and these two together function as a *ḥaṭṭāʾt* even though they have different practical forms.[6]

It seems possible that the scapegoat ritual on its own does not have the "praxemic" form of a *ḥaṭṭāʾt*. Indeed, it seems most likely that the statement of the scapegoat being "לעזאזל" does not refer to an otherwise unheard of deity named "Azazel." Rather, following the LXX, the Vulgate, and several scholars including Douglas, the term "עזאזל" is mostly likely the name of a particular ritual form or function, which in English is traditionally something like "the goat that goes away" thus "scapegoat."[7] To me the most persuasive argument for this position is the analogy of "Azazel" with "Molech." In 1935 Otto Eissfeldt argued, rather conclusively, that the term "מלך" does not refer to some unknown deity of child sacrifice but is the direct cognate of the Punic term *molk*, which clearly refers to an offering in the established ritual form of a burnt child or animal, as famously found in the "tophet" at Carthage and other Punic sites.[8] A child is not given

5 N.S. Meshel, *The "Grammar" of Sacrifice: A Generativist Study of the Israelite Sacrificial System in the Priestly Writings* (New York: Oxford University Press, 2014) 130–70.

6 See similarly the substitution of two birds for a ewe in the *ḥaṭṭāʾt* rite of cleansing for skin disease in Lev 14:10, 21, 22.

7 M. Douglas, "The Go-Away Goat," in R. Rendtorff/R.A. Kugler (ed.), *The Book of Leviticus: Composition and Reception* (Leiden: Brill, 2003), especially 126–7. Douglas makes the excellent point that there is no other deity in the Hebrew Bible to whom an offering should be made, and that the very next chapter, 17:7 explicitly prohibits making offerings to goat deities in the wilderness. The meaning of the term "Azazel" has been debated since antiquity. This translation assumes it derives from the phrase עז אזל (from the words עז "goat" and אזל "to go away"). I do not feel certain of that etymology, thought as indicated, to me it seems likely that the name is related to its action. The LXX translates it as τω αποπομπαιω ("the one who carries away evil") like the Vulgate's *caper emissarius*, both of which describe the purpose of the goat. Compare also the use of *lamed* in 16:3, 5 to determine the kind of offering it an animal will be used for.

8 O. Eissfeldt, *Molk als Opferbegriff im Punischen und Hebräischen und das Ende des Gottes Moloch* (Halle: Max Niemeyer, 1935).

"to Moloch," but rather, "as" or "for a *molek* offering" (למלך).[9] The evidence for a cognate ritual term for עזאזל is scant. It is beyond the scope of this essay to survey the many possibilities for its etymology.[10] But in any case, it seems more likely that this unusual ritual has an unusual name, rather than that there is some strange but apparently powerful deity who is only known in this unusual circumstance. Moreover, Leviticus is a book largely about ritual terminology; it is a logical place to find additions to the lexicon of ritual terms and descriptions.

It is thus possible that the scapegoat ritual on its own does not have the "praxemic" form of a *ḥaṭṭāʾt*—and instead has one of an "עזאזל"—but it does have the function of a *ḥaṭṭāʾt*. Indeed, its purpose is quite clearly stated in verse 10, as "to make atonement" (לכפר), which is the specific, main function of *ḥaṭṭāʾt* rites according to Lev 4:26, 31, 35; 5:6; 16:6, etc. Therefore, the writer may use this sense of the term *ḥaṭṭāʾt* in verse 5. Milgrom also says that in verse 5 the scapegoat is called a *ḥaṭṭāʾt* for what he says is its "philological meaning 'that which removes sin'" which he says, precisely defines its function.[11] Similarly, Roy Gane suggests that the term *ḥaṭṭāʾt* in verse 5 should not be understood necessarily to mean a "sacrifice" but rather is a term meaning "purification ritual."[12] Yet, if I understand him correctly, he feels that translation is only the case here in verse 5 and not that the term *ḥaṭṭāʾt* should be understood in this broader way in every circumstance. In any event, these scholars illustrate that the definition of the term cannot be limited just to the form of offerings discussed in Lev 4 and 5.

Therefore, one possibility for the language in verse 5 is that the scapegoat is a *ḥaṭṭāʾt* in this purpose and function alone. However, the text seems to imply that the two goats together are the *ḥaṭṭāʾt*. And just as it is possible for two birds to function as one *ḥaṭṭāʾt*, even though they have two different ritual forms,[13] so the two goats of the Yom Kippur *ḥaṭṭāʾt* may have the overall purpose and form of a *ḥaṭṭāʾt*, but individually one has the "praxemic" form of a "burnt" *ḥaṭṭāʾt* while the other has the "praxemic" form of an "עזאזל," whatever that specifically entails.

9 Lev 18:21, 20:2–5. Compare the use of ל here to 16:3, 5, 8, 11, though the pointing of למלך is a matter of debate and a point of criticism against Eissfeldt's argument.—See also the contribution by T. Hieke, "The Prohibition of Transferring an Offspring to 'the Molech,'" in this volume, pp. 171–199.

10 The literature is too extensive to list here. For entrees to the possible meanings of the term, see the commentaries, D. P. Wright, "Azazel," *ABD* I (New York: Doubleday, 1992) 536–7, and Aron Pinker's article "A Goat to Go to Azazel" (in *JHS* 7/8 [2007]). Pinker summarizes the options for its meaning and suggests that solutions fall into four types: "name of a supernatural entity," "name or description of a place," "abstract noun," "description of the dispatched goat" as well as other miscellaneous options.

11 *Leviticus 1–16*, 1018.

12 *Cult and Character*, 258–60.

13 I.e. one with the form of a *ḥaṭṭāʾt* and the other having the form of an עלה in Lev 5:7–10.

2 Features of *Ḥaṭṭāʾt* Rituals

It should be said, however, that the exact means by which the goat "makes atonement" is not entirely clear. The syntax of verse 10's phrase לכפר עליו is problematic since כפר rites are usually done with blood, and an animal is not otherwise the object of the phrase כפר על, so that it is unclear whether "atonement" is made for the goat, or on the goat for someone else, and how it is done. Moreover, it is also not clear how the particular ritual of the scapegoat fits in with the rest of the complex of rites in Lev 16, whose overall function is to "make atonement" (16:16, 20, 33, 34). Granted, the purpose of the goat is to carry away the negativity that has been put onto it, but how specifically does that happen? And how would the rest of the rituals work without the scapegoat? For example, is it possible that although the scapegoat has had wrongdoings (עונת) and transgressions (פשעים) and sins (חטאות) put on its head, it only actually carries away wrongdoings (עונת) as stated literally in verse 22, while the transgressions and sins are expunged through the other rituals? This suggestion seems unlikely, but it highlights the problem of the specificity of the scapegoat rite.

The lack of clarity about the precise mechanism by which the scapegoat "atones" is indicative of the general imprecision of *ḥaṭṭāʾt* rites in general. Even in their most basic forms, *ḥaṭṭāʾt* rites' mechanisms of action are unclear and extremely difficult to understand. Many aspects of their operation are highly debated. For example, as James Watts asks about *ḥaṭṭāʾt* rites in *Ritual and Rhetoric in Leviticus*:

> [I]s it a 'separation offering' to put distance between the sinner and pollution (Marx) or an 'empowerment ritual' to restore the status of person or altar (Baumgarten)? And is it the sanctuary that is purified (Milgrom) or the worshipper (Marx, Gane) or both (Kiuchi, Schwartz)?[14]

To continue this line of questioning, we can also ask how impurities are transferred to the animal: Do sins and impurities enter the victim when offerers put their hands on the victim's head (Zohar)? Or does the carcass absorb the impurity that the blood has cleansed (Milgrom)? If so, how, and when? Is it because the blood, which is part of the body, has absorbed the impurity and in a "*pars pro toto*" manner also infects the carcass (Milgrom)? What if the blood has not yet touched

14 Watts, *Ritual and Rhetoric,* 80–1, and see the other issues and sources he raises there. Sources he mentions are: A. Marx, "Sacrifice pour les péchés ou rites de levée de sanction," *ZAW* 100 (1988) 183–98; Baumgarten, "HATTAʾT Sacrifices," 337–42; Gane, *Cult and Character*; Kiuchi, *Purification Offering*; Milgrom, *Leviticus 1–16*; B.J. Schwartz, "The Bearing of Sin in Priestly Literature" in D.P. Wright/D.N. Freedman/A. Hurvitz (ed.), *Pomegranates and Golden Bells: Studies in Biblical, Jewish, and Near Eastern Ritual, Law and Literature in Honor of Jacob Milgrom* (Winona Lake: Eisenbrauns, 1995) 3–21.

the impurity? Does it work "prospectively" for its future purpose (Wright)?[15] Does the blood absorb the impurities from the sanctuary (Milgrom)? Or does it actually bring impurity into the sanctuary instead of removing it from there (Zohar)?

While progress continues to be made in understanding these details, indeed often by scholars in this volume, I fear that these questions may never be fully answered. The texts are too opaque. Even the most recent detailed and exhaustive study of *ḥaṭṭāʾôt* takes positions that it cannot prove definitively.[16] Given these difficulties, it seems questionable whether the priests or priestly writers themselves engaged in this kind of explication of their rituals. Obviously, they had an understanding of what they were doing or describing, but they might not have worried about these specifics of mechanics and fact as we do. One might expect that if they had they would be more forthcoming in their explanations and the details of their rites. Moreover, I dare say that many biblical scholars who work on priestly texts have been reluctant to fully consider the concept articulated long ago by Frits Staal, that rituals do not have single meanings, and by extension lack certain kinds of logic and precision.[17]

Since this kind of detailed debate about the workings of *ḥaṭṭāʾt* rites may have reached something of an impasse, it might be helpful to step back, away from these particulars, and look at *ḥaṭṭāʾt* rituals in an objective, broad light, outside of the rhetoric of the text. In an attempt both to understand the nature of *ḥaṭṭāʾt* rites in general, and to explain how it might be possible for the scapegoat and the burnt *ḥaṭṭāʾt* goat to together be one *ḥaṭṭāʾt*, I want to articulate a specific element of all *ḥaṭṭāʾt* rituals. It may be overly obvious, but I think it is worth stating clearly, that rites which are given the label "*ḥaṭṭāʾt*," be they the scapegoat, the "burnt" and "eaten" *ḥaṭṭāʾôt* or the ritual of the red cow in Numbers 19, all have a common feature: unlike almost all other forms of priestly rituals, they make divisions of the material at hand into two main portions and then treat one of the two as dangerous and negative.[18] In addition, and also obviously, all *ḥaṭṭāʾt* rituals generally remedy things or situations that are characterized as negative and

---

15 D.P. Wright, *The Disposal of Impurity: Elimination Rites in the Bible and in Hittite and Mesopotamian Literature* (SBLDS 101; Atlanta: Scholars Press, 1987) 129–35.

16 Y. Feder, *Blood Expiation in Hittite and Biblical Ritual: Origins, Context, and Meaning* (Atlanta: SBL Press, 2011).

17 "The Meaninglessness of Ritual," *Numen* 26 (1979) 2–22.

18 The ritual in Leviticus 14 to restore the purity of people and houses contaminated with disease is similar. This rite is not termed a *ḥaṭṭāʾt* but has a great deal in common with both the scapegoat and the red cow *ḥaṭṭāʾt* rites; indeed, it is said to fulfill the *ḥaṭṭāʾt*'s function of כפר (14:53). The priest orders two live birds, has one of the birds slaughtered, then he mixes its blood with ritual materials, dips the living bird into the blood mixture and sprinkles the recovered person seven times with the mixture. Then he releases the bird to fly away into the countryside (Lev 14:4–7, 53). Here again two parts are created, the first is destroyed and its blood is exposed for ritual use, while the other, which would take on negativity, is expelled.

dangerous—be they impurities, sins, transgressions, or otherwise. In response to a negative event they ritually construct a part, a character, or an object that also is negative or dangerous, that might appear unclean, or at least relatively so. The rituals culminate in the elimination of the negative part, be it though burning, washing, or expulsion. The result of this successful creation and destruction of the negative element is atonement.

To be clear, what I am calling "constructing" impurity or sin is what priestly texts explain as exposing or recognizing it. I am arguing that what priests do on Yom Kippur and in other *ḥaṭṭāʾt* rites is materially create "sin" and then destroy it. This is a highly simplistic statement; however, it is one that takes an objective viewpoint and that also assumes impurity or sin does not exist except insofar as one defines it. Performing *ḥaṭṭāʾt* rituals and other rites of purification and atonement creates and materially actualizes a particular worldview. It defines what is positive and negative, what belongs and what does not, who has the power to make these determinations, and who can benefit from them. Approaching *ḥaṭṭāʾt* rites from this perspective takes seriously the prospect that rituals do not have meanings, or at least do not have single finite meanings. This is a departure from the more common approaches to *ḥaṭṭāʾt* rites (including my own!) which have often attempted to nail down the exact purpose of each and every ritual act, when in fact these acts might not have distinct meanings at all. Priests might not have focused on the logic of the mechanisms by which sin adheres to a sacrificial victim, or how exactly impurity becomes manifest in the sanctuary, but rather they centered on explaining that certain people or things or behaviors are potentially harmful and dangerous and that the priest has the means to decide what they are and what should be done about them. The concept and ritual complex of the *ḥaṭṭāʾt* do have a particular function, however, which is to define certain things as negative, to show how they can be controlled, and to destroy them, thereby giving the sense that they have temporarily been overcome, i.e. that atonement has been achieved.

3 *Ḥaṭṭāʾt* Rites as Separation, Definition, Valuation and Destruction

Again, what is most vital for *ḥaṭṭāʾt* procedure is the separating out of a negative, dangerous or rejected part of its victim(s). For example, the burnt *ḥaṭṭāʾt*, which is offered by the priest or the whole congregation, includes separating out an animal into specific body parts, defining some of these parts (i.e. the blood and fat), which are placed on the altar, as holy, and defining others (i.e. the skin, dung, head, legs, and flesh), which are burned outside the camp, as inferior and negative (Lev 4:1–21, 6:23 [30]). These negative pieces become so defined by the use of space—they are burned in a place (outside the camp) that is diametrically opposed to the altar, and which is the site of disposal for the detritus of other offerings (4:11–12). They cannot be eaten or used. And they must be burned there in a "secular" burning (שרף) juxtaposed to the sacred "turning to smoke" (הקטיר) on the altar. If the altar is the locus of the holy, and thus the good and the perfect, then what becomes juxtaposed to it spatially appears to be its opposite. In comparison, the rites for the עלה, the שלמים and the מנחה do not create this sort of negative, inverted characterization of any part of their offerings.

The dynamic of creating a negative part also appears in the rite of the "eaten" *ḥaṭṭāʾt* (Lev 4:22–35; 6:18–22 [24–29]), though the nature of the expelled element is less clear. In the eaten *ḥaṭṭāʾt*, the victim's body is also divided into two distinct elements, the first being the parts that are burned on the altar and the blood that is poured out at its base. But the second and negative element, the meat of the carcass, is not sent outside the camp and burned; it is eaten by priests, in a specific way. Unlike the description of any other offering that priests eat, the text stresses that this meat is dangerous and needs to be handled with great care. 6:20–21 [27–28] states:

> Whatever touches its flesh will become holy, and when its blood is sprinkled on a garment, you will wash it off in a holy place. Any clay vessel in which you cook it will be broken, but if it is cooked in a metal vessel, it will be washed and rinsed.

Although the priests can eat other offerings, the flesh and blood of the "eaten" *ḥaṭṭāʾt* require specific rules that give the impression it is not only dangerous but contagious. Moreover, although eating the *ḥaṭṭāʾt* meat is a prerogative of priestly service, it is also a requirement, which seems like eating it is a form of disposal. According to the story of Nadab and Abihu (Lev 10), priests must eat the *ḥaṭṭāʾt* meat "to bear the guilt of the community to atone for them before Yahweh" (10:17). The status of the *ḥaṭṭāʾt* meat is extremely unclear and the meaning of its special treatment is hotly debated (i.e. is it clean, is it holy, does it defile, does it make people holy, are the priests absolutely required to eat it, and in what way is their eating it comparable to burning the meat of the burnt *ḥaṭṭāʾt* outside the camp?). However, the law and the ritual clearly characterize it as special, dangerous and contagious. No other ritual food requires washing, scouring, and the destruction of its cooking vessel. The law also indicates that the meat should be eliminated by being eaten in a specific way, and by washing or destroying any parts of it that remain.

As rites that create and define a negative element that is eliminated, *ḥaṭṭāʾôt* correspond to what they remedy, namely, sins and impurities. I have argued elsewhere that one of the most fundamental ways of creating impurity is by making separations.[19] To say, for instance, that one kind of animal is pure while

19 N.J. Ruane, *Sacrifice and Gender in Biblical Law* (New York: Cambridge University Press, 2013), chapter 5.

another kind is impure is to separate species and to define and characterize each differently. Similarly, to say that one kind of skin eruption is clean but another is impure is not only to separate them, but to give each definition as well as relative value. As just discussed, separation is also crucial to the process of creating the negative elements or "sacred impurities" in *ḥaṭṭāʾôt* and other purification rites, such as the *ḥaṭṭāʾt* meat that must be burned outside of the camp. Therefore, the whole priestly discourse of impurity is one of separation, definition, characterization and valuation. Rituals that make separations reflect the separations inherent in what they remedy. In fact, *ḥaṭṭāʾôt* and other rituals of elimination are fundamental to the construction and definition of impurities, which is why most descriptions of impurity include its ritual remedies. The impurity is created by the ritual itself and so the remedy is part of its definition. Indeed, texts about impurity almost never state reasons why something is impure, or sinful; they only show how it can be overcome. For example, Lev 12, which discusses the impurity of childbirth, never explains why a new mother is impure; it only states that she is, and it details the rituals she needs to follow in order to overcome her impure state and re-enter the community. The ritual instructions highlight her separation for 40 or 80 days, indicate that in that state she is ritually excluded, but then they give her the means to overcome that characterization. Apart from these rituals of separation, exclusion and expiation, it is hard to say how she is defined as impure; the rituals define her as such.

4 Two Goats as a *Ḥaṭṭāʾt*

In the Yom Kippur rites, the two goats together have the form of a *ḥaṭṭāʾt* when they are presented together and then separated and divided.[20] They appear as one, but the process of casting lots, giving the goats alternate fates, and placing them in different locations, begins the process of division necessary for creating materi als that actualize impurity. The process of separating and defining then continues through the regular *ḥaṭṭāʾt* protocol as the goat that is "for the LORD" becomes the burnt *ḥaṭṭāʾt* which itself becomes divided again, into the fat and blood, which stay on the altar, and the meat, which is taken outside the camp and burned. The extra layer of ritual complexity in casting lots over the goats adds to the gravity and authority of the larger Yom Kippur ritual and articulates a more extensive experience of sin and impurity, and their removal, than more common *ḥaṭṭāʾt* rites. The scapegoat is a part of the process of relative separation and definition as

20 On this idea of the separation of the goats being a part of the rite, see also Douglas, "The Go-Away Goat," 129; on the two as one *ḥaṭṭāʾt*, though from a different perspective, see Kiuchi, *Purification Offering*, 149.

it becomes designated as לעזאזל and then is transformed from a potentially sacred offering into an entity laden with all bad things, which then must be eliminated.

But the logistics of how the goat becomes filled with sin lie not in the metaphysical mechanics of transferring sins. Rather, the goat's separation and elimination, as well as the bathing required by the one who drives it out (16:26), enact its characterization as filled with sins and transgressions. In other words, objectively speaking, one cannot say that the goat takes on the sins of the people, which are then eliminated from the community; rather, the goat becomes negatively characterized as the priest confesses the sins and transgressions while his hands are on it, and then he enacts the goat's negativity, as well as the resolution of that negativity, as he (and the man) drives it out. The performance of the ritual has both constructed a physical manifestation of the negative (sinful and impure) and has created its own ability to overcome it, which it understands as "making atonement" (כפר). This does not mean that the rite is not efficacious, but it is efficacious insofar as the reality the ritual creates is persuasive and fulfilling to those encountering it.

Similarly, the red cow ritual (Num 19), which is also called a *ḥaṭṭāʾt*, works as both an articulation of the negative and a means of relieving it. This complicated ritual produces a remedy for death impurity.[21] In it, a perfectly red cow is brought outside the camp, possibly where the apparently excluded parts of the burnt *ḥaṭṭāʾt* are burnt. There it is almost entirely burnt, save for some of its blood, which is sprinkled in the direction of the sanctuary. The rest of its blood is then burnt along with its skin, dung and all other parts. The ritual creates something that is impure, or at least something that resembles the impure, because it takes place at a site of disposal, and because those who are involved in burning the ashes and collecting them for aspersion become impure. Thus again, ritual creates its own impurity, but here the impurity becomes capable of defining and valuing what is negative, since it will be applied to those who have come into contact with death. As long as a person has death impurity—for seven days—he or she wears the ashes. So the ashes quite clearly articulate and show impurity, both their own and that of the wearer. At the end of the seven days the wearer washes off the ashes and simultaneously becomes rid of impurity. The rite of the red cow has always been a conundrum because its logic is elusive. Yet despite its illogic, its power lies in the fact that for a community it presented a credible worldview that understood death as negative and harmful and yet offered a means of controlling that harm. Moreover, like the scapegoat, scholars have wanted to say it is neither a sacrifice nor Israelite. Yet if we consider that it works as a *ḥaṭṭāʾt* by making divisions, articulating a negative part, and creating its own means of eliminating that negativity, perhaps we can see how it, like the two parts of the scapegoat, is a clear form of the *ḥaṭṭāʾt* system in priestly ritual.

---

21 For a more comprehensive discussion, see my *Sacrifice and Gender*, chapter 4.

So to conclude, while we cannot know exactly all of the mechanisms by which *ḥaṭṭā ʾt* rituals were thought to work, it is possible that in fact the people who created those rituals did not know all these details themselves and did not always have a clear rationale for each of their acts. What we can say, clearly and objectively, though also roughly, is that *ḥaṭṭā ʾôt* involved separation and the creation of a negative, dangerous part that can then be eliminated—be it through killing, eating, burning, washing or driving out. The ability to achieve this creation and destruction is atonement, which stabilizes the community's sense of wellbeing.

In this aspect of function and form, we can say, as in Lev 16:5, that the two goats are a *ḥaṭṭā ʾt*. They begin together as one, but then the two are separated and embody the division, and then partial negative characterization, of all *ḥaṭṭā ʾôt* as the scapegoat becomes the carrier of sin while the other goat become a sacrificial and holy offering. The goat "for YHWH" becomes a "burnt" *ḥaṭṭā ʾt*, which on its own then further enacts the process of separation and characterization necessary for atonement as its blood and fat stay on the altar but the meat and hide and dung are expelled from the community. The scapegoat itself fulfills the purpose of atonement, and thus the function of a *ḥaṭṭā ʾt*, as it eliminates sin, though its "praxemic" form, on its own, is that of an עזאזל.

Bibliography

Baumgarten, A. I., "HATTA ʾT Sacrifices," *RB* 103 (1996) 337–42.

Dennis, J., "The Function of the *ḥaṭṭā ʾt* Sacrifice in the Priestly Literature: An Evaluation of the View of Jacob Milgrom," *ETL* 78 (2002) 108–29.

Douglas, M., "The Go-Away Goat," in R. Rendtorff/R. A. Kugler (ed.), *The Book of Leviticus: Composition and Reception* (Leiden: Brill, 2003), 121–41.

Eissfeldt, O., *Molk als Opferbegriff im Punischen und Hebräischen und das Ende des Gottes Moloch* (Halle: Max Niemeyer, 1935).

Feder, Y., *Blood Expiation in Hittite and Biblical Ritual: Origins, Context, and Meaning* (Atlanta: SBL Press, 2011).

Gane, R., *Cult and Character: Purification Offerings, Day of Atonement, and Theodicy* (Winona Lake: Eisenbrauns, 2005).

Gilders, W. K., *Blood Ritual in the Hebrew Bible* (Baltimore: Johns Hopkins University Press, 2004).

Kiuchi, N., *The Purification Offering in the Priestly Literature: Its Meaning and Function* (JSOTSup 56; Sheffield: JSOT Press, 1987).

Levine, B. A., *Leviticus* (JPSTC; Philadelphia: Jewish Publication Society, 1989).

Marx, A., "Sacrifice pour les péchés ou rites de levée de sanction," *ZAW* 100 (1988) 183–98.

Marx, A., "Sacrifice pour les péchés ou rites de passages?: Quelques réflexions sur la fonction du hatta ʾt," *RB* 96 (1989) 27–48.

Meshel, N. S., *The "Grammar" of Sacrifice: A Generativist Study of the Israelite Sacrificial System in the Priestly Writings* (New York: Oxford University Press, 2014).

Milgrom, J., "Sin Offering or Purification Offering?," *VT* 21 (1971) 237–9.

Milgrom, J., "Israel's Sanctuary: The Priestly 'Picture of Dorian Gray,'" *RB* 83 (1976) 390–9.

Milgrom, J., "The Paradox of the Red Cow (Num XIX)," *VT* 31 (1981) 62–72.

Milgrom, J., "The Modus Operandi of the *Hatta ʾt*: A Rejoinder," *JBL* 109 (1990) 112–13.

Milgrom, J., *Leviticus 1–16* (AB 3; New York: Doubleday, 1991).
Pinker, A., "A Goat to Go to Azazel," *JHS* 7/8 (2007) (http://www.jhsonline.org/Articles/article_69.pdf doi:10.5508/jhs.2007.v7.a8).
Ruane, N. J., *Sacrifice and Gender in Biblical Law* (New York: Cambridge University Press, 2013).
Schenker, A., "Interprétations récentes et dimensions spécifique du sacrifice *ḥaṭṭāʾt*," *Biblica* 75 (1994) 59–70.
Schwartz, B. J., "The Bearing of Sin in Priestly Literature" in D. P. Wright/D. N. Freedman/A. Hurvitz (ed.), *Pomegranates and Golden Bells: Studies in Biblical, Jewish, and Near Eastern Ritual, Law and Literature in Honor of Jacob Milgrom* (Winona Lake: Eisenbrauns, 1995) 3–21.
Sklar, J., *Sin, Impurity, Sacrifice, Atonement: The Priestly Conceptions* (Sheffield: Sheffield Phoenix, 2005).
Snaith, N. H., "The Sin Offering and the Guilt Offering," *VT* 15 (1965) 73–80.
Staal, F., "The Meaninglessness of Ritual," *Numen* 26 (1979) 2–22.
Watts, J. W., *Ritual and Rhetoric in Leviticus: From Sacrifice to Scripture* (New York: Cambridge University Press, 2007).
Wright, D. P., "Azazel," *ABD* I (New York: Doubleday, 1992) 536–7.
Wright, D. P., *The Disposal of Impurity: Elimination Rites in the Bible and in Hittite and Mesopotamian Literature* (SBLDS 101; Atlanta: Scholars Press, 1987) 129–35.
Zohar, N., "Repentance and Purification: The Significance and Semantics of *ḥaṭṭāʾt* in the Pentateuch," *JBL* 107 (1988) 609–18.

Thomas Hieke

Participation and Abstraction in the Yom Kippur Ritual According to Leviticus 16

1 Introduction

Yom Kippur, the Day of Atonement,[1] is widely observed as a Holy Day among Jewish people all over the world. Although it goes back to the description of the ritual in Leviticus 16, the actual celebration of the day differs widely from the biblical text. A long and intensive process of abstraction took place over centuries. The issue of abstraction lies at the roots of the ritual itself; abstraction already occurred at the time when the ritual was actually carried out at the Second Temple in Jerusalem (before 70 CE). Yet the inner logic and concern of Yom Kippur was central for the composers of the book of Leviticus and the Torah: They placed the description within the center of the Torah.[2] The following essay demonstrates that the central position of Leviticus 16 (the Day of Atonement) is also justified and corroborated by content related aspects. In Leviticus 16, all parts of the people of Israel participate (the High Priest, the priests, the Israelites), all sorts of sins and impurities are eliminated, and the ritual itself shows the highest degree of abstraction (a minimal amount of blood in an empty room suffices for the efficacy of the ritual).

Methodologically, an exegetical commentary has to explore the inner logics of the text and to detect its semantic concepts. In this sense, Leviticus 16 represents a comprehensive reset of cultic and social relationships; the concept includes purification as well as reconciliation (or atonement), collectively and individually. By means of abstraction, the ritual itself turns into a metaphor, even at the time when it still actually took place in Jerusalem. Jews all over the diaspora abstained from food consumption and thus participated spiritually in the ritual of the Holy Day.

---

1 On the history of research on the concept and the term "atonement" see, e.g., C. A. Eberhart, "Introduction: Constituents and Critique of Sacrifice, Cult, and Atonement in Early Judaism and Christianity," in H. L. Wiley/C. A. Eberhart (ed.), *Sacrifice, Cult, and Atonement in Early Judaism and Christianity. Constituents and Critique* (Resources for Biblical Study 85; Atlanta: SBL Press, 2017) 1–29, on pp. 12–24.

2 See, e.g., C. A. Eberhart, "To Atone or Not to Atone: Remarks on the Day of Atonement Rituals according to Leviticus 16 and the Meaning of Atonement," in H. L. Wiley/C. A. Eberhart (ed.), *Sacrifice, Cult, and Atonement in Early Judaism and Christianity. Constituents and Critique* (Resources for Biblical Study 85; Atlanta: SBL Press, 2017) 197–231, on p. 198.

These concepts constitute the basis and starting point for multiple transformations and further abstractions as well as metaphorical charging in Judaism (the liturgy in the synagogue, fasting, rest from working) and Christianity (Rom 3:25: Christ as *hilasterion*—expiation or place of atonement, etc.).

2 Formal and Semantic Abstraction

What is the center of the Torah? The answer is easy: Leviticus 11:42,

> Whatever moves on its *belly*, and whatever moves on all fours, or whatever has many feet, all the creatures that swarm upon the earth, you shall not eat; for they are detestable.

The medieval scribes marked the letter *waw* in the Hebrew word *gāḥōn*, "belly," by using a larger script. Here, they found out, is the middle of the Torah—according to a painstaking calculation of its entire letters. This feature shows the meticulous care the scribes applied when they produced manuscripts of the Hebrew Bible or the Torah,[3] and it marks a certain way of *formal* abstraction to deal with the text.

However, an exegetical commentary on a biblical book has a different task and pursues some kind of *semantic* abstraction. A commentary explores the inner logic of the text and interprets its semantic concepts. Asking for the center of the Torah in this sense, the book of Leviticus with Leviticus 16 (the Day of Atonement) as the center of its theology is probably the best candidate. Various scholars (e.g., Rolf Rendtorff and Erich Zenger) have already pointed this out.[4] This essay will add some more reasons that the central position of Leviticus 16 within the book of Leviticus also stands for a semantic and theological center. This assumption is justified and corroborated by conceptual reasons regarding textual logic: In Leviticus 16, all constituents of the people of Israel participate, all sorts of sins and impurities are eliminated, and the ritual itself shows the highest degree of abstraction. From here, the ritual turns into a metaphor and

3 See W.G. Plaut (ed.), *Die Tora in jüdischer Auslegung. Band III: Wajikra/Levitikus*, ed. B.J. Bamberger; Übersetzung, Bearbeitung und Gestaltung von A. Böckler (Gütersloh: Gütersloher Verlagshaus, 2001), 110.

4 See R. Rendtorff, "Leviticus 16 als Mitte der Tora," *BibInt* 11 (2003); E. Zenger, "Das Buch Levitikus als Teiltext der Tora/des Pentateuch. Eine synchrone Lektüre mit kanonischer Perspektive," in H.-J. Fabry/H.-W. Jüngling (ed.), *Levitikus als Buch* (BBB 119; Berlin et al.: Philo, 1999) 47–83, on pp. 76–80; B. Janowski, "Das Geschenk der Versöhnung. Leviticus 16 als Schlussstein der priesterlichen Kulttheologie," in T. Hieke/T. Nicklas (ed.), *The Day of Atonement. Its Interpretations in Early Jewish and Christian Traditions* (Themes in Biblical Narrative 15; Leiden/Boston: Brill, 2012) 189–209, on p. 6. See also J.W. Watts, *Leviticus 1–10* (HCOT; Leuven: Peeters, 2013), 19–20: Leviticus 11–16 as the third of five parts with emphasis on Leviticus 16.

becomes the starting point of multiple transformations, further abstractions and metaphorical charging in Judaism and Christianity.

3 Participation of All Parts of the People of Israel

The rituals regarding the sacrifices in Leviticus 1–7 refer to a limited number of participants: the person bringing the animal or semolina to be sacrificed, the family or group celebrating the well-being offering, the priests carrying out the tasks that refer to the altar. The inauguration of the cult in Leviticus 8–10 mainly concerns "Aaron and his sons," the priests. The Israelites only receive the blessing, and when they see the divine fire consuming the burnt offering and the fat of the sin offering and well-being offering on the altar, they shout and fall on their faces (Lev 9:22–24). This accompanying reaction took place only once at the inauguration of the ritual. It is not an integral part of the ritual, and the participants should not repeat it.[5] The following prescriptions regarding purity and impurity, Leviticus 11–15, all focus on the individual. Under certain circumstances, the individual Israelite or priest has to refrain from partaking in the cult. If these circumstances disappear, and after a certain amount of time and some washing and perhaps other rituals, the individual was reintegrated into the cultic community.

Although it starts almost in the same way as the preceding chapters, Leviticus 16 as a whole shows a remarkable interest in integrating *all parts of the people of Israel*—and thus differs in perspective from the preceding and the following chapters. This programmatic integration of all members of the people as active participants of the ritual is probably the result of a longer editorial process and the literary growth of the chapter. I can summarize this process only briefly here:[6] While the reference back to Leviticus 10 in Lev 16:1 is probably due to the redaction of the entire book, the main part of the chapter, vv. 2–28, belongs to a priestly layer and focuses on the actions and provisions of the High Priest as Aaron's successor. V. 34bc originally concluded that part. Verses 29–34a, however, pursue a different agenda and use a slightly different terminology. These additional verses originated from priests responsible for or at least associated with

5 The divine fire lighting the sacrifice on the altar and thus inaugurating the cult is of an exceptional nature. Its famous repetitions corroborate the extraordinariness. All cases are marked as unique instances at crucial points of the history of Israel, i.e., David's founding of the altar on Ornan's threshing floor (1 Chron 21:26, not in the *Vorlage* 2 Sam 24:25), Solomon's dedication of the new built temple (2 Chron 7:1–3, not in the *Vorlage* 1 Kings 8:54), Elijah's demonstration of Yahweh's uniqueness on Mount Carmel (1 Kings 18:38–39).

6 See, e.g., T. Hieke, *Levitikus 16–27* (HThKAT; Freiburg i. Br.: Herder, 2014), 568–70, based on the work of C. Nihan, *From Priestly Torah to Pentateuch: A Study in the Composition of the Book of Leviticus* (FAT.2 25; Tübingen: Mohr Siebeck, 2007), 340–79; Janowski, "Geschenk," 8–9.

the so-called "Holiness Code" (Leviticus 17–26).[7] This second part of Leviticus 16 focusses on the people, including the resident alien (v. 29), and their conduct during the entire Day of Atonement. The effects of this literary development are manifold: The two large blocks of the book of Leviticus, chapters 1–16 and 17–26, are welded together. Leviticus 16 gets the role of a literary and theological center, because *now all parts of the entire people of Israel are actively involved*, the priests, the High Priest, as well as "all the people of the assembly" (*kōl ʿam ha-qāhāl*).[8] Lev 16:29 describes the active part of the people: "you shall deny yourselves, and shall do no work, neither the citizen nor the alien who resides among you" (NRSV). The phrase "you shall deny yourselves" (*tᵉʿannū ʾæt napšotē-kæm*) soon becomes a cipher for various spiritual and corporeal abstentions. The Mishnah summarizes in m. Yoma 8:1 that, on Yom Kippur, it is prohibited to eat and drink, to wash or anoint with oil, to wear shoes and to have marital relations.[9] By these actions that heavily interrupt everyday life, especially the cycle of eating, drinking, and working, the entire people spiritually participate in the ritual process of the Day of Atonement. However, this kind of participation transgresses the limits of space already within the biblical text: All Israelites all over the world (or better the diaspora) take part, wherever they are. The road to metaphorization and abstraction starts here.

4 Elimination of All Sorts of Sins and Impurities

Another aspect that qualifies Leviticus 16 as the center of the Book of Leviticus and thus of the Torah has to do with the matter that is removed by its rituals. Again, the diachronically identified two parts of the chapter complement each other to form an overall picture. The first part, Leviticus 16:2–28, usually attributed to P, relates closely to the immediately preceding chapters on purity and impurity. It focuses on the purification of the sanctuary. Especially in 16:14–15 and 16:18–19, the ritual applies the blood of the sin offering (or purification offering) to all parts of the sanctuary, thus connecting them symbolically with the sacrifice on the altar and the presence of the LORD on the *kapporæt* in the Holy of Holies. This act of

7 See, e.g., J. M. Vis, "The Purgation of Persons through the Purification Offering," in H. L. Wiley/C. A. Eberhart (ed.), *Sacrifice, Cult, and Atonement in Early Judaism and Christianity. Constituents and Critique* (Resources for Biblical Study 85; Atlanta: SBL Press, 2017) 33–57, on p. 42.

8 This combination in Lev 16:33 is new within the sequence of Leviticus; the chapters before mention either the people (*ʿam*) or the assembly (*qāhāl*).

9 See, e.g., G. Stemberger, "Yom Kippur in Mishna Yoma," in T. Hieke/T. Nicklas (ed.), *The Day of Atonement. Its Interpretations in Early Jewish and Christian Traditions* (Themes in Biblical Narrative 15; Leiden/Boston: Brill, 2012) 121–37, on pp. 134–5. He summarizes on p. 136: "Considering the Mishnaic description in its totality, it depicts a largely expanded Temple ritual in which the people play their part."

a deep ritual purification was probably the concern of the text in its first version. Lev 16:16a summarizes, "Thus he shall make atonement for the sanctuary."

However, the final form of the explanation of the ritual in Lev 16:16 specifies more matter to be removed and thus goes beyond the paradigm of purity and impurity and the purification of the sanctuary only:

> Thus he shall make atonement for the sanctuary, because of the uncleannesses of the people of Israel, and because of their transgressions, [that is:] all their sins; and so he shall do for the tent of meeting, which remains with them in the midst of their uncleannesses (NRSV with additions).

To the *uncleannesses* (*ṭumʾōt*) that need purification the verse adds *their transgressions* (*pišʿē-hæm*). These are the crimes and wrongdoings that are committed deliberately and intentionally, wrongdoings and offences that normally a ritual act never can remove. However, they are now included in the process of *kipper*, Hebrew for "to make atonement"[10] or "to mitigate" (James Watts' translation). Thus, "*all* their sins," as the verse expressly states, are incorporated. The phrase "all their sins" does not refer to an additional matter but rather functions as a collective term for uncleannesses and transgressions. "Sin" (Hebrew: *ḥaṭṭāʾt*), however, is to be understood here in a wider sense: all matter that separates a human being from God, matter that causes impurity by nature, and matter caused by human deliberate wrongdoing. The two parts of the ritual of the Day of Atonement remove all of that: the blood rites and the elimination rite with the scapegoat (Lev 16:20–21).[11]

Within the context of the eliminatory scapegoat ritual, Lev 16:21 repeats almost the same phraseology as in Lev 16:16: "all the iniquities (*ʿawonot*) of the people of Israel, and all their transgressions (*pišʿē-hæm*), [that is:] all their sins (*ḥaṭṭōʾt-am*)." Thus, Lev 16:16, 21, two verses within the *first* half of Leviticus 16, are expanded by terms and concepts from the *second* half of the chapter. Furthermore, Lev 16:30 explains the reason for the people's self-denial and abstention from work, "For on this day atonement shall be made (*kipper*) for you, to cleanse you; from all your sins (*mi-kol ḥaṭṭōʾtē-kæm*) you shall be clean before the LORD."

Lev 16:29–34a, the addition to the older P version in the style of the Holiness Code thus widens the idea of a general purification of the sanctuary to a general removal of *all* sorts of sin, all matter that disconnects the human being and the entire community from God. In order to weld the two parts and concepts together, verses 16:16, 21 are enlarged by the term "transgressions" (i. e., deliberately committed crimes) and the collective term "sins" that covers all, the unintentionally committed offences, the impurities, and the deliberately perpetrated crimes. Thus, the Day of Atonement in its entirety becomes a unique and comprehensive

10 On the term see, e.g., Eberhart, "To Atone," 216.

11 See, e.g., Janowski, "Geschenk," 12–21; Eberhart, "To Atone," 204.

reset of cultic and social relationships among human beings and between human beings and God. The concept includes purification as well as reconciliation (or, atonement), in a collective and individual way as well.[12]

Consequently, Lev 16:33 summarizes the effect of the entire ritual by way of a catalogue:

> He [the anointed priest] shall make atonement for *the sanctuary*,[13] and he shall make atonement for *the tent of meeting* and for *the altar*, and he shall make atonement for *the priests* and *for all the people of the assembly*.

Therefore, it becomes clear that it is essential and indispensable that all parts of the people of Israel take part in the ritual in some way or another.

5 Highest Degree of Abstraction

At the same time, the ritual itself reaches the highest degree of abstraction. A few drops of blood sprinkled within an empty room suffice for the efficacy of the ritual. Of course, the fiction narrative set in the wilderness of Sinai mentions the mysterious *kapporæt* on the Ark of the Covenant within the Tent of Meeting. However, this fiction is the result of a retro-projection of the rituals at the Second Temple back to the wandering in the wilderness. All persons involved knew very well that the Holy of Holies of the Second Temple was empty. However, obviously this emptiness and the physical absence of the Ark of the Covenant with the *kapporæt* was no obstacle to the effective performance of the ritual and the spiritual success of the entire Day of Atonement. The core process within the cultic community already received such a degree of abstraction that the physical requirements in the Holy of Holies no longer mattered. The biblical text itself hints at this abstraction: From the huge amount of blood gained from a bull and a goat, only seven drops (and a little bit more for daubing onto the altar) are essential.

---

12 See also Vis, "Purgation," 46–7.

13 This translation of the NRSV interprets the term *miqdaš ha-qodæš*, which occurs only here, as a summary term for all the following items ("the sanctuary, *i.e.*, the tent, the altar etc."). However, it is also and perhaps more probable that the text forms an anti-climax, an enumeration with a decreasing grade of holiness. Thus, the *miqdaš ha-qodæš* functions as a synonym for *qodæš qodāšīm* and should be translated as "the holy of holies." See, e.g., Hieke, *Levitikus 16–27*, 565.

6 From Abstraction to Metaphor

Based on these levels of abstraction within the text itself, processes of transformation transmitted the core of the Day of Atonement to different modes of expression. The ritual itself turns into a metaphor, even at the time when the priests still performed the actual cult in Jerusalem. Jews from all over the diaspora spiritually took part in the ritual through their fasting, acts of self-denial, and abstention from work. Thus, the basic idea of purification and reconciliation moves beyond the limits of space and time and is preserved in Judaism over the destruction of the Second Temple in 70 CE up to the present time. The possibility of spiritual instead of factual participation and the idea of abstraction give rise to multiple transformations and metaphorical charging. Today, celebrating the liturgy in a synagogue, fasting, and abstaining from work make the Day of Atonement a Holy Day for most of the Jews. The seed of metaphorization also grew in Christianity. The mystical place of the *kapporæt*, never physically present in the Second Temple, became the spiritual location where God removes all impurities and transgressions, that is: all the sins, and grants a new beginning. Thus the *kapporæt* of Leviticus 16 was already a metaphor, and thus Paul could use its Greek equivalent *hilasterion* without problems and in the full sense for Jesus Christ (Rom 3:25):[14] For Christianity, the core message of the Day of Atonement became manifest in the life, death, and resurrection of Jesus Christ. Thus, the Day of Atonement described in Leviticus 16 marks the literary and theological center of the Torah, and its basic concept of purification and reconciliation stands at the center of Judaism and Christianity.

Bibliography

Eberhart, C. A., "Introduction: Constituents and Critique of Sacrifice, Cult, and Atonement in Early Judaism and Christianity," in H. L. Wiley/C. A. Eberhart (ed.), *Sacrifice, Cult, and Atonement in Early Judaism and Christianity. Constituents and Critique* (Resources for Biblical Study 85; Atlanta: SBL Press, 2017) 1–29.

–, "To Atone or Not to Atone: Remarks on the Day of Atonement Rituals according to Leviticus 16 and the Meaning of Atonement," in H. L. Wiley/C. A. Eberhart (ed.), *Sacrifice, Cult, and Atonement in Early Judaism and Christianity. Constituents and Critique* (Resources for Biblical Study 85; Atlanta: SBL Press, 2017) 197–231.

Hieke, T., *Levitikus 16–27* (HThKAT; Freiburg i. Br.: Herder, 2014).

14 See, e.g., M. Tiwald, "Christ as Hilasterion (Rom 3:25): Pauline Theology on the Day of Atonement in the Mirror of Early Jewish Thought," in T. Hieke/T. Nicklas (ed.), *The Day of Atonement. Its Interpretations in Early Jewish and Christian Traditions* (Themes in Biblical Narrative 15; Leiden/Boston: Brill, 2012) 189–209; Janowski, "Geschenk," 26; Eberhart, "To Atone," 228.

Janowski, B., "Das Geschenk der Versöhnung. Leviticus 16 als Schlussstein der priesterlichen Kulttheologie," in T. Hieke/T. Nicklas (ed.), *The Day of Atonement. Its Interpretations in Early Jewish and Christian Traditions* (Themes in Biblical Narrative 15; Leiden/Boston: Brill, 2012) 189–209.

Nihan, C., *From Priestly Torah to Pentateuch: A Study in the Composition of the Book of Leviticus* (FAT.2 25; Tübingen: Mohr Siebeck, 2007).

Plaut, W. G. (ed.), *Die Tora in jüdischer Auslegung. Band III: Wajikra/Levitikus*, ed. B. J. Bamberger; Übersetzung, Bearbeitung und Gestaltung von A. Böckler (Gütersloh: Gütersloher Verlagshaus, 2001).

Rendtorff, R., "Leviticus 16 als Mitte der Tora," *BibInt* 11 (2003) 252–8.

Stemberger, G., "Yom Kippur in Mishna Yoma," in T. Hieke/T. Nicklas (ed.), *The Day of Atonement. Its Interpretations in Early Jewish and Christian Traditions* (Themes in Biblical Narrative 15; Leiden/Boston: Brill, 2012) 121–37.

Tiwald, M., "Christ as Hilasterion (Rom 3:25): Pauline Theology on the Day of Atonement in the Mirror of Early Jewish Thought," in T. Hieke/T. Nicklas (ed.), *The Day of Atonement. Its Interpretations in Early Jewish and Christian Traditions* (Themes in Biblical Narrative 15; Leiden/Boston: Brill, 2012) 189–209.

Watts, J. W., *Leviticus 1–10* (HCOT; Leuven: Peeters, 2013).

Vis, J. M., "The Purgation of Persons through the Purification Offering," in H. L. Wiley/C. A. Eberhart (ed.), *Sacrifice, Cult, and Atonement in Early Judaism and Christianity. Constituents and Critique* (Resources for Biblical Study 85; Atlanta: SBL Press, 2017) 33–57.

Zenger, E., "Das Buch Levitikus als Teiltext der Tora/des Pentateuch. Eine synchrone Lektüre mit kanonischer Perspektive," in H.-J. Fabry/H.-W. Jüngling (ed.), *Levitikus als Buch* (BBB 119; Berlin et al.: Philo, 1999) 47–83.

William K. Gilders

Is There an Incense Altar in This Ritual?

A Question of Ritual-Textual Interpretive Community

1 Introduction

How do we know what we know? Or rather, how do we *think* or *believe* that we know something? Specifically, how do we think or believe that we know that the ritual complex for the "Day of Atonement" set out in Lev 16 included the application of blood to a golden incense altar inside the tent-shrine—or, that it *did not*? In raising these questions, I make my theoretical start from the work of Stanley Fish on the authority of interpretive communities, presented in his influential 1980 book, *Is There a Text in This Class?* That title, rather obviously, is reflected in the title of my paper. In answer to his titular question, Fish writes:

> There isn't a text in this or any other class if one means by text what E. D. Hirsch and others mean by it, 'an entity which always remains the same from one moment to the next' (*Validity in Interpretation*, pg. 46); but there is a text in this and every class if one means by text the structure of meaning that is obvious and inescapable from the perspective of whatever interpretive assumptions happen to be in force.[1]

In line with Fish's hermeneutical perspective, I would answer my own titular question by affirming that there *is* an incense altar in the ritual in Lev 16, if one means by incense altar that shrine appurtenance "that is obvious and inescapable from the perspective of whatever interpretive assumptions happen to be in force." By the very same standard—of "whatever interpretive assumptions happen to be in force"—it is also possible to hold that the *absence* of an incense altar is "obvious and inescapable"! It is those interpretive assumptions, with the incense altar and the blood rituals it receives instantiated on the basis of those assumptions—or, the altar and rituals *not* instantiated—that are the focus of this paper.

1 S. Fish, *Is There a Text in This Class? The Authority of Interpretive Communities* (Cambridge, MA.: Harvard University Press, 1980), vii.

2 Where is the Incense Altar?

According to the ritual instructions set out in Lev 16:14–15, Aaron is required to take blood from a bullock offered as a "sin offering" (חטאת)[2] on his behalf and on behalf of his household (Lev 16:3, 6, and 11) into the adytum of the tent-shrine, where he is to sprinkle it with his finger upon and in the direction of the cover (כפרת) of the Ark of the Pact. He is then to repeat this manipulation with the blood of a goat offered on behalf of the whole people (Lev 16:5, 9). Then, according to verse 16b, "and so is he to do [וכן יעשה] for the Tent of Meeting that resides with them in the midst of their impurities." Then, according to verses 18–19, he is to go out [ויצא] to "the altar that is before Yahweh" to perform further blood manipulations, placing the mixed blood of the bullock and the goat onto the horns of the altar and sprinkling this blood with his finger seven times upon the altar, with the effect of cleansing and re-consecrating it "from the impurities of the Israelites."

On what I judge to be a straightforward reading of the text, Lev 16:16b refers to blood manipulation actions performed in the outer room of the shrine, referred to in Lev 16 as the "Tent of Meeting," in distinction from the adytum, which is designated as "the Holy Place" (הקדש).[3] According to Lev 4, an incense altar stood within the outer room of the tent-shrine and blood was applied to its horns from sin offerings brought on behalf of the high priest and the whole congregation of Israel (Lev 4:7, 18). However, that incense altar, the construction, placement, and use of which is dealt with in Exod 30:1–10, 37:25–29, and 40:26–27, is not explicitly mentioned in Lev 16. The altar referred to in verses 18–19 is not that altar, but the bronze altar of burnt offerings located in the shrine courtyard. This conclusion follows naturally from the reference at the beginning of verse 18 to Aaron going out (ויצא), which comes directly after the reference to his actions in the outer room. Aaron is instructed to leave the outer room and proceed to an altar, which must, therefore, be the one in the shrine courtyard. This understanding of the text is reinforced by verse 20, which refers to Aaron effecting removal (כפר) on *three* loci—the Holy Place (הקדש, the adytum), the Tent of Meeting, and the altar—after which he is to proceed immediately to dealing with the so-called

2 On the retention of this translation, see W.K. Gilders, "חטאת as 'Sin Offering': A Reconsideration," in C.J. Hodge/S.M. Olyan/D. Ullucci/E. Wasserman (ed.), *"One Who Sows Bountifully": Essays in Honor of Stanley K. Stowers* (BJS 356; Providence, RI: Brown Judaic Studies, 2013) 119–28.

3 This terminological combination is unique to Lev 16. Elsewhere in Aaronide priestly texts, the adytum is referred to as the "Holy of Holies" (קדש הקדשים) in distinction from the outer room, which is specified as the "Holy Place" (הקדש); see, e.g., Exod 26:33; Lev 6:23.

"scapegoat." This interpretation of the text holds a near complete consensus in modern biblical scholarship.[4]

Near complete, because there are a few exceptions. Most notably, Baruch A. Levine asserts that the altar referred to in verses 18–19 is, in fact, the incense altar inside the Tent.[5] In this, he follows the line of ancient Rabbinic interpretations of Lev 16 found in the Mishnah (m. Yoma 5:5) and the Tannaitic midrash, Sifra (Ahare Mot 4:8). These rabbinic works reflect an evident concern to make the presence of the incense altar explicit both in the ritual and in its foundational prescriptive text, Lev 16, which m. Yoma 1:3 designates the "Order of the Day" (סדר היום). Their reason for wanting the incense altar to be part of the rite is clear. Exodus 30:10 refers explicitly to the performance of blood manipulations on the incense altar *once each year*. This verse must be referring to the ritual complex set out in Lev 16, where the concluding verses of the chapter (29–34a) indicate that the rite is a once-a-year performance.

The rabbinic solution to the problem of the presence of the incense altar in the ritual complex of Lev 16—as I have noted—is rejected by the vast majority of modern interpreters of the text, who identify the altar of Lev 16:18–19 as the altar of burnt offerings in the shrine courtyard. Indeed, the rabbinic interpretation was already rejected by the medieval Jewish commentator, Abraham ibn Ezra, in a characteristically terse comment on Lev 16:18, in which he states that the altar referred to there is the altar of burnt offering (without making his dissent against the received rabbinic interpretation explicit).[6]

However, although they reject the manner in which the Rabbis attempted to put an incense altar into the Tent of Lev 16, many modern scholars have nevertheless sought their own way of achieving the same goal. Rather than transporting the altar from Lev 16:18 into the Tent, they convey the incense altar from

4 See, e.g., M. Noth, *Leviticus: A Commentary* (OTL; Philadelphia: Westminster, 1965), 124; G.J. Wenham, *The Book of Leviticus* (NICOT; Grand Rapids, MI: Eerdmans, 1979), 232; J. Milgrom, *Leviticus 1–16: A New Translation with Introduction and Commentary* (AB 3; New York: Doubleday, 1991), 1036; J.E. Hartley, *Leviticus* (WBC 4; Dallas: Word Books, 1992), 240–1; E. Gerstenberger, *Leviticus: A Commentary* (OTL; Louisville, KY: Westminster John Knox, 1996), 217; C. Nihan, *From Priestly Torah to Pentateuch: A Study in the Composition of the Book of Leviticus* (FAT.2 25; Tübingen: Mohr Siebeck, 2007), 141, 162; T. Hieke, *Levitikus 16–27* (HThKAT; Freiburg: Herder, 2014), 585–6.

5 B.A. Levine, *Leviticus: The Traditional Hebrew Text with the New JPS Translation* (Philadelphia: Jewish Publication Society, 1989), 105. Carol Meyers affirms and follows Levine's interpretation; see "Realms of Sanctity: The Case of the 'Misplaced' Incense Altar in the Tabernacle Texts of Exodus," in M.V. Fox et al. (ed.), *Texts, Temples, and Traditions: A Tribute to Menahem Haran* (Winona Lake, IN: Eisenbrauns, 1996) 33–46, on pp. 42–3. Amongst non-Jewish interpreters, there are two notable exceptions to the consensus: R.K. Harrison, *Leviticus: An Introduction and Commentary* (TOTC; Downers Grove, IL: Inter-Varsity, 1980), 173; T.B. Dozeman, *Commentary on Exodus* (ECC; Grand Rapids, MI: Eerdmans, 2009), 663.

6 Noted by Milgrom (*Leviticus 1–16*, 1036); see also Josephus, *Ant.* 3.243.

Exod 30:10 with a detour through Lev 4:3–21 (particularly, verses 5–7 and 16–18) to pick up the details of the blood ritual performed on the altar. For example, Jacob Milgrom, comments on Leviticus 16:16b:

> the shrine should be purged in the same manner as the adytum. Specifically, one object (the incense altar) is to be purged by direct contact with the purgation blood, and the rest of the shrine is to be purged by a sevenfold sprinkling of the purgation blood on the shrine floor. Thus, "likewise" refers to the 1 + 7 sequence … employed in the adytum … There is, however, no need to specify how the purgation of the incense altar takes place, for the procedure was already given in 4:6–7, 17–18.[7]

Milgrom adds a reference to "the explicit requirement of Exod 30:10."[8] *This latter point is decisive.* In the absence of Exod 30:10, it *might* be possible, even in the case of a holistic, synthesizing, final-form reading of Leviticus, to argue that the ritual complex of Lev 16 lacked a blood ritual directed at the incense altar. It would not be *necessary* to project the blood rites of Lev 4:3–21 into Lev 16. Putting this in Fishian terms, we can imagine various readers who are members of an interpretive community that prioritizes holistic, final-form reading of the Pentateuch coming to different conclusions about the presence of the incense altar in the ritual complex of Lev 16, with some of these readers developing complex explanations of the ritual and theological significance of the absence of that altar from the Day of Atonement rite. Thus, I conclude that envisaging the application of blood to the incense altar inside the Tent on the Day of Atonement depends *essentially* on a single pentateuchal verse: Exod 30:10; it is decisively because of this verse that readers of the received form of the text *know* that blood was applied to the incense altar.

But this is only the case if we accord Exod 30:10 the authority to determine our understanding of Lev 16. As an alternative to this approach, I turn now to interpretations of Lev 16 that emphasize the complex compositional history of the Aaronide priestly material in the Pentateuch, readings that are sharply diachronic rather than synchronic, treating the present text non-holistically and non-harmonistically. Anyone who has investigated the history of critical scholarship on Lev 16 will agree with Christophe Nihan's declaration that "discussion of the genesis of Lev 16 is remarkably complex, so much so that it is even difficult to summarize."[9] Rather than attempt such a difficult summary here, I will commend Nihan's detailed and cogent survey,[10] which is followed by a compelling argument for the essential compositional unity of Lev 16:2–28, with which he concludes,

7 Milgrom, *Leviticus 1–16*, 1034–5.
8 Milgrom, *Leviticus 1–16*, 1035.
9 Nihan, *Priestly Torah*, 340.
10 Nihan, *Priestly Torah*, 340–5.

"the bulk of ch. 16 should be regarded as a unified composition from the hand of the Priestly writers."[11]

Milgrom also holds that the bulk of Lev 16:2–28 is a coherent composition, which is "a discrete literary unit that was not originally composed by the author or redactor of P."[12] In support of this argument for the non-P origin of this material, Milgrom notes:

> Verses 2–28 contain unique terms that differentiate them from P ... Hence vv 2–28 must stem from an earlier source, which was only subsequently incorporated into P.[13]

Of particular significance to Milgrom is the distinctive use of הקדש to designate the adytum. Nihan challenges Milgrom's claim about the prior independent existence of Lev 16:2–28, arguing that the text "already presupposes P's broader narrative context in Gen—Lev, and ... the language and theology of these verses clearly betray the influence of P." However, he then argues that,

> if ... P adapted freely an older ritual on the purification ... of the sanctuary, one may surmise that such specific use of הקדש was taken from his source. Alternatively, this could also suggest that Lev 16 was composed by a scribe other than that responsible for Lev 1–9,[14]

a hypothesis that Nihan develops at some length.[15] In my view, the difference between Milgrom's proposal and Nihan's is really quite small. Both assert that the material in Lev 16:2–28 reflects an older source used by P, which contains distinctive vocabulary. Their arguments for this basic hypothesis have much to commend them.

If Lev 16:2–28 did exist, in some form, independent of and prior to the composition of Lev 4 and, especially, Exod 30:10, must we assume that this older form of the rite included the incense altar inside the shrine? There is certainly no explicit reference to the incense altar in the text (unless, of course, we follow the rabbinic understanding of Lev 16:18–19). A number of scholars have, in fact, argued that the oldest form of the ritual complex presented in Lev 16 lacked the incense altar. On this view, most influentially set out by Julius Wellhausen, that appurtenance was a later addition to the Aaronide shrine.[16] This claim is supported not simply by an argument from silence—the lack of explicit reference

11 Nihan, *Priestly Torah*, 362.
12 Milgrom, *Leviticus 1–16*, 1013.
13 Milgrom, *Leviticus 1–16*, 1063.
14 Nihan, *Priestly Torah*, 368.
15 Nihan, *Priestly Torah*, 379–82.
16 J. Wellhausen, *Die Composition des Hexateuchs und der historischen Bücher des Alten Testaments* (Berlin: Georg Reimer, ³1899), 138, 147. See also, M. Noth, *Exodus: A Commentary* (OTL; Philadelphia: Westminster, 1962), 234; idem, *Leviticus*, 122–3; Nihan, *Priestly Torah*, 162–3.

to the incense altar in Lev 16, where we would expect it—but by the strong evidence for the secondary compositional nature of Exod 30:10. I will refer here to Milgrom's argument,[17] which particularly emphasizes the insistence in Exod 30:10 that the incense altar is treated to a ritual of removal (כפר) just *once a year*. This ritual prescription corresponds with secondary material in Lev 16 (verse 29–34a), and with Lev 23:26–32, which reflects the transformation of the ritual complex of Lev 16:2–28 from an emergency rite, which could be conducted at any time, into a once-a-year event with a set date (an understanding anticipated by Leviticus Rabbah and considered by Elijah, the Vilna Gaon, in the late 18th century, prior to its articulation by a number of modern critical scholars[18]).

Thus, it is entirely possible to understand the ritual complex of Lev 16:2–28 as first having been composed by a tradent who knew nothing of an incense altar and who, therefore, did not envisage the ritual he recorded as including any blood manipulations performed thereon. Rather, this tradent apparently imagined a simple repetition of the sprinkling actions in the outer room[19] (perhaps in front of the curtain, similar to what Lev 4:6 and 17 prescribe).

My effort here to identify and distinguish this particular incense-altar-free version of the text is not an exercise in textual deconstruction and atomization for its own sake. Rather, I regard compositional criticism as an ethical activity, which has the goal of recovering and hearing suppressed cultural voices. This is part of the ethnographic program of my work, to seek out and listen to a variety of indigenous informants, who reflect diverse aspects of the society being investigated. So, we have a once-suppressed voice, which we can now hear. But we also have the voices that suppressed it by incorporating Lev 16:2–28 into the larger context of Leviticus within the larger context of Aaronide priestly redactional work. Within this larger context, we are compelled, specifically by Exod 30:10, to see an incense altar in the ritual.

However, we are left to puzzle over how exactly the rituals of removal (כפר) were performed on this altar. As Carol Meyers puts it: "The exact sequence of this ritual, meant to maintain the sanctity of the sanctuary, is tantalizingly vague."[20] The diversity of suggestions about this "tantalizingly vague" performance reflects the vagueness and ambiguity of the text before us. Meyers asserts (following Levine) that we should, in fact, draw on m. Yoma 5:3–5 to reconstruct the ritual, and she agrees with the Rabbis and Levine that the altar of Lev 16:18–19 is the incense altar.[21] While I am not convinced that this approach to Lev 16:16b reflects the intent of the tradent behind the original version of Lev 16:2–28 posited by

17 Milgrom, *Leviticus 1–16*, 1061–3.
18 As noted by Milgrom, *Leviticus 1–16*, 1012–13.
19 Noth, *Leviticus*, 124; Nihan, *Priestly Torah*, 163, n. 247.
20 Meyers, "'Misplaced' Incense Altar," 42.
21 Meyers, "'Misplaced' Incense Altar," 42–3.

Milgrom and Nihan, I am prepared to consider that the Rabbis may well have correctly deducted the intention of the Aaronide redactors who combined Lev 16:2–28 with material that included the incense altar. They, like the Rabbis, certainly may have understood the altar of Lev 16:18–19 to be the incense altar. Thus, Levine, Meyers, and others may be correct in their interpretation of the present contextual form of Lev 16, against the mainstream consensus, although this interpretation does require a less straightforward understanding of the instruction for Aaron to go out (Lev 16:18a); on this reading, the text emphasizes that his application of blood to the incense altar takes place after his departure from the adytum, as he situates himself in front of the altar.[22]

Meyers goes further, however, than simply presenting a way to make sense of the current form of the redacted text. She argues that material about the incense altar was not a secondary compositional addition to the Aaronide work, as Wellhausen and those who have followed him posit, but an original and integral part of the composition; the incense altar, therefore, is not an addition to the shrine pictured in the Aaronide texts, but an integral element. To advance and sustain this argument, she asserts that the incense altar of Exod 30:1–10 is not "misplaced" or "displaced," but quite logically placed.[23]

In both of her essays on the incense altar—contributions to the 1996 Festschrift for Menhem Haran and the 2008 Festschrift for Richard E. Friedman—Meyers first marshals textual and archaeological evidence for the antiquity of cultic incense altars, against the position that the tradents responsible for the prescriptive tabernacle texts could not have known of such appurtenances.[24] On the basis of this evidence, she concludes that "the incense altar was an integral part of the furnishings of the outer sanctum of the tabernacle, just as the descriptive section stipulates."[25] It follows, she insists, that the textual material about the incense altar in Exod 30 is an integral part of the composition and that its location has to be accounted for in terms of conceptual logic, synchronically, rather than by appeal to stages of composition.

In her 1996 article, she argues that the organization of Exod 25:1–31:17 as a unified composition is governed by the logic of "ordered sacred reality." Under this conceptual logic, although the golden incense altar was an appurtenance of the outer shrine room (along with the lampstand and table), its construction could not be prescribed in the same textual unit with them because of its unique

22 This is how Rashi (*ad loc.*) explains the instruction, as noted by Hartley, *Leviticus*, 240–1.

23 C. Meyers, "Framing Aaron: Incense Altar and Lamp Oil in the Tabernacle Texts," in S. Dolansky, *Sacred History, Sacred Literature: Essays on Ancient Israel, the Bible, and Religion in Honor of R. E. Friedman on His Sixtieth Birthday* (Winona Lake, IN: Eisenbrauns, 2008) 13–21. This essay depends and builds on her earlier piece, "'Misplaced' Incense Altar."

24 Meyers, "'Misplaced' Incense Altar," 36–8; idem, "Incense Altar and Lamp Oil," 16–17.

25 Meyers, "'Misplaced' Incense Altar," 38; see also, Milgrom, *Leviticus 1–16*, 236–7.

characteristics, the most important of which is its strong connection with elements external to the tent-shrine, especially with the altar of burnt offerings, with which it shared the application of sacrificial blood.[26] Thus, the incense altar,

> appears outside the carefully graduated sequence of the core of the prescriptive texts precisely because it crosses the realms of sanctity that the texts represent with such exquisite precision.[27]

In her 2008 piece, Meyers carries her analysis further in response to Jacob Milgrom's explanation of the location of the incense altar material in terms of the appurtenance's functionality; according to Milgrom, the incense altar is treated separately from the other appurtenances of the outer shrine room due to the text's attention to its cultic usage.[28] Meyers affirms that Milgrom is on the right track in his approach, but argues that his explanation does not fully account for the entire context in which the incense altar material is situated. To address this problem, she emphasizes that the material about the lamp oil (Exod 27:20–21) and the material on the incense altar (Exod 30:1–10) frames the prescriptions for Aaron's vestments and his ordination in relation to the larger theme of sacred order:

> By framing [Exod 28–29] with directions for the lamp oil and the incense altar, the writer signifies the integral nature of priesthood, structure, and ritual in the tabernacle texts.[29]

Meyers clearly views her identification of the conceptual logic governing the placement of the incense altar material in Exodus as decisive proof that the material was composed by the same tradents who produced the material about the lampstand and table in Exod 25, who made a conscious decision to separate the incense altar from the other appurtenances of the outer shrine room. From Meyers' perspective, this identification of literary coherence makes the conclusion "obvious and inescapable," that Exod 25:1–31:17 (inclusive of Exod 30:1–10) is a literary unity. However, it is possible to affirm the coherence of the present document without accepting its synchronic composition. Compositional coherence need not be equated with compositional unity. Material could have been added to an older composition with a unifying rationale in play. Against the notion that Exod 30:1–10 could be a secondary addition, Meyers approvingly cites U. Cassuto's argument that, if the incense altar were really a later addition to

---

26 Meyers, "'Misplaced' Incense Altar," 44–5.

27 Meyers, "'Misplaced' Incense Altar," 46.

28 Milgrom, *Leviticus 1-16*, 236–7.

29 Meyers, "Incense Altar and Lamp Oil," 21. Meyers notes (p. 21, n. 22) that Exod 27:20–Exod 30:10 constitutes one of the weekly Torah portions, indicating rabbinic recognition of the material as "a meaningful unit."

the text, it would have been inserted into Exod 25.[30] Cassuto's argument, however, fails to take into account the evidence for how scribal editors added blocks of new material to older works in the form of appendices that follow concluding notes like the one found in Exod 29:43–46.[31] Thus, it remains possible to argue that Exod 30:1–10 (and everything that follows it) was added to an earlier composition. The tradent who made this addition could very well have understood this addition in the conceptual terms identified by Meyers. Or the identified conceptual logic may well be the creation of a modern reader seeking to find literary coherence in a work that achieved its present form primarily under technological-compositional constraints, with larger conceptual concerns playing a distinctly secondary role.

But why posit that Exod 30:1–10 is a secondary addition when such an elegant case can be made for the compositional unity of Exod 25:1–31:17? To answer this question, I return to Lev 16 and the absence of explicit reference to the incense altar. The absence of explicit mention of such a significant appurtenance in that context strongly suggests that it was unknown to the tradent who composed Lev 16:2–28; if it was unknown to that tradent, then it seems reasonable to suggest that it was unknown to the tradent who composed Exod 28:1–29:46. The two blocks of Aaronide composition can then be read together as representing a cultural stage during which an incense altar was not imagined to be part of the Tabernacle complex. The result of this reading is that a suppressed cultural voice can be heard.

As I noted previously, given the evidence that Exod 30:10 is an addition to Exod 30:1–9 (in line with the reconceptualization of the Day of Atonement as a once-a-year event), it is also possible to read Lev 16:2–28 along with a version of the Tabernacle prescriptions that includes the incense altar (but not Exod 30:10) and to conclude that the incense altar did not figure in the Day of Atonement rituals even though it did stand in the outer room of the shrine. This approach highlights, again, the crucial significance of Exod 30:10 in the final form of the text.

3 Conclusion

I have highlighted the identification of two significant ritual-textual interpretive communities that engage with Lev 16 and the ritual complex it presents: those who adopt a largely holistic and synthesizing approach to the text and those who

30 Meyers, "'Misplaced Incense Altar,'" 37. Meyers does not specify where this argument appears, but is apparently referring to U. Cassuto, *A Commentary on the Book of Exodus* (Jerusalem: Magnes Press, 1967), 390.

31 Compare, e.g., the material in Lev 23:39–44 added on to Lev 23:1–38 after its concluding notes (vv. 37–38) and the supplemental material in Lev 16:29–34a added to Lev 16:1–28.

attend to what David Carr calls the "fractures" in the textual corpus.[32] These interpretive communities have porous borders. There is no huge wall between them; indeed, they are best thought of as two end points on a spectrum. As I have emphasized in the articulation of my own approach to the text, it is possible to attend equally to the diverse voices that can be recovered through source and compositional analysis *and* to the voice or voices of the received form of the text. All of those indigenous voices are important for a commentator who treats a text ethnographically, because an ethnographic approach requires close attention to a cultural formation's complexity and conflicts.

As my discussion of Meyers' work indicates, it is necessary to make a careful distinction between compositional coherence and compositional unity. I do not believe that identifying compositional coherence—the product of the redactional creation of a work that makes sense as a whole—necessitates the conclusion that the work in question is a compositional unity. Specifically, the fact that we can find ways of making sense of the placement of the incense altar material in Exodus does not mean that this placement was always an organic and original feature of the work.

Finally, I wish to reiterate the crucial role played by Exod 30:10 for interpretive decisions to see an incense altar and blood rites directed at that altar in Lev 16. If that single verse did not exist, we would almost certainly find holistic interpreters and "fracture" interpreters coming to the same fundamental conclusion by very different routes: there is no incense altar in this ritual. They would then, quite certainly, diverge in their answers to the question, "What should we do about that absent altar?" The holistic interpreters would likely seek to explain why the incense altar (which must be there in the outer room of the Tent, given the references to it in Lev 4) is not a participant in the ritual, while, of course, the "fragment" interpreters would look at the empty spot in front of the curtain, note that the incense altar was a later addition to the tradition, and wonder what all the fuss is about!

So, is there an incense altar in this ritual? It depends on whom you ask!

Bibliography

Carr, D. M., *Reading the Fractures of Genesis: Historical and Literary Approaches* (Louisville, KY: Westminster John Knox, 1996).

Cassuto, U., *A Commentary on the Book of Exodus* (Jerusalem: Magnes Press, 1967).

Dozeman, T. B., *Commentary on Exodus* (ECC; Grand Rapids, MI: Eerdmans, 2009).

Fish, S., *Is There a Text in This Class? The Authority of Interpretive Communities* (Cambridge, MA.: Harvard University Press, 1980).

32 D. M. Carr, *Reading the Fractures of Genesis: Historical and Literary Approaches* (Louisville, KY: Westminster John Knox, 1996).

Gerstenberger, E., *Leviticus: A Commentary* (OTL; Louisville, KY: Westminster John Knox, 1996).
Gilders, W. K., "חטאת as 'Sin Offering': A Reconsideration," in C. J. Hodge/S. M. Olyan/D. Ullucci/E. Wasserman (ed.), *"One Who Sows Bountifully": Essays in Honor of Stanley K. Stowers* (BJS 356; Providence, RI: Brown Judaic Studies, 2013) 119–28.
Harrison, R. K., *Leviticus: An Introduction and Commentary* (TOTC; Downers Grove, IL: Inter-Varsity, 1980).
Hartley, J. E., *Leviticus* (WBC 4; Dallas: Word Books, 1992).
Hieke, T., *Levitikus 16–27* (HThKAT; Freiburg: Herder, 2014).
Levine, B. A., *Leviticus: The Traditional Hebrew Text with the New JPS Translation* (Philadelphia: Jewish Publication Society, 1989).
Meyers, C., "Realms of Sanctity: The Case of the 'Misplaced' Incense Altar in the Tabernacle Texts of Exodus," in M. V. Fox et al. (ed.), *Texts, Temples, and Traditions: A Tribute to Menahem Haran* (Winona Lake, IN: Eisenbrauns, 1996) 33–46.
–, "Framing Aaron: Incense Altar and Lamp Oil in the Tabernacle Texts," in S. Dolansky, *Sacred History, Sacred Literature: Essays on Ancient Israel, the Bible, and Religion in Honor of R. E. Friedman on His Sixtieth Birthday* (Winona Lake, IN: Eisenbrauns, 2008) 13–21.
Milgrom, J., *Leviticus 1–16: A New Translation with Introduction and Commentary* (AB 3; New York: Doubleday, 1991).
Nihan, C., *From Priestly Torah to Pentateuch: A Study in the Composition of the Book of Leviticus* (FAT.2 25; Tübingen: Mohr Siebeck, 2007).
Noth, M., *Exodus: A Commentary* (OTL; Philadelphia: Westminster, 1962).
–, *Leviticus: A Commentary* (OTL; Philadelphia: Westminster, 1965).
Wellhausen, J., *Die Composition des Hexateuchs und der historischen Bücher des Alten Testaments* (Berlin: Georg Reimer, [3]1899).
Wenham, G. J., *The Book of Leviticus* (NICOT; Grand Rapids, MI: Eerdmans, 1979).

Thomas Hieke

The Prohibition of Transferring an Offspring to "the Molech"

No Child Sacrifice in Leviticus 18 and 20

1 Introduction

Contemporary language uses the term "Moloch" as a metaphor for a monstrous entity that devours everything. "Moloch" nowadays functions as a social or political allegory, e.g., the automobile or industrial civilization or non-transparent institutions, to which human beings fall victim in some way or another. The term stems from the Bible, yet its meaning and usage in biblical literature are by no means clear or unproblematic. Despite the alleged confidence in popular encyclopedias (like "Wikipedia"), the historical existence of a deity or demon called "Moloch" can by no means be taken for granted. Many scholarly publications stress the enormous difficulties regarding the epigraphical and archaeological evidence.[1] However, in most cases, scholars stick to the opinion that there was a practice of child sacrifice in Iron Age Judah "for the Molech" or as a *molk*-sacrifice. But it is methodologically and hermeneutically inacceptable to infer the existence of a practice of child sacrifice from the ambiguous biblical texts alone and then to try to find archaeological evidence in similarly vague texts and remains far away from the Levant. Hence, the problem is by no means settled, and the evidence as well as the biblical texts deserve new considerations. I elaborated the following contribution while working on my commentary on Leviticus for the series "Herders Theologischer Kommentar zum Alten Testament," when I was deeply dissatisfied with the scholarly literature about the verses Lev 18:21 and 20:1–5. There was a clear tendency to cast doubt on most epigraphical and archaeological remains; however, authors still opt for the existence of child sacrifice in the Levant

1 See, e.g., two collections of essays from 2007: J.N. Bremmer (ed.), *The Strange World of Human Sacrifice* (Studies in the History and Anthropology of Religion 1; Leuven: Peeters, 2007); K. Finsterbusch/A. Lange/K.F.D. Römheld (ed.), *Human Sacrifice in Jewish and Christian Tradition* (Numen Book Series 112; Leiden: Brill, 2007). See also the short overview by T. Staubli, "The 'Pagan' Prehistory of Genesis 22:1–14: The Iconographic Background of the Redemption of Human Sacrifice," in I.J. de Hulster/B.A. Strawn/R.P. Bonfiglio (ed.), *Iconographic Exegesis of the Hebrew Bible/Old Testament: An Introduction to Its Method and Practice* (Göttingen: Vandenhoeck & Ruprecht, 2015) 77–101, on pp. 96–9.

in the Iron Age.[2] This is, however, avoidable, if one is ready to interpret the related biblical passages in a different way as the "classical" reading that more or less sees in the texts historical information to be taken at face value. Hence, I identified the necessity to look for a new approach to at least the two passages I had to comment on. As there is no archaeological evidence for child sacrifice in the Levant[3] and as there is unanimity about the absence of child sacrifice in post-exilic times, the verses in Leviticus 18 and 20[4] cannot speak about a practice that is no longer in use and that perhaps never existed. Maybe the "Molech" in these verses functions as a cipher and camouflage for a completely different practice, which was virulent and which the priests as authors wanted to prohibit under all circumstances, but which they could not address in plain language. I had an idea, which I am still convinced of, and I presented it at a regional meeting in Frankfurt/Main (Sankt Georgen) in 2010. From this paper, a publication in the German journal

2 This also holds true for the study from 2017 by H. D. Dewrell, *Child Sacrifice in Ancient Israel* (Winona Lake, IN: Eisenbrauns). Dewrell distinguishes three different rites that involved the sacrifice of children to Yahweh in the Iron Age Israel: general sacrifice of firstborn sons by an "ultra-pious" group of Yahwists (p. 90), the offering of a firstborn child during times of crisis, and the *lmlk* sacrifices (pp. 191–2).—With good reasons, M. Bauks, "The Theological Implications of Child Sacrifice in and Beyond the Biblical Context in Relation to Genesis 22 and Judges 11," in K. Finsterbusch/A. Lange/K. F. D. Römheld (ed.), *Human Sacrifice in Jewish and Christian Tradition* (Numen Book Series 112; Leiden: Brill, 2007) 65–86, on pp. 75–9, 83, excludes the possibility that real child sacrifices occurred as acts of dedication of the firstborn son to the Creator (Exod 22:29–30).—For an analysis of all the biblical passages on the firstborn as an offering to Yahweh, see K. Finsterbusch, "The First-Born between Sacrifice and Redemption in the Hebrew Bible," in eadem/A. Lange/K. F. H. Römheld (ed.), *Human Sacrifice in Jewish and Christian Tradition* (Numen Book Series 112; Leiden: Brill, 2007) 87–108. She prepares Dewrell's position that it cannot be ruled out that some early Israelites at a particular time sacrificed firstborn sons to Yahweh according to Exod 22:28 (note the vague terminology on p. 108!). However, she also points out that the *first* law of the firstborn in the canonical order, Exod 13:11–16, carries a hermeneutical key function and indicates that readers shall understand all following laws in the sense of a *redemption* of the firstborn (see p. 108). On the ancient Babylonian, Syrian, and Canaanite tradition of redeeming and thereby saving humans dedicated as victims for a sacrifice, see Staubli, "Prehistory," passim.

3 See, e.g., E. Noort, "Child Sacrifice in Ancient Israel: The Status Quaestionis," in J. N. Bremmer (ed.), *The Strange World of Human Sacrifice* (Studies in the History and Anthropology of Religion 1; Leuven: Peeters, 2007) 103–26, on p. 104.—It is indeed one of the great achievements of Dewrell's study (Dewrell, *Child Sacrifice*, 37–71) that he summarizes the archaeological evidence of the items usually presented as "proof" for child sacrifice. He convincingly demonstrates for most of them that they in fact cannot bear the burden of proof. Either the objects definitely have nothing to do with child sacrifice, or the evidence is so ambiguous or dubious that one cannot accept them as a compelling proof. According to Dewrell, the best (and only) "evidence for child sacrifice in the Near East and the Mediterranean during the first millennium BCE remains the Punic evidence." (*Child Sacrifice*, 68).

4 I hereby presuppose a post-exilic origin of most of the texts and the book of Leviticus in its entirety; see T. Hieke, *Levitikus 1–15* (HThKAT; Freiburg i. Br.: Herder, 2014), 65–74.

Die Welt des Orients emerged (2011).[5] I further refined the hypothesis in my German commentary for the series "Herders Theologischer Kommentar zum Alten Testament" (2014).[6] The following pages are an English translation and revising of these German works. During the work on my commentary, I learned very much from earlier commentators on the book of Leviticus, notably from the magisterial work of Jacob Milgrom. Thus, in most places I adopted the most probable interpretations I could get from the secondary literature, as it is usual when writing a commentary. In the Molech case, however, I was not satisfied with the suggestions made by scholars so far, and thus I dared to present an entirely new proposal for understanding these elusive verses. This is one of the few cases where I had to present a single opinion against the predominant scholarly opinion. Still, wherever I present my idea orally, my conversation partners regard it as worthy of consideration. Hence, I am using this opportunity to delineate my theory in detail in English language. Although it is not possible to cover the entire spectrum of purported passages on child sacrifice in the Hebrew Bible here, I will say a few words on the other texts, too, while I will primarily focus on a new interpretation of the "Molech" texts in Leviticus 18 and 20.

2 The Context and the Text: Leviticus 18 and 20

2.1 The Context

The main topic of Leviticus 18 and 20 is the prohibition of illegitimate sexual relations between biological relatives, which are considered incest. Other persons related by marriage are socially and juridically on equal terms. In addition, both chapters mention the prohibition to give of one's offspring in order to transfer him/her to (or: "for") "the Molech" (Molech practice). If this injunction—as many presume—refers to a cultic ritual, even child sacrifice, it would hardly fit the overarching topic of prohibited sexual relations. In Lev 18:21, the banned Molech practice is mentioned between the prohibition of sexual relationship with a menstruant or a married woman (Lev 18:19–20) and the prohibition for a man to have sex with another man (18:22). Leviticus 20 adds sanctions to most of the commandments of Leviticus 18; here the Molech practice is mentioned at the beginning and is secured with a variety of sanctions, followed by the prohibition to turn to mediums and wizards (20:6), a basic paraenesis (20:7–8), and the sanctions for incest and other forbidden sexual relationships (20:9–21). Hence,

5 T. Hieke, "Das Verbot der Übergabe von Nachkommen an den 'Molech' in Lev 18 und 20. Ein neuer Deutungsversuch," *WO* 41 (2011) 147–67.

6 T. Hieke, *Levitikus 16–27* (HThKAT; Freiburg i. Br.: Herder, 2014), 643–4, 679–88, 695, 781–7.

the question emerges whether the Molech practice is an inadequate insertion—or whether perhaps the context provides a key for an appropriate understanding.

2.2 Lev 18:21

Lev 18:21 reads as follows in the Hebrew Bible (the Masoretic text):

וּמִזַּרְעֲךָ לֹא־תִתֵּן לְהַעֲבִיר לַמֹּלֶךְ וְלֹא תְחַלֵּל אֶת־שֵׁם אֱלֹהֶיךָ אֲנִי יְהוָה׃

> [21]And you shall not give any of your offspring to allow passing over to/for the Molech. And you shall not profane the name of your God. I am the LORD.

Most standard translations render the Hebrew text by inserting ritual terms like "immolation," "sacrifice," or "offering up."[7] However, the verbs are "to give" (*NTN*) and "to cause/allow to pass" (*ʿBR* hiph). This is followed by "to/for Molech;" here the Hebrew reads לַמֹּלֶךְ, in consonants: *l-m-l-k*. The Masoretes set the article and thus cause a double determination, if one understands "Molech" as a proper name (for, e.g., a deity). The Septuagint reads:

> ἀπὸ τοῦ σπέρματός σου οὐ δώσεις λατρεύειν ἄρχοντι

> and you shall not give any of your offspring to serve a ruler

Who could be meant by the "ruler"? Probably the Septuagint reads the verb עבד, "to serve," instead of עבר hiph, "to cause to pass," hence the translation with λατρεύω. "In the Septuagint, this verb almost always has God or gods as its object. This suggests that, in this context, the translator understood ἄρχων as referring to a deity or a leader who usurped divine prerogatives."[8] Does the Greek translator think about the prohibition of a cooperation or collaboration with pagan rulers (Ptolemaics, Seleucids) and their officials, as some suggest?[9] Does this

7 E.g., "You shall not give any of your offspring *to sacrifice* them to Molech" (New Revised Standard Version, NRSV); "And thou shalt not let any of thy seed pass through *the fire* to Molech" (King James Version); "You shall not offer any of your offspring *for immolation* to Molech" (New American Bible); "Do not allow any of your offspring *to be offered up* to Molech" (Jewish Publication Society Tanakh); "Und von deinen Nachkommen sollst du nicht *einen* hingeben, um sie dem Moloch durch *das Feuer* gehen zu lassen (Elberfelder Bibel); "Und von deinen Nachkommen sollst du keinen hingeben und ihn dem Moloch *darbringen*" (Zürcher Bibel 2007). The new German *Einheitsübersetzung* comes closer to the Hebrew wording: "Von deinen Nachkommen darfst du keinen hingeben, um ihn für Moloch hinübergehen zu lassen."

8 J. Lust, "Molek and ΑΡΧΩΝ," in E. Lipiński (ed.), *Phoenicia and the Bible. Proceedings of the Conference held at the University of Leuven on the 15th and 16th of March 1990* (OLA 44; StPhoe 11; Leuven: Peeters, 1991) 193–208, on p. 197.

9 Lust, "Molek," 203; D. Büchner, "'You Shall Not Give of Your Seed to Serve an Archon.' Lev 18,21 in the Septuagint," in H. Ausloos/J. Cook/F. García Martínez/B. Lemmelijn/M. Vervenne

interpretation have a clue in the Hebrew text (consonants: *lmlk*, "for Molech" or even "for the king")? For the intention of the translator, Büchner suggests a very vague paraphrase: "improper placement of semen by the worshiper in cultic service of one sort or another."[10]

The Jewish recensions Aquila, Symmachus and Theodotion transcribe the term with τῷ Μολοχ. The Peshitta replaces the difficult term by *(b)nwkrjtʾ*, "foreign woman," and thus thinks about a marriage with a non-Israelite woman (prohibition of exogamy; see Deut 7:3–4). The Targum Pseudo-Jonathan on Leviticus follows the same line at Lev 18:21:

> You shall not give any of your offspring *to have sexual intercourse with a pagan woman* impregnating her to the benefit of *idolatry*, and you shall not profane the name of your God. I am the Lord.[11]

However, the same Targum on Lev 20:2–5 as well as Targum Neofiti I on Lev 18:21 and 20:2–5 speak about a dedication of children in the context of idolatry:

> And you shall not give any of *your children* to be passed *through fire before an idol* (lit.: before an idolatrous cult) and *you* shall not profane the name of *your* God. *Says* the Lord.[12]

The prohibition of transferring one's offspring to "the Molech" yields at least two questions: First, what exactly is meant, i. e., who or what is "the Molech"? Second, why does this prohibition occur in this particular context?

2.3 Lev 20:1–5

Lev 20:1–5 receives its terminology from Lev 18:21 and speaks in the same way about giving one's offspring to "the Molech" (יִתֵּן מִזַּרְעוֹ לַמֹּלֶךְ). The section reads (NRSV adapted):

> [1]YHWH spoke to Moses, saying: [2]Say further to the people of Israel: Any of the people of Israel, or of the aliens who reside in Israel, who give any of their offspring to the Molech shall be put to death; the people of the land shall stone them to death. [3]I myself will set my face against them, and will cut them off from the people, because they have given of their offspring to the Molech, defiling my sanctuary and profaning my holy name. [4]And if the people of the land should ever close their eyes to them, when they give of their offspring to the Molech, and do not put them to death,

(ed.), *Translating a Translation. The LXX and its Modern Translations in the Context of Early Judaism* (BETL 213; Leuven: Peeters, 2008) 183–96, on pp. 195–6.

10 Büchner, "Lev 18,21," 188, 195.

11 M. Maher, *Targum Pseudo-Jonathan: Leviticus* (ArBib 3; Edinburgh: Clark, 1994), 174.

12 Targum Neofiti I on Lev 18:21, see M. McNamara/R. Hayward, *Targum Neofiti 1: Leviticus* (ArBib 3; Edinburgh: Clark, 1994), 69.

> [5]I myself will set my face against them and against their family, and will cut them off from among their people, them and all who follow them in prostituting themselves to the Molech.

3 The Terminology

For a correct understanding of these prescriptions, one has to investigate the terminological field. The "Molech" instances alone do not cover the entire problem, since several passages do not use the name "Molech," but address the same or at least similar issues. The sole biblical passage that contains *all* terms of this semantic field[13] is 2 Kings 23:10 in the context of the cult reform of King Josiah (NRSV adapted):

וְטִמֵּא אֶת־הַתֹּפֶת אֲשֶׁר בְּגֵי בְנֵי־הִנֹּם לְבִלְתִּי לְהַעֲבִיר אִישׁ אֶת־בְּנוֹ וְאֶת־בִּתּוֹ בָּאֵשׁ לַמֹּלֶךְ׃

> He defiled Topheth, which is in the valley of Ben-hinnom, so that no one would allow a son or a daughter pass over in fire to the Molech.

Again, the original NRSV inserts the words "as an offering," which have no equivalent in the Hebrew text. The Jewish Publication Society Tanakh translation reads instead,

> … so that no one might consign his son or daughter to the fire of Molech.

The relevant terms are as follows: "to allow to pass" or "transfer" (עבר hiph), "in/by fire" (בָּאֵשׁ), "son or daughter" or "children/offspring," "for the Molech" (לַמֹּלֶךְ; the Septuagint reads here: τῷ Μολοχ).

At all other instances, at least one of these elements is missing or replaced by another one. The following table provides a partial overview:

Missing element	*Verb*	*References*
Molech	to allow to pass (*ʿBR*)	Deut 18:10; 2 Kings 16:3; 17:17; 21:6; 2 Chronicles 33:6; Ezek 20:31
Molech	to burn (*ŚRP*)	Deut 12:31; 2 Kings 17:31; Jer 7:31; 19:5

13 See J. Milgrom, *Leviticus 17–22* (AB 3A; New York et al.: Doubleday, 2000), 1554.

Missing element	*Verb*	*References*
Molech	to burn (*BʿR*)	2 Chronicles 28:3
fire	to allow to pass (*ʿBR*)	Lev 18:21 (+to give); Jer 32:35
fire	to give (*NTN*)	Lev 20:2–4
Molech, fire	to allow to pass (*ʿBR*)	Ez 20:26
Molech, fire	to slaughter (*ŠḤṬ*)	Ezek 16:21; 23:39
Molech, fire	to sacrifice (*ZBḤ*)	Ps 106:37

Lev 18:21 and 20:2–4 use the verb "to give" (namely, offspring to/for the Molech). The expression "give for" (נתן ל, *NTN l-*) is never used as a technical term for the offering of a bloody victim.[14] Lev 20:5 calls the practice "prostituting themselves to Molech" (לִזְנוֹת אַחֲרֵי הַמֹּלֶךְ).[15]

Only a few biblical passages (2 Kings 23:10; Jer 7:31–32; 19:6, 11–14) mention the "Topheth." It appears to be a fireplace for the deity behind the term *l-mlk*. Staubli assumes that premature births and dead infants were cremated there in a ritual in front of the deity.[16] In the same vein, Staubli explains the archaeological evidence in the Phoenician areas. He points to the observation that the Greeks regarded the ritual of cremating dead children as distasteful; thus, they repelled this practice with polemic expressions and declared it as "child sacrifice."—Lipiński[17] uses the term "Topheth" also for the alleged archaeological evidence of child sacrifices in Carthage. He connects these issues several times with the biblical texts. In addition, he explains child sacrifices as a kind of selection legitimated by the society (elimination of the supposedly weaker firstborn) or as an act of birth control and thus as a reaction to demographic circumstances (problem of overpopulation). These speculations as well as the all too rashly

14 See P.A. Enger, *Die Adoptivkinder Abrahams. Eine exegetische Spurensuche zur Vorgeschichte des Proselytentums* (BEAT 53; Frankfurt am Main: Lang, 2006), 150.

15 U. Rüterswörden, "Die Stellung der Deuteronomisten zum alttestamentlichen Dämonenwesen," in A. Lange/H. Lichtenberger/K.F.D. Römheld (ed.), *Die Dämonen. Demons. Die Dämonologie der israelitisch-jüdischen und frühchristlichen Literatur im Kontext ihrer Umwelt* (Tübingen: Mohr Siebeck, 2003) 197–210, on pp. 199–200, provides an overview over the terminology, too.

16 See T. Staubli, *Die Bücher Levitikus, Numeri* (NSK.AT; Stuttgart: Katholisches Bibelwerk, 1996), 164; M. Bauks, "Menschenopfer in den Mittelmeerkulturen," *VF* 56 (2011) 33–44, on p. 36. See also J.H. Schwartz/F. Houghton/R. Macchiarelli/L. Bondioli, "Skeletal Remains from Punic Carthage Do Not Support Systematic Sacrifice of Infants," *PLoS ONE* 5(2) (2010): e9177 (https://doi.org/10.1371/journal.pone.0009177), passim.

17 E. Lipiński, "Sacrifices d'enfants à Carthage et dans le monde sémitique oriental," in idem (ed.), *Carthago. Acta Colloquii Bruxellensis habiti diebus 2 et 3 mensis Maii anni 1986* (OLA 26; Leuven: Peeters, 1988) 151–85, on pp. 160–2.

drawn lines between Carthage and Jerusalem are not convincing.[18] One has to bear in mind that there is no attestation of the word "Topheth" in Phoenician or Punic inscriptions.[19]

4 Directions of Research

Research on "the Molech" produced a variety of studies, but due to the ambiguous evidence, no finally convincing explanation has emerged so far. Studies typically follow one of the three following trajectories.[20]

4.1 A Deity

According to the classical interpretation, one has to reckon with sacrifices of children to a Canaanite deity. This old custom was revived in the eighth or seventh century BCE under Phoenician influence. The name with the consonants *m-l-k* that can also stand for "king" relates to various deities, especially to the god of the Netherworld, Malik.[21] However, archaeological evidence only exists in the Punic colonies of northern Africa (Carthage), Sardinia, and Sicily—but even those instances are disputed.[22] According to the consonantal

18 See, e.g., the critique by Noort, "Child Sacrifice," 114–15.

19 See B.H. Reynolds, "Molek: Dead or Alive? The Meaning and Derivation of *mlk* and מלך," in K. Finsterbusch/A. Lange/K.F.D. Römheld (ed.), *Human Sacrifice in Jewish and Christian Tradition* (Numen Book Series 112; Leiden: Brill, 2007) 133–50, on p. 135.

20 See, e.g., R. Albertz, *Religionsgeschichte Israels in alttestamentlicher Zeit* (ATD Ergänzungsreihe 8; Göttingen: Vandenhoeck & Ruprecht, 1992), 297–300; T. Seidl, "Der 'Moloch-Opferbrauch'—ein 'rite de passage'? Zur kontroversen Bewertung eines rätselhaften Ritus im Alten Testament," *OTE* 20 (2007) 432–55, on pp. 438–42. On the history of research see also G.C. Heider, *The Cult of Molek. A Reassessment* (JSOTS 43; Sheffield: JSOT Press, 1984), 1–92; Noort, "Child Sacrifice," 103–25; Dewrell, *Child Sacrifice*, 8–36.

21 See J. Day, *Molech: A God of Human Sacrifice in the Old Testament* (Cambridge: Cambridge University Press, 1989), 84.

22 See the critique by Rüterswörden, "Stellung," 204–7; Bauks, "Menschenopfer," 44. C. Levin, "Das Kinderopfer im Jeremiabuch," in idem, *Fortschreibungen. Gesammelte Studien zum Alten Testament* (BZAW 316; Berlin/New York: De Gruyter, 2003) 227–41, on pp. 258–60, assumes a cult of child sacrifices for Adadmelek (see below) from the Syro-Aramaic area. On the discussion see also H.-P. Müller, "Genesis 22 und das mlk-Opfer. Erinnerungen an einen religionsgeschichtlichen Tatbestand," in A. Lange/K.F.D. Römheld (ed.), *Wege zur Hebräischen Bibel. Denken – Sprache – Kultur. In memoriam Hans-Peter Müller* (FRLANT 228; Göttingen: Vandenhoeck & Ruprecht, 2009) 201–13, on pp. 204–8, who opts for the interpretation of *mlk* as a technical term for a sacrifice; M. Bauks, "Opfer, Kinder und mlk. Das Menschenopfer und seine Auslösung," in Lange/Römheld (ed.), *Wege zur Hebräischen Bibel*, 215–32, on p. 216, agrees. Staubli, "Prehistory," 96, concludes: "But a closer look at the sources reveals most theories

text, one can read *ha-mōlek* as a determined participle, as "king," or as a divine name.[23]

4.2 A Technical Term for a Sacrifice

A second position follows the results of the research by Otto Eißfeldt.[24] He interprets *molk* as a general technical term for a sacrifice ("offering" or "the offered"), because this term denotes the child sacrifice or the replacement by an animal on Punic votive stelae. Israel took over this Punic custom and offered *lmlk* sacrifices to Yahweh.[25] However, King Josiah denunciated it as idolatry and reinterpreted the term for the sacrifice as a term for a deity and thus, an idol.[26]

---

about child sacrifices to be groundless and based on misperceptions." A recent summary of the archaeological and textual research on "Tophets" by A. Orsingher, "Understanding Tophets: A Short Introduction," in The Ancient Near East Today 6 (2018) (http://www.asor.org/anetoday/2018/02/Understanding-Tophets-Short; last visited on February 23, 2018), concludes: "The question of child sacrifice remains unresolved, but the necropolis-sanctuary dichotomy now seems outdated. Today many scholars agree that *Tophets* were multipurpose sacred areas where a variety of rites was performed."

23 See Seidl, "Moloch-Opferbrauch," 434–5.

24 See O. Eißfeldt, *Molk als Opferbegriff im Punischen und Hebräischen und das Ende des Gottes Moloch* (BRGA 3; Halle: Niemeyer, 1935), passim. Two recent studies (R.M. Kerr, "In Search of the Historical Moloch," in idem/R. Miller/P.C. Schmitz [ed.], *"His Word Soars Above Him". Biblical and North-West Semitic Studies Presented to Professor Charles R. Krahmalkov* [Ann Arbor, MI, 2018]) 59–80, on p. 79; Dewrell, *Child Sacrifice*, 36) confirm Eißfeldt's view; see also Noort, "Child Sacrifice," 117–18; Reynolds, "Molek," 150. There seems to emerge a growing consensus in current scholarship to interpret *lmlk* as a technical term for sacrifices and thus put the god *Molek* to rest (Reynolds).

25 According to Dewrell, *Child Sacrifice*, 143, King Ahaz introduced *lmlk* offerings into the Jerusalem cult. "Ahaz borrowed the rite from Phoenicia, the original homeland of the Punic colonists" (ibid., 145).

26 See A. Michel, *Gott und Gewalt gegen Kinder im Alten Testament* (FAT 37; Tübingen: Mohr Siebeck, 2003), 276–7 (with reference to further secondary literature). Reynolds also interprets *lmlk* as a technical term for a sacrifice built from the root *hlk* hiph as a causative ("Molek," 133–50; see also M. Bauks, "Kinderopfer als Weihe- oder Gabeopfer. Anmerkungen zum *mlk*-Opfer," in M. Witte/J.F. Diehl (ed.), *Israeliten und Phönizier. Ihre Beziehungen im Spiegel der Archäologie und der Literatur des Alten Testaments und seiner Umwelt* (OBO 235; Göttingen: Vandenhoeck & Ruprecht, 2008) 233–51, on p. 248; F. Stavrakopoulou, *King Manasseh and Child Sacrifice. Biblical Distortions of Historical Realities* (BZAW 338; Berlin/New York: De Gruyter, 2004), 240–61; K. Koch, "Molek astral," in A. Lange/H. Lichtenberger/D. Römheld (ed.), *Mythos im Alten Testament und seiner Umwelt. Festschrift für Hans-Peter Müller zum 65. Geburtstag* (BZAW 278; Berlin/New York: De Gruyter, 1999) 29–50, on pp. 29–45, Kerr, "Search," passim). Dewrell, *Child Sacrifice*, 68–9, again opts for Eißfeldt's hypothesis. Bauks, Reynolds, Stavrakopoulou, Koch, Kerr and Dewrell treat the Punic epigraphy in detail (see also S. Brown, *Late Carthaginian Child Sacrifice and Sacrificial Monuments in their Mediterranean Context* [Sheffield: JSOT Press, 1991], passim). However, Dewrell has to conclude that there "is

In the wake of Josiah's centralization of the cult at the temple in Jerusalem, the traditional Canaanite sacrificial cult was abolished.[27] T. Seidl interprets the term as an abstract substantive due to the determination by the article and thus opts for a technical term for a sacrifice.[28] He correctly points to the problem that the Punic evidence is comparably young and disputed and thus cannot bear the burden of proof.[29] In addition, a recent study by J. H. Schwartz et al. suggests the following:

> In sum, while the Carthaginians may occasionally have practiced human sacrifice, as did other circum-Mediterranean societies ... our analyses do not support the contention that all humans interred in the Tophet had been sacrificed. Rather, it would appear that the Carthaginian Tophet, and by extension Tophets at Carthaginian settlements in general, were cemeteries for the remains of human prenates and infants who died from a variety of causes and then cremated and whose remains, sometimes on a catch-as-catch-can basis, interred in urns.[30]

However, this is not the end of the discussion; other studies seem to prove that child sacrifices actually took place in the Punic colonies. Dewrell recently correlates the archaeological and textual evidence and concludes:

> Thus, although archaeological evidence must always be interpreted with caution, the combined data, both textual and archaeological, points to child sacrifice as having been a very real practice in the Punic colonies of the central Mediterranean.[31]

---

as yet no strong material evidence for child sacrifice in Phoenicia proper, or Syria-Palestine in general ... Thus, in order to maintain a connection between Punic *mlk* and Hebrew מֹלֶךְ, as I do, circumstantial evidence remains, for now, the only basis" (69). According to my view, this basis is not sufficient. Hence, I do not ignore the Punic material, as Kerr, "Search," 74 n. 72, insinuates, but I do not accept the alleged direct connection between the inscriptions and the biblical term *l-mlk*.—Koch suggests that the *molek* ritual belongs to an astral cult with child sacrifices, and Noort, "Child Sacrifice," 124–5, seems to follow him with caution, but these guesses are in sum less convincing.

27 See Kerr, "Search," 79.

28 Seidl, "Moloch-Opferbrauch," 434.

29 See also A. Michel, "Gewalt gegen Kinder im alten Israel. Eine sozialgeschichtliche Perspektive," in A. Kunz-Lübcke (ed.), *"Schaffe mir Kinder ...". Beiträge zur Kindheit im alten Israel und in seinen Nachbarkulturen* (ABIG 21; Leipzig: Evangelische Verlagsanstalt, 2006) 137–63, on pp. 154–7, and Rüterswörden, "Stellung," 204–7.

30 Schwartz et al., "Skeletal Remains," Discussion. See also Dewrell, *Child Sacrifice*, 46–50, who conveniently summarizes the recent discussion.

31 Dewrell, *Child Sacrifice*, 49.

4.3 A Kind of Worship

The third position opts for a certain kind of worship that existed in Judah in the eighth and seventh century. M. Weinfeld[32] takes this view and interprets Molech as a parody of the divine epithet *mælæk*, "king." The parody builds on the vowels of the term *bošæt*, "shame."[33] The "king" is the deity *Adad-milki*, "King Adad," the Aramaic-Assyrian weather god Adad.[34] The phrase "to let pass through fire" does not literally mean an immolation as a child sacrifice but a rite of consecration and dedication, by which the children are integrated in the service of this deity.[35] The children became priestesses or priests or a lower clergy or even female and male cult prostitutes.[36] Extra-biblical occurrences appear in Assyrian vassal treaties from the ninth to the seventh century BCE.[37] For R. Albertz it is clear that this weather god stands behind Molech and that the biblical passages are about a rite of dedication and purification of children for this deity.[38] T. Seidl essentially adopts this interpretation and sees this "dedication" as a rite of adolescence in the transition from youth to adulthood.[39]

5 The Problem of Polemic

The basic problem for the reconstruction of the history behind the Molech practice results from the following observation. Many claimed proof texts, especially biblical texts from later periods, constitute a metaphorically alienated and exaggerated polemic to defame certain groups.[40] Michel evaluates all pertinent

32 See M. Weinfeld, "The Worship of Molech and of the Queen of Heaven and its Background," *UF* 4 (1972) 133–54.

33 As early as 1857, A. Geiger suggested this interpretation, see G. C. Heider, "Molech," *ABD* 4 (1992) 895–8, on p. 896; Reynolds, "Molek," 143–4; Milgrom, *Leviticus 17–22*, 1556; Kerr, "Search," 60. Most scholars no longer accept this solution, see ibid., 68.

34 On the discussion about Adadmilki and the problematic passage in 2 Kings 17:31 see D. Schwemer, *Die Wettergottgestalten Mesopotamiens und Nordsyriens im Zeitalter der Keilschriftkulturen. Materialien und Studien nach den schriftlichen Quellen* (Wiesbaden: Harrassowitz, 2001), 636–7. Schwemer opts for interpreting Adrammelek as a Phoenician deity and separating him from Adadmilki (and Adad).

35 See also Rashi's Commentary on the Pentateuch on Leviticus 18:21, English translation by Rabbi A. J. Rosenberg on https://www.chabad.org/library/bible_cdo/aid/9919#showrashi=true.

36 See, e.g., N. Snaith, "The Cult of Molech," *VT* 16 (1966) 123–4, on p. 124.

37 See, e.g., K. Hecker, "Akkadische Rechts- und Verwaltungsurkunden," in *TUAT (AF) Ergänzungslieferung* (Gütersloh: Gütersloher Verlagshaus, 2001) 21–33, on p. 29.

38 Albertz, *Religionsgeschichte*, 301.

39 Seidl, "Moloch-Opferbrauch," 441–2.

40 See in particular Ezek 16; Ezek 23; Ps 106:37–38; cf. Michel, *Gott und Gewalt*, 287–8, who also regards Deut 12:31 and 2 Kings 17.31 as a later atrocity propaganda in analogy to Wis 12:3–6.

passages diachronically and draws the following conclusion: The ritual "to burn by fire" (*ŚRP bā-ʾēš*) is a literary and polemical construction by late or even post-Deuteronomistic writers that reveals much about the mentality of their creators, but less to nothing about historical conditions. Briefly and as a summary for most passages in Ezekiel and Jeremiah: Especially with the occurrences of *ZBḤ/ŠḤṬ* (to slaughter) and *ŚRP bā-ʾēš* (to burn by fire), one cannot surmise that the Molech practice included child sacrifice or the killing of children.[41] Michel's analysis proceeds very carefully and plausible; thus one has to admit that all passages, which terminologically point to a bloody sacrifice ("slaughter," "burn"), proffer a biased polemic. This sort of propagandistic polemic works with an imagination that is commonly rated as absurd in order to arouse abhorrence. This literary strategy can only operate if the ritual killing of children was *not* a common or accepted practice.

A few examples may illustrate this consideration. In Judges 11[42], Jephthah made a vow and thus had to offer up his daughter, his only child. However, the biblical text does not regard Jephthah's sacrifice as a great deed. According to the judgment of the Deuteronomist, Jephthah's reign is limited to six years only; thus, he comes off significantly worse than his predecessors and successors.[43] The story is by no means a proof for the reality of child sacrifice,[44] but a polemical fiction with the parenetic aim to warn against thoughtless vows. There is a tendency in scholarship to construct a general practice of child sacrifice from single passages like Judges 11; 2 Kings 16:3; 2 Kings 3:27 (and finally also Genesis 22[45]) and

41 See Michel, *Gott und Gewalt*, 291; Kerr, "Search," 70.

42 See, e.g., M. Bauks, *Jephtas Tochter. Traditions-, religions- und rezeptionsgeschichtliche Studien zu Richter 11,29–40* (FAT 71; Tübingen: Mohr Siebeck, 2010); eadem, "Theological Implications" (including a comparison of Judges 11 with Genesis 22). In the latter contribution, Bauks distinguishes Judges 11, Genesis 22, and 2 Kings 3 clearly from "the sacrifice to *mlk*" (see p. 84). She makes clear that Genesis 22 does not function as an etiology of the substitution for child sacrifice indicating some sort of "religious progress" with regard to neighboring cultures (p. 85).

43 See Michel, *Gott und Gewalt*, 302.

44 Pace, A. Lange, "'They Burn Their Sons and Daughters—That Was No Command of Mine' (Jer 7:31). Child Sacrifice in the Hebrew Bible and in the Deuteronomistic Jeremiah Redaction," in K. Finsterbusch/A. Lange/K. F. D. Römheld (ed.), *Human Sacrifice in Jewish and Christian Tradition* (Numen Book Series 112; Leiden: Brill, 2007) 109–32, on pp. 118–19.

45 See in particular Müller, "Genesis 22," 210–13: abolishing child sacrifice. On the reception history in Early Judaism, see K. Berthelot, "Jewish Views of Human Sacrifice in the Hellenistic and Roman Period," in K. Finsterbusch/A. Lange/K. F. D. Römheld (ed.), *Human Sacrifice in Jewish and Christian Tradition* (Numen Book Series 112; Leiden: Brill, 2007) 151–73. According to Berthelot, human sacrifices are not a major theme in Jewish literature from the Hellenistic and Roman period. The literature shows almost no references to pagan human sacrifices, presents human sacrifices as inspired by demons (e.g., Prince Mastema), and reinterprets biblical human sacrifices as self-sacrifices with a positive value (Jephthah's daughter, Isaac). Apart from these specific cases, condemnation of human sacrifices prevails in Jewish literature from this period (ibid., 173).

to insist on the historical reality of child sacrifice[46] in spite of all difficulties to reconstruct this practice from external evidence. However, this conclusion is unwarranted. The passages claimed as proof for the practice child sacrifice operate in the logic of the text (within the world of the text) as extreme exceptions, and they unfold their literary effectiveness only if one does *not* presuppose a generally accepted practice of child sacrifice.

Occasionally, the following passages are presented as proof texts for the historical reality of child sacrifice in Israel in the seventh to sixth century (NRSV adapted):

> Will the Lord be pleased with thousands of rams, with ten thousands of rivers of oil? Shall I give my firstborn for my transgression, the fruit of my body for the sin of my soul? (Micah 6:7)

> 25Moreover I gave them statutes that were not good and ordinances by which they could not live. 26I defiled them through their very gifts, in their setting aside all their firstborn, in order that I might horrify them, so that they might know that I am the Lord. (Ezek 20:25–26)

Nevertheless, even these passages do not gain their effectiveness from the regular practice of child sacrifice.[47] The punch line rather emerges from the fact that such a thing is beyond imagination and considered by the addressees as utterly absurd.[48] C. Levin goes so far to state that Jer 7:31 is the *only* passage in the Hebrew Bible that can be considered as a proof for the practice of child sacrifice in Israel/Judah.[49] All other occurrences are deductions from this text with polemical interests. At the same time, Levin lists several reasons to cast doubt on the historical relevance of Jer 7:31: Even this statement has the notion of a harsh polemic and looks back from a considerable chronological distance during the time of the Exile to an obscure practice of the pre-exilic era. In sum, there is no clear and positive evidence for child sacrifice in Israel (with or without the term *l-mlk*, Molech).

Hence, the case remains open whether "Molech" is a technical term for a sacrifice or the name of a deity as the receiver of gifts. What is no longer possible, at least according to my view, is to take the existence of child sacrifices for "Molech"

46 E.g., Levin, "Kinderopfer," 259; Bauks, "Opfer," 232; Dewrell, *Child Sacrifice*, 111, 189–90. Regarding Genesis 22, however, Dewrell admits that this chapter "is far too overlaid with legend and etiology to provide reliable information about either the historical practice of child sacrifice or even biblical rhetoric surrounding the practice" (p. 172 n. 48).

47 Pace, Bauks, "Theological Implications," 78–9; eadem, "Kinderopfer," 248; eadem, *Jephtas Tochter*, 56; Noort, "Child Sacrifice," 112–13; Lange, "They Burn," 116–17.

48 See Michel, *Gott und Gewalt*, 294–5.

49 See Levin, "Kinderopfer," 239; Lange, "They Burn," 129–32.

for granted, especially on a large scale.[50] For this, any clear textual and archaeological evidence is entirely missing.[51] On the other hand, it is clear that all biblical texts reject child sacrifice as well as any Molech practice.[52] Unfortunately it is no longer discernible which historical practice stood behind this sharply worded polemic. It was definitely not a regular cult; we do not even have evidence of an *ultima ratio* in a military crisis (as it was in the case of the sacrifice by the king of Moab in 2 Kings 3:27[53]). Maybe there was some cult of the dead in connection with a royal deity that was worshipped as king of the Sheol (Malik, Milku, Milki or Adad) *next to* Yahweh[54] or that was used for mantic practices (see the closeness of Lev 20:2–5 to 20:6, the prohibition of necromancy and divination). This cult for a chthonic deity did perhaps not include sacrifices of living children, but used the ritual cremation of miscarriages and infants that died early.[55] The place of this cult of the dead was probably the Topheth in the Hinnom valley near Jerusalem. King Josiah of Judah is said to have profaned this Topheth in order to abolish this parallel cult (2 Kings 23:10, see above).

An alternative interpretation[56] that considers these observations assumes a royal deity behind the Masoretic *ha-molæk* (even Yahweh himself). In a ritual act, young people were consecrated and dedicated to this deity. The phrase "to burn in/by fire" might designate a fire ceremony for the purgation of the candidates. The *w-qatal* form in 2 Kings 21:6 (*wᵉ-hæʿæbīr*, "he made his son pass through fire") points to a *repeated* procedure[57] like the other practices mentioned in this verse, i. e., Manasseh made his son pass through fire several times in the same way as he practiced soothsaying etc. continuously (several *w-qatal* forms). Consequently, one must assume that the rite did not include the killing of the

50 See, e.g., Enger, *Adoptivkinder*, 150–1.

51 See, e.g., Bauks, "Kinderopfer," 244–5, for the second millennium BCE; Lange, "They Burn," 119: no archaeological traces of child sacrifice in Iron Age Israel; the evidence mentioned by Stavrakopoulou, *Child Sacrifice*, 261–99, cannot bear the burden of proof; for the critique of Stavrakopoulou's results see Michel, "Gewalt gegen Kinder," 152–4. See also the very cautious results mentioned by Heider, *Cult*, 222; Dewrell, *Child Sacrifice*, 68–9.

52 See Dewrell, *Child Sacrifice*, 148–90.

53 See J. Ebach/U. Rüterswörden, "ADRMLK, 'Moloch' und BAʿAL ADR. Eine Notiz zum Problem der Moloch-Verehrung im alten Israel," *UF* 11 (1979) 219–26, on p. 220; Bauks, "Opfer," 226; Noort, "Child Sacrifice," 109–10.

54 See Milgrom, *Leviticus 17–22*, 1564–5; Heider, *Cult*, 401.

55 See Staubli, *Levitikus, Numeri*, 164.

56 Seidl, "Moloch-Opferbrauch," 446–9; similarly, C. Frevel, "Moloch und Mischehen. Zu einigen Aspekten der Rezeption von Gen 34 in Jub 30," in U. Dahmen/J. Schnocks (ed.), *Juda und Jerusalem in der Seleukidenzeit. Herrschaft – Widerstand – Identität. Festschrift für Heinz-Josef Fabry* (BBB 159; Göttingen: V&R unipress, 2010) 161–87, on p. 167.

57 See Gesenius-Kautzsch-Cowley, Hebrew Grammar (1909), § 112e; B. K. Waltke/M. O'Connor, *An Introduction to Biblical Hebrew Syntax* (Winona Lake, IN: Eisenbrauns, 1990), 524 (§ 32.1.3c).

son.[58] The proximity to the incest laws in Lev 18 and 20 might indicate a rite of adolescence as a *rite de passage* on the occasion of sexual maturity. However, one cannot understand all *mlk* texts along these lines.

K. A. D. Smelik suggests that the alleged deity Molech is an invention from the Persian period with the following function: The cipher "Molech" serves to blur the traces of child sacrifices for Yahweh in Judah in pre-exilic times.[59] However, this suggestion is less convincing. On the one hand, a pre-exilic practice of child sacrifice is by no means proven, since the proofs mentioned by Smelik can be interpreted differently. On the other hand, this suggestion does not explain why post-exilic authors invented exactly *this* name.

Hence the terminology remains peculiarly open: Clear sacrificial terms (to burn, to slaughter) do not appear in direct connection with the occurrences of "the Molech." Sacrificial terms without "the Molech" turn out to be atrocity propaganda.[60] It is possible that the commandments in Leviticus 18 and 20 prohibit an alien cult practice that we cannot reconstruct any longer: the text rebukes it as dreadful and associates it with the proscribed child sacrifice.[61]

6 The Alternative: a Cipher

In particular, the open terminology invites the attempt to understand "for the Molech" (לַמֹּלֶךְ; without vowels למלך, *lmlk*) as a cipher for something entirely different. Two preliminary considerations may introduce this line of thought.

6.1 Preliminary Considerations

(1) The consonantal version without vowels is the same as the stamp seal impressions on vessels from the pre-exilic period. Archaeologists found hundreds and thousands of sherds with these seal impressions. The word *lmlk* on a vessel indicated that the vessel and its content belonged to the king (in Jerusalem).[62] One can translate the formula *lmlk* thus "for the king/belonging to the king/destined for the king," or, more freely translated, "state property."

58 Seidl, "Moloch-Opferbrauch," 447.

59 K. A. D. Smelik, "Moloch, Molekh or Molk-Sacrifice?," *SJOT* 9 (1995) 133–42.

60 See Michel, *Gott und Gewalt*, 288.

61 See the interpretations by Milgrom, *Leviticus 17–22*, 1555, 1558; Enger, *Adoptivkinder*, 152; Stavrakopoulou, *Child Sacrifice*, 301–22. Most scholars no longer accept the suggestion that the voweling of Molech emerged by the use of the vowels of *bošæt*, "shame," by which the Masoretes wanted to mock the term (see above, n. 33).

62 See the internet platform http://www.lmlk.com/research/ for examples and further research.

Fig 1: Stamp seal impression from Lachish (size: 35 × 23 mm)
Text on top: *LMLK*—למלך "for the king"
Text on bottom: *HBRN* "Hebron"
(D. Ussishkin, "The Royal Judean Storage Jars and Seal Impressions from the Renewed Excavations," in idem [ed.], *The Renewed Archaeological Excavations at Lachish [1973–1994]*, Vol. IV [Tel Aviv: Yass Publications in Archaeology, 2004] 2133–47, on p. 2140, No. 4)

(2) The Septuagint transcribes the Hebrew word as Μολοχ only in 4Bas 23:10 (2 Kings 23:10) and Jer 39:35LXX (Jer 32:35MT). The Greek version translates the Leviticus passages as ἄρχοντι, "for the ruler, leader" (also "for the supreme authority"), or εἰς τοὺς ἄρχοντας (plural, 20:5). The related verb in Lev 18:21LXX reads λατρεύειν, "to serve."—If one follows the broad consensus within scholarship that the commandments in Leviticus presuppose post-exilic (Persian period) conditions, a different assumption emerges that I would like to outline here.

6.2 A Cipher for the Collaboration with the Occupying Power

Is it plausible to imagine that the term "Molech" operated subliminally as a cipher for a certain way of collaboration with the occupying power? Leviticus 18 and 20 do not speak of fire, but only of "giving" and "allowing to pass/transfer"—"for/to the Molech," or, more clearly, "for the (foreign) king" and his governors. This could refer to the provision of children for different services for the foreign power. For the motivation as well as for the services a variety of options is possible. Family heads in Yehud and Jerusalem might sell (or, give) one of their children permanently in order to solve a situation of financial distress (see Nehemiah 5:5) or accommodate a child as servant for a foreign master, thus having one mouth less to feed. Alternatively, they place one of their offspring as a courtesy at the disposal of the Persian authority in order to gain a favor. Perhaps career opportunities in the service of the occupation power made fathers to allow their sons to transfer to the foreign troops. Of course, this kind of "provision of children" happened voluntarily or was an option to pay debts. If the occupation power requisitioned the children as laborers, the family heads had no choice; thus, the priestly ban would be useless and ineffective. We thus do not speak about enforcement measures of the foreign masters. The actions of the Judeans (Yehudites) rather oscillates in the grey scale between collaboration and ingratiation for the sake of one's own profit.

The services, for which the children were provided, certainly covered a wide variety: taking care of smaller children of the Persian officials, serving in the households and the agriculture, even hard physical work or military service as arms bearers. Implicitly and unavoidable, the transferred children got alienated from their own religious-cultural identity, they adopted the religious and social values of their masters—and thus, the small Israelite/Jewish community lost them forever.

6.3 A Patristic Testimony

A patristic testimony in the works of Theodoret of Cyrus (393–458/460/466 CE) corroborates this interpretation. In his commentary on Leviticus 18:21, Theodoret refers an opinion that interprets the Septuagint equivalent ἄρχοντι for Hebrew *lmlk* as an earthly ruler or master. It is not allowed to transfer one's offspring as house-slaves or arms bearers to these foreign masters, since the foreigner might seduce his servants to idolatry. Theodoret writes:

> What is the meaning of "You shall not give any of your offspring in worship of a ruler and shall not profane my holy name: I am the Lord"?—The Hebrew has "Moloch," which the other translators have also used. This was an idol. Hence, God also said through the prophet, "Surely you did not offer victims and sacrifices to me in the desert for forty years, sons of Israel? You took up the tent of Moloch and the star of your god Rephan, the images you made to worship." So he forbade the offering of their children as attendants on idols. On the other hand, some commentators have claimed that the purpose of this law was to prohibit the assignment of children as servants or bodyguards to foreign rulers, to prevent them from participating in their idolatry. (Theodoret of Cyrus, Question XXV on Lev 18:21)

6.4 Loss of the Children

Whether our imagination has to go so far as to think of profane and cultic sexual "services," including the decoration of festivals by neat child slaves or orgies with child abuse remains an open question.[63] In any case, the children are either corrupted or even killed—or they make their career and marry into the foreign society. The common denominator of all these considerations is that the children who have been "given" and "passed over" were lost to their own community and their people; they lose their own religion and identity forever. However, the "seed" or "sperm" (*zēra*ʿ, translated in Lev 18:21 with "offspring") is "holy," as Ezra 9:2 underscores; it must not mix with "the peoples of the land." Hence the penitential prayer and the subsequent action in Ezra 9–10 explicitly inculcates the prohibition of mixed marriages in the Torah (Exod 34:16; Deut 7:1–4). One would suspect such a ban on marriages with foreign women also in Leviticus 18 and 20.[64] Maybe it is included in the much wider prohibition of "giving one's offspring" (one's own children) to the foreign occupying power—for whatever purpose, perhaps also for a profitable mixed marriage. It is illuminating that Jub 30:10 and b. Meg. 25a connect the mixed marriage with the giving of "semen" to Molech.[65]

6.5 The Encryption

The priestly authors of the book of Leviticus cannot convey the prohibition against transferring one's offspring to the occupying power (i. e., the Persian authorities) in explicit language. Hence they use a polemic against child sacrifices for "the Molech" as a disguise, camouflage, or encryption. *Ad extra*, they avoid a direct attack on the foreign king: If the Persian authorities become suspicious because of this wording, the priests could point to the "plain" meaning and claim that *lmlk* does not mean the (Persian) king but a foreign deity.[66] *Ad intra*, the atrocious propaganda already connected with the term "Molech" strengthens the deterrent effect: If you give your child in the service of the foreign king and his

63 Lust, "Molek," 203–4, points to this possibility but also expresses some reservations.

64 See Milgrom, *Leviticus 17–22*, 1553. 1584–6.

65 See Weinfeld, "Worship," 142–4; Frevel, "Moloch," 161–87; G. Vermes "Leviticus 18:21 in Ancient Jewish Bible Exegesis," in J. J. Petuchowski/E. Fleischer (ed.), *Studies in Aggadah, Targum and Jewish Liturgy in Memory of Joseph Heinemann* (Jerusalem: Magnes, 1981) 108–24, on pp. 111–12.

66 Michel, *Gott und Gewalt*, 298, regards Molech as a probably fictitious divine name; see also Stavrakopoulou, *Child Sacrifice*, 301. The problem of a code or cipher is that one can hardly find any "solid evidence." Insofar, Kerr's allegation is correct (see Kerr, "Search," 74 n. 72). On the other hand, I consider the alleged connection between *l-mlk* and the Punic stelae no "solid evidence" either.

officials or in a mixed marriage with the alien masters, you act like an idolater who sacrifices to "Molech"![67] One can even explain the "prostituting" in Lev 20:5 in the same way: The people who "prostitute themselves" are those who obsequiously collaborate with the foreign power and who in their ingratiation give away their own children and thus hand them over to idolatry.

6.6 Profaning the Divine Name

In the aforementioned interpretation, how then can one understand the final phrase of Lev 18:21, the profanation of the divine name? All who give away one of their children in the described way, be it in order to pay debts, to ingratiate the foreign rulers, or to attempt a bribery, diminishes the number of the people of God, despise the "holy seed" and thus profane the name of God. They deprive God of a person that in the future could praise God. At the same time, if the child is transferred to the service for the foreigners, it will become acquainted with their religion and cult, and it will take over these practices. This child is lost for Yahweh. Hence, the suggested alternative interpretation also fits the prohibition to profane God's name. Such profanation not only happens by worshipping foreign gods (sacrifices for Molech, Malik, or the like), but also by distracting one's own children from the worship of Yahweh by transferring them to the foreign power.[68]

---

67 One could also apply the terminology coined by James C. Scott (*Domination and the Arts of Resistance*): On the level of the "public transcript," i.e., the official communication of the priests and the Judahites with the Persian authorities, the prohibition refers to a (fictitious) foreign cult, perhaps including child sacrifices. The authorities would accept such a prohibition without any suspicion. On the level of the "hidden transcript," however, the priests address their own community and intend something different: the prohibition to collaborate with the Persian authorities by transferring offspring to the foreign power. The Persian officials would not accept that injunction if they understood this sort of offstage communication or "hidden transcript." As Scott demonstrates in his entire book, it is a strategy of resistance by subordinate groups to employ different interactions among their peers than with the dominators. The open, public interactions between dominators and oppressed are called "public transcript," while the critique of the superordinate power goes on offstage as "hidden transcript." With the *lmlk* cipher, the priests could prohibit transfers of children to the Persian authorities on the level of "hidden transcript" without ever informing the foreign authority about this prohibition.

68 According to Amos 2:7, the profanation of Yahweh's holy name happens by sexual misconduct (father and son have sex with the same girl). Other passages mention social (Jer 34:16) and cultic wrongdoings (Lev 19:12; 21:6; 22:2.32; Ezek 20:39; 36:20–23).

6.7 The Relationship to the Context: No Progeny

The exposure of children to the occupying power (Lev 18:21) diminishes the number of the people of God that depends heavily on progeny. Here one finds the connection to the two following prohibitions: same-sex relationship among men (18:22) and sexual relationship with an animal (18:23). All three practices have in common that they inhibit progeny for Yahweh. If an Israelite man wastes his "holy seed" by transferring his offspring to the service for the foreigners or by having sex with a male or with an animal, or if a woman has sex with an animal, in all cases these wrongdoers prevent the emergence of future Yahweh worshipers and supporters of the people's identity. Thus, these persons do not justice to their responsibility towards the people as a unity. In biblical texts, sexuality is always connected with a mean responsibility, not only on a personal level, but especially in view of the people—hence, sexuality is never detached from its social function.[69]

7 Verification of the Suggested Interpretation by Means of Lev 20:1–5

7.1 The Seriousness of the Crime

The suggestion for an alternative understanding of the Molech practice in Lev 18:21 needs now a verification by means of the parallel in Lev 20:1–5. As already demonstrated, many texts dealing with "Molech" and the related terminology unleash a massive polemic; they exalt the associated practice to something quite disgusting.[70] Lev 20:2–5, too, pronounces the harshest sanctions against the "transferring of offspring to Molech." Is it plausible that such harsh warnings refer to child sacrifices that took place at most as an *ultima ratio* in desperate situations of distress?[71] Is it probable that such harsh warnings refer to a certain cult for a chthonic royal deity, for which no archaeological, epigraphical, and literary sources exist? It is not easy to align the parenetical texts with the most plausible assumptions about the Molech practice that scholarship normally asserts. The intensity with which particularly Lev 20:2–5 rebukes the transfer of offspring to "the Molech" suggests a more commonplace, even regular procedure; and perhaps

---

69 Vermes, "Leviticus 18:21," 122–4, points to the importance of this context for the interpretation of Lev 18:21.

70 See E. S. Gerstenberger, *Das 3. Buch Mose. Leviticus* (ATD 6; Göttingen: Vandenhoeck & Ruprecht, 1993), 267.

71 See 2 Kings 3:27: The king of Moab sacrifices his firstborn son as a burnt offering.

larger parts of the Israelite community in Yehud did not perceive this procedure as all too bad. Hence I suggest interpreting the Molech practice as a cipher for the surrender of children to the occupying power, the Persian authorities and officials. By this practice, the Israelite community loses these children; they forfeit their cultural and religious identity and take over the culture, faith, and religion of their new suzerains. For the priestly theologians who developed the concept of "holiness in everyday life" and the *imitatio Dei* as representation of Yahweh's justice and holiness by the people of Israel in the world, this transfer of children to foreign rulers is the biggest accident to be assumed. It is an idea that contradicts the priests' fundamental principles in the most absurd way. For the priests, this procedure is like murdering one's own children in combination with apostasy from Yahweh. Of course, the priests may not speak frankly in this manner: If the priests explicitly condemn the collaboration with the Persian authorities by incriminating the surrender of children for various services, these very authorities would become suspicious. If the Persian governor and his officials had become aware of the fact that the priests warn of them with the threat of the death penalty, they could interpret this warning as a call for disloyalty and protest. Hence, the priests camouflage their intensive warning of transferring children to the Persian officials and the rich foreigners by using the cipher of the "Molech practice." The consonants *lmlk* may function as a remembrance of the many stamp seal impressions from the era of the kings, in which *lmlk* indicated "for the king, state property"—and now it is the *foreign* king and his governors, to whom the children shall not be given.

> The resident aliens (גרים), who the Israelites shall treat not differently than the natives among them and who they shall love as themselves (Lev 19:34), are understandably subject to the same law. The resident aliens who joined Israel as a labor migrant may attend Israel's festivals, sacrifice for Yahweh (and no other god!), and should keep the days of rest (the Sabbath and the holidays)—they are thus already (almost) part of the people of Israel. It would be absurd to allow them to give their offspring to the occupying power. As pointed out above, the children adopt the culture and religion of the occupiers, and maybe they return temporarily to their own families. This would open the doors for foreign cults: The resident alien who adopted Israel's religion (later the term denotes "proselyte") might turn to the gods of the foreign masters for the sake of his children. This is an unthinkable scenario for the priestly writers, and they prevent it by including the stranger in the prohibition of "Molech" practice.

From a priestly viewpoint, the "Molech" practice, understood in the sense outlined above, is so grave that immediate killing is required—with no intervening examination, witness testimony, trial, verdict, or even legal assistance instruction. Of course, it is historically unlikely that such an approach would have been practicable for a long time without causing serious abuses. It would quickly lead to the removal of unpopular persons through false accusations without much investigation. Therefore, the purpose (the pragmatics) of the text may not be to describe the practice of punishment, but rather to achieve maximum deterrence through the horror scenario of uncontrolled lynching.

7.2 God's Punishment

God's punishment is added to the "stoning," i.e., human lynch justice:[72] God will set his face against the evildoer. The Hebrew text uses the same verb "to give" (*NTN*) as for the "giving" of offspring "to the Molech." Thus a mirror penalty emerges, which corresponds to the facts:[73] In the same way as someone gives his offspring to the Molech, God will give his face against him, and this implies a hostile and punishing effect. God will personally call the evildoers to account and "cut them off from the people" (*karet*). This is a mirror penalty, too, that works as follows: If the person who gives one of his children "to the Molech" (be it a dedication, a sacrifice, or the transfer to the occupying power) expects some personal advantages in return (a "growth"), God himself ("my face") will personally arrange that this person has no longer any future. The Hebrew text is as vague as this statement sounds. It does not say whether this person will die on the spot, or if so, how this will happen. It suffices to state clearly that God will cut off that person from the lineage (*karet*), namely from the past (the person will not be "joined with the fathers") and from the future (the person will not live on among the descendants).[74]

7.3 Profaning God's Sanctuary and God's Name

The last sentence of Lev 20:3 summarizes the reason for the harsh threats: By giving one of his offspring "to the Molech," that person has profaned God's sanctuary and God's holy name. These phrases are likewise formulated in an open way in order to fit both interpretations of "the Molech:" If one assumes the cult of a foreign (chthonic) deity (of the Netherworld), the worshipping of Molech contradicts the First Commandment and thus prohibits a direct encounter between Israel and Yahweh, between human and God in the sanctuary. As it is told in the story of the Golden Calf (Exod 32–34) in a paradigmatic way, worshipping a

72 It is an addition, not a replacement, so correctly Milgrom, *Leviticus 17–22*, 1733.

73 Ibid.

74 It is also clear that it is up to God to put it into practice in his day—human institutions are not involved in this kind of "punishment." One should also emphasize that the *karet* sanction, the "cutting off," must not be identified with the human-juridical punishment of excommunication in the sense of exclusion from the community of living and faith (see Milgrom, *Leviticus 17–22*, 1737).

foreign deity makes it impossible for Yahweh to dwell amidst his people (see also Jer 7:30; Ezek 5:11; 2 Chronicles 36:14). The sanctuary is no longer suitable for the encounter with God; it is ritually impure. Ezek 23:38–39 develops a rather similar concept: God raises accusations against the inhabitants of Judah and Jerusalem that they sacrifice their children to the idols (does this refer to "Molech"?) and on the very same day, they come into the sanctuary and thus profane it. One can understand this reproach in a way that the people were so hardhearted that they sacrificed children in the Hinnom Valley just below the temple and then moved to the temple of Yahweh.[75] However, such an interpretation sounds all too ruthless and appears unlikely. Is it imaginable that the "slaughtering" of children for the idols operates as a cipher for the transfer of children to the service for the foreign occupying power and the rich foreigners? Many Israelites had perhaps no qualms to betray their own identity and future by this surrender, and they even went to the temple the same day. At least for the post-exilic era, one can understand Lev 20:3 and Ezek 23:38–39 as a warning of such a practice. The profanation of God's holy name becomes understandable in the same way: From the very beginning, the Israelites live in a special covenant with Yahweh, and regarding the boys, this covenant is sealed by circumcision on the eighth day. If Israelites transfer the children to the service for foreign occupiers, they expose their offspring to the danger of apostasy from their own religion and faith in the one and only God Yahweh. They disregard the holy name of God, under whom God called the Israelites and freed them from slavery in Egypt. At the same time, such people make it impossible for their children to realize the call to holiness in everyday life (*imitatio Dei*) in a foreign environment; thus, God's holiness gets no representation by the way of life of the Israelites in the world.

7.4 The Danger of the Cover-Up

One can imagine the following scenario: Despite an Israelite knows about the coded prohibition by the priests, he nevertheless surrenders one of his children "to the Molech"—in perfect secrecy and with approval of his family and the entire people who in fact should sanction this crime. The biblical text knows about the danger of the cover-up, and hence, Lev 20:4–5 makes clear that Yahweh himself will intervene. However, the text does not say how this will happen exactly. God himself will "cut off" the trespasser and all those who disguise his deed. In particular, the addition of 20:4–5 demonstrates that the people probably was not all too ready to punish the "Molech" practice (whatever it was) immediately by stoning. Thus, it becomes more and more improbable that real child sacrifices were at issue. In post-exilic times, it should have been not too difficult to find an

75 See, e.g., Milgrom, *Leviticus 17–22*, 1734.

outraged group to proceed the stoning in the case of real child sacrifice. Hence, it seems to be more plausible to interpret the "Molech" practice as something acceptable—outside of priestly circles, though. The priestly text, however, tries to foster some formation of conscience among the addressees by using harsh polemic. The priests declare the "Molech" practice as irreconcilable with the call for holiness. Anyway, in the post-exilic era, the monotheistic faith was more or less established, and hence it is improbable that people regarded a "Molech" cult with child sacrifices as compatible with the worshipping of Yahweh at the temple.[76] Thus, the suggested new interpretation becomes even more probable: The "transfer of offspring to the Molech" operates as a cipher for the collaboration with the occupying power by way of giving children in the service for the occupiers. Many inhabitants of Jerusalem and Judah (Yehud) probably had no scruples about that, and the priestly texts had to point out the theological and ideological scope of this practice.

7.5 To Prostitute Themselves (Whoring After)

One can even understand the expression "to prostitute oneself" properly within this line of thought. Normally, "to prostitute" operates as a rude, sexually connoted metaphor for idolatry ("whoring," see in particular Ezek 16 and 23). This does not necessarily imply that "Molech" is a deity.[77] In 1QpHab 5:7, the phrase "to prostitute" (or "fornication") seems to point to a violation of God's commandments in general:

1. 'You have marked them for judgement; O Rock, You have made them for rebuke. Eyes too pure
2. to see evil, You cannot even watch wrongdoing.' (Hab 1:12–13a) vacat
3. This passage means that God will not exterminate his people through the Gentiles;
4. on the contrary, He will give the power to pass judgement on the Gentiles to his chosen, and it is at their rebuke that
5. all the wicked of His people shall be condemned. The chosen are those who have observed His commandments
6. in the time of their distress, for that is what it means when it says, 'eyes too pure to see
7. evil;' vacat that means that they have not let their eyes lead them into fornication (לוא זנו אחר עיניהם) during the time of
8. wickedness. …[78]

76 See, e.g., Kerr, "Search," 72.

77 Pace, Milgrom, *Leviticus 17–22*, 1738; Seidl, "Moloch-Opferbrauch," 435; G.C. Heider, "Molech," *DDD* (^{2}1999) 581–5, on p. 583.

78 1QpHab, translated by M. Wise, M. Abegg, and E. Cook with N. Gordon, in E. Tov (ed.), *The Dead Sea Scrolls Electronic Library* (Leiden/Boston: Brill, 2006).

The semantic *tertium comparationis* of this metaphorical manner of speaking is that the whore submissively chums up to allow that one can buy her sexuality at a cheap price. In the same way, the unfaithful sisters Israel and Judah offer themselves to the foreign gods in willing venality, as Ezek 16 and 23 formulates as a reproach against the people. This corresponds exactly to the surrender of children for the service of the occupying power, since this practice is also a cheap ingratiation. He who transfers one of his offspring *lmlk*, collaborates in an obsequious manner with the foreign power, he sells himself and his identity, he "prostitutes himself."

8 Summary, Conclusion and Reception

8.1 Summary and Conclusion

In this contribution I suggest to understand the phrase "for the Molech" (Hebrew without vowels *l-mlk*) in Leviticus 18 and 20 as a code word for the handing over of children from the Jewish community of Yehud to the Persian authorities for various services, such as sons for military services and daughters for concubines. This was possibly a common practice and provided economic advantages for Jewish families. In doing so, however, the offspring loses its connection with the Jewish community; the children lose their identity and leave the path of holiness. If they come back to their families, they might import not only a different culture but also a foreign religion. Hence the priests condemn the practice of giving children away like the worshipping of foreign gods and impose the harshest penalties. However, the priests could not address the issue explicitly since the authorities would have regarded it as disloyalty or an act of rebellion. Hence the priests skillfully invented the cipher *l-mlk*: Outsiders like the Persian authorities would have understood this as the prohibition of a foreign cult (*l-mlk* as a technical term for a sacrifice or as a royal deity of the Netherworld). For the own Israelite-Jewish community, however, *lmlk* resembled the pre-exilic stamp seal impressions, which marked taxes "for the king" ("state property"). Now, in the post-exilic Persian period, the practice "to allow one's offspring to pass *l-mlk*" denotes the transfer of children to the Persian king and his officials. Again, this was attractive for the families in order to get an economic support of their children; however, for the priests who designed the texts and who safeguarded their own Jewish identity, it was a horrible violation of God's call for holiness—like the worship of foreign gods and a breach of the covenant and the First Commandment. The polemic against the "Molech" practice in later texts will present it as "child sacrifice." Thus, the "Molech/Moloch" becomes the horrible monster that it is still in today's contemporary usage: a metaphor for something that devours the most precious items that one has.

8.2 Reception

The issue of collaboration with the occupying power does obviously not prevail in the history of reception. The monstrous figure of an obscure deity "Molech," in the Greek version "Moloch," appears to be much more fascinating. However, if there were any rituals or sacrifices in pre-exilic times, we do not have any traces of them and do not know any details. If it ever existed, the post-exilic era preserves at most some distorted remembrances. Anyway, the warnings in the biblical texts had a strong effect in the history of reception, resulting in a veritable horror scenario of a dreadful and disgusting deity. The most prominent examples are Milton's "horrid King besmear'd with blood"[79] (1667) and the shocking and scary scenery in Gustave Flaubert's novel "Salammbô" (1862). The term "Moloch" as a quasi-supernatural being or system devouring everything, including human beings, became a standing metaphor in contemporary language.[80] Perhaps these new manifestations also contain something of the camouflage interpretation: The Jewish inhabitants of the Persian province Yehud would probably describe the situation of the occupation as a condition, which nowadays language would call a "Moloch." Whoever collaborates with such inhuman systems, sacrifices to the Moloch.

Bibliography

Albertz, R., *Religionsgeschichte Israels in alttestamentlicher Zeit* (ATD Ergänzungsreihe 8; Göttingen: Vandenhoeck & Ruprecht, 1992).

Bauks, M., "The Theological Implications of Child Sacrifice in and Beyond the Biblical Context in Relation to Genesis 22 and Judges 11," in K. Finsterbusch/A. Lange/K. F. D. Römheld (ed.), *Human Sacrifice in Jewish and Christian Tradition* (Numen Book Series 112; Leiden: Brill, 2007) 65–86.

–, "Kinderopfer als Weihe- oder Gabeopfer. Anmerkungen zum *mlk*-Opfer," in M. Witte/ J. F. Diehl (ed.), *Israeliten und Phönizier. Ihre Beziehungen im Spiegel der Archäologie und der Literatur des Alten Testaments und seiner Umwelt* (OBO 235; Göttingen: Vandenhoeck & Ruprecht, 2008) 233–51.

–, "Opfer, Kinder und mlk. Das Menschenopfer und seine Auslösung," in A. Lange/K. F. D. Römheld (ed.), *Wege zur Hebräischen Bibel. Denken – Sprache – Kultur. In memoriam Hans-Peter Müller* (FRLANT 228; Göttingen: Vandenhoeck & Ruprecht, 2009) 215–32.

–, *Jephtas Tochter. Traditions-, religions- und rezeptionsgeschichtliche Studien zu Richter 11,29–40* (FAT 71; Tübingen: Mohr Siebeck, 2010).

–, "Menschenopfer in den Mittelmeerkulturen," *VF* 56 (2011) 33–44.

Berthelot, K., "Jewish Views of Human Sacrifice in the Hellenistic and Roman Period," in

79 See, e.g., Dewrell, *Child Sacrifice*, 4.

80 Just one of the examples to be found on the internet: "look at Los Angeles, the largest metropolis in the world by area: a virtual Moloch that seems to be perpetually on the verge of collapse."

K. Finsterbusch/A. Lange/K. F. D. Römheld (ed.), *Human Sacrifice in Jewish and Christian Tradition* (Numen Book Series 112; Leiden: Brill, 2007) 151–73.
Bremmer, J. N. (ed.), *The Strange World of Human Sacrifice* (Studies in the History and Anthropology of Religion 1; Leuven: Peeters, 2007).
Brown, S., *Late Carthaginian Child Sacrifice and Sacrificial Monuments in their Mediterranean Context* (Sheffield: JSOT Press, 1991).
Büchner, D., "'You Shall Not Give of Your Seed to Serve an Archon'. Lev 18,21 in the Septuagint," in H. Ausloos/J. Cook/F. García Martínez/B. Lemmelijn/M. Vervenne (ed.), *Translating a Translation. The LXX and its Modern Translations in the Context of Early Judaism* (BETL 213; Leuven: Peeters, 2008) 183–96.
Day, J., *Molech: A God of Human Sacrifice in the Old Testament* (Cambridge: Cambridge University Press, 1989).
Dewrell, H. D., *Child Sacrifice in Ancient Israel* (Winona Lake, IN: Eisenbrauns, 2017).
Ebach, J./Rüterswörden, U., "ADRMLK, 'Moloch' und BAʿAL ADR. Eine Notiz zum Problem der Moloch-Verehrung im alten Israel," *UF* 11 (1979) 219–26.
Eißfeldt, O., *Molk als Opferbegriff im Punischen und Hebräischen und das Ende des Gottes Moloch* (BRGA 3; Halle: Niemeyer, 1935).
Enger, P. A., *Die Adoptivkinder Abrahams. Eine exegetische Spurensuche zur Vorgeschichte des Proselytentums* (BEAT 53; Frankfurt am Main: Lang, 2006).
Finsterbusch, K./Lange, A./Römheld, K. F. D. (ed.), *Human Sacrifice in Jewish and Christian Tradition* (Numen Book Series 112; Leiden: Brill, 2007).
Finsterbusch, K., "The First-Born between Sacrifice and Redemption in the Hebrew Bible," in eadem/A. Lange/K. F. H. Römheld (ed.), *Human Sacrifice in Jewish and Christian Tradition* (Numen Book Series 112; Leiden: Brill, 2007) 87–108.
Frevel, C., "Moloch und Mischehen. Zu einigen Aspekten der Rezeption von Gen 34 in Jub 30," in U. Dahmen/J. Schnocks (ed.), *Juda und Jerusalem in der Seleukidenzeit. Herrschaft – Widerstand – Identität. Festschrift für Heinz-Josef Fabry* (BBB 159; Göttingen: V&R unipress, 2010) 161–87.
Gerstenberger, E. S., *Das 3. Buch Mose. Leviticus* (ATD 6; Göttingen: Vandenhoeck & Ruprecht, 1993).
Gesenius-Kautzsch-Cowley, Hebrew Grammar (Oxford: Clarendon Press, 1909).
Hecker, K., "Akkadische Rechts- und Verwaltungsurkunden," in *TUAT (AF) Ergänzungslieferung* (Gütersloh: Gütersloher Verlagshaus, 2001) 21–33.
Heider, G. C., *The Cult of Molek. A Reassessment* (JSOTS 43; Sheffield: JSOT Press, 1984).
–, "Molech," *ABD* 4 (1992) 895–8.
–, "Molech," *DDD* (^{2}1999) 581–5.
Hieke, T., "Das Verbot der Übergabe von Nachkommen an den 'Molech' in Lev 18 und 20. Ein neuer Deutungsversuch," *WO* 41 (2011) 147–67.
–, *Levitikus 1–15*; *Levitikus 16–27* (HThKAT; Freiburg i. Br.: Herder, 2014).
Kerr, R. M., "In Search of the Historical Moloch," in idem/R. Miller/P. C. Schmitz (ed.), *"His Word Soars Above Him". Biblical and North-West Semitic Studies Presented to Professor Charles R. Krahmalkov* (Ann Arbor, MI, 2018) 59–80.
Koch, K., "Molek astral," in A. Lange/H. Lichtenberger/D. Römheld (ed.), *Mythos im Alten Testament und seiner Umwelt. Festschrift für Hans-Peter Müller zum 65. Geburtstag* (BZAW 278; Berlin/New York: De Gruyter, 1999) 29–50.
Lange, A., "'They Burn Their Sons and Daughters—That Was No Command of Mine' (Jer 7:31). Child Sacrifice in the Hebrew Bible and in the Deuteronomistic Jeremiah Redaction," in K. Finsterbusch/A. Lange/K. F. D. Römheld (ed.), *Human Sacrifice in Jewish and Christian Tradition* (Numen Book Series 112; Leiden: Brill, 2007) 109–32.
Levin, C., "Das Kinderopfer im Jeremiabuch," in idem, *Fortschreibungen. Gesammelte Studien zum Alten Testament* (BZAW 316; Berlin/New York: De Gruyter, 2003) 227–41.

Lipiński, E., "Sacrifices d'enfants à Carthage et dans le monde sémitique oriental," in idem (ed.), *Carthago. Acta Colloquii Bruxellensis habiti diebus 2 et 3 mensis Maii anni 1986* (OLA 26; Leuven: Peeters, 1988) 151–85.

Lust, J., "Molek and ΑΡΧΩΝ," in E. Lipiński (ed.), *Phoenicia and the Bible. Proceedings of the Conference held at the University of Leuven on the 15th and 16th of March 1990* (OLA 44; StPhoe 11; Leuven: Peeters, 1991) 193–208.

Maher, M., *Targum Pseudo-Jonathan: Leviticus* (ArBib 3; Edinburgh: Clark, 1994).

McNamara, M./Hayward, R., *Targum Neofiti 1: Leviticus* (ArBib 3; Edinburgh: Clark, 1994).

Michel, A., *Gott und Gewalt gegen Kinder im Alten Testament* (FAT 37; Tübingen: Mohr Siebeck, 2003).

–, "Gewalt gegen Kinder im alten Israel. Eine sozialgeschichtliche Perspektive," in A. Kunz-Lübcke (ed.), *"Schaffe mir Kinder …". Beiträge zur Kindheit im alten Israel und in seinen Nachbarkulturen* (ABIG 21; Leipzig: Evangelische Verlagsanstalt, 2006) 137–63.

Milgrom, J., *Leviticus 17–22* (AB 3A; New York et al.: Doubleday, 2000).

Müller, H.-P., "Genesis 22 und das mlk-Opfer. Erinnerungen an einen religionsgeschichtlichen Tatbestand," in A. Lange/K. F. D. Römheld (ed.), *Wege zur Hebräischen Bibel. Denken – Sprache – Kultur. In memoriam Hans-Peter Müller* (FRLANT 228; Göttingen: Vandenhoeck & Ruprecht, 2009) 201–13.

Noort, E., "Child Sacrifice in Ancient Israel: The Status Quaestionis," in J. N. Bremmer (ed.), *The Strange World of Human Sacrifice* (Studies in the History and Anthropology of Religion 1; Leuven: Peeters, 2007) 103–26.

Orsingher, A., "Understanding *Tophets*: A Short Introduction," in *The Ancient Near East Today* 6 (2018) (http://www.asor.org/anetoday/2018/02/Understanding-Tophets-Short; last visited on February 23, 2018).

Rashi's Commentary on the Pentateuch, English translation by Rabbi A. J. Rosenberg online on https://www.chabad.org/library/bible_cdo/aid/9919#showrashi=true.

Reynolds, B. H., "Molek: Dead or Alive? The Meaning and Derivation of *mlk* and מלך," in K. Finsterbusch/A. Lange/K. F. D. Römheld (ed.), *Human Sacrifice in Jewish and Christian Tradition* (Numen Book Series 112; Leiden: Brill, 2007) 133–50.

Rüterswörden, U., "Die Stellung der Deuteronomisten zum alttestamentlichen Dämonenwesen," in A. Lange/H. Lichtenberger/K. F. D. Römheld (ed.), *Die Dämonen. Demons. Die Dämonologie der israelitisch-jüdischen und frühchristlichen Literatur im Kontext ihrer Umwelt* (Tübingen: Mohr Siebeck, 2003) 197–210.

Schwartz, J. H./Houghton, F./Macchiarelli, R./Bondioli, L., "Skeletal Remains from Punic Carthage Do Not Support Systematic Sacrifice of Infants," *PLoS ONE* 5(2) (2010): e9177. (https://doi.org/10.1371/journal.pone.0009177).

Schwemer, D., *Die Wettergottgestalten Mesopotamiens und Nordsyriens im Zeitalter der Keilschriftkulturen. Materialien und Studien nach den schriftlichen Quellen* (Wiesbaden: Harrassowitz, 2001).

Scott, J. C., *Domination and the Arts of Resistance: Hidden Transcripts* (New Haven: Yale University Press, 1990).

Seidl, T., "Der 'Moloch-Opferbrauch'—ein 'rite de passage'? Zur kontroversen Bewertung eines rätselhaften Ritus im Alten Testament," *OTE* 20 (2007) 432–55.

Smelik, K. A. D., "Moloch, Molekh or Molk-Sacrifice?," *SJOT* 9 (1995) 133–42.

Snaith, N., "The Cult of Molech," *VT* 16 (1966) 123–4.

Staubli, T., *Die Bücher Levitikus, Numeri* (NSK.AT; Stuttgart: Katholisches Bibelwerk, 1996).

–, "The 'Pagan' Prehistory of Genesis 22:1–14: The Iconographic Background of the Redemption of Human Sacrifice," in I. J. de Hulster/B. A. Strawn/R. P. Bonfiglio (ed.), *Iconographic Exegesis of the Hebrew Bible/Old Testament: An Introduction to Its Method and Practice* (Göttingen: Vandenhoeck & Ruprecht, 2015) 77–101.

Stavrakopoulou, F., *King Manasseh and Child Sacrifice. Biblical Distortions of Historical Realities* (BZAW 338; Berlin/New York: De Gruyter, 2004).

Theodoret of Cyrus, *The Questions on the Octateuch* (LEC 2; English translation by Robert C. Hill; Washington, D.C.: The Catholic University of America Press, 2007).
Tov, E. (ed.), *The Dead Sea Scrolls Electronic Library* (Leiden/Boston: Brill, 2006).
Ussishkin, D., "The Royal Judean Storage Jars and Seal Impressions from the Renewed Excavations," in idem (ed.), *The Renewed Archaeological Excavations at Lachish (1973–1994)*, Vol. IV (Tel Aviv: Yass Publications in Archaeology, 2004) 2133–47.
Vermes, G., "Leviticus 18:21 in Ancient Jewish Bible Exegesis," in J. J. Petuchowski/E. Fleischer (ed.), *Studies in Aggadah, Targum and Jewish Liturgy in Memory of Joseph Heinemann* (Jerusalem: Magnes, 1981) 108–24.
Waltke, B. K./O'Connor, M., *An Introduction to Biblical Hebrew Syntax* (Winona Lake, IN: Eisenbrauns, 1990).
Weinfeld, M., "The Worship of Molech and of the Queen of Heaven and its Background," *UF* 4 (1972) 133–54.

David P. Wright

Law and Creation in the Priestly-Holiness Writings of the Pentateuch*

Writing a biblical commentary involves two mutually interactive dimensions of research and writing: ascertaining the meaning of textual details, word by word and passage by passage, and making sense of the meaning of the text broadly and collectively. Doing the latter for the book of Leviticus, however, is not a simple matter. The contextual boundaries of the book are not the canonical book, but the entire Priestly or, as I call it, Priestly-Holiness (PH) corpus. This requires wading into the marsh of pentateuchal studies broadly to determine exactly what belongs to the PH corpus and studying texts throughout this corpus—in Genesis, Exodus, Numbers, and Deuteronomy—and relating them to Leviticus. Some of my first work on Leviticus has consequently been devoted to assessing the big picture, including the essay that follows.

In the ancient Near East, nature and law, cosmos and norm, order and ordinance, regularity and regulation—Greek φύσις and νόμος, if you will—were conceptually relatable. This was possible by virtue of a mythological worldview, where the natural world was believed to have been created by the gods, and whatever system of law or ethics prevailed, be this a general sense of justice or specific laws set down in writing, was championed and inspired, if not authored, by the gods. The natural and legal worlds were interlaced, and the latter was the inexorable outcome of the former, ordained by the gods. Thus it is not a coincidence to find expressions where the promulgation of law is tied in some way to the divine establishment of the cosmos.

An example of this connection is found in the prologue and epilogue of the Laws of Hammurabi. The prologue starts with a short history of kingship among the gods and the call of Hammurabi as king:[1]

* This essay was originally published in the volume *Laws of Heaven—Laws of Nature: Legal Interpretations of Cosmic Phenomena in the Ancient World* (ed. K. Schmid and C. Uehlinger; OBO 276; Fribourg: Academic Press; Göttingen: Vandenhoeck & Ruprecht, 2016) 71–101. This version has been slightly updated for the present volume.

1 On the prologue and epilogue, see V. A. Hurowitz, *Inu Anum ṣīrum: Literary Structures in the Non-Juridical Sections of Codex Hammurabi* (Occasional Publications of the Samuel Noah Kramer Fund 15; Philadelphia: University Museum, 1994); D. P. Wright, *Inventing God's Law: How the Covenant Code of the Bible Used and Revised the Laws of Hammurabi* (Oxford: Oxford University Press, 2009), 286–321.

> When exalted Anu, king of the Anunnaki gods, and Enlil, the lord of heaven and earth, who ordains the destinies of the land, ordained lordship for Marduk, the first son of Ea, magnified him among the Igigi gods, named Babylon with its exalted name, made it excellent in the world, and established for him in its midst eternal kingship, whose foundations are as firm as heaven and earth—at that time, to bring well-being to the people, the gods Anu and Enlil, for the well-being of the people, named me by name, Hammurabi, the pious prince, the one who worships the gods, in order to make justice appear in the land, to eradicate the wicked and evil, so that the strong not wrong the weak, to rise like Shamash over humanity, to enlighten the land (col 1:1–49).

The epilogue augments this description and is more specific about Hammurabi's promulgation of law:

> So that the strong not wrong the weak and to secure justice for the destitute girl and widow, in Babylon, the city whose heights Anu and Enlil elevated, (specifically) in the Esagil, the temple whose foundations are firm like the heaven and earth, for the purpose of setting down the law of the land, to render the verdicts of the land and to secure justice for the wronged, I have written my treasured words on my stele and set it up before the image of me, the king of justice (col. 47:59–78).

The story reflected in these passages is that Anu and Enlil gave rule to Marduk and established Babylon in the primordium, akin to the story expressed in detail in the later Babylonian creation story *Enuma elish*. Then, subsequently in history, the gods named Hammurabi king in that city so that, among other royal activities, he could set down and publish laws that would be just. Hammurabi's rule and laws were a result of the goals, indeed fate, inaugurated at creation.

A Near Eastern text in which the correlation between creation and law is extensively developed is the Priestly-Holiness corpus (PH) of the Pentateuch (what is referred to classically as the Priestly corpus or P). The conceptual center of this broad and complex work is a divine revelation of prescriptions about the building and operation of the wilderness tabernacle. The other parts of the PH narrative orbit this sun. The chapters that follow this revelation deal with events in the wilderness and flesh out the consequences of this revelation, both the positive aspects of cultic inauguration as well as the negative aspects of rebellion, often associated with cultic matters. The preceding chapters provide a prelude to the tabernacle revelation, from the creation of the world, through the epoch of the patriarchs, to the call of Moses as the prophet who founds the cult. The first part of the story has been carefully crafted to prepare for the tabernacle revelation and its cultic regulations. The priestly creation story does not simply end with the seventh day when the deity rested from his creative work. The culmination of this process is in the revelation of the tabernacle, the basic regulations associated with it, and its dedication. Thus the revelation of law, cultic regulation in particular, is the fulfillment of creation.[2]

2 I acknowledge the valuable stimulus of my student S. E. Tanchel in discussions we had as I advised her on a chapter in her dissertation, which argued that Gen 1:1–2:4a is to be attributed

This paper will outline the details and nuances of this picture, several of which have been recognized by others. I bring these together with new insights within the context of my understanding of the composition of the PH work.

1 The Priestly-Holiness Corpus

This is not the place for a treatise on the difficult question about the nature and development of the PH corpus. I must, however, outline my working hypothesis because the themes discussed in this essay relate to the goals of what might be considered the *Grundschrift* of this corpus and the realization and extension of those goals in later portions of the text.[3] According to my evolving view, the revelation of details for building the tabernacle and regulations about sacrifice and purity constitute the compositional and conceptual core of PH (mainly and roughly in Exodus 25–29a*; Leviticus 1–5*, 11–16*).[4] This core was never intended to stand alone, but was equipped with an ideologically supporting narrative. The first part or panel of this narrative included much of the material that various analyses have assigned to the P corpus from Genesis 1 to Leviticus 16. This comprised the P stories in Genesis through the first half of Exodus and the material that fleshed out tabernacle prescriptions and the description of its building and consecration

---

to H rather than P (*Honoring Voices: Listening to the Texts and the Teacher, the Scholars and the Students* [PhD diss.; Waltham MA: Brandeis University, 2006], 13–114).

3 This summary advances preliminary considerations about PH in D.P. Wright, "Ritual Theory, Ritual Texts, and the Priestly-Holiness Writings of the Pentateuch," in S. Olyan, *Social Theory and the Study of Israelite Religion: Essays in Retrospect and Prospect* (SBLRBS 71; Atlanta: SBL, 2012), 195–216 (especially pp. 214–16).

4 Here I differ from other approaches that argue that the Priestly *Grundschrift* (Pg) consists of a limited narrative from creation to the revelation or building of the tabernacle with little cultic legislation. See the summary of views in C. Nihan, *From Priestly Torah to Pentateuch: A Study in the Composition of the Book of Leviticus* (FAT 25; Tübingen: Mohr Siebeck, 2007), 1–68; and the convenient tabulation of earlier scholarship in P.P. Jenson, *Graded Holiness: A Key to the Priestly Conception of the World* (JSOTSup 106; Sheffield: Sheffield Academic Press, 1992), 220–4. For helpful descriptions of and arguments for a limited Pg, see also A. de Pury, "Pg as the Absolute Beginning," in T. Römer/K. Schmid (ed.), *Les dernières rédactions du Pentateuque, de l'Hexateuque et de l'Ennéateuque* (BETL 203; Leuven: University Press/Peeters, 2007) 99–128; idem, "The Jacob Story and the Beginning of the Formation of the Pentateuch," in T. Dozeman/K. Schmid (ed.), *A Farewell to the Yahwist? The Composition of the Pentateuch in Recent European Interpretation* (SBLSS 34; Atlanta: SBL, 2006) 51–72; M. Bauks, "La signification de l'espace et du temps dans 'l'Histoire Sacerdotale'," in T. Römer (ed.), *The Future of the Deuteronomistic History* (BETL 147; Leuven: University Press/Peeters, 2000) 29–45; J.C. Gertz/A. Berlejung/K. Schmid/M. Witte, *T&T Clark Handbook of the Old Testament* (London: T&T Clark, 2012), 263–5; K. Schmid, *The Old Testament: A Literary History* (Minneapolis: Fortress Press, 2012), 147–52. Nihan argues that some cultic legislation and detail must have belonged in the basic P text.

(the latter approximately include Exodus 29b–31*, 35–40*; Leviticus 8–9*). The so-called Holiness Code (Leviticus 17–26) was added to this to expand the scope of legislation beyond cultic matters. The writers of this collection also augmented some of the cultic regulations in the first panel. The second narrative panel, in the book of Numbers, about rebellions in the wilderness and the appointment of the Levites along with various legal supplements, was then added. The work probably also ended with description of entry into the land.

The first panel of law and narrative can be provisionally and broadly labeled P in distinction to the Holiness Code and second panel of narrative and law, which can be labeled H.[5] Nevertheless, the distinction between P and H is not always clear. The first panel anticipates the ideas and language of H in many respects or has been updated with H material, especially to tie individual pericopae of P together or fill in gaps. In some cases it looks like H completes an unfinished or inchoate P narrative.[6] At the same time, the second panel takes up and emphasizes some of the narrative themes from Genesis and Exodus. Some materials in the second panel, especially basic narratives, may have been drafted early on, to be included in the larger work as it developed. In addition, textual production at each major stage of development reflects what I call inner-compositional development, i. e., refinement of the text in the drafting or basic compositional process.[7]

Internally, my analysis of the development of PH proceeds by determining which passages in the corpus presuppose other passages. For example, the narrative from the beginning of Genesis to mid-Exodus presupposes the essential

---

5 I. Knohl (*Sanctuary of Silence* [Minneapolis: Fortress, 1995]) and J. Milgrom (*Leviticus 17–22* [AB 3A; New York: Doubleday, 2000], 1319–66) have been influential on my distinguishing of P and H. I agree that H includes more than just the Holiness Code and that H is chronologically later than and supplementary to P. I do not agree, however, with their early dating of P and much of H (see below). For more recent considerations, see the analyses and bibliographies in Nihan, *Priestly Torah*; J. Stackert, *Rewriting the Torah: Literary Revision in Deuteronomy and the Holiness Legislation* (FAT 52; Tübingen: Mohr Siebeck, 2007); D. M. Carr, *The Formation of the Hebrew Bible: A New Reconstruction* (Oxford: Oxford University Press, 2011), 292–303.

6 For the notion of an unfinished P from a different point of view, see E. Blum, "Issues and Problems in the Contemporary Debate Regarding the Priestly Writings," in S. Shectman/ J. S. Baden (ed.), *The Strata of the Priestly Writings* (ATANT 95; Zürich: Theologischer Verlag, 2009), 31–44, on p. 42.

7 While additions to a base text might be recognized or hypothesized, I am not sanguine about being able to definitively determine intermediate stages of a text and ultimately an original text by a process of peeling off perceived additions, though such analyses must be ventured. Multiple factors, including the reworking and combination of source texts (as well as traditions), are responsible for introducing complexity and inconsistency into even an original or unitary composition (see Wright, *Inventing*, 352–5 and passim; idem, "The Origin, Development, and Context of the Covenant Code [Exod 20:23–23:19]," in T. Dozeman/C. Evans/J. Lohr (ed.), *The Book of Exodus: Composition, Reception, and Interpretation* [FIOTL; VTSup 164; Leiden: Brill, 2014] 220–44). Thus I share—for different reasons—Carr's realization that determining an original text may elude our methods and abilities (*Formation*, 4, 112–14, 148, 255–6, 336–7).

content of the revelation of the tabernacle and its basic cultic laws, as this essay will point out later. Externally, my study increasingly indicates that the PH work knew and *recast* some of the materials found for the most part in the non-PH portions of Genesis through Numbers.[8] PH reacted to the description of institutions and content in this earlier material to produce a "corrected" version of non-PH stories, laws, and larger history to suit its ideology. This essay will make reference to where such dependence and recasting seems possible, but, because of space and the goals, the present paper cannot enter into a full treatment of the issues and secondary literature. That various places across the whole PH work reflect the reworking of non-PH, even though executed over time by different hands, indicates that these scribes followed and fulfilled a compositional plan conceived at the beginning of P's composition largely dictated by non-PH. This textual dependence also indicates to me that the non-PH materials already existed in one

8 For P's ideological revision of the non-P (i.e., J's) flood story, see D. P. Wright, "Profane Versus Sacrificial Slaughter: The Priestly Recasting of the Yahwist Flood Story," in R. Gane and A. Taggar-Cohen (ed.), *Current Issues in Priestly and Related Literature: The Legacy of Jacob Milgrom and Beyond* (SBLRBS; Atlanta: SBL, 2015) 125–54. Recent models of the development of the Pentateuch assess the relationship of P to non-P in other ways (see also n. 10). In very rough outlines, the last quarter of the twentieth century witnessed a move by various scholars from a documentary to a supplementary model. This viewed P and H texts as redactional additions to a non-PH base text. See F. M. Cross, *Canaanite Myth and Hebrew Epic* (Cambridge, MA: Harvard University Press, 1973), 294, 324–5; R. Rendtorff, *The Problem of the Process of Transmission in the Pentateuch* (JSOTSup 89; Sheffield: JSOT Press, 1990 [originally 1977]), 156–70 (esp. 169–70); E. Blum, *Studien zum Komposition des Pentateuch* (BZAW 189; Berlin: De Gruyter, 1990), 221–85; idem, "Issues and Problems" (Blum views P as somewhat independent but also a supplement); J.-L. Ska, *Introduction to Reading the Pentateuch* (Winona Lake: Eisenbrauns, 2006), 146–61. For this thesis in studies relevant to the general theme of this essay, see R. Albertz, *A History of Israelite Religion in the Old Testament Period* (2 vols.; Louisville: Westminster John Knox Press, 1994), 1:42–3, 55; 2:480–93; M. S. Smith, *The Priestly Vision of Genesis 1* (Minneapolis: Fortress Press, 2010), 2, 4, 117–38. Around the beginning of the twentieth-first century, the perceived relationship between PH and non-PH began to be inverted: P was seen as the base text to which non-P (or post-P) materials were added. See, for example and with different points of emphasis, K. Schmid, *Genesis and the Moses Story* (Siphrut 3; Winona Lake: Eisenbrauns, 2010 [originally 1999]); de Pury, "Pg as the Absolute Beginning"; R. Achenbach, *Die Vollendung der Torah: Studien zur Redaktionsgeschichte des Numeribuches im Kontext von Hexateuch und Pentateuch* (BZABR 3; Wiesbaden: Harrassowitz, 2002); and the summaries in Schmid, *Old Testament*, 147–8; Gertz et al., *Handbook*, 265. For arguments that P is the base text in the creation or flood stories, see J. Blenkinsopp, "P and J in Genesis 1:1–11:26: An Alternative Hypothesis," in A. B. Beck/A. H. Bartelt/P. R. Raabe/C. A. Franke (ed.), *Fortunate the Eyes That See: Essays in Honor of David Noel Freedman* (Grand Rapids: Eerdmans, 1995) 1–15; R. Kratz, *The Composition of the Narrative Books of the Old Testament* (London: T&T Clark, 2005), 257–8); K. Schmid (ed.), *Schöpfung* (Themen der Theologie 4; Stuttgart: UTB, 2012), 77–98; J.-L. Ska, *The Exegesis of the Pentateuch* (FAT 66; Tübingen: Mohr Siebeck, 2009), 1–22 (this essay originally appeared in 1994). My analysis of the dependence of PH on non-PH has been enriched by discussions with my student M. DeMarco.

or more narratives that recounted the early history and the origins of Israel.[9] It also helps demonstrate that PH, with its various strata as sketched above, was an independent composition before non-PH materials were blended with it.[10]

The date of PH is not of great importance for this essay. I should briefly note, however, that in my view the answer is chiefly determined by the relationship of PH to other biblical literature (principally non-PH narrative and law in Genesis to Numbers and the books of Deuteronomy and Ezekiel) rather than the sociological portrait of PH or possible correlations with historical events. Social and historical data have been skewed to fit the pseudoarchaeographic contextualization of the story in the time of Moses.[11] The relationship of PH to other texts suggest that its formulation may have begun just prior to 586 BCE, but developed mainly in the exile (586–539 BCE), with the H material stemming from the late exile or early post-exile.

In the following, I will sometimes refer to the material in PH from Genesis through Leviticus 16 simply as P, material after that as H, and the whole work as PH, adding precision or qualification when necessary.

---

9 This claim differs from recent scholarship that views P as the first text to join together stories and traditions about the pre-Mosaic and Mosaic ages into a long narrative (see Schmid, *Genesis*; similarly Achenbach, *Vollendung*, argues that pre-priestly traditions in Numbers were unified only through post-priestly redactional activity).

10 A documentary hypothesis seems the most viable way of explaining the literary complexity of the Pentateuch and, in particular, the evidence of textual dependence that I see. My summary in this part of this essay indicates to me that there existed at least an independent PH text and a pre-PH independent non-PH (and non-D) text. But the non-PH/D textual material has contradistinctive elements and cannot be considered a unity (e.g., n. 65). Moreover, as I argued in *Inventing*, 332–45, the Covenant Code was created in a narrative context, and this was not J. Therefore a hypothesis of a J and non-J narratives (i. e., E) seems plausible, even though the latter is less visible or complete. For a recent restatement of the documentary hypothesis, see J. Baden, *The Composition of the Pentateuch* (AYBRL; New Haven: Yale University Press, 2012). A major difference in my approach from Baden's is the view that PH used non-PH narratives as a source (Baden resists this; see his *Composition*, 63–5, 178–9, 188–92). For critique of Baden and discussion of current approaches, see T. Römer, "Zwischen Urkunden, Fragmenten und Ergänzungen: Zum Stand der Pentateuchforschung," *ZAW* 125 (2013) 2–24; Carr, *Formation*, 102–49; K. Schmid, "Has European Scholarship Abandoned the Documentary Hypothesis? Some Reminders on Its History and Remarks on Its Current Status," in T. B. Dozeman/K. Schmid/B. J. Schwartz (ed.), *The Pentateuch* (FAT 78; Tübingen: Mohr Siebeck, 2011) 17–30.

11 See B. D. Sommer, "Dating Pentateuchal Texts and the Perils of Pseudo-Historicism," in T. B. Dozeman/K. Schmid/B. J. Schwartz (ed.), *The Pentateuch* (FAT 78; Tübingen: Mohr Siebeck, 2011) 85–108. On the effects of pseudoarchaeographic contextualization, see Wright, *Inventing*, 171–4, 297, 301; idem, "Ritual Theory," 199–209.

2 The Purpose of Creation

A problem looms in the creation story of Genesis 1:1–2:4a, which serves as a preface to the PH work.[12] Nowhere in it do we find a clear reason for the creation of humans, the climax of the seven-day event in terms of life-forms created. To be sure, humans are given dominion over animals and the earth (vv. 26, 28), but this is not the purpose for which they were created as much as an administrative benefit or custodial responsibility marking the primacy of humans over the animals.[13] Human dominance is greatly restricted in that they are not allowed to eat animals (1:29–30). Legal carnivorism begins only after the flood (9:3–5). This dietary relaxation, granted only later in history, indicates that illegal killing and consumption of animals was part of the "violence" (חָמָס) that brought about the flood (6:11, 13). Another problem with identifying human dominion over animals as the reason for human creation is that this is not characterized as something done for the benefit of the deity. The grant of dominion also begs the question of why the animals and the rest of the world were created in the first place.

The absence of a clear purpose for creating humans in P's story contrasts with J's creation and garden story that immediately follows (Gen 2:4–3:24). The man there is created to provide labor for the deity. The story opens by saying there are no plants, in part because there is no man to work the earth. As soon as the man is created, he is placed in the garden of Eden to work and guard it (2:15). This

12 Already with this first P text we have to contend with a possibly complex redactional history; see recently T. Krüger, "Genesis 1:1–2:3 and the Development of the Pentateuch," in T.B. Dozeman/K. Schmid/B.J. Schwartz (ed.), *The Pentateuch* (FAT 78; Tübingen: Mohr Siebeck, 2011) 125–38. He posits an original text that described creation by act, not speech. One of his points, observed by others before, is that the passage on the seventh day in 2:2–3 appears to be a rather late addition. For me, these verses are integral to a Near Eastern ritual or mythic pattern that expects culmination on the seventh day. Further, as we will see, they tie the passage to the larger tabernacle narrative. To remove them eviscerates a basic P narrative. Nevertheless, it is possible that these verses are part of a *planned* inner-compositional expansion that tied the text to the larger narrative. The verses on vegetarianism (1:29–30) have a similar character and function, to tie the creation and flood stories together (Krüger keeps v. 29 in his base text). I have argued ("Profane versus Sacrificial Slaughter") that vegetarianism in Genesis 1 is a foil for the grant of profane slaughter in Genesis 9. It is possible—even probable in view of PH's use of non-P pentateuchal narrative and law—that the PH creation story used an unknown source. But here is the rub: we should expect that the PH writers transformed this unattested source as they did attested non-P pentateuchal narrative and law that served as sources. Just as we cannot recover the J flood story by working backward from the P flood story, so we cannot expect to recover the creation text that may have inspired P. We can only speculate about motifs that it contained and its possible outline.

13 For a recent study, see J. Wöhrle, "*dominium terrae:* Exegetische und religionsgeschichtliche Überlegungen zum Herrschaftsauftrag in Gen 1,26–28," *ZAW* 121 (2009) 171–88. This includes examination of the motif in its Near Eastern context relevant to the broader argument here.

garden is the deity's reserve or estate.[14] An assistant is made for the man, first the animals, and after this fails, the woman. When the humans are expelled from the garden, they continue to toil for the god in presenting offerings, as found in the stories of Cain and Abel, Noah, and the later patriarchs.[15]

J's view of creation (Gen 2:4b–3:24) is broadly consistent with the Mesopotamian stories of *Atrahasis* and *Enuma elish*, where humans are created to work for the gods. This includes manual labor such as digging canals, but also providing them with food (i. e., through offerings). In *Atrahasis*, for example, when humans are made, they take up tools and work on canals "for the hunger of the people [i. e., to feed them] and sustenance of the gods" (*bubūtiš niši tîtiš ilī*; I 339). In *Enuma elish* Marduk says:

> Let me create a first-man. The labor of the gods shall be imposed (on him), so they (the gods) may rest
>
> (*lubnima lullâ* [LÚ.U$_{18}$.LU-*a*] *amēlu lū endu dullu ilī* [DINGIR.DINGIR]-*ma šunu lū pašḫū*; VI 7–8, cf. 34, 36).

This mythic depiction of human labor dovetails with Mesopotamian cultic phenomenology that considers offerings as the food of the gods.[16]

3 The Age of Sacrifice

If we limit our vision to Gen 1:1–2:4a, P does not have much in common with J's or the Mesopotamian view of creation. However, the way that P treats the motif of sacrifice and related matters makes it clear that it does share a similar, though ideologically distinctive and more complex, perspective. As already noted briefly, the non-PH narratives of Genesis into Exodus portray sacrifice as a custom operative from the earliest times.[17] In J's early history, Cain, Abel, and Noah offer sacrifice (Gen 4:3–7; 8:20–22). In later non-PH narrative in Genesis, the patriarchs build

14 See D. P. Wright, "Holiness, Sex, and Death in the Garden of Eden," *Bib* 77 (1996) 305–29, on pp. 306–12.

15 For an insightful analysis of the purpose of creation in J, set against data from the ancient Near East, see E. L. Greenstein, "God's Golem: The Creation of the Human in Genesis 2," in H. G. Reventlow/Y. Hoffman (ed.), *Creation in Jewish and Christian Tradition* (JSOTSup 319; Sheffield: Sheffield Academic Press, 2002) 219–39.

16 See the discussion and references in D. P. Wright, "The Study of Ritual in the Hebrew Bible," in F. Greenspahn (ed.), *The Hebrew Bible: New Insights and Scholarship* (Jewish Studies in the 21st Century; New York: New York University Press, 2008) 120–38.

17 See mainly W. K. Gilders, "Sacrifice before Sinai and the Priestly Narratives," in S. Shectman/J. S. Baden (ed.), *The Strata of the Priestly Writings* (ATANT 95; Zürich: Theologischer Verlag, 2009) 57–72; W. Zwickel, "Die Altarbaunotizen im Alten Testament," *Bib* 73 (1992) 533–46, on pp. 538–9; see also K. van der Toorn, *Family Religion in Babylonia, Syria and Israel:*

altars, and Abraham and Jacob are described as offering sacrifice (12:7, 8; 13:4, 18; 22:9; 33:20; 35:1, 3, 7). A number of other cult related activities are recounted (tithe payment to a priest, pillar erection, anointing, and libation; Gen 14:20; 28:18, 22; 31:13, 45, 51, 52; 35:14, 20).[18] At the dawn of the age of Moses, the J plague narrative describes sacrifice as the pretext to get Pharaoh to loosen his grip on the Israelites so they might escape (described with the roots זבח "sacrifice;" חגג "celebrate a festival;" עבד "[cultically] serve;" 3:18; 4:23; 5:1, 3; 7:16, 26; 8:4, 16, 21–25; 9:1, 13; 10:3, 7–8, 10–11, 24–26).[19]

In contrast, PH does not mention sacrifice at all until the revelation of the tabernacle to Moses at Sinai (e.g., Exod 27:1–8; 28:43; 29:1–46). This is part of its ideological rewriting of history, noted earlier. PH reacted to and recast non-PH narrative to create its own, more acceptable, portrayal of the cult over the course of history. The case of the flood narrative illustrates this in a nutshell.[20] P's flood story followed the template of J's account in general but altered cultic details. It removed the distinction between pure and impure animals. It also eliminated Noah's sacrifice and replaced it with profane slaughter, the non-cultic companion to sacrifice and a practice that a mind thinking cultically would consider alongside sacrifice. Holiness and Deuteronomic laws on sacrifice in Leviticus 17 and Deuteronomy 12, for example, include discussion of profane slaughter.

P also purged the record of sacrifice in the patriarchal and early Mosaic ages. Abraham demonstrates his piety through circumcision (Genesis 17). This becomes the basis for promises made to him. This contrasts with non-P stories where promises are attached to sacrificial or quasi-sacrificial performances in Genesis 22 (the near sacrifice of Isaac) and Genesis 15 (the rite involving dividing animals). P may in part be responding to these portrayals and, as in the flood story, replaces sacrifice with a non-cultic ritual.[21] P's story of the plagues of Egypt,

---

Continuity and Change in the Forms of Religious Life (SHCANE 7; Leiden: Brill, 1996), 255–64; Wright, *Inventing*, 358–9. That Gen 35:14 is not P, see Baden, *Composition*, 230–45.

18 Calling on the name of Yahweh in J is often associated with cultic activity (see Gen 4:26; 12:8; 13:4; 21:33; 26:25; cf. 4:1; see Wright, *Inventing*, 358 and 474 n. 21). J's motif has a climax in the revelation of the *kavod* to Moses (Exod 33:19; 34:5; see n. 69 below).

19 For P and J in the plague stories, see n. 57 below.

20 In Gen 6–9, P consists of 6:9–22; 7:6–7, 8bβ–9, 11, 13–16a, 17b–22; 8:1–2a, 3b–7, 13a, 14–19; 9:1–17, and J consists of 6:1–8; 7:1–5, 8abα, 10, 12, 16b, 17a, 23; 8:2b–3a, 6, 8–12, 13b, 20–22. There are neither significant redactional additions (perhaps only the definite article on "the ark" in 7:1 and maybe all of 7:5) nor deletions (perhaps only a verb for taking animals prefacing J's 7:8abα similar to 7:2 and mention of land and air animals at the beginning of P's 7:8bβ). Each reads as a complete story. For the argument summarized here, see Wright, "Profane Versus Sacrificial Slaughter."

21 Preliminary study suggests to me that Genesis 17 is a recasting of J promises to Abraham and Sarah in Genesis 18 (compare especially 17:15–21 with 18:10–14), blended with motifs from Genesis 15 (cf. 17:17–19 and 15:2–4) and Genesis 21 (cf. 17:20 with 21:17–18). See provisionally S. McEvenue, *The Narrative Style of the Priestly Writer* (AnBib 50; Rome: Biblical Institute Press,

which in my analysis is based in part on J's story (see below), removes all reference to sacrifice. Indeed, negotiations with Pharaoh about sacrifice take up a large part of J's narrative. With this sacrificial component removed, there is nothing to talk about, and P can present its sign-plagues in a rapid series with no speech to Pharaoh and portray them as performed in one day (up to the darkness plague). The only other place where PH has animal killing prior to the tabernacle is in the first Passover in Exod 12:1–20.[22] Although this text has some elements that relate to sacrifice-like elements,[23] and though later instances of the Passover would be sacrificial (cf. the implication in Numbers 9), this first instance was not. It was a home rite, with no altar and manipulation of blood on it, no requirement of purity (contrast the second Passover in Num 9:4–14), and no priesthood.[24]

This portrait of cultic practice demonstrates that for PH the culmination of creation is really in the age of Moses. It is only with the revelation of the tabernacle and its laws that the purpose for the creation of humans and all of creation becomes clear. The world and humans were created so that eventually Israel could serve the deity in the cult. This culmination, however, had to wait until the time of Moses because of a reality that could not be denied in view of the Near Eastern cultural and historiographical reality that Israel was a latecomer to the scene. PH could not realistically describe the birth of Israel and the command to build the tabernacle in the early years of human history. P had to provide a preliminary history of humanity in Genesis. Its emphasis on family lines is partly to describe the process by which Israel's DNA was differentiated from the rest of humanity. Only then could cultic performances begin. P thus actually agrees with J and Near Eastern texts that creation has the goal of providing workers for the deity.

1971), 145–78; D.M. Carr, *Reading the Fractures of Genesis: Historical and Literary Approaches* (Louisville: Westminster John Knox Press, 1996), 82–5. Recognition of the use of sources in Genesis 17 will necessarily temper redactional analyses of this chapter (e.g., P. Weimar, *Studien zur Priesterschrift* [FAT 56; Tübingen: Mohr Siebeck, 2008], 185–225; J. Wöhrle, "The Integrative Function of the Law of Circumcision," in R. Achenbach/R. Albertz/J. Wöhrle (ed.), *The Foreigner and the Law: Perspectives from the Hebrew Bible and the Ancient Near East* [BZABR 16; Wiesbaden: Harrassowitz, 2011], 71–87). This type of analysis also affects the understanding of promise passages in non-P Genesis as late additions (for a recent history of scholarship and reassessment, see J. Baden, *The Promise to the Patriarchs* (Oxford: Oxford University Press, 2013). For Genesis 15 as part of the "Covenant Code Narrative," see D.P. Wright, "The Adaptation and Fusion of Near Eastern Treaty and Law in Legal Narrative of the Hebrew Bible," in B. Levinson (ed.), *Law, Society, and Religion*: George E. Mendenhall Symposium, October, 2016 (*Maarav* special issue; forthcoming).

22 For the H character of this passage, see the section on the calendar below.

23 Sacrificial motifs include requirement of a blemish free animal (v. 5), slaughtering described with שחט (v. 6), concern about how it is cooked (v. 8–9), the accompaniment of unleavened bread (v. 8), concern about the head, legs, and entrails (v. 9), and not leaving over until morning (v. 10).

24 See Gilders, "Sacrifice," 60–61. Not all ritualistic animal killing is *sacrifice* (Wright, "The Study of Ritual").

In this respect, P also concurs with other texts and Mesopotamian cult practice more generally in viewing sacrifice as a meal for the deity, in analogy to feasting human kings and elites.

4 The Revelation of Yahweh's Name

A number of other features complement this broad understanding of creation in PH. One of these is the disclosure of the proper name of the deity. The call of Moses in Exod 6:2–8, which reflects H tendencies[25] but must be part of the basic narrative constructed from Genesis to the tabernacle, refers back to covenants with the patriarchs and notes that in the earlier age the deity did not reveal his name Yahweh, but spoke to them as El Shaddai (Gen 17:1; 28:3; 35:11; 48:3). This appears to build on and interpret the notice of the revelation of the divine name in non-P's Exod 3:14–15.[26] P's revelation of the proper divine name in the age of Moses is an enlargement of theological knowledge and is necessary for the functioning of the cult, as several passages show, some of which augment a basic P text.

For example, Aaron wears a gold ornament (צִיץ זָהָב טָהוֹר) on his turban. The phrase קֹדֶשׁ לַיהוָה "Holiness to Yahweh" is engraved on it (Exod 28:36). The ornament is not mere decoration, but has the cultic function of bearing sin. A similar concrete use of the divine name in the cult may be in the Day of Atonement ritual. A lot (גּוֹרָל), perhaps inscribed with the phrase "for Yahweh," is placed on one of two goats provided by the people for the purgation offering (Lev 16:8–9). The divine name is used in various types of ritual speech. When the tabernacle is consecrated, Aaron and Moses bless the people (Lev 9:22, 23). This presumably

25 The declaration of the deity as אֲנִי יְהוָה (vv. 2, 6, 7, 8), especially אֲנִי יְהוָה (אֱלֹהֵיכֶם) וְהוֹצֵאתִי/ הַמּוֹצִיא אֶתְכֶם מִ ... מִצְרָיִם (in vv. 6 and 7), have affinities with H (cf. Exod 29:46; Lev 19:36; 21:12; 22:33; 23:43; 25:38, 55; 26:13, 45; Num 15:41; see Knohl, *Sanctuary*, 17–18 n. 24). The writing of Exod 6:2–8 may have occurred chronologically closer to H than other parts of the P narrative in Genesis and Exodus. For the integrity of 6:2–8, its necessity in the narrative, and a critique of Knohl, see Nihan, *Priestly Torah*, 35–6 n. 72; 65 n. 237.

26 This dependence is to be understood in a larger context of PH's possible dependence on non-PH in the first chapters of Exodus. Moses' objection, the appointment of Aaron, and initial charge to go to Pharaoh in PH (6:12, 30; 7:1–3) may be a reworking of J (4:10, 14–16, 21–23; see n. 58 for context why P, for example, changes Aaron from Moses' "mouth" to his "prophet"). P also appears to revise J's plagues in Exod 7–10, including conversion of J's faith signs (Exod 4) into signs before Pharaoh. For the dependence of PH's 12:1–20 on J, see also n. 36. A notable difference in the case of Exod 6:2–8 is that its possible source (3:14–15) is E, not J. (Source analysis in Exod 3–7a for me is, provisionally: J = 3:2–4a, 5, 6b–8, וְעַתָּה of v. 9, 16–20; 4:1–16, 19–20a, 21–31; 5:1–6:1, E = 3:1, 4b [without מִתּוֹךְ הַסְּנֶה, a redactional gloss], 6a, 9 [without initial וְעַתָּה], 10–15, 21–22; 4:17, 18, 20aγ [shared with J], 20b, and PH = 6:2–7:7; see J. Baden, *J, E, and the Redaction of the Pentateuch* [FAT 68; Tübingen: Mohr Siebeck, 2009], 176–7, 185, 218–21, 226, 227, 234–39, 269–270, 273–5, 279, 281). For PH's dependence on both J and E elsewhere, see n. 69.

involves the use of the divine name. The supplementary priestly blessing in Num 6:22–27 may seek to indicate how the people were blessed at this inaugural event as well as at other times.[27] This blessing employs the Tetragrammaton thrice and is how the divine name is "placed" on the people. The curses for the suspected adulteress use the divine name in speech and as a ritual object. The priest speaks the curses to the woman, which include the phrase: "may Yahweh make you a curse and imprecation among your people, when Yahweh makes your genitals fall and womb swell." These are written out, dissolved in water, and given to the woman to drink (Num 5:21–24). The rejoicing of the people "before Yahweh" on the festival of Sukkot in Lev 23:40 indirectly suggests invocation of the divine name in praise. In addition to these cultic examples of the legitimate use of the name, the story about blasphemy in Leviticus 24, which in part builds on prescriptions about the divine name in the Covenant Code (cf. Exod 20:24; 22:27; 23:13) in creative combination with the miscarriage and talion law in that collection (21:22–25), explores a counter example where the divine name is abused.[28]

In sum, the use of the name Yahweh is necessary for a variety of cultic purposes and it becomes functional precisely in the age of the tabernacle. Knowing the divine name allows the people to fully engage the deity and his presence. While blessings and promises can be communicated to individuals under a different divine appellation in the pre-cultic age, the revelation of deity's proper name in the age of the tabernacle marks and directs the renewal of those promises to the entire nation.

5 The Calendar

Similar to sacrifice and the use of the divine name, PH makes no mention of humans' observing cultic or quasi-cultic calendric events—festivals or the Sabbath—prior to the revelations to Moses.[29] The deity's rest on the seventh day

27 Neighboring Numbers 7 puts 6:22–27 in the context of the erection of the tabernacle. For a recent study of the Ketef Hinnom amulets with phrases paralleling this blessing, A. Berlejung, "Theologisches Wort und anthropologischer Ort der Silberamulette von Ketef Hinnom," *ZAW* 120 (2008) 204–30.

28 See D. P. Wright, "Source Dependence and the Development of the Pentateuch: The Case of Leviticus 24," in J. Gertz/B. Levinson/D. Rom-Shiloni/K. Schmid (ed.), *The Formation of the Pentateuch: Bridging the Academic Cultures of Europe, Israel, and North America* (Tübingen: Mohr Siebeck, 2016), 651–82; C. Nihan, "Murder, Blasphemy and Sacral Law: Another Look at Lev 24,10–23," *ZABR* 17 (2011) 211–40; M. Leuchter, "The Ambiguous Details in the Blasphemer Narrative: Sources and Redaction in Lev 24:10–23," *JBL* 130 (2011) 431–50.

29 While the Sabbath in P is not observed cultically, it does have cultic associations. As we will see it is first revealed in connection with the building of the tabernacle: its observance supersedes work on the structure. H in particular enhanced the status of the Sabbath and brought it into the list of festivals and other occasions that are cultic (Lev 23:2–3; cf. Knohl, *Sanctuary*, 8–45).

at creation involves him alone (Gen 2:2–3). If the PH manna story in Exodus 16, which involves the Sabbath, originally appeared later in the context of PH (around Num 15:32–36),[30] then the Sabbath is first revealed to humans in connection with the building of the tabernacle in Exod 31:12–17.[31] This passage directly prohibits work on the seventh day. It introduces the Sabbath as a "sign" (אוֹת) and observance by the Israelites is binding "for their generations, an eternal covenant" (לְדֹרֹתָם בְּרִית עוֹלָם). This wording is similar to that found in connection with P's rainbow and circumcision (Gen 9:12; Gen 17:7, 9; see also 9:13, 17).[32] The content and rhetoric of Exod 31:12–17, combined with the call of Moses in 6:2–8, indicate that, though PH did not use the term "covenant" בְּרִית for the broad relationship between deity and the nation Israel at the birth of the nation, it is phenomenologically this type of relationship.[33]

The full festival calendar is found (revised by H) in Leviticus 23 of the Holiness Code, but aspects of the calendar are revealed for the first time in prescriptions for the first Passover in Exod 12:1–20. Verse 2 drops a pin on the temporal map for the people: "*This month* for you is the beginning of months" (הַחֹדֶשׁ הַזֶּה לָכֶם רֹאשׁ חֳדָשִׁים). For the first time in history humans are informed about the calendar, which will be important in cultic practice soon to be unfolded.

It is not entirely clear how this passage fits in the composition of PH. As a whole it has a number of H features. Yet omitting the entirety of this passage would deprive a basic P narrative of an account of the first Passover and reference to killing the firstborn of Egypt.[34] An argument can be made for a shorter P textual

30 See J. Baden, "The Original Place of the Priestly Manna Story in Exodus 16," *ZAW* 122 (2010) 491–504.

31 For an analysis of P and H in Exod 31:12–17, see J. Stackert, "Compositional Strata in the Priestly Sabbath: Exodus 31:12–17 and 35:1–3," *JHS* 11 (2011) article 15 (http://www.jhsonline.org; accessed 09/21/13); idem, "The Composition of Exodus 31:12–17 and 35:1–3 and the Question of Method in Identifying Priestly Strata in the Torah," in R. Gane/A. Taggar-Cohen (ed.), *Current Issues in Priestly and Related Literature: The Legacy of Jacob Milgrom and Beyond* (SBLRBS; Atlanta: SBL, 2015) 175–96. For him, basic P consists of the introduction, main prohibition, and the following phrases with third person plural formulation in 31:12–13aα, 15 (without שַׁבָּתוֹן קֹדֶשׁ and מוֹת), 16, 17 (without וַיִּנָּפַשׁ). The original passage is partly determined by the more minimally worded 35:1–3 (for Stackert vv. 1–2 here, without יִהְיֶה לָכֶם קֹדֶשׁ and שַׁבָּתוֹן, are P). It should be noted, however, that 31:12–17 as a whole has features indicative of H (including chiastic formulation and repetition), it appears in a section of the tabernacle prescriptions that seems largely associable with H (Exod 29:38–31:18), and it features, less characteristically, the supposed H addition *before* the basic P material rather than after.

32 See the discussion by S.M. Olyan, "An Eternal Covenant with Circumcision as Its Sign: How Useful a Criterion for Dating and Source Analysis?" in T.B. Dozeman/K. Schmid/B.J. Schwartz (ed.), *The Pentateuch* (FAT 78; Tübingen: Mohr Siebeck, 2011) 347–58.

33 On the topic, see C. Nihan, "The Priestly Covenant, Its Reinterpretations, and the Composition of 'P'," in S. Shectman/J.S. Baden (ed.), *The Strata of the Priestly Writings* (ATANT 95; Zürich: Theologischer Verlag, 2009) 87–134.

34 For example, Knohl (*Sanctuary*, 19–23) attributes the whole of Exod 12:1–20 to H (and multiple levels of H). For the similar narrative problem of seeing Exod 6:2–8 as a later H addition,

nucleus that consisted of text lacking second person plural forms (i.e., 12:1, 3 without לֵאמֹר בֶּעָשֹׂר לַחֹדֶשׁ הַזֶּה, 6b–8, 12) and that this was expanded by H. In this analysis the notice "This month for you is the beginning of months" would be an H supplement.[35]

On the other hand, the larger passage parallels and thus appears to be built on J's Passover and unleavened bread prescriptions in 12:21–27 and 13:3–10.[36] Unless both P and H contributors went back to the same J text to formulate 12:1–20—which is not impossible in view of the broad recourse to non-PH by different strata of PH—this source dependence may indicate that 12:1–20 is a

---

see n. 25. For a significant differing assessment, see C. Nihan, "Israel's Festival Calendars in Leviticus 23, Numbers 28–29 and the Formation of the 'Priestly' Literature," in T. Römer (ed.), *The Books of Leviticus and Numbers* (BETL 215; Leuven: Uitgeverij Peeters, 2008) 177–231.

35 J. Stackert, "Why Does the Plague of Darkness Last for Three Days? Source Ascription and Literary Motif in Exodus 10:21–23, 27," *VT* 61 (2011) 657–76, on pp. 660, 669 attributes a slightly larger text (i. e., 12:1, 3–13) to the basic P narrative.

36 Exod 12:1–14 closely parallels 12:21–24, and the following verses about unleavened bread in 12:15–20 parallel 13:6–10. Exod 12:21–27 and 13:6–10, for their part, are two of three passages that share a common thematic structure and have a pronounced Deuteronomistic character: 12:21–27 (Passover), 13:3–10 (unleavened bread), and 13:11–16 (the firstborn). Because of this coherence and distinctive character, they appear to belong to a source different from PH. Other considerations bear this out. The passage Exod 12:21b–27a does not make sense as the continuation of PH, outlining what Moses told the people to do, because they omit instruction of important elements commanded in 12:1–14 (including the meal and requirement not to leave flesh over until morning). The instructions of 12:21b–27a also appear in a J narrative frame (vv. 21a, 27b; cf. 4:29–31). Furthermore (if 13:1–2 is put aside for the moment), the passage on unleavened bread in 13:3–10 follows nicely on the last narrative verse in J about unleavened dough (12:39; J in Exod 12 would consist of vv. 21–27, 29–34, 39). Though 12:21–27 and 13:3–16 in this analysis are part of the J text, they may not be original therein. Moreover, J's basic Passover instructions in 12:21b–23 with their narrative frame (vv. 21a, 27b) may even be an addition, perhaps introduced along with the contextually extraneous cameo about circumcision in 4:24–26. Like the rite in 12:21–27, the circumcision story features an apotropaic blood rite that protects a son. Notably J's little circumcision story immediately follows J's announcement of the future firstborn plague (4:22–23). The circumcision event thus narratively anticipates J's culminating firstborn plague with its blood rite. The injunction of the Passover on future generations in 12:24–27b as well as the unleavened bread and firstborn regulations in 13:3–16 may be further additions to J and part of might be termed the "legification" of J. J may not have originally included lawgiving, but was updated to parallel the Covenant Code narrative (E). The so-called ritual or cultic decalogue in Exod 34:10–27, based largely on the Covenant Code but endowed with a distinctive Deuteronomistic flavor, would be part of this addition of law to J. (The firstborn command in 13:1–2, which interrupts the parallel patterning of 12:21–27, 13:3–10, and 11–16, might be considered a further addition in J). That PH is secondary to and dependent on J's 12:21–27 and 13:3–10 is indicated, among other things, by portraying the slaughter, not merely as the source of apotropaic blood, but also providing a meal and added detail in regulation. For the argument that 12:21–27 is actually part of PH and 13:1–16 as later expansion that provides and alternative to 12:1–28, with incisive discussion of the various issues involved, see S. Gesundheit, *Three Times a Year: Studies on Festival Legislation in the Pentateuch* (FAT 82; Tübingen: Mohr Siebeck, 2012).

rather unified composition. Additionally, the change of number to second plural is not a definitive sign of textual strata.[37] This may mean that Exod 12:1–20 was composed somewhat later in the overall formulation of the P narrative and completes it according to a predetermined plan. Its composition may have been delayed in order to coordinate it with the development of the H version of festival legislation in Leviticus 23.

Even though announced only in these Exodus passages, the world's calendar, according to the broad view of PH, did not begin ticking with these revelations to the Israelites. The clock was wound and started at the beginning of creation. The Israelites were only made privy to this cosmological secret and reality at the time of Moses. On the fourth day of creation the deity creates the sun, moon, and stars. They are to be "for signs, set times, days and years" (לְאֹתֹת וּלְמוֹעֲדִים וּלְיָמִים וְשָׁנִים; 1:14). The term אֹתֹת "signs" here must include Sabbaths and anticipates the revelation in Exod 31:12–17, which uses this term for the Sabbath, as noted earlier. The term מוֹעֲדִים, often translated "set times," includes the festivals (cf. Lev 23:2,4, 37; Num 28:2; 29:39).[38] These terms in Gen 1 thus presage the later revelation of these occasions in the age of Moses. Their observance by humans, as with sacrifice, remains dormant until that age. In contrast to this, the marking of "days and years" by the sun and moon begins at the creation. "Days" actually begin on the first day of creation when light is created (1:5). This allows the counting of days across the week of creation leading up to divine rest on the seventh day. "Years" operate from the beginning of human history and are visible in P's detailed chronology punctuated with "generations" (תּוֹלְדוֹת) notices (Gen 2:4; 5:1; 6:9; 10:1, 32; 11:10, 27; 25:12, 13, 19; 36:1, 9; 37:2; Exod 6:16, 19).

6 Purity and Holiness

Before the establishment of the tabernacle, PH does not depict the operation of purity and holiness customs. The mention of pure and impure animals in the flood story (Gen 7:2, 8; 8:20) belongs to J, not P. J requires bringing a surplus (seven pairs) of pure animals so that some of them may be used as food on the ark (implied in Gen 7:2) and more importantly in sacrifice after the flood (8:20–22). P's Noah brings only one pair of each kind of animal, including pure animals, because they are neither eaten (6:21) nor sacrificed (9:1–17).[39] Jacob's disposal of foreign gods and accompanying purification in Gen 35:1–7, the sexual pollution

37 For example, phrases with second person plural forms in passages such as Gen 17:9–14; Exod 25:1–7; Num 15:37–41; 19:2–3; 35:1–8 cannot be eliminated leaving a sensible text in terms of syntax or context.

38 It is possible to argue that the detail about the heavenly lights, whose form and content seems belabored, is an addition, attributable to H. See Krüger, "Genesis 1:1–2:3."

39 See Wright, "Profane versus Sacrificial Slaughter."

of Dinah in Gen 34:5, 13, 27,[40] the holiness of theground at the burning bush (Exod 3:5), and the three-day advance purification for the theophany at Mt. Sinai (19:6, 20, 13, 22) are all non-PH.[41]

The story of the first Passover in PH anticipates aspects of holiness concerns that only come into operation after the revelation of the tabernacle. The verse Exod 12:16 prescribes the observance of a "sacred declaration" (מִקְרָא־קֹדֶשׁ) on the first and seventh day of the observance of unleavened bread (cf. the term in Lev 23:2–4, 7–8, 21, 24, 27, 35–37). This is presumably not observable at the inaugural event. H is responsible for adding this somewhat out of place datum.

But though PH avoids matters of purity and holiness prior to the time of Moses, its early narrative nonetheless anticipates later pollution concerns, much as the grant of profane slaughter to Noah in Gen 9:3–5 anticipates sacrifice. In fact, sacrifice and purity concerns are integrally related in P. The grant of animal flesh in the human diet after the flood is the foundation of a pyramid of dietary rules matching social gradations, which are fully unveiled at the time of Moses, as summarized in Figure 1.[42] The deity's diet in sacrifice (e.g., Leviticus 1–7) complements dietary rules for the people (mainly Leviticus 11), and these together reflect a cultic-cosmic hierarchy. God has the most limited diet, whereas lowly animals have the broadest. The rules to Noah anticipate this full system, but they deal with the bottom two registers, which are not yet concerned with matters of purity.

Being or Creature	*Consumable Quadruped Flesh*	*Sample References*
Deity	Sacrifices of unblemished domestic animals including visceral fat (blood is placed on/at altar but technically not *offered* like the flesh)	e.g., Lev 1–7
Priests	Portions of sacrifices and properly killed permissible domestic or game animals, but no blood or visceral fat	e.g., Lev 6–7; 11; 22:8
Israelites	Permissible domestic or game animals and dead or improperly killed animals of the permissible category as long as purification follows, but no blood or visceral fat	Lev 11 (note vv. 39–40); 17:15–16

40 For sorting out P and non-P in Genesis 34 and 35, see Baden, *Composition*, 230–45. He attributes to E specifically 35:1–8, 14 (excluding בַּמָּקוֹם אֲשֶׁר־דִּבֶּר אִתּוֹ), 16b, 17–18, 19 (וַתָּמָת רָחֵל, common with P), 20. The analysis of Gen 34 is more complex, but it is not P. The question is whether it is composite. See the considerations about composition and the motif of impurity in the story in E. S. Feinstein, *Sexual Pollution in the Hebrew Bible* (PhD Diss.; Cambridge MA: Harvard University, 2010), 153–209. She views it as an essential unity belonging to E (p. 170). Baden, *Composition*, 233–4 (see also 72, 73–4, 237, 242, 318 n. 6) views Gen 34 as a blend of J and E.

41 For Exod 3, see n. 26. For the Sinai pericope, see Wright, *Inventing*, 338–9.

42 See further Wright, "Profane versus Sacrificial Slaughter;" J. Milgrom, *Leviticus 1–16* (AB 3; New York: Doubleday, 1991), 722.

Being or Creature	*Consumable Quadruped Flesh*	*Sample References*
Non-Israelites	All animal flesh and (implicitly) visceral fat, but no blood	Gen 9:4–6
Animals	All animal flesh, blood, visceral fat allowed	implied

Figure 1: Allocation of Animal Flesh in PH Sacrificial and Dietary Regulations

This sacrificial-dietary schema drove P's rewriting of J's flood story, noted above. Because of its different view of the cult, P could not simply revise J's story but had to radically retool it to serve the ideology of its broad narrative. The conceptual relationship of the flood story to the basic legislation on sacrifice and purity is one of the pieces of evidence that shows the priority of the cultic regulations in the formation of the PH corpus.[43]

P's flood story also encodes the system of personal sin and external pollution effect found in later PH legislation. In P legislation, sin causes impurity that pollutes the sanctuary from afar and sacrificial blood of the purgation or sin offering (חַטָּאת) removes that impurity (Leviticus 4 and 16). In H legislation, which broadens the scope of P legislation beyond the context of the sanctuary, sin pollutes the land and this becomes the mechanism for exile from the land (Lev 18:25–28; 19:29; Num 35:33).[44] P's flood story displays these same mechanics, but uses neutral or non-cultic terminology. At the beginning of the story, the deity surveys creation and finds that "the earth had become corrupt (נִשְׁחָתָה), because all flesh (כָּל־בָּשָׂר) had corrupted (הִשְׁחִית) its behavior on the earth" (Gen 6:12). P here solves two conceptual problems in the J account. It attributes sin to "all flesh," including animals, as opposed to just humans in J (cf. 6:5–7; 8:21), to explain why the flood affects humans and land animals.[45] Further P portrays the

43 It can be wondered whether Gen 9:4–6 is secondary because of its divergent style, its character as an aside (especially with אַךְ in vv. 4 and 5), its legal rather than narrative orientation, and the prominent poetic verse about homicide in v. 6a. Several considerations, however, point to the originality of the verses: The poetic form in v. 6, is consistent with 1:27, which is presumably original. The verses make clear that the reason for the flood was the shedding of blood by and finally explain why in P "all flesh," including animals, is guilty (see n. 45). Further, P, dependent on J and interested in responding to J's portrayal of animal killing in sacrifice, would be expected to make some concrete reference to animal killing. This is only clear in the context of vv. 4–6. In addition, the fronting of "and as for you" (וְאַתֶּם) in v. 7 contrasts the people's obligation with that of the deity, which begins with "and as for me" (וַאֲנִי) in v. 9. If v. 9 is original, v. 7 should also be original; but v. 7 operates also as a resumptive repetition of v. 1, which seems to require the digression in vv. 4–6.

44 See D.P. Wright, "Unclean and Clean (OT)," *ABD* 6 (1992) 729–41; idem, "Holiness in Leviticus and Beyond," *Interpretation* 53/4 (1999) 351–64.

45 P uses "all flesh" a key term to describe the object of destruction (6:12, 13, 17, 19; 7:15, 16a, 21, 8:17; 9:11, 15, 16, 17). The guilt of animals is characterized indirectly in 9:5.

sin of all flesh as affecting the earth to explain why it is covered by water. The flood implicitly removes the earth's corruption and restores it to a pristine state.

Another foreshadowing of purity and holiness rules and the broader ontology of its cultic system may be in P's use of the verb הִבְדִּיל "to divide" in its creation story.[46] This verb is used of distinguishing between light and darkness (Gen 1:4), the upper and lower waters (v. 6, 7), and day and night (v. 14, 18). Other pairs are prominent in the creation story though the verb הִבְדִּיל is not used to describe them. These include morning versus evening, land versus water, water and air animals versus land animals, male versus female, and activity versus rest. This verb reappears in the description (attributable to H) of the priestly role to "distinguish between the holy and the profane and between the impure and the pure" (וּלֲהַבְדִּיל בֵּין הַקֹּדֶשׁ וּבֵין הַחֹל וּבֵין הַטָּמֵא וּבֵין הַטָּהוֹר; Lev 10:10; cf. Ezek 22:26; 44:23) and in dietary laws that speak of distinguishing pure and impure animals (Lev 11:47). The passage Lev 20:24–26 employs the verb in an analogy rationalizing divine election. The deity separated Israel off from the other nations (vv. 24, 26). Israel should similarly distinguish between pure and impure animals. Thus they become holy, as the deity is holy. Thus the act of separation begun at creation continues up to the constitution of Israel as a nation at the time when the people are freed from Egypt and the tabernacle is established.[47]

While the use of הִבְדִּיל in PH legislation may be attributable specifically to H, it makes explicit notions that operate in P's cultic system. Every object, place, person, or event is ritually definable by the presence of one quality from two sets of pairs: (A) impure versus pure, and (B) holy versus profane (see the Hebrew terminology in Lev 10:10; "profane" here means merely lacking holiness). These qualities are graphed in Figure 2, as a "doughnut" displaying four possible combinations (the "barbells" point to the nexuses of categories).[48] For example, the tabernacle, ideally, is both pure and holy (e.g., Lev 8:10); an Israelite person eating impure flesh is both impure and profane (e.g., Lev 11:39–40); this same Israelite, after purification, is pure and profane (e.g., Lev 17:15–16); and, uniquely and perhaps surprisingly, the purgation offering while holy is also impure after it is used for purification (e.g., Lev 4:1–12; 6:18–23; 16:27–28).

Paired criteria or binary oppositions are found in other parts of the PH cultic system. Pure land animals have split hooves and chew the cud, and pure water animals that have fins and scales are pure (Leviticus 11). In the leprosy laws, lesions that are immediately identifiable as a scale or surface disease (צָרַעַת) are those that have at the same time white hair and deepness (13:3). The male

---

46 For some discussion, see Krüger, "Genesis 1:1–2:3," 135–6.

47 The verb הִבְדִּיל is also used of separating the Levites off as cultic servitors (Num 8:14; 16:9; the verb in 16:21 is a literary play against v. 9).

48 This bends the diagram in Milgrom, *Leviticus 1–16*, 732, into a circle to add the holy-impure combination.

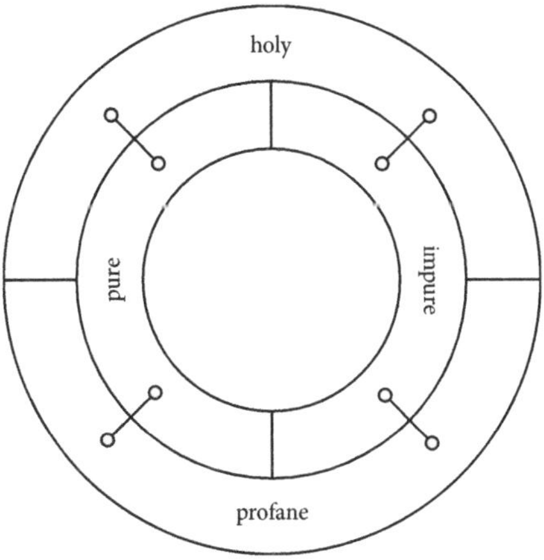

Figure 2: Paired combinations of cultic statuses

gonorrheic is one whose flesh runs or whose flesh is stopped up (Lev 15:3). In the sacrificial laws, options between cattle and flock animals are counterpoised (e.g., Lev 1:2). In matters of ritual space, P and PH broadly are concerned about inside versus outside the camp, and inside versus outside the tabernacle.[49] P's more complex graded systems, which appear in connection with space or in the diet (discussed above), can be analyzed as a system of interlocking binary oppositions.

In various ways, then, P's portrayal of division at creation structurally anticipates the intellectual shape of its legal system. This portrayal of binary conceptualization at creation, however, is likely not representative of its actual generative history. It would seem that binary patterning had its home in the cultic and legal system and that this was applied secondarily to the mythological description of creation. The reversal of the relationship in the PH narrative made the world the sounding board on which the strings of the cultic and legal system resonated.

7 The Birth of the Nation

The foregoing section of this essay noted the use of the verb הִבְדִּיל ("divide") to describe the election of Israel as a nation (Lev 20:24–26), which can be viewed as an extension and culmination of acts of division starting at creation. By this separation, the deity makes the people his possession ("to be mine" לִהְיוֹת לִי; v. 26). This echoes the call of Moses in Exod 6:2–8 where the people are formally appro-

49 See the discussion of ritual space in Jenson, *Holiness*; J. Z. Smith, *To Take Place: Toward Theory in Ritual* (Chicago: University of Chicago Press, 1987), 47–73; D. P. Wright, *The Disposal of Impurity* (SBLDS 101; Atlanta: Scholars Press, 1987).

priated: “I take you (the Israelites) to me as a people and I will be your god” (וְלָקַחְתִּי אֶתְכֶם לִי לְעָם וְהָיִיתִי לָכֶם לֵאלֹהִים; v. 7; cf. also Lev 26:12). This is an adoption formula which, as a speech act and comparable to the speech acts in the creation story, officially creates the divine-human relationship. It fulfills a promise given to Abraham where the deity becomes the god of Abraham’s descendants through the covenant and promise (לִהְיוֹת לְךָ לֵאלֹהִים וּלְזַרְעֲךָ אַחֲרֶיךָ and וְהָיִיתִי לָהֶם לֵאלֹהִים; Gen 17:7–8).

P’s motif of being fruitful, increasing, and filling the land (varied formulation but often with the verbs פרה, רבה, מלא) is related to the birth of the nation. As a command and blessing this is directed to the fish and birds and then to humans at creation (1:22, 28). It is renewed after the flood and is directed to all life (8:17), particularly humans (9:1, 7). Along the way, the deity uses this language saying that he will make Ishmael fruitful (17:20). Isaac blesses Jacob to multiply (28:3). God tells Jacob to multiply (35:11, recounted in 48:4). Finally when Israel is in Egypt, the idiom is used again. But it is no longer a matter of blessing or command, but a matter of fact. At the beginning of the sojourn in Egypt P observes: “Israel dwelt in the land of Egypt …,”[50] and they took possession of it. They were fruitful and multiplied greatly” (47:27). Then at the dawn of the age of Moses, P’s Exodus tells us, with a climactic piling up of terminology: “The Israelites had become fruitful, had swarmed, had multiplied and had become numerous very greatly and the land was full of them” (וּבְנֵי יִשְׂרָאֵל פָּרוּ וַיִּשְׁרְצוּ וַיִּרְבּוּ וַיַּעַצְמוּ בִּמְאֹד מְאֹד וַתִּמָּלֵא הָאָרֶץ אֹתָם; Exod 1:7). Israel had now fulfilled the directive and expectations set down at creation.[51] It is important to note that this climaxing verse is only *five* verses before the call of Moses where the people are officially adopted (PH here consists of Exod 1:1–5, 7, 13–14; 2:23aβb–25; 6:2–8). The “generations” (תּוֹלְדוֹת) formulae that run through Genesis (see the discussion on the calendar, above) contribute to this thematic arc constituted by the fertility motif. The intent to get to an account of the establishment of Israel also partly helps explain why P does not write a detailed account of the patriarchs but focuses, sometimes schematically, on family lineages.[52]

The establishment of the nation or laying the foundations for later human political activity as part of creation is consistent with other ancient Near Eastern creation stories. For example, *Enuma elish* is not just about the creation of humans and their service to the gods, but also about the foundation of Babylon, its cult, and the promotion of Marduk to chief executive.[53] A national or political

50 In a paper delivered at the annual meeting for the Society of Biblical Literature, B. Schwartz has suggested reading in this ellipsis “in the land of Ramses” for “in the land of Goshen.”

51 On this as fulfillment see Schmid, *Genesis*, 62–4, 240; Bauks, “Signification,” 43.

52 See Schmid, *Genesis*, 246–7.

53 My colleague T. Abusch has suggested to me that the description of the foundation of Babylon in the text may be secondary though the basic story of the elevation of a deity would have a political significance.

orientation is missing in P's seven day creation story when read by itself. One might even make the mistake of thinking that P had a universalistic orientation, according to which its deity looked equally on all nations of the earth. It is only with the rest of PH that its particularistic message becomes clear, where Israel is favored over other nations.[54]

8 The Revelation of the Kavod

Comparable to other phenomena discussed to this point, the deity's physical presence, described with the technical term כָּבוֹד (which I will render in simplified transliteration as *kavod*), is fully disclosed only in the age of Moses.[55] The deity's presence is described in other ways prior to the revelation at Mt. Sinai. The creation story refers to a "divine wind" (רוּחַ אֱלֹהִים; 1:2). This is echoed in the flood story where it says "God sent a wind across the land" (וַיַּעֲבֵר אֱלֹהִים רוּחַ עַל־הָאָרֶץ; 8:1). Revelations to pious men prior to Moses often involve only auditions (Noah in Gen 6:13; 8:15; 9:1, 8, 12, 17; Moses' inaugural revelation in Exod 6:2–8; Moses and sometimes Aaron in the plagues in Exod 7:8, 19; 8:1, 12; 9:8, 22; 10:12, 21; 11:9). The deity does appear to Abraham and Jacob, but these events do not feature the god's *kavod* (Gen 17:1; 35:9; cf. 48:3).

The picture changes in P's story about the parting of the sea in Exod 14 (= vv. 1–4, 8–9, 10bγ, 15–18, 21aα, 21b–23, 26–27a, 28–29). This uses the root of *kavod* in a verbal form to describe divine glorification obtained or displayed in the parting of the sea that saves the Israelites: "I will obtain/display glory through Pharaoh and all his army" (וְאִכָּבְדָה בְּפַרְעֹה וּבְכָל־חֵילוֹ: v. 4, 17; with different syntax v. 18).[56] The people do not yet witness the full revelation of the *kavod* at this point. Nonetheless, this is the type of miraculous event that is accompanied by description of the presence of the *kavod* in later stories. The use of this verb in the sea event had an effect on P's description of the hardening of Pharaoh's heart

---

54 A reflex of this is in H's debt-slave legislation (Lev 25:39–47), which makes a distinction between Israelite debt-slave and foreign chattel-slave, and allows harsh treatment of the latter (see Wright, *Inventing*, 123–53; idem, "'She Shall Not Go Free as Male Slaves Do:' Developing Views About Slavery and Gender in the Laws of the Hebrew Bible," in B.J. Brooten [ed.], *Beyond Slavery: Overcoming Its Religious and Sexual Legacy* [New York: Palgrave Macmillan, 2010], 125–42).

55 For a discussion, see B.D. Sommer, *The Bodies of God and the World of Ancient Israel* (New York: Cambridge University Press, 2009), 58–62. For a broad study of *kavod* in the Hebrew Bible and in its Near Eastern context, see S. Aster, *The Unbeatable Light:* Melammu *and Its Biblical Parallels* (AOAT 384; Münster: Ugarit-Verlag, 2012).

56 The nif'al stem of כבד is paralleled by the nif'al of קדש with reference to the deity ("obtain/display holiness, be holy"; Exod 29:43; Lev 10:3; 22:32; Num 20:13) and, more broadly, with references to the deity's holiness (Lev 11:44–45; 19:2; 20:26; 21:8) that appear in H or material with H tendencies.

in the preceding plague stories. In my view, P's plague stories recast J's plague stories.[57] J regularly uses the root כבד for the hardening of Pharaoh's heart. P had to reserve this root and verb for deity. It therefore chose another verb (חזק) to describe the obstinacy of Pharaoh.[58] This allowed P to contrast the "strengthening" that Pharaoh and Yahweh display. That this was P's intent is indicated by the juxtaposition of Pharaoh's heart hardening and Yahweh's glorification in the sea story: "I will harden (וְחִזַּקְתִּי) Pharaoh's heart so that he pursues them, and I will then obtain/display glory (וְאִכָּבְדָה) …" (v. 4, 17; cf v. 8).[59]

---

57 I sort out the sources in plague stories in Exod 7b–11 as follows: P consists of 7:8–13 (rod-reptile); 7:19–20aα, 21b–22 (water-blood); 8:1–3a, 11aβb (frogs); 8:12–15 (lice); 9:8–12 (boils); 9:22–23aα1, 24aα, 25, 31–32, 35 (hail); 10:12–13aα1, 14aα, 15aα2βb, 20 (locusts); 10:21–23, 27 (darkness); 11:9–10 (transition). J consists of 7:14–18, 20aβb–21a, 23–25 (water-blood); 7:26–29, 8:3b–11aα (frogs); 8:16–28 (flies); 9:1–7 (animal death); 9:13–21, 23aα2βγb, 24aβb, 26–30, 33–34 (hail); 10:1–11, 13aα2βb, 14aβb–15aα1, 16–19, 24–26, 28–29 (locusts); 11:4–8 (start of firstborn). The only E material may be in 11:1–3. For Exod 3–7a see n. 26 and for Exod 12 see n. 36. For discussion of some aspects of source division, see Stackert, "Plague of Darkness."

58 P's חזק appears in 7:13, 22; 8:15; 9:12, 35; 10:20, 27 (it should have also appeared in 8:11, but was omitted when the Pentateuch was compiled). J's כבד appears in 7:14; 8:11, 28; 9:7, 34; 10:1. P and J each once use another root in their first references to heart hardening: P קשה in 7:3, and J 4:21 חזק (see the circumlocution of the idiom in J's 14:5 with הפך; Baden, *Redaction*, 273–5, sees J's exceptional verb in 4:21 as redactional). In addition to regularizing J's heart-hardening motif, P's dependence on J in the plague stories appears in its replication of the binary pattern of prediction and fulfillment in J and filling in the problematic narrative gap between these elements. Dependence is also visible in P's incorporation of J's belief-signs for the people (Exod 4) into the series of sign-plagues for Pharaoh. P has the rod-reptile sign performed before Pharaoh rather than before the people as in J. P's more widespread conversion of water into blood, affecting even water in vessels, may be due in part to refiguring J's faith sign of water turning to blood when poured from a vessel. P's boil plague relates to J's sign of Moses' hand turning leprous in view of P's symptomatology of צָרַעַת, in which a שְׁחִין "boil" has the potential of developing into the disease (Lev 13:18–23). P may be seeking to dissociate this impure condition from its foundational prophet and cult originator, Moses, and, at the same time, cast opprobrium on Pharaoh's magicians and effect a transition to a direct confrontation between Moses and Pharaoh. In any case, the dependence of the P's plague series on J shows that P's series is essentially a unified composition. P's change of agent in plague performance (first Aaron then Moses) and from intransitive to transitive forms of חזק for heart hardening are part of an intentionally crafted climaxing pattern where subordinate representative "prophets" (Aaron and Pharaoh's magicians) are replaced by direct competition between the human "gods" of the story (Moses and Pharaoh). This helps explain why P described Aaron as Moses' prophet in 7:1–2, presumably a rewriting of J's 4:14–16 (see n. 26).

59 Baden, "Original Place," 498 n. 33, critiques Ska's and Ruprecht's connection of the verb in Exod 14 with the *kavod* (Ska, *Introduction*, 157; E. Ruprecht, "Stellung und Bedeutung der Erzählung vom Mannawunder [Ex 16] im Aufbau der Priesterschrift," *ZAW* 86 [1974] 269–307, 291–8). It is true that the *kavod* is not being revealed here, but it is a significant down payment, so to speak, on the fulfillment at Mt. Sinai. Baden is right, however, in arguing that the PH quail and manna story, which mentions the *kavod*, actually appeared later in the PH narrative. See the discussion about the calendar, above.

The *kavod* appears in PH after this and for the first time in the theophany at Mt. Sinai (Exod 24:15–18). A cloud (הֶעָנָן) covers the mountain and the *kavod*, enveloped by the cloud, settles (שכן) on the mountain. The people witness the appearance of the *kavod* as a burning fire. The deity speaks to Moses from the cloud and Moses enters it for the revelation of the tabernacle. A similar phenomenology occurs when the tabernacle is set up and before it is publicly consecrated. The cloud covers or settles on the tent and the *kavod* fills the tabernacle (40:34–35). The deity then delivers revelations to Moses from the tent (Lev 1:1). After the tabernacle and its priests are consecrated (Leviticus 8–9), the *kavod* appears to the people as a fire issuing from the tent that consumes offerings on the altar (9:6, 23–24). The people fall on their faces in fearful awe. The appearance of the *kavod* at the tent is part of the basic phenomenological plan for the tabernacle (Exod 29:43: וְנֹעַדְתִּי שָׁמָּה לִבְנֵי יִשְׂרָאֵל וְנִקְדַּשׁ בִּכְבֹדִי).

The narrative trajectory of the *kavod* continues in later PH stories of rebellion.[60] Immediately after its inaugural display to the people at the consecration of the tabernacle, the same divine fire issues from the tabernacle to destroy two of Aaron's sons who committed cultic error (Lev 10:1–3; their illicit "fire" plays against the destructive divine "fire").[61] In the PH spy story (= Num 13:1–17a, 21, 25–26bα*, 32; 14:1a, 2–10, 26–39) the *kavod* appears at the tent of meeting to all the Israelites when they threaten to stone Moses and Aaron (14:10).[62] When the people complain about the lack of food in the PH manna and quail story

60 See Achenbach, *Vollendung*, for a different assessment of Numbers, including the wilderness stories. His works views Numbers as a post-priestly development reflecting a three-staged redactional process out of which the Pentateuch arises (see also his "Die Erzählung von der gescheiterten Landnahme von Kadesch Barnea [Numeri 13–14] als Schlüsseltext der Redaktionsgeschichte des Pentateuchs," *ZABR* 9 [2003] 56–123).

61 In my view, the sin of Aaron's sons and the consequent controversy about not eating the חַטָּאת sacrifice in Leviticus 10 is a reflex of non-P stories of the golden calf and the Levites in Exodus 32. Main correlations include: dedication of the Levites/priests with מִלֵּא יָד (Lev 8:33; Exod 32:29); the triangulation of Jeroboam's bulls and the golden calf and his and Aaron sons' names (Lev 10:1; Exod 32:4, 8, 19, 20, 24, 35; Kings 15:25, 28, 32; 19:1); a cultic sin in the context of a public celebration (Leviticus 9; Exod 32:5-6); a sin that comes immediately after the revelation of foundational law; preoccupation with Aaron's responsibility; Moses' anger and questioning of Aaron (or his sons) after the sin and Aaron's defense (Lev 10:16–20; Exod 32:19–24); bearing sin נָשָׂא חַטָּאת/עָוֹן in connection with כִּפֶּר (Lev 10:17; Exod 32:30, 32); consuming divine anger with the root אכל (Lev 10:2; Exod 32:10); resolution of tensions by Moses (Lev 10:20; 32:14); and the appearance of the root פרע referring to illicit behavior (Lev 10:6; Exod 32:25). The PH Korah story in Numbers 16–17 is a complement to Leviticus 10 (see n. 65) and reflects golden calf motifs (Num 16:22 // Exod 32:33; Num 17:10 // Exod 32:20) including a preoccupation with the status of Levites. PH's transformation of motifs from Exodus 32 is consistent with its imbuing post-exodus rebellions with PH cultic-ideological concerns.

62 The divine *kavod* in Num 14:21–22 is J. The correlations between PH's and J's spy stories are not as dense as in other wilderness stories surveyed in this essay. Some of the correlations, apart from general similarity in plot and some common characters, include (PH // J): seeing giants 13:32 // 13:28, 33; weeping 14:1a // 1b; divine response with 11 עַד־אָנָה // 14.27 עַד־מָתַי,

(= Exod 16:1, 2–3, 6–25, 31–36), Moses and Aaron tell the people that they will see the divine *kavod* (v. 7).[63] The fulfillment says "they turned to the wilderness and Yahweh's *kavod* appeared in a cloud" (v. 10). This PH story likely originally appeared around Numbers 15 (hence between the spy and Korah stories). In its original context, v. 10 may have read "they turned to the tent of meeting and Yahweh's *kavod* appeared in the cloud," similar to the wording in Num 17:7.[64] In the Korah story (PH = Num 16:1a, 2aβ [starting אֲנָשִׁים]–11, 16–24, 26–27a, 35) the *kavod* appears at the tent of meeting for the ordeal attending Korah's rebellion (v. 19). As in Leviticus 10, fire issues from Yahweh and consumes the rebels (v. 35). In the aftermath when the whole congregation complains, the *kavod* appears at the tent of meeting (17:7). This launches a plague that Aaron stops with his fire pan.[65] Finally, in the water from the rock episode (20:1–13*), when Moses and Aaron offend the deity, the *kavod* appears again at the tent of meeting

oath with 21 // 14:28 חַי־אָנִי; the punishment that the exodus generation would not enter the land, except for Caleb (the PH text adds Joshua) 14:28–35 // 21–24; reference to the land as promised in oath 14:30 // 23; and the *kavod* 14:10 // 21–22.

63 For source analysis of Exodus 16, see Baden, "Original Place." PH's manna and quail story appear to combine and transform J's separate stories about manna (Exod 16:4–5, 26–30) and quail (Num 11:1–10, 13, [16aα], 18–24a, 31–34; for source division of Numbers 11, see Baden, "Original Place," 501–2 n. 43; *Composition*, 82–102). An indication of the derivative character of the PH story is the disappearance of the quail theme in the latter part of its story. PH's story starts as a complaint following the context of J's quail story and then becomes focused on manna in the context of the Sabbath, the theme in J's manna story. PH, however, turns the manna story into miracle tale about preservation of the double portion on the Sabbath as opposed to J's story about transgressing the Sabbath prohibition. Correlations in motifs and language include (PH // J): the good food enjoyed in Egypt (Exod 16:3 // Num 11:5), consuming flesh (אכל בָּשָׂר; Exod 16:3, 12 // Num 11:4, 18), giving flesh to the people (נתן בָּשָׂר; Exod 16:8 // Num 11:13, 21), description of appearance and taste of manna, including being like coriander seed (Exod 16:14, 31 // Num 11:7–8), the manna's connection with dew (Exod 16:13, 14 // Num 11:9); its covering the camp (Exod 16:13 // Num 11:9, 31), hearing the complaint (Exod 16:7, 8, 9, 12 // Num 11:10), the complaint being "before" the deity (Exod 16:9 // Num 11:20); seeing the deity's power (Exod 16:10 // Num 11:23); the connection of manna with Sabbath regulation (Exod 16:23, 25 // 16:26, 29, 30), gathering with לקט (Exod 16:16, 17, 18, 21, 22; // 16:4, 5, 26, 27; Num 11:8), a person gathering a little (הַמַּמְעִיט; Exod 16:17 // Num 11:32). PH adds a cultic dimension to the manna event, including the motif of preservation and rotting that parallels sacrificial flesh (Exod 16:19–20, 23–24; cf. Exod 12:10; Lev 7:16–18; 19:5–8) and storage of the omer at the sanctuary (Exod 16:33–34).

64 Note the similarity in wording: וַיִּפְנוּ אֶל־הַמִּדְבָּר וְהִנֵּה כְּבוֹד יְהוָה נִרְאָה בֶּעָנָן (Exod 16:10) and וַיִּפְנוּ אֶל־אֹהֶל מוֹעֵד וְהִנֵּה כִסָּהוּ הֶעָנָן (Num 17:7). That Exod 16:10 originally referred to the tent is supported by the context. Exodus 16:9 says the people are to approach "before Yahweh," i.e., gather at the tabernacle. Verses 11–12 has Yahweh speaking to Moses, presumably from the tabernacle (see n. 69). The editor of the Pentateuch presumably changed the geographical referent in Exod 16:10 when he moved the PH quail and manna story to a position before the revelation of the *kavod* and the tabernacle.

65 This shows the relationship of the Korah story in Numbers 16*–17 to that about Aaron's sons in Leviticus 10. These stories revolve around divine fire (from the *kavod*) and legitimate fire offered by legitimate priestly representatives (Lev 9:24; 10:1–2; Num 16:7, 18, 35).

(v. 6).[66] Moses and Aaron fall on their faces as the people did at the inauguration of the sanctuary (Lev 9:24).[67]

The movement of the cloud from the sanctuary to signal when the Israelites are to travel is part of the *kavod* phenomenology in PH (Exod 40:36–38; Num 9:15–23; 10:11–12). These passages describe the wonder more elaborately as a cloud during the day and a fire at night. This fiery display correlates with the fiery phenomenon of the *kavod* seen in passages discussed earlier. The darkness of night makes it visible. The analogy is a fire with hot coals. During the day the *kavod* smolders, and what is mainly visible is smoke. At night the coals become visible. Nevertheless, during times of rebellion or heightened devotion the *kavod* heats up and becomes visible even in the daytime. In the examples of rebellion surveyed above, the cloud is implicitly in place at the tabernacle. They describe the amplification of the *kavod* where it becomes visible in daylight.[68]

The stories of the *kavod* in the wilderness dovetail with the *kavod* theme developed through the consecration of the tabernacle. This shows that, whatever may be argued about the complex literary development of PH, its plan was not merely to tell how the *kavod* came to occupy the tabernacle, but how the *kavod* and the tabernacle operated in the continuing early history of the Israelite nation.[69] Just

---

66 On Num 20:1–13 as a réécriture of Exod 17:2–7, see Nihan, *Priestly Torah*, 25–30. In my view, however, this rewriting is not post-priestly, but part of the PH transformation of non-P rebellion stories, as described throughout this essay.

67 This motif appears in the other PH wilderness stories surveyed here: Num 14:5; 16:4, 22; 17:10.

68 The PH story of Moses' glowing face after revelation on Mt. Sinai (Exod 34:29–35) reflects the contagious nature the *kavod*. The cloud of incense smoke created to shield the high priest from the deity in the Day of Atonement rite is also associated with the *kavod* theme (Lev 16:2, 13).

69 The cloud-*kavod* motif in PH appears to recombine motifs from non-P narratives, and these non-P motifs themselves appear to have a genetic relationship. E has two separate motifs: (1) a cloud (not involving fire) on the inaugural mountain of revelation and later at the tent of meeting outside the camp (Exod 33:7–11; Num 11:16, 24–27, 30; 12:4, 9–15) and (2) the vanguard motif of a messenger, terror, and "hornet" that guide the Israelites to their land (Exod 23:20–33). The latter passage may be a reworking of themes form Assyrian royal inscriptions along with the curses at the end of the epilogue of the Laws of Hammurabi (itself a royal inscription; see Hurowitz, *Inu Anum ṣīrum*) and arose as part of the process that produced the Covenant Code that immediately precedes (for this argument, see D. P. Wright, "The Covenant Code Appendix [Exod 23:20–33], Neo-Assyrian Sources, and Implications for Pentateuchal Study," in J. Gertz/B. Levinson/D. Rom-Shiloni/K. Schmid [ed.], *The Formation of the Pentateuch: Bridging the Academic Cultures of Europe, Israel, and North America* [Tübingen: Mohr Siebeck, 2016, 47–85]; idem, "Origin, Development, and Context of the Covenant Code"). J combined the vanguard motif with the motif of the theophany cloud and expanded the phenomenology to a cloud by day and fire by night (Exod 13:21–22; 14:19–20, 24). (For J's dependence otherwise on the narrative in which the Covenant Code appears, i. e., E, see Wright, *Inventing*, 358.) It is not clear how J's Exod 33:1–6bα, 12–23; 34:2–3, 4*, 5aβ–9, which relate negotiations between Moses and Yahweh about divine accompaniment in the wilderness, relate to this picture (for attribution

as the story of creation does not end on the seventh day but continues to the establishment of the tabernacle, the story of the tabernacle does not end with its erection becomes the basis for the next stage of the narrative, about the people Israel and the divine presence among them.

9 Creation Language in the Tabernacle Construction and Beyond

Many have recognized phraseological ties between P's seven-day creation story and the building of the tabernacle, particularly those sections that refer to Sabbath prohibitions or provide summary notes about the building of the tabernacle.[70] For example Exod 31:15–17, the commands about the Sabbath mentioned above, make explicit reference to creation: "For in six days Yahweh made the heaven and earth, and on the seventh day he rested" כִּי־שֵׁשֶׁת יָמִים עָשָׂה יְהוָה אֶת־הַשָּׁמַיִם וְאֶת־הָאָרֶץ וּבַיּוֹם הַשְּׁבִיעִי שָׁבַת (see also 31:15; 35:2). This summarizes Gen 1:1–2:4a and echoes the language of 2:2–3 specifically (see these verses cited below).

Some of the incidental language of creation is also found in the description of the building of the tabernacle. These include the motif of seeing the product with a judgment about its quality with a הִנֵּה ("behold") clause, blessing, and doing

---

of these verses to J, see Baden, *Composition*, 78; *Redaction*, 169; "On Exodus 33,1–11," *ZAW* 124 [2012] 329–40 and specifically 338–9 n. 30). Exodus 33:2 uses language from E's 23:20, 23 but portrays the "messenger" as a lesser substitute for Yahweh's personal guidance (the latter is represented by the smoke and fire pillar according to Exod 13:21–22; 14:24). It thus contradicts and seems to react to 23:20–33. Baden has recently argued that 33:2 is an addition ("On Exodus 33,1–11"). But its apparent extraneousness may be due to sources used in an original composition (see n. 7). In any case, the mention of the messenger in Exod 14:19a may be secondary (v. 19a duplicates v. 19b and is in tension with 13:21–22). Thus J's story of the sea event may have featured only a pillar of cloud and fire representing Yahweh's guidance (14:19b–20, 24). The negotiations over divine accompaniment in J's Exodus 33–34 describe the divine presence with פָּנִים (33:14, 15, 20) and כָּבוֹד (vv. 18, 22). It can be argued that PH regularized the connection of the *kavod* with the day-cloud and night-fire of J, but followed E in having a tent of meeting, tying the cloud-*kavod* phenomenon to this structure, and describing the tent as a means of revelation that continues the mode of revelation inaugurated at the mountain (cf. Lev 1:1; Num 1:1; 7:89; implied revelation from the tent in Exod 34:34–35; Lev 9:23; Num 3:14; 9:1). PH did not follow E and J in describing the phenomenon as an עַמּוּד "pillar."

70 See, for example, J. Blenkinsopp, "The Structure of P," *CBQ* 38 (1976) 275–92; E. Blum, *Studien*, 306–12; B. Janowski, "Tempel und Schöpfung: Schöpfungstheologische Aspekte der priesterschriftlichen Heiligtumskonzeption," *JBTh* 5 (1990) 37–69; J. Levenson, *Creation and the Persistence of Evil* (San Francisco: Harper & Row, 1988), 84–9; Schmid, *The Old Testament*, 148–9; M. Weinfeld, "Sabbath, Temple and the Enthronement of the Lord: The Problem of the *Sitz im Leben* of Genesis 1:1–2:3," in A. Caquot/M. Delcor (ed.), *Mélanges bibliques et orientaux en l'honneur de M. Henri Cazelles* (AOAT 212; Kevelaer: Butzon & Bercker, 1981) 501–12; see also the broader considerations in Weimar, *Studien*, 269–317 (with the section "Die Errichtung der Wohnung Jahwes als Vollendung der Schöpfung," pp. 291–305, esp. 297–302).

and finishing work, with the noun מְלָאכָה ("work") and the verbs כלה ("finish/be finished") and עָשָׂה ("do, make"), as in the following texts:

Exod 39:32 וַתֵּכֶל כָּל־עֲבֹדַת מִשְׁכַּן אֹהֶל מוֹעֵד וַיַּעֲשׂוּ בְּנֵי יִשְׂרָאֵל כְּכֹל אֲשֶׁר צִוָּה יְהוָה אֶת־מֹשֶׁה כֵּן עָשׂוּ׃

39:43 וַיַּרְא מֹשֶׁה אֶת־כָּל־הַמְּלָאכָה וְהִנֵּה עָשׂוּ אֹתָהּ כַּאֲשֶׁר צִוָּה יְהוָה כֵּן עָשׂוּ וַיְבָרֶךְ אֹתָם מֹשֶׁה׃

40:33 ... וַיְכַל מֹשֶׁה אֶת־הַמְּלָאכָה

Exod 39:32 All the construction of the tabernacle of the tent of meeting was finished. The Israelites made it according to all that Yahweh commanded Moses, thus they did.

39:43 Moses saw the work, and they had made it just as Yahweh commanded, thus they did. Then Moses blessed them.

40:33 ... Moses finished the construction.

Gen 1:31 וַיַּרְא אֱלֹהִים אֶת־כָּל־אֲשֶׁר עָשָׂה וְהִנֵּה־טוֹב מְאֹד וַיְהִי־עֶרֶב וַיְהִי־בֹקֶר יוֹם הַשִּׁשִּׁי׃ 2:1 וַיְכֻלּוּ הַשָּׁמַיִם וְהָאָרֶץ וְכָל־צְבָאָם׃ 2 וַיְכַל אֱלֹהִים בַּיּוֹם הַשְּׁבִיעִי מְלַאכְתּוֹ אֲשֶׁר עָשָׂה וַיִּשְׁבֹּת בַּיּוֹם הַשְּׁבִיעִי מִכָּל־מְלַאכְתּוֹ אֲשֶׁר עָשָׂה׃ 3 וַיְבָרֶךְ אֱלֹהִים אֶת־יוֹם הַשְּׁבִיעִי וַיְקַדֵּשׁ אֹתוֹ כִּי בוֹ שָׁבַת מִכָּל־מְלַאכְתּוֹ אֲשֶׁר־בָּרָא אֱלֹהִים לַעֲשׂוֹת׃

Gen 1:31 God saw all that he had made, and it was very good. ... 2:1 The heaven and earth and all their hosts were finished. 2 On the seventh day God finished his work that he made. He rested on the seventh day from all his work that he made. 3 God blessed the seventh day and sanctified it, because on it he rested from all the work that God creatively made.

Sanctification of the seventh day in Gen 2:3 (just cited) is also paralleled by the sanctification of the tabernacle Exod 40:9, 10, 11 and Lev 8:10, 11, 15.

Incidental motifs include the presence of the "spirit/wind of God" at the beginning of creation as a force inspiring the sanctuary craftsman Bezalel in constructing the tabernacle (Gen 1:2; Exod 31:3; 35:31). Besides the corresponding Sabbath motif already mentioned, the deity waits six days at the beginning of the revelation of the tabernacle before speaking to Moses on the seventh (Exod 24:16). This structurally echoes the week of creation.

A recurring syntactic feature in the tabernacle texts is extended to a description of construction with pronominal resumption as in Gen 1:27 (the translations here are somewhat literal in order to reflect the Hebrew syntax):

וַיִּבְרָא אֱלֹהִים אֶת־הָאָדָם בְּצַלְמוֹ
בְּצֶלֶם אֱלֹהִים בָּרָא אֹתוֹ
זָכָר וּנְקֵבָה בָּרָא אֹתָם

God created man in his image;
in the image of God (or: divine beings; cf. v. 26) he created him;
male and female he created them.

Compare texts such as:

Exod 25:18 וְעָשִׂיתָ שְׁנַיִם כְּרֻבִים זָהָב
מִקְשָׁה תַּעֲשֶׂה אֹתָם מִשְּׁנֵי קְצוֹת הַכַּפֹּרֶת

Exod 25:18 You shall make two cherubim of gold;
of wrought metal you shall make them at the ends of the ark cover.

Exod 25:29 וְעָשִׂיתָ קְּעָרֹתָיו וְכַפֹּתָיו וּקְשׂוֹתָיו וּמְנַקִּיֹּתָיו אֲשֶׁר יֻסַּךְ בָּהֵן
זָהָב טָהוֹר תַּעֲשֶׂה אֹתָם

Exod 25:29 You shall make its bowls, cups, jugs, and vessels for making libations;
of pure gold you shall make them.

Exod 26:7 וְעָשִׂיתָ יְרִיעֹת עִזִּים לְאֹהֶל עַל־הַמִּשְׁכָּן
עַשְׁתֵּי־עֶשְׂרֵה יְרִיעֹת תַּעֲשֶׂה אֹתָם

Exod 26:7 You shall make hangings of goat hair for the tent over the tabernacle;
eleven hangings you shall make them.

See also Exod 25:29; 26:1; 28:11, 14; 29:2; 30:1, 7; 37:7, 23–24; 38:7. Of these different sets of attestations, it appears that the syntax in the descriptions of tabernacle construction is primary and that Genesis 1 has been crafted in their image.[71] Signs that Gen 1:27 is an elaboration of the usage in the construction texts are its use of the theologically colored verb בָּרָא instead of the quotidian עָשָׂה and its more poetic formulation.

Creation language in the description of the tabernacle forms a literary inclusio with the language of Gen 1:1–2:4a. Some see this as an indication that the original P work ended with the erection of the tabernacle. Certainly, the repetition of the language marks a climax in the first panel of the narrative and shows that the tabernacle is a piece of PH's broad picture of creation. Yet creation language reappears briefly but significantly in PH's pivotal spy story, in Num 14:7:

וַיֹּאמְרוּ אֶל־כָּל־עֲדַת בְּנֵי־יִשְׂרָאֵל לֵאמֹר
הָאָרֶץ אֲשֶׁר עָבַרְנוּ בָהּ לָתוּר אֹתָהּ טוֹבָה הָאָרֶץ מְאֹד מְאֹד

They said to the whole Israelite community:
"The land that we scouted is *very very* good."

The double adverb in this passage echoes and at the same time intensifies the summary description of creation on the seventh day in Gen 1:31: "God saw all that he had made, and it was *very good*" (וַיַּרְא אֱלֹהִים אֶת־כָּל־אֲשֶׁר עָשָׂה וְהִנֵּה־טוֹב מְאֹד).

That the double adverb of Num 14:7 relates to creation is indirectly supported by the double adverb Exod 1:7 that describes Israel's fulfillment of expecta-

71 This has implications for positing an Ur-text of Gen 1:1–2:4a. Krüger ("Genesis 1:1–2:3," 132) sees Gen 1:27a as original, but this already reflects the tabernacle construction syntax.

tions for fertility set down at creation: "The Israelites were fertile, swarmed, became many, and became *very very* numerous and the land was full with them" (וּבְנֵי יִשְׂרָאֵל פָּרוּ וַיִּשְׁרְצוּ וַיִּרְבּוּ וַיַּעַצְמוּ בִּמְאֹד מְאֹד וַתִּמָּלֵא הָאָרֶץ אֹתָם). As noted earlier in this essay, this verse is the climax of the fertility motif about humans that begins in Gen 1:28. The verses Num 14:7 and Exod 1:7 have parallel narrative functions, describing different stages in the nation's fulfillment of the divine creative plan. Exodus 1:7 refers to the *biological* dimension: Israel at the beginning of the Mosaic era is *quantitatively* ready for divine adoption as Yahweh's people in Exod 6:2–8. Numbers 14:7 refers to the *geographical* dimension: Israel after deliverance from Egypt is at the threshold of acquiring the land, a land that is *qualitatively* the best of all the deity has created.

The spy story relates more complexly to the initial call of the nation Israel. The punishment imposed includes the decree: "You will not come to the land in which I swore to settle you" (אִם־אַתֶּם תָּבֹאוּ אֶל־הָאָרֶץ אֲשֶׁר נָשָׂאתִי אֶת־יָדִי לְשַׁכֵּן אֶתְכֶם בָּהּ; Num 14:30). This echoes the promise to the nation in Moses' call: "I will bring you to the land which I swore to give to Abraham, Isaac, and Jacob" (וְהֵבֵאתִי אֶתְכֶם אֶל־הָאָרֶץ אֲשֶׁר נָשָׂאתִי אֶת־יָדִי לָתֵת אֹתָהּ לְאַבְרָהָם לְיִצְחָק וּלְיַעֲקֹב; Exod 6:8). This, in turn, has reference back to the promises to the patriarchs in Genesis (Gen 17:8; 28:3–4; 35:11–12; 48:3). This web of associations shows that the promise texts, even though they do not use creation story language, are part of the unfolding of creation in PH.[72] The deity creates the world at the beginning of Genesis and then promises part of it to the patriarchs' posterity. It is fulfilled at the end of the wilderness period.

10 Conclusion

Just as PH's schema of creation over seven days grows logically, with the action of each day forming the foundation for the events on the next and subsequent days in a folk-evolutionary way, so PH's larger history, from this creation through the various epochs described in Genesis, gradually but inevitably sets up what is conceptually the culmination of creation: the establishment of the nation Israel and its system of serving the deity in the cult. Further, as the last sections of this essay have indicated, this culmination is not the end of the story, but is itself the stage for telling how the people came to the land promised them. In the larger picture, creation is not really complete—the people are not fully the deity's and their cultic

---

72 PH's spy story builds on other motifs it set down in the first part of its story in Exodus: in contrast to knowing (יָדַע) Yahweh (Exod 6:7), the exodus generation will know the deity's opposition (Num 14:34) and only their children will know the land (14:31). Too, the deity's hearing of the complaint (Num 14:27) plays against the deity's hearing of the cry of the oppressed Israelites (Exod 2:23aβb–25; 6:5).

practice is not fully realized until they get to their national-geographical home. Thus, neither the PH narrative nor its depiction of creation ends at Sinai.[73]

The goal of PH's long and intricate narrative is partly to rationalize and justify Yahweh's election of Israel and the obligation of cultic practice and the broader behaviors associated therewith. These matters, as the intended and even natural outgrowth and result of creation, are normative. The story of PH thus marries two somewhat distinct themes found in ancient Near Eastern literature: the birth of the nation politic as part of creation, as exampled in the current formulation of *Enuma elish*, and the establishment of cosmic order through the revelation of law at the behest of the gods, as found, for example, in the Laws of Hammurabi. But PH also appears to be imposing reason and order on native materials, be those traditions or sources. If PH is the first to join pre-Mosaic and Mosaic traditions together, PH is the first to bring creation and lawgiving together. The creativity involved in this would rise in proportion to the degree of ideological innovation PH employed relative to traditions that were influential. If PH used pre-existing documentary sources, J and E, and if original J had no or little lawgiving and E had no creation story, then PH has still brought together previously uncombined materials and made them speak to each other. In either case, PH has blended and integrated divergent materials and scenes. In short, PH may be said to have created the world in the image of its law. This ideological picture colors the force of the details of legislation in the book of Leviticus.

Bibliography

Achenbach, R., *Die Vollendung der Torah: Studien zur Redaktionsgeschichte des Numeribuches im Kontext von Hexateuch und Pentateuch* (BZABR 3; Wiesbaden: Harrassowitz, 2002).

–, "Die Erzählung von der gescheiterten Landnahme von Kadesch Barnea (Numeri 13–14) als Schlüsseltext der Redaktionsgeschichte des Pentateuchs," *ZABR* 9 (2003) 56–123.

Albertz, R., *A History of Israelite Religion in the Old Testament Period* (2 vols.; Louisville: Westminster John Knox Press, 1994).

Aster, S., *The Unbeatable Light: Melammu and Its Biblical Parallels* (AOAT 384; Münster: Ugarit-Verlag, 2012).

Baden, J., *J, E, and the Redaction of the Pentateuch* (FAT 68; Tübingen: Mohr Siebeck, 2009).

–, "The Original Place of the Priestly Manna Story in Exodus 16," *ZAW* 122 (2010) 491–504.

–, *The Composition of the Pentateuch* (AYBRL; New Haven: Yale University Press, 2012).

–, "On Exodus 33,1–11," *ZAW* 124 (2012) 329–40.

–, *The Promise to the Patriarchs* (Oxford: Oxford University Press, 2013).

Bauks, M., "La signification de l'espace et du temps dans 'l'Histoire Sacerdotale,'" in T. Römer (ed.), *The Future of the Deuteronomistic History* (BETL 147; Leuven: University Press/Peeters, 2000) 29–45.

73 An intentional echo of L. Schmidt's title "Die Priesterschrift—kein Ende am Sinai!" *ZAW* 120 (2008) 481–500.

Berlejung, A., "Theologisches Wort und anthropologischer Ort der Silberamulette von Ketef Hinnom," *ZAW* 120 (2008) 204–30.
Blenkinsopp, J., "The Structure of P," *CBQ* 38 (1976) 275–92.
–, "P and J in Genesis 1:1–11:26: An Alternative Hypothesis," in A.B. Beck/A.H. Bartelt/P.R. Raabe/C.A. Franke (ed.), *Fortunate the Eyes That See: Essays in Honor of David Noel Freedman* (Grand Rapids: Eerdmans, 1995) 1–15.
Blum, E., *Studien zur Komposition des Pentateuch* (BZAW 189; Berlin: De Gruyter, 1990).
–, "Issues and Problems in the Contemporary Debate Regarding the Priestly Writings," in S. Shectman/J.S. Baden (ed.), *The Strata of the Priestly Writings* (ATANT 95; Zürich: Theologischer Verlag, 2009) 31–44.
Carr, D.M., *Reading the Fractures of Genesis: Historical and Literary Approaches* (Louisville: Westminster John Knox Press, 1996).
–, *The Formation of the Hebrew Bible: A New Reconstruction* (Oxford: Oxford University Press, 2011).
Cross, F.M., *Canaanite Myth and Hebrew Epic* (Cambridge, MA: Harvard University Press, 1973).
Feinstein, E.S., *Sexual Pollution in the Hebrew Bible* (PhD Diss.; Cambridge MA: Harvard University, 2010).
Gertz, J.C./Berlejung, A./Schmid, K./Witte, M., *T&T Clark Handbook of the Old Testament* (London: T&T Clark, 2012).
Gesundheit, S., *Three Times a Year: Studies on Festival Legislation in the Pentateuch* (FAT 82; Tübingen: Mohr Siebeck, 2012).
Gilders, W.K., "Sacrifice before Sinai and the Priestly Narratives," in S. Shectman/J.S. Baden (ed.), *The Strata of the Priestly Writings* (ATANT 95; Zürich: Theologischer Verlag, 2009) 57–72.
Greenstein, E.L., "God's Golem: The Creation of the Human in Genesis 2," in H.G. Reventlow/Y. Hoffman (ed.), *Creation in Jewish and Christian Tradition* (JSOTSup 319; Sheffield: Sheffield Academic Press, 2002) 219–39.
Hurowitz, V.A., Inu Anum ṣīrum: *Literary Structures in the Non-Juridical Sections of Codex Hammurabi* (Occasional Publications of the Samuel Noah Kramer Fund 15; Philadelphia: University Museum, 1994).
Janowski, B., "Tempel und Schöpfung: Schöpfungstheologische Aspekte der priesterschriftlichen Heiligtumskonzeption," *JBTh* 5 (1990) 37–69.
Jenson, P.P., *Graded Holiness: A Key to the Priestly Conception of the World* (JSOTSup 106; Sheffield: Sheffield Academic Press, 1992).
Knohl, I., *Sanctuary of Silence* (Minneapolis: Fortress, 1995).
Kratz, R., *The Composition of the Narrative Books of the Old Testament* (London: T&T Clark, 2005).
Krüger, T., "Genesis 1:1–2:3 and the Development of the Pentateuch," in T.B. Dozeman/K. Schmid/B.J. Schwartz (ed.), *The Pentateuch* (FAT 78; Tübingen: Mohr Siebeck, 2011) 125–38.
Leuchter, M., "The Ambiguous Details in the Blasphemer Narrative: Sources and Redaction in Lev 24:10–23," *JBL* 130 (2011) 431–50.
Levenson, J., *Creation and the Persistence of Evil* (San Francisco: Harper & Row, 1988).
McEvenue, S., *The Narrative Style of the Priestly Writer* (AnBib 50; Rome: Biblical Institute Press, 1971).
Milgrom, J., *Leviticus 1–16* (AB 3; New York: Doubleday, 1991).
–, *Leviticus 17–22* (AB 3A; New York: Doubleday, 2000).
Nihan, C., *From Priestly Torah to Pentateuch: A Study in the Composition of the Book of Leviticus* (FAT 25; Tübingen: Mohr Siebeck, 2007).
–, "Israel's Festival Calendars in Leviticus 23, Numbers 28–29 and the Formation of the 'Priestly' Literature," in T. Römer (ed.), *The Books of Leviticus and Numbers* (BETL 215; Leuven: Uitgeverij Peeters, 2008) 177–231.

–, "The Priestly Covenant, Its Reinterpretations, and the Composition of 'P'," in S. Shectman/J.S. Baden (ed.), *The Strata of the Priestly Writings* (ATANT 95; Zürich: Theologischer Verlag, 2009) 87–134.
–, "Murder, Blasphemy and Sacral Law: Another Look at Lev 24,10–23," *ZABR* 17 (2011) 211–40.
Olyan, S.M., "An Eternal Covenant with Circumcision as Its Sign: How Useful a Criterion for Dating and Source Analysis?" in T.B. Dozeman/K. Schmid/B.J. Schwartz (ed.), *The Pentateuch* (FAT 78; Tübingen: Mohr Siebeck, 2011) 347–58.
de Pury, A., "The Jacob Story and the Beginning of the Formation of the Pentateuch," in T. Dozeman/K. Schmid (ed.), *A Farewell to the Yahwist? The Composition of the Pentateuch in Recent European Interpretation* (SBLSS 34; Atlanta: SBL, 2006) 51–72.
–, "Pg as the Absolute Beginning," in T. Römer/K. Schmid (ed.), *Les dernières rédactions du Pentateuque, de l'Hexateuque et de l'Ennéateuque* (BETL 203; Leuven: University Press/Peeters, 2007) 99–128.
Rendtorff, R., *The Problem of the Process of Transmission in the Pentateuch* (JSOTSup 89; Sheffield: JSOT Press, 1990).
Römer, T., "Zwischen Urkunden, Fragmenten und Ergänzungen: Zum Stand der Pentateuchforschung," *ZAW* 125 (2013) 2–24.
Ruprecht, E., "Stellung und Bedeutung der Erzählung vom Mannawunder (Ex 16) im Aufbau der Priesterschrift," *ZAW* 86 (1974) 269–307, 291–8.
Schmid, K., *Genesis and the Moses Story* (Siphrut 3; Winona Lake: Eisenbrauns, 2010).
–, "Has European Scholarship Abandoned the Documentary Hypothesis? Some Reminders on Its History and Remarks on Its Current Status," in T.B. Dozeman/K. Schmid/B.J. Schwartz (ed.), *The Pentateuch* (FAT 78; Tübingen: Mohr Siebeck, 2011) 17–30.
–, *The Old Testament: A Literary History* (Minneapolis: Fortress Press, 2012).
–, (ed.), *Schöpfung* (Themen der Theologie 4; Stuttgart: UTB, 2012).
Schmidt, L., "Die Priesterschrift—kein Ende am Sinai!" *ZAW* 120 (2008) 481–500.
Ska, J.-L., *Introduction to Reading the Pentateuch* (Winona Lake: Eisenbrauns, 2006).
–, *The Exegesis of the Pentateuch* (FAT 66; Tübingen: Mohr Siebeck, 2009).
Smith, J.Z., *To Take Place: Toward Theory in Ritual* (Chicago: University of Chicago Press, 1987).
Smith, M.S., *The Priestly Vision of Genesis 1* (Minneapolis: Fortress Press, 2010).
Sommer, B.D., *The Bodies of God and the World of Ancient Israel* (New York: Cambridge University Press, 2009).
–, "Dating Pentateuchal Texts and the Perils of Pseudo-Historicism," in T.B. Dozeman/K. Schmid/B.J. Schwartz (ed.), *The Pentateuch* (FAT 78; Tübingen: Mohr Siebeck, 2011) 85–108.
Stackert, J., *Rewriting the Torah: Literary Revision in Deuteronomy and the Holiness Legislation* (FAT 52; Tübingen: Mohr Siebeck, 2007).
–, "Why Does the Plague of Darkness Last for Three Days? Source Ascription and Literary Motif in Exodus 10:21–23, 27," *VT* 61 (2011) 657–76.
–, "Compositional Strata in the Priestly Sabbath: Exodus 31:12–17 and 35:1–3," *JHS* 11 (2011) article 15 (http://www.jhsonline.org/Articles/article_162.pdf doi:10.5508/jhs.2011.v11.a15).
–, "The Composition of Exodus 31:12–17 and 35:1–3 and the Question of Method in Identifying Priestly Strata in the Torah," in R. Gane/A. Taggar-Cohen (ed.), *Current Issues in Priestly and Related Literature: The Legacy of Jacob Milgrom and Beyond* (SBLRBS; Atlanta: SBL, 2015) 175–96.
Tanchel, S.E., *Honoring Voices: Listening to the Texts and the Teacher, the Scholars and the Students* (PhD diss.; Waltham MA: Brandeis University, 2006).
van der Toorn, K., *Family Religion in Babylonia, Syria and Israel: Continuity and Change in the Forms of Religious Life* (SHCANE 7; Leiden: Brill, 1996).
Weimar, P., *Studien zur Priesterschrift* (FAT 56; Tübingen: Mohr Siebeck, 2008).
Weinfeld, M., "Sabbath, Temple and the Enthronement of the Lord: The Problem of the *Sitz*

im Leben of Genesis 1:1–2:3," in A. Caquot/M. Delcor (ed.), *Mélanges bibliques et orientaux en l'honneur de M. Henri Cazelles* (AOAT 212; Kevelaer: Butzon & Bercker, 1981) 501–12.
Wöhrle, J., "dominium terrae: Exegetische und religionsgeschichtliche Überlegungen zum Herrschaftsauftrag in Gen 1,26–28," *ZAW* 121 (2009) 71–88.
–, "The Integrative Function of the Law of Circumcision," in R. Achenbach/R. Albertz/J. Wöhrle (ed.), *The Foreigner and the Law: Perspectives from the Hebrew Bible and the Ancient Near East* (BZABR 16; Wiesbaden: Harrassowitz, 2011) 71–87.
Wright, D. P., *The Disposal of Impurity* (SBLDS 101; Atlanta: Scholars Press, 1987).
–, "Unclean and Clean (OT)," *ABD* 6 (1992) 729–41.
–, "Holiness, Sex, and Death in the Garden of Eden," *Bib* 77 (1996) 305–29.
–, "Holiness in Leviticus and Beyond," *Interpretation* 53 (1999) 351–64.
–, "The Study of Ritual in the Hebrew Bible," in F. Greenspahn (ed.), *The Hebrew Bible: New Insights and Scholarship* (Jewish Studies in the 21st Century; New York: New York University Press, 2008) 120–38.
–, *Inventing God's Law: How the Covenant Code of the Bible Used and Revised the Laws of Hammurabi* (Oxford: Oxford University Press, 2009).
–, "'She Shall Not Go Free as Male Slaves Do:' Developing Views About Slavery and Gender in the Laws of the Hebrew Bible," in B. J. Brooten (ed.), *Beyond Slavery: Overcoming Its Religious and Sexual Legacy* (New York: Palgrave Macmillan, 2010) 125–42.
–, "Ritual Theory, Ritual Texts, and the Priestly-Holiness Writings of the Pentateuch," in S. Olyan (ed.), *Social Theory and the Study of Israelite Religion: Essays in Retrospect and Prospect* (SBLRBS 71; Atlanta: SBL, 2012) 195–216.
–, "The Origin, Development, and Context of the Covenant Code (Exod 20:23–23:19)," in T. Dozeman/C. Evans/J. Lohr (ed.), *The Book of Exodus: Composition, Reception, and Interpretation* (FIOTL; VTSup 164; Leiden: Brill, 2014) 220–44.
–, "Profane Versus Sacrificial Slaughter: The Priestly Recasting of the Yahwist Flood Story," in R. Gane and A. Taggar-Cohen (ed.), *Current Issues in Priestly and Related Literature: The Legacy of Jacob Milgrom and Beyond* (SBLRBS; Atlanta: SBL, 2015) 125–54.
–, "The Covenant Code Appendix (Exod 23:20–33), Neo-Assyrian Sources, and Implications for Pentateuchal Study," in J. Gertz/B. Levinson/D. Rom-Shiloni/K. Schmid (ed.), *The Formation of the Pentateuch: Bridging the Academic Cultures of Europe, Israel, and North America* (Tübingen: Mohr Siebeck, 2016) 47–85.
–, "Source Dependence and the Development of the Pentateuch: The Case of Leviticus 24," in J. Gertz/B. Levinson/D. Rom-Shiloni/K. Schmid (ed.), *The Formation of the Pentateuch: Bridging the Academic Cultures of Europe, Israel, and North America* (Tübingen: Mohr Siebeck, 2016) 651–82.
–, "The Adaptation and Fusion of Near Eastern Treaty and Law in Legal Narrative of the Hebrew Bible," in B. Levinson (ed.), *Law, Society, and Religion*: George E. Mendenhall Symposium, October, 2016 (*Maarav* special issue; forthcoming).
Zwickel, W., "Die Altarbaunotizen im Alten Testament," *Bib* 73 (1992) 533–46.

James W. Watts

Drawing Lines

A Suggestion for Addressing the Moral Problem of Reproducing Immoral Biblical Texts in Commentaries and Bibles

The book of Leviticus contains many norms and instructions that have fallen into abeyance in later Jewish and Christian congregations and cultures. Normative forms of Judaism and Christianity do not follow the plain meaning of these verses. Such verses therefore pose an interesting problem for interpreting their continuing theological and cultural significance.[1]

A subset of this material, however, also poses a moral problem for commentators and bible publishers. Some verses of Leviticus express norms that explicitly conflict with the legal and ethical teachings of contemporary Jewish and Christian denominations, and also with the laws of modern nations. Among them are texts mandating that readers treat some other people in ways now widely regarded as immoral, cruel, inhumane, and exploitive—texts that call for and/or have historically justified genocide, indiscriminate capital punishment, slavery, and the subjugation of women by men. National and international law today declares most of these behaviors illegal and subject to criminal prosecution.

The moral problem for commentators and publishers is that, by publishing bibles and commentaries that reproduce these texts, we continue to promulgate claims of divine approval for immoral and illegal behavior. I call this a "moral" problem rather than an "ethical" quandary because the issue does not require difficult ethical reasoning. The moral imperative to not perpetrate or condone genocide, indiscriminate capital punishment, slavery, and patriarchy are quite clear to most or, in the case of patriarchy, at least many Jews and Christians. For these people, therefore, this is not a problem of ethical reasoning but of moral will, because reproducing these particular texts prioritizes the religious ideal of preserving scripture unaltered over these moral imperatives.

1 See my other essay in this volume, "Unperformed Rituals in an Unread Book," pp. 25–33.

1 The Problem of Latent Normative Texts

The negative social impact of immoral biblical norms has often been restrained by long-standing traditions of *halakhah*, preaching, canon law, and commentary. For example, whereas Pentateuchal texts mandate the death penalty for a wide variety of offenses ranging from murder (Gen 9:6) and blasphemy (Lev 24:14, 16–17) to hitting or cursing one's parents (21:15, 17), rabbinic *halakhah* intensified the biblical requirement of two witnesses for conviction (Num 35:30; Deut 20:15) to the point of making it virtually impossible to carry out capital punishment.[2] Modern national legislation has, over time, steadily reduced the number of offenses that may be punished by the death penalty to only first-degree murder and, sometimes, treason. In many countries, capital punishment has been abolished entirely.[3]

Commentators often use historical context to argue that biblical texts raised moral standards at the time they were written, even if they seem immoral today. So 19th-century abolitionists argued that slavery contradicts the moral teachings of the Bible, despite verses that seem to validate the practice. Interpreters today continue to argue that the Bible's moral trajectory supports liberty and justice.[4]

However, the iconic status of the biblical text has often overridden these interpretive traditions. The example of slavery is instructive for the tension between violent biblical norms and restraining commentary traditions. Despite the prominence of Christian leaders in the abolitionist movement, Christian slaveholders could cite solid biblical precedents for defending their right to own slaves.[5] The

2 b. Sanh. 37B, 161; b. Ketub. 30A, 30B; B.A. Berkowitz, *Execution and Invention: Death Penalty Discourse in Early Rabbinic and Christian Cultures* (New York: Oxford University Press, 2006); C.T. Halberstam, *Law and Truth in Biblical and Rabbinic Literature* (Bloomington: Indiana University Press, 2010), 85–91.

3 W. Schabas, *The Abolition of the Death Penalty in International Law* (Cambridge: Cambridge University Press, [3]2002); J.J. Megivern, *The Death Penalty: An Historical and Theological Survey* (Mahwah, NJ: Paulist Press, 1999).

4 For a recent example of this deep and widespread commentary traditions, see R.H. Gnuse, *Trajectories of Justice: What the Bible Says about Slaves, Women and Homosexuality* (Eugene, OR: Cascade, 2015). I have myself argued that Second-Temple-period priests used the Torah to promote more inclusive and accomodationist policies regarding intermarriage and foreigners than did other Jewish literature that has survived from this period: see J.W. Watts, *Ritual and Rhetoric in Leviticus: From Sacrifice to Scripture* (Cambridge: Cambridge University Press, 2007), 142–172, or idem, "The Torah as the Rhetoric of Priesthood," in G. Knoppers/B.M. Levinson (ed.), *The Pentateuch as Torah: New Models for Understanding Its Promulgation and Acceptance* (Winona Lake, IN: Eisenbrauns, 2007), 319–32.

5 P.J. Wogaman, *Christian Ethics: A Historical Introduction* (Louisville: Westminster John Knox, 1993), 29–30; 180–6. On the influence of biblical slave texts, see J.A. Glancy, *Slavery in Early Christianity* (Oxford: Oxford University Press, 2002); D.M. Goldenberg, *The Curse of Ham: Race and Slavery in Early Judaism, Christianity, and Islam* (Princeton, NJ: Princeton

issue was settled in 19th-century America not by scriptural interpretation or by moral reasoning, but by a bloody and brutal civil war.[6] The racist legacy of the African slave trade continues today to haunt cultures on at least four continents.

The Bible's latent potential for preserving abhorrent norms is exacerbated by Jewish and Christian religious movements that have, at one time or another, embraced the rhetoric of "back to the Bible." Though the sixteenth-century Protestant Reformation is most famous for this rhetoric, it began much earlier with the Karaites, who already in the eighth-to-ninth centuries rejected rabbinic traditions codified by the Talmuds and focused sustained attention on Torah and Tanak. In twelfth-century France and Italy, the Waldensians challenged Catholic authorities with a popular appeal to the teaching of Jesus in the Gospels, as did the fourteenth-century Lollards in England. More recently, in colonial and post-colonial Africa and Asia, new ethnic churches have turned the Bible against the colonizing Europeans by revitalizing biblical practices, often from Pentateuchal law, to establish themselves as more authentically biblical than the colonizers.[7] In Europe and Palestine, the Zionists found the Tanak more useful than the Talmud for establishing a modern Jewish state in the territory of ancient Israel.[8]

University Press, 2009); S. R. Haynes, *Noah's Curse: The Biblical Justification of American Slavery* (Oxford: Oxford University Press, 2002).

6 Historians debate the degree to which Christian ethics ultimately influenced the outcome of these debates. While many credit the tradition for influencing the culture's morals for the better (e.g. R. Stark, *For the Glory of God: How Monotheism Led to Reformations, Science, Witch-Hunts, and the End of Slavery* [Princeton: Princeton University Press, 2004]), others think the bad effects outweigh the good (e.g. H. Avalos, *Slavery, Abolitionism, and the Ethics of Biblical Scholarship* [Sheffield: Sheffield Phoenix Press, 2013]). Of course, sweeping evaluations of the Bible's influence, much less of entire religious traditions, are too general to offer much historical insight. The influence of particular biblical verses is easier to trace and evaluate through the history of their citation and use.

7 J. W. Watts, *Leviticus 1–10* (HCOT; Leuven: Peeters, 2013), 84; R. S. Sugirtharajah, *The Bible and Empire: Postcolonial Explorations* (Cambridge: Cambridge University Press, 2005), 175–89; P. Jenkins, *The New Faces of Christianity: Believing the Bible in the Global South* (Oxford: Oxford University Press, 2006), 50–2, 55, 65–6; N. J. Savishinsky, "African Dimensions of the Jamaican Rastafarian Movement," in N. S. Murrell et al. (ed.), *Chanting Down Babylon: The Rastafari Reader* (Philadelphia: Temple University Press, 1998) 125–44, on p. 139; D. C. van Zyl, "In Africa, Theology is Not Thought Out but Danced Out: On the Theological Significance of Old Testament Symbolism and Rituals in African Zionist Churches," *OTE* 8 (1995) 425–38, on pp. 429-34; S. W. D. Dube, "Hierophanies: A Hermeneutic Paradigm for Understanding Zionist Ritual," in G. C. Oosthuizen et al. (ed.), *Afro-Christianity at the Grassroots: Its Dynamics and Strategies* (Leiden: Brill, 1994), 105–18, on p. 114; A. F. Walls, *The Cross-Cultural Process in Christian History* (New York: Continuum, 2001), 131.

8 Watts, *Leviticus 1–10*, 81–2; Z. J. Braiterman, "The Emergence of Modern Religion: Moses Mendelssohn, Neoclassicism, and Ceremonial Aesthetics," in C. Wiese/M. Urban (ed.), *German-Jewish Thought Between Religion and Politics* (Berlin: De Gruyter, 2012) 11–29; A. Saposnik, "The Desert Comes to Zion: A Narrative Ends its Wandering," in P. Barmash/W. D. Nelson (ed.), *Exodus in the Jewish Experience: Echoes and Reverberations* (Lanham, MD: Lexington, 2015), 213–46.

The religious and moral power of such movements to bring about reform and even revolution is undeniable. But the biblical text that they revive also contains material that can justify abhorrent social practices. In turning people's attention to the original scriptures of Christian and Jewish traditions, bible-based reforms risk also empowering immoral texts. Recent examples include legislation introduced in the Ugandan parliament in 2009 mandating the death penalty for homosexual acts[9] and a movement among some ultra-Orthodox rabbis in Israel to revive the biblical mandates for holy war to defend Jewish occupation of Palestinian land.[10] In the United States, political conflicts over the death penalty involve religious arguments invoking biblical texts on both sides of the issue.[11]

2 The Moral Impact of Bible Publishing

Historians record the prominent role of biblical interpretation in these ethical debates, but have paid little attention to the influence of bible publishing. For more than 500 years, technological advances in printing along with rising literacy rates have steadily expanded access to all parts of the biblical text, and are doing so again through the current digital revolution.[12] Previously, when most people heard biblical texts read aloud rather than reading them for themselves, lectionaries mediated biblical texts through interpretive lenses. Glossed bibles, rabbinic bibles and, now, "study" bibles still encase the biblical texts with interpretation on every page, but they also privilege the biblical text by their typography and layout. The visual format distinguishes scripture from commentary, and invites the

9 A bill calling for capital punishment for "aggressive" homosexual acts was introduced in the Ugandan parliament in 2009. The penalty had been reduced to life imprisonment when it passed into law in 2014, but the legislation was invalidated by Ugandan courts on procedural grounds later the same year. Anti-gay legislation in Uganda and elsewhere in Africa is widely supported by local Christian leaders and by Evangelical organizations from America. See J. Gettlemanjan, "Americans' Role Seen in Uganda Anti-Gay Push," *New York Times*, January 3, 2010 (https://www.nytimes.com/2010/01/04/world/africa/04uganda.html; accessed April 17, 2018). On the broader historical and cultural context, see the essays in A. van Klinken/E. Chitando (ed.), *Public Religion and the Politics of Homosexuality in Africa* (London: Routledge, 2016); and J. Sadgrove/R. M. Vanderbeck/J. Andersson/G. Valentine/K. Ward, "Morality Plays and Money Matters: Towards a Situated Understanding of the Politics of Homosexuality in Uganda," *Journal of Modern African Studies* 50/1 (2012) 103–29.

10 R. Firestone, *Holy War in Judaism: The Fall and Rise of a Controversial Idea* (Oxford: Oxford University Press, 2012); idem, "Holy War: Rabbinic to Modern Judaism," *EBR* 12 (2015); and more generally, R. Eisen, *The Peace and Violence of Judaism: From the Bible to Modern Zionism* (New York: Oxford University Press, 2011).

11 A. Santoro, "Religion and Capital Punishment in the United States," *Religion Compass* 8/5 (2014), 159–74 (https://doi.org/10.1111/rec3.12105).

12 J. S. Siker, *Liquid Scripture: The Bible in the Digital World* (Minneapolis: Fortress, 2017).

reader's eye to dwell on the ancient text more than on its modern interpretation. Many printed and digital bibles contain no explanatory commentary at all.

Recent studies of the iconic dimension of sacred texts have demonstrated the powerful influence that ritualizing the material form and visual appearance of books has over readers, congregations, religious movements, and even nations.[13] The stereotypical bindings and distinctive page formats of many bibles legitimize the religious identity and status of their readers and handlers.[14] Congregational rituals, visual art and mystical traditions combine to identify the book of scripture with God or Christ. For Jews and many Christians, the Torah scroll or the codex Bible is the most sacred or, even, the only sacred object in their religious experience.[15]

The history of Jewish and Christian controversies over war, slavery, anti-Semitism and patriarchy shows that biblical texts retain their power to justify actions and institutions despite considerable moral teaching and commentary to the contrary. History therefore demonstrates that it is not enough for commentaries simply to argue that particular verses of scripture have been superseded by changing cultural contexts or that, in their original contexts, these verses advocated improvements over existing norms. The iconic status of their continuing appearance in the sacred text preserves their latent power to be invoked malevolently again and again.

So I question the morality of my profession which insists on reproducing these verses as written. If I found an ancient manuscript that omitted them or if I advanced a compositional theory that identified them as secondary additions, the established practices of biblical studies would allow me to alter them or delete them from my commentary's translation. If sufficient numbers of other biblical scholars agreed with my judgment, the change might be reflected in new Bible translations for the mass market.[16] But the discipline of modern biblical studies provides no similar precedents for dealing with immoral verses that have been used to justify pervasive and malevolent violence.

The practice of encouraging scholars to emend the biblical text for historical but not for moral reasons is 200-hundred-years old, as Stephen D. Moore and Yvonne Sherwood have shown.[17] Enlightenment thought of the seventeenth

---

13 See the essays collected in J. W. Watts (ed.), *Iconic Books and Texts* (Sheffield: Equinox, 2013).

14 J. W. Watts, "The Three Dimensions of Scriptures," in *Iconic Books and Texts*, 8–30.

15 See the essays collected in J. W. Watts/Y. Yoo (ed.), *Books As Sacred Beings* (Sheffield: Equinox, forthcoming).

16 E.g., how most bibles today reflect the text-critical indeterminacy of the end of Mark's Gospel.

17 S. D. Moore/Y. Sherwood, "Biblical Studies 'after' Theory: Onwards Towards the Past," *Biblical Interpretation* 18 (2010) 1–27, 87–113, 191–225, reprinted and expanded in Moore/Sherwood, *The Invention of the Biblical Scholar* (Minneapolis: Fortress, 2011).

and eighteenth centuries included serious moral criticism of Biblical teachings. Leading philosophers thought about how to modify or adapt the text to meet the standards of rational thought.[18] Subsequent biblical scholarship, however, sidelined the ethical problems posed by biblical texts by instead focusing on historical research into the origins and development of biblical literature and ideas.[19]

This poses a moral problem for the discipline because it implicates the field of biblical studies in the evil perpetuated by people citing these texts. It is not just the Bible itself that is implicated in justifying genocide by providing the model of conquering Canaan to justify settler colonialism, as well as divine support for slavery, religious inquisitions of heretics, witch-hunts, pogroms, and misogyny of all sorts. Present-day biblical scholars are also implicated for failing to take corrective measures and instead preserving and publishing immoral norms.

We are, of course, already implicated by the violent heritage of our history and society, in different ways depending on our own identities and social locations. For example, a 1790 census lists my ancestor, James Watts, who farmed former Cherokee land[20] in Laurens County, South Carolina, as the owner of seven slaves. His brothers, George and John, owned ten more. Neither the census nor family records provide any more information about these slaves or how my ancestors justified owning them.[21] In that time and location, the slaves were presumably Africans or descendants of Africans forcibly brought to America. Given the times and my family name suggesting descent from English Protestants, these slave owners probably believed that the Bible justified their actions. More than two centuries later, I now find myself facing the task of reproducing in my Leviticus commentary some of the texts that excused my ancestors for violently enslaving these people. For me, then, as a white, male, U. S. citizen whose family has resided in North America for more than 300 years, the problem of immoral latent norms in the Bible not only implicates my ancestors for violent actions which they most likely justified by biblical texts, it also implicates me for promoting the career of

18 One product of such thinking took the form of two editions of *The Life and Morals of Jesus of Nazareth* published by Thomas Jefferson in 1804 and 1820. See H. Rubenstein/B. Clark Smith/J. Stagnitto Ellis, *The Jefferson Bible, Smithsonian Edition: The Life and Morals of Jesus of Nazareth by Thomas Jefferson* (Washington, DC: Smithsonian, 2011).

19 Moore/Sherwood, "Biblical Studies 'After' Theory," 91–107.

20 Ceded in 1755 by the Cherokee in a treaty with the English governor of South Carolina. On treaties between colonial powers and Native American nations, see R.N. Clinton, "Treaties with Native Nations: Iconic Historical Relics or Modern Necessity?" in S. Shown Harjo (ed.), *Nation to Nation: Treaties Between the United States and American Indian Nations* (Washington, DC: Smithsonian, 2014) 14–33.

21 The 1790 South Carolina census recorded the names of only the male heads of household. It counted other male and female adults in the household, as well as the number of children and slaves. My family's records have preserved the names of these men's wives and children, but make no mention of slaves at all.

these texts through my teaching and research about them, not least by writing a commentary and new translation of Leviticus.

Moore and Sherwood pointed out that feminist, ideological and post-colonial critiques are restoring ethical criticism to the repertoire of biblical scholars.[22] I add that commentary's long history of failing to restrain immoral uses of biblical texts shows the need to extend ethical critique to how the biblical text itself gets reproduced. Biblical commentators and translators usually focus our attention on the semantic dimension of the text and leave its visual features—the type-face, page layout, and binding—to printers and publishers. That practice conforms to the strong and ancient belief of scholars that what counts, what is most important, is interpreting the semantic text. Scholars usually regard iconic ritualization of the text's appearance and material form as, at best, a concession to the ignorance of lay people or, at worst, an encouragement to idolatry.[23] By taking this position, we have ceded to publishers and book sellers the power to legitimize religious identities and ideas through the iconic dimension of scriptures. The problem of immoral norms in biblical texts needs to be corrected iconically by altering their appearance to make clear in the text itself that Jewish and Christian traditions have repudiated them, as well as by notes and comments explaining the reasons for doing so and the history that makes it necessary.

3 How to Strike Through Immoral Biblical Norms

Modern software for editing documents provides a ready means for marking legible text as no longer applicable: the strikethrough (or cross-out). The practice of striking through mistakes to add corrections above the line or in the margins dates back to manuscript cultures. For example, even the rigid guidelines for copying Torah scrolls in the Talmud allow up to three corrections per page.[24] Though parchment can usually be corrected by scraping away the ink, ancient biblical manuscripts sometimes also contain strikethrough corrections.[25] Now digital texts use strikethrough to track changes in evolving documents. It is so easy that striking through one's own or other's comments is a popular (and frequently

---

22 Moore/Sherwood, "Biblical Studies 'After' Theory," 107.

23 D. Miller Parmenter, "Material Scripture," in T. Beal (ed.), *The Oxford Encyclopedia of the Bible and the Arts* (Oxford: Oxford University Press, 2015, from *Oxford Biblical Studies Online*, http://www.oxfordbiblicalcstudies.com/article/opr/t454/e97 [accessed June 4, 2018]); J.W. Watts, "Ancient Iconic Texts and Scholarly Expertise," in Watts, *Iconic Books and Texts*, 374–84.

24 b. Menaḥ. 29b.

25 E.g. the Qumran Isaiah scroll (*1QIsa*[a]) at Isa 21:1; Latin Codex Laudianus (E) at Acts 8:37. For pictures of more elaborate strikethroughs in medieval manuscripts of all sorts, see B.C. Keene, "Medieval Copyediting," *The Iris: Behind the Scenes at the Getty*, April 8, 2014 (http://blogs.getty.edu/iris/medieval-copyediting/; accessed April 18, 2018).

ridiculed) practice on blogs and social media.[26] However, strikethrough was also used philosophically by Martin Heidegger and became prominent in the writings of Jacque Derrida. He struck through words to place them *sous rature* "under erasure" to mark their meaning as problematically undecidable despite the fact that he must use them. Gayatria Spivak observed about Derrida's practice: "Since the word is inaccurate, it is crossed out. Since it is necessary, it remains legible."[27]

I propose that commentators and other bible translators should use strikethrough to mark normative statements in biblical verses that contemporary Jewish and Christian interpretive traditions have strongly repudiated as contradicting the moral teachings of scripture and of the traditions themselves. The judgment indicated by striking through biblical verses would not be text-critical and historical as in traditional biblical scholarship, nor epistemological as in philosophy, but rather moral. I propose that strikethroughs should mark biblical texts that fail even the lowest standards of moral decency, specifically texts that advocate or excuse human acts of genocide (including violent anti-Semitism), indiscriminate capital punishment, slavery, and patriarchy. For example, Leviticus 20:26–27 should be printed like this:

> 26 You are holy to me because I, YHWH, am holy. I have separated you from the nations to be mine. 27 ~~Any man or woman who is possessed by a ghost or spirit must certainly be killed. They must stone them with rocks. Their blood is on themselves.~~

The strikethrough will mark this text's mandates as immoral. I do not suggest deleting such texts, because doing so would erase the literary context and the historical record. Instead, the strikethrough indelibly marks this verse as superseded by basic moral standards expressed in other verses in Leviticus, most famously in 19:18, 34, and elsewhere in the Bible and its interpretive traditions.

My suggestion to strike through immoral normative texts is not just a salve to my own conscience for reproducing them. A technical commentary offers a new translation as a model for mass-market publishers to follow. In the same way, my commentary will strike through these verses to suggest to publishers of mass-market translations of the Bible that they should do the same thing. Strikethrough has an advantage over other typographical means of marking a text (e.g. italics, different fonts, rubrication) because its meaning is intuitively obvious: the text is abrogated while remaining legible. Of course, no textual feature is

---

26 On the popularity of strike-through in digital media, see N. Cohen, "Crossing Out, for Emphasis," *New York Times*, July 23, 2007 (https://www.nytimes.com/2007/07/23/business/media/23link.html; accessed April 8, 2018); M. Ticak, "Strikethrough and Why It's so Popular," *Grammerly Blog* (https://www.grammarly.com/blog/strikethrough-formatting-popularity/; accessed January 2, 2017).

27 G. Spivak, "Translator's Preface," in J. Derrida, *Of Grammatology* (Baltimore: Johns Hopkins University Press, 1976), xiv. See the discussion of using strikethrough for composition in C. Barker/E. A. Jane, *Cultural Studies: Theory and Practice* (Los Angeles: Sage, ^{5}2016), 98–9.

immune to misunderstanding, so notes and introductions are still needed to explain the moral judgment conveyed by strikethrough. But the implications of strikethrough are more obvious than most other typographical marks. Another advantage is that bible owners can strike through immoral verses themselves, without waiting for publishers or denominations to do it for them. Everyone is empowered to strikethrough immoral texts in their own bibles, just like other ways of ritualizing the iconic dimension of scriptures.[28]

4 Criteria for Striking Through Verses

The problem, of course, is deciding what to strike through—literally, where to draw the line. I suggest striking through only laws, instructions, curses and proverbs, but not stories, and only those norms with a known history of malevolent applications and consequences. Normative texts that fall most obviously into this category endorse slavery, indiscriminate capital punishment, genocide including violent anti-Semitism, and patriarchy.

Even though modern countries disagree about whether capital punishment is ever an appropriate punishment, with some still executing murderers and traitors, all agree in principle that it should be restricted to the most heinous and violent crimes and that it can only be lawfully applied by the courts after a fair trial. Leviticus does not reflect such restrictions. I therefore strike all biblical endorsements of capital punishment, because they make adultery, idolatry, blasphemy and sexual offenses equivalent to murder by treating all of them as capital offenses. That rhetoric has created many victims over time and does not stand the moral test of the recommended practices of either Christianity or Judaism. So I suggest striking through all verses calling for capital punishment. I do not strike through verses that threaten divine punishment, such as the threat to כרת "cut off" offenders (e.g. Lev 17:9–10), because these threats do not explicitly authorize human violence (even though they have often been read that way). Biblical literature and its commentary traditions often emphasize God's monopoly over such retribution.[29] Biblically-based traditions have regularly made creative use of divine threats of retribution to understand their own history and teach responsibility. The rhetoric of divine punishment shapes the histories of Israel (Judges-Kings, Chronicles, and Ezra-Nehemiah) as well as the prophetic and apocalyptic books and related narratives (such as the Gospels), and has

---

28 Watts, *Three Dimensions*, 22–3, 27–8; idem, *Understanding the Pentateuch as a Scripture* (Oxford: Wiley Blackwell, 2017), 70, 74–7, 86–7.

29 E.g. Deut 32:35 was interpreted as limiting human vengeance in Rom 12:17–19, 2 Enoch 50:4–5, the *Testament of Gad* 6:7, and *Sifre* 325. Cf. also warnings against judging other people (e.g. Rom 2:1–8).

generated sustained theological reflections in the books of Job and Romans. On the other hand, the rhetoric of God's judgment on the Canaanites' immorality which justifies the Israelites' conquest of their land (Lev 18:24–25, 27; 20:23) has often served subsequently as a justification for crusades and colonial conquests around the world, and therefore deserves to be struck through.[30]

It will be clear to most readers that verses that justify enslaving others and committing acts of genocide and indiscriminate capital punishment do not reflect the Bible's moral ideals according to the consensus of Jewish and Christian ethical thought, even though people in various times have continued to cite them to justify their violent actions. However, verses that justify patriarchy, misogyny, and second-class status for women have not yet achieved such a broad consensus. Jewish and Christian denominations continue to be divided about these issues. Some still use these verses to justify limiting clerical roles (as priests, ministers, rabbis, and scribes) to men and to defend patriarchy within families. Others have opened all of their leadership roles to women and actively denounce patriarchy in families and societies as a severe moral failure. My proposal calls upon congregations and denominations that champion women's rights, such as my own United Church of Christ, to use bibles consistent with their own moral stance.

You may think that striking through immoral norms will introduce divisiveness into bible publishing. The Bible is often lauded for unifying various denominations and even providing common ground between Jews and Christians. The cultural reality, however, is quite different. The material forms of biblical books as scrolls or codices have historically differentiated the two religions. Christian liturgical use of translated bibles has also distinguished churches from each other and fueled schisms along ethnic and doctrinal lines.[31] Today, publishers produce bibles customized for denominations as well as for different age-groups, genders, and many other social distinctions.[32] The ideal of the Bible's unifying function does not accord with the cultural reality of diverse bible translations and publications. Therefore, the proposal to strike through biblical verses that endorse patriarchy and other forms of discrimination against women cannot be criticized for introducing divisiveness into bible publishing. Doctrinal, ethnic, and denominational divisions have long since been entrenched there by translations and bible editions.

---

30 For example, the European conquest of the Western hemisphere frequently invoked the biblical rhetoric of a "promised land" inhabited by pagan "Canaanites" or, even, as an uninhabited land. See C. Cherry, *God's New Israel: Religious Interpretations of American Destiny* (Englewood Cliffs, NJ: Prentice Hall, 1971); R. Warrior, "Canaanites, Cowboys, and Indians: Deliverance, Conquest, and Liberation Theology," *Christianity and Crisis* 29 (1989) 261–5.

31 Watts, *Understanding the Pentateuch*, 92–105, 138–41.

32 T. Beal, *The Rise and Fall of the Bible: The Unexpected History of an Accidental Book* (Boston: Houghton Mifflin Harcourt, 2011), 41–84, 129–45.

You may wonder why I do not strike more normative passages that have fallen into abeyance in many religious communities, such as the rules for offerings in Leviticus 1–7 and the purity regulations of Leviticus 11–16. I do not strike through them because the history of the interpretation and use of these texts is not as negative as the cases described above. Though Jews and Christians since 70 CE have not practiced animal offerings (much), they have made productive theological and devotional use of the offering instructions. The purity rules have prompted extensive debates about ethics, especially around issues of social difference and inclusion. Minority religious and ethnic communities have often used purity instructions to distinguish and legitimize themselves against oppressors and colonizers.[33]

My criteria for striking through some verses as immoral—namely, explicitly mandating human violence and/or a history of oppressive use—enable clear decisions in some cases, but they inevitably lead to drawing ever finer distinctions in others. The complications of this kind of moral decision-making are illustrated by surveying the influence of Leviticus 18 on restrictions on sexual activity, past and present.[34] In its Israelite cultural context, Leviticus 18 emphasized maintaining purity by protecting bodily and group boundaries. That motivation accords poorly with the contemporary Western emphasis on protecting individual autonomy by prohibiting coercive sex. However, both motivations agree on outlawing intercourse among close relatives (incest), differing only over exactly which relationships should be permitted. On the other hand, Lev 18:22 prohibits sex between males (it does not mention females) while the ethic of individual autonomy has led recently to decriminalizing homosexual intercourse in many jurisdictions. But a different set of interpretive trends have manifested around the next verse. Bans on bestiality (sex with animals) in Christian countries, which were inspired by 18:23 and which sodomy laws often conflated with 18:22, were gradually abandoned under the influence of Enlightenment legal reforms, but are now being strengthened again by the moral argument against animal cruelty.[35] Thus Leviticus 18 continues to play a role in ethical debates over how to justify restrictions on sex. I leave most of these issues for the more nuanced discussion in the commentary, but I suggest striking through 18:22 and 20:13 because of their continuing and widespread use today to justify violence and discrimination against gays, lesbians, and others with non-hetero-normative sexual orientations.[36]

33 For a summary and citations of further literature, see Watts, *Leviticus 1–10*, 84–5.

34 Most of the counter-part sex rules in Leviticus 20 that include penalties will already be struck through because they apply the death penalty indiscriminately.

35 For a recent example, see Humane Society Legislative Fund, "U.S. Senate unanimously passes bill to prohibit animal cruelty, bestiality," December 14, 2017 (http://www.humanesociety.org/news/press_releases/2017/12/PACT-passes-Senate-12142017.html; accessed May 28, 2018).

36 G.D. Comstock, *Violence Against Lesbians and Gay Men* (New York: Columbia University Press, 1992), 122–4. Recent news stories include: D. Henry, "West Auckland pastor preaches gay

I do not advocate striking through normative texts simply because modern people no longer follow them. But normative regulations that explicitly mandate violence or that have been used in the past and present to justify oppression should be struck through to mark clearly their moral rejection by congregations and denominations.

5 The Strikethrough Verses

On these criteria, I suggest striking through the mandates for capital punishment for false worship (Lev 20:2, 3–5), sexual offenses (20:10–16), magical practices (20:27), and other capital offenses (20:9; 21:9; 24:14, 16–17, 21b; 27:29), as well as the slave laws (Lev 19:20–22; 25:44–46; 27:2–8), the justifications for genocide (18:24–25, 27; 20:23b–24a), and the purity laws that endorse a double standard for men and women (12:5; 21:7a, 13–15) and that ban gay sex (18:22; 20:13). In other biblical books, verses should also be struck through that endorse indiscriminate capital punishment and taking revenge (Gen 9:6a; Exod 21:12, 14–17, 29c; 22:17–19 [Eng. 22:18–20]; Num 35:16c, 17c, 18c, 19, 21b–c, 27b, 31, 33b; Deut 13:5, 8b–11, 15–16; 17:5, 7, 12–13; 19:12b–13; 21:21–23b; 22:20–25; 24:7b, 16c; Psalm 137:8b–9), genocide (Num 31:2–3, 15–18; 33:52–53, 55; Deut 7:2b, 16a; 20:11, 13–18; 25:17–19), slavery (Gen 9:25, 26c, 27c; Exod 21:2–11, 20–21, 26–27, 32; Deut 15:12, 16–17), and patriarchy (Gen 3:16; Exod 22:15–16 [Eng 22:16–17]; Num 5:11–31; 30:3–16; Deut 21:10–14; 22:28–29; 24:1–4; 25:12). Verses in the Deutero-canon/Apocrypha and New Testament should be struck through that have justified genocide in the form of violent anti-Semitism (Matt 27:24c–25; John 8:44; 1 Thess 2:14c–16), slavery (Eph 6:5–8; Col 3:22–25; Titus 2:9–10; Philemon 8–21; 1 Peter 2:18–21a), persecuting same-sex relations (Rom 1:26–27), and patriarchy in families and in religious communities (Sir 25:24–26; 1 Cor 11:3, 7–10; 14:33b–35; Eph 5:22–24; Col 3:18; 1 Tim 2:11–15; Titus 2:5c "submissive to their husbands"; 1 Peter 3:1–6, 7c "as the weaker vessel").

Many readers will no doubt judge my strikethroughs as modern overreach. However, though my suggestion to use strikethroughs for this purpose is novel, the editing of biblical texts by scholars is not new. In fact, both Jewish and Christian traditions since ancient times have granted scribes and scholars various

people should be shot," *The New Zealand Herald*, August 15, 2017 (https://www.nzherald.co.nz/nz/news/article.cfm?c_id=1&objectid=11904818; accessed May 28, 2018); J. Moyo, "Living with HIV and AIDS, and unwelcome in Zimbabwe's churches," *Religion News Service*, November 15, 2017 (https://religionnews.com/2017/11/15/living-with-hiv-and-aids-and-unwelcome-in-zimbabwes-churches/; accessed May 28, 2018); G. Karol, "Baptist pastor stands by anti-gay Orlando shooting sermon," *ABC 10*, June 15, 2016 (https://www.abc10.com/article/news/local/sacramento/baptist-pastor-stands-by-anti-gay-orlando-shooting-sermon/243921283; accessed May 28, 2018).

means for editing their sacred texts. Suspected additions have been marked in the margins of manuscripts, while rubrication has been used to emphasize especially significant verses (such as the words of Jesus in red-letter bibles). Modern scholars have rearranged biblical texts to match their literary reconstructions.[37] Religious traditions have also placed restrictions on reading certain scriptural texts. The ancient rabbis restricted study of the *merkaba* texts of Ezekiel to only the most advanced scholars.[38] They also prohibited translating certain embarrassing verses in the golden calf story in Exodus.[39] The medieval Masoretes preserved the consonantal Hebrew text of the Tanak scrupulously, but noted their corrections in the vowels and marginal comments (*masorah*) that they added to the text, including instructions to read (*qere*) differently than what is written (*kethib*).[40] Most English translations follow in this tradition of reading something other than what is written by printing "the LORD" rather than transliterating the Hebrew name of God, YHWH (יהוה). Christian lectionaries since antiquity have rendered mute large swaths of the scriptures, including all of the Leviticus texts I listed above, by not including them in weekly or even daily readings for liturgies.[41] The Protestant Reformers segregated parts of the Christian Old Testament that do not appear in the Jewish Tanak as a separate section of the Bible, the Apocrypha, and considered it of secondary authority. Later publishers unilaterally decided to drop the Apocrypha from most Protestant bibles, thereby omitting roughly 17 % of what had been Christian scripture.[42]

Such modifications to the biblical text are modeled by the biblical writers and editors themselves, most obviously in the Chronicler's additions and deletions to Samuel-Kings and Luke's editing and supplementing of Mark's Gospel. The Pentateuch even models a process of legal revision in several passages, such as when the daughters of Zelophehad complain about their lack of inheritance. God responds by granting inheritance to daughters without brothers (Num 27:9–10).

37 E.g. Exod 22:2–4 in the NEB and NRSV.

38 m. Hag. 2:1. See D. J. Halperin, *The Faces of the Chariot: Early Jewish Responses to Ezekiel's Vision* (Tübingen: Mohr Siebeck, 1988).

39 Exod 32:21–25 in m. Meg. 4:10; t. Meg. 3:31–38; y. Meg. 75c; b. Meg. 25a–b, all of which refer to Aaron's speech in the golden calf story, though their lists of prohibited passages do not quite agree with each other. See L. H. Feldman, "Philo's Account of the Golden Calf Incident," *JJS* 56 (2005) 245–64, on pp. 245–46; P. Lindqvist, *Sin at Sinai: Early Judaism Encounters Exodus 32* (Studies in Rewritten Bible 2; Turku: Åbo Akademi; Winona Lake, IN: Eisenbrauns, 2008), 168–9, who pointed out that *Targum Neofiti* seems to have observed a form of the rabbinic proscription (178–80).

40 E. Würthwein/A. A. Fischer, *The Text of the Old Testament: An Introduction to the Biblia Hebraica* (tr. E. F. Rhodes; Grand Rapids: Eerdmans, [3]2014), 15–38.

41 F. Just, "Lectionary Statistics" on the Roman Catholic *Lectionary for Mass* (2009) (http://catholic-resources.org/Lectionary/Statistics.htm).

42 A. E. Hill, "The King James Bible Apocrypha: When and Why Lost?" in D. G. Burke/J. F. Kutsko/P. H. Towner (ed.), *The King James Version at 400: Assessing Its Genius as Bible Translation and Its Literary Influence* (Atlanta: SBL, 2013) 345–58.

However, when tribal leaders complain about possible loss of land because of this legal innovation, Moses restricts the daughter's potential marriage partners to their tribal cousins (Num 36:1–12).[43] Legal reasoning and revision were thus features of biblical law, and marking and proscribing deleterious verses has deep precedents in both Jewish and Christian scribal traditions.

While some readers may think my proposal to strike through immoral biblical verses goes too far, others will likely think it does not go far enough. Why not also strike through the many stories about divine and human violence? And why not simply delete offensive verses? Though my list of strikethrough verses includes some curses and rulings in quoted dialogue within narratives, I do not suggest striking through entire stories of the Bible, no matter how violent and terrible. Stories work rhetorically in different ways than explicit norms like commands, laws, instructions, blessings and curses. It is possible to learn positive lessons even from stories of terror, violence, and evil. Besides, it would be the height of hypocrisy for me, a 21st-century American whose culture glorifies and profits from narrating violence in fictional books and films, to presume to pass judgement on the Bible for its violent stories. That discussion is best left to the commentary literature, where moral interpretation has been strengthened in recent decades by feminist and post-colonial critiques.

The situation is very different in the realms of law and morality. Here modern secular culture joins Jewish and Christian ethical reflection in rejecting indiscriminate capital punishment, slavery, genocide and, increasingly, patriarchy. The Bible's visual text should therefore strike through these verses, so that this judgment is immediately apparent to anyone who opens a bible to that page.

I do not propose deleting verses, however. Deleting offensive texts, besides confusing the literary form of biblical books, would whitewash the biblical tradition. It would obscure its complicity in fueling violence within and between religious communities as well as more broadly in the politics and economies of many societies. Deletion would hinder rather than advance the moral education of readers.

Instead, I recommend striking through immoral biblical norms. The strikethrough preserves the position of these verses in biblical literature while clearly marking the interpretive traditions' repudiation of their normative force. It is time for the texts of commentaries and of mass-market bibles to strike through verses that justify evil behavior rather than good.

---

43 Num 27:1–10; 36:1–12. See M. Fishbane, *Biblical Interpretation in Ancient Israel* (Oxford: Clarendon, 1985), 105; J.W. Watts, *Reading Law: the Rhetorical Shaping of the* Pentateuch (Sheffield: Sheffield Academic Press, 1999), 105–106. Nevertheless, B.M. Levinson observed correctly that Pentateuchal editors also attempted to conceal their innovations by misquotation or by failing to credit superseded rules to God or by reinterpreting them against their plain meaning ("The Human Voice of Divine Revelation: the Problem of Authority in Biblical Law," in M.A. Williams et al. [ed.] *Innovations in Religious Traditions* [Berlin: De Gruyter, 1992] 35–71, on pp. 43–63).

Postscript

As I was finishing this essay, the news broke that 300 French politicians and cultural leaders had issued a manifesto calling for the Qur'an to be edited to eliminate texts that fuel anti-Semitic violence.[44] Despite superficial similarities to my proposal here, the French manifesto expresses a very different political and moral position. Most obviously, it calls on members of a different religion, Islam, to conform to the standards of its non-Muslim writers. The manifesto obscures the deep and continuing anti-Semitic tendencies in French culture that stem from Christian, not Muslim, roots. The manifesto claims that Catholic culture shed its anti-Semitism through the reforms of the Second Vatican Council (1962–1965), but that is belied by the history of on-going anti-Semitic incidents in France as well as in other majority-Christian countries.[45] Though very many Christian denominations have disavowed anti-Semitism in the 20th century, just as they disavowed slavery in the 19th, neither the Second Vatican Council nor any other ecclesiastical bodies have modified the text of bibles to constrain their immoral use in justifying violence and oppression.

My proposal calls instead for bible translators and publishers to strike through immoral norms in our own scriptures. The strikethrough marks these norms as abrogated by Christian and Jewish traditions, but leaves them legible to acknowledge the traditions' complicity in perpetuating them.[46]

44 The manifesto recounted the history of recent murders of elderly Jews by Muslim immigrants and emphasized the vital role of Jewish contributions to French culture. Its second-to-last paragraph then demanded: "Nous demandons que les versets du Coran appelant au meurtre et au châtiment des juifs, des chrétiens et des incroyants soient frappés d'obsolescence par les autorités théologiques, comme le furent les incohérences de la Bible et l'antisémite catholique aboli par Vatican II, afin qu'aucun croyant ne puisse s'appuyer sur un texte sacré pour commettre un crime" ("Manifeste 'contre le nouvel antisémitisme,'" *Le Parisien*, April 21, 2018 [http://www.leparisien.fr/societe/manifeste-contre-le-nouvel-antisemitisme-21-04-2018-7676787.php; accessed May 5, 2018]).

45 "Anti-Semitism Worldwide 2017," Kantor Center for the Study of Contemporary European Jewry, Tel Aviv University (http://kantorcenter.tau.ac.il/sites/default/files/Doch_full_2018_110418.pdf; accessed May 14, 2018).

46 This essay has benefitted from the comments and encouragement of Nicole Ruane, William K. Gilders, Thomas Hieke and Christian A. Eberhart, to whom I am very grateful. Of course, I alone am responsible for its contents and arguments.

Bibliography

Academic Publications

Avalos, H., *Slavery, Abolitionism, and the Ethics of Biblical Scholarship* (Sheffield: Sheffield Phoenix Press, 2013).

Barker, C./Jane, E. A., *Cultural Studies: Theory and Practice* (Los Angeles: Sage, [5]2016).

Beal, T., *The Rise and Fall of the Bible: The Unexpected History of an Accidental Book* (Boston: Houghton Mifflin Harcourt, 2011).

Berkowitz, B. A., *Execution and Invention: Death Penalty Discourse in Early Rabbinic and Christian Cultures* (New York: Oxford University Press, 2006).

Braiterman, Z. J., "The Emergence of Modern Religion: Moses Mendelssohn, Neoclassicism, and Ceremonial Aesthetics," in C. Wiese/M. Urban (ed.), *German-Jewish Thought Between Religion and Politics* (Berlin: De Gruyter, 2012) 11–29.

Cherry, C., *God's New Israel: Religious Interpretations of American Destiny* (Englewood Cliffs, NJ: Prentice Hall, 1971).

Clinton, R. N., "Treaties with Native Nations: Iconic Historical Relics or Modern Necessity?" in S. Shown Harjo (ed.), *Nation to Nation: Treaties Between the United States and American Indian Nations* (Washington, DC: Smithsonian, 2014) 14–33.

Comstock, G. D., *Violence Against Lesbians and Gay Men* (New York: Columbia University Press, 1992).

Dube, S. W. D., "Hierophanies: A Hermeneutic Paradigm for Understanding Zionist Ritual," in G. C. Oosthuizen et al. (ed.), *Afro-Christianity at the Grassroots: Its Dynamics and Strategies* (Leiden: Brill, 1994) 105–18.

Eisen, R., *The Peace and Violence of Judaism: From the Bible to Modern Zionism* (New York: Oxford University Press, 2011).

Feldman, L. H., "Philo's Account of the Golden Calf Incident," *JJS* 56 (2005) 245–64.

Firestone, R., *Holy War in Judaism: The Fall and Rise of a Controversial Idea* (Oxford: Oxford University Press, 2012).

–, "Holy War: Rabbinic to Modern Judaism," *EBR* 12 (2015).

Fishbane, M., *Biblical Interpretation in Ancient Israel* (Oxford: Clarendon, 1985).

Glancy, J. A., *Slavery in Early Christianity* (Oxford: Oxford University Press, 2002).

Gnuse, R. H., *Trajectories of Justice: What the Bible Says about Slaves, Women and Homosexuality* (Eugene, OR: Cascade, 2015).

Goldenberg, D. M., *The Curse of Ham: Race and Slavery in Early Judaism, Christianity, and Islam* (Princeton, NJ: Princeton University Press, 2009).

Halberstam, C. T., *Law and Truth in Biblical and Rabbinic Literature* (Bloomington: Indiana University Press, 2010).

Halperin, D. J., *The Faces of the Chariot: Early Jewish Responses to Ezekiel's Vision* (Tübingen: Mohr Siebeck, 1988).

Haynes, S. R., *Noah's Curse: The Biblical Justification of American Slavery* (Oxford: Oxford University Press, 2002).

Hill, A. E., "The King James Bible Apocrypha: When and Why Lost?" in D. G. Burke/J. F. Kutsko/P. H. Towner (ed.), *The King James Version at 400: Assessing Its Genius as Bible Translation and Its Literary Influence* (Atlanta: SBL, 2013) 345–58.

Jenkins, P., *The New Faces of Christianity: Believing the Bible in the Global South* (Oxford: Oxford University Press, 2006).

Klinken, A. van/Chitando, E. (ed.), *Public Religion and the Politics of Homosexuality in Africa* (London: Routledge, 2016).

Levinson, B. M., "The Human Voice of Divine Revelation: the Problem of Authority in Biblical

Law," in M. A. Williams et al. (ed.), *Innovations in Religious Traditions* (Berlin: De Gruyter, 1992) 35–71.
Lindqvist, P., *Sin at Sinai: Early Judaism Encounters Exodus 32* (Studies in Rewritten Bible 2; Turku: Åbo Akademi; Winona Lake, IN: Eisenbrauns, 2008).
Megivern, J. J., *The Death Penalty: An Historical and Theological Survey* (Mahwah, NJ: Paulist Press, 1999).
Moore, S. D./Sherwood, Y., "Biblical Studies 'after' Theory: Onwards Towards the Past," *Biblical Interpretation* 18 (2010) 1–27, 87–113, 191–225, reprinted and expanded in Moore/Sherwood, *The Invention of the Biblical Scholar* (Minneapolis: Fortress, 2011).
Parmenter, D. Miller, "Material Scripture," in T. Beal (ed.), *The Oxford Encyclopedia of the Bible and the Arts* (Oxford: Oxford University Press, 2015, from *Oxford Biblical Studies Online*, http://www.oxfordbiblicalcstudies.com/article/opr/t454/e97; accessed June 4, 2018).
Rubenstein, H./Clark Smith, B./Stagnitto Ellis, J., *The Jefferson Bible, Smithsonian Edition: The Life and Morals of Jesus of Nazareth by Thomas Jefferson* (Washington, DC: Smithsonian, 2011).
Sadgrove, J./Vanderbeck, R. M./Andersson, J./Valentine, G./Ward, K., "Morality Plays and Money Matters: Towards a Situated Understanding of the Politics of Homosexuality in Uganda." *Journal of Modern African Studies* 50/1 (2012) 103–29.
Santoro, A., "Religion and Capital Punishment in the United States," *Religion Compass* 8/5 (2014) 159–74 (https://doi.org/10.1111/rec3.12105).
Saposnik, A., "The Desert Comes to Zion: A Narrative Ends its Wandering," in P. Barmash/W. D. Nelson (ed.), *Exodus in the Jewish Experience: Echoes and Reverberations* (Lanham, MD: Lexington, 2015) 213–46.
Savishinsky, N. J., "African Dimensions of the Jamaican Rastafarian Movement," in N. S. Murrell et al. (ed.), *Chanting Down Babylon: The Rastafari Reader* (Philadelphia: Temple University Press, 1998) 125–44.
Schabas, W., *The Abolition of the Death Penalty in International Law* (Cambridge: Cambridge University Press, ^{3}2002).
Siker, J. S., *Liquid Scripture: The Bible in the Digital World* (Minneapolis: Fortress, 2017).
Spivak, G., "Translator's Preface," in J. Derrida, *Of Grammatology* (Baltimore: Johns Hopkins University Press, 1976) ix–xc.
Stark, R., *For the Glory of God: How Monotheism Led to Reformations, Science, Witch-Hunts, and the End of Slavery* (Princeton: Princeton University Press, 2004).
Sugirtharajah, R. S., *The Bible and Empire: Postcolonial Explorations* (Cambridge: Cambridge University Press, 2005).
Walls, A. F., *The Cross-Cultural Process in Christian History* (New York: Continuum, 2001).
Warrior, R., "Canaanites, Cowboys, and Indians: Deliverance, Conquest, and Liberation Theology," *Christianity and Crisis* 29 (1989) 261–5.
Watts, J. W., *Reading Law: the Rhetorical Shaping of the* Pentateuch (Sheffield: Sheffield Academic Press, 1999).
–, *Ritual and Rhetoric in Leviticus: From Sacrifice to Scripture* (Cambridge: Cambridge University Press, 2007).
–, "The Torah as the Rhetoric of Priesthood," in G. Knoppers/B. M. Levinson (ed.), *The Pentateuch as Torah: New Models for Understanding Its Promulgation and Acceptance* (Winona Lake, IN: Eisenbrauns, 2007), 319–32.
–, *Leviticus 1–10* (HCOT; Leuven: Peeters, 2013).
–, (ed.), *Iconic Books and Texts* (Sheffield: Equinox, 2013).
–, "Ancient Iconic Texts and Scholarly Expertise," in Watts, *Iconic Books and Texts* (2013) 374–84.
–, "The Three Dimensions of Scriptures," in Watts, *Iconic Books and Texts* (2013) 8–30.
–, *Understanding the Pentateuch as a Scripture* (Oxford: Wiley Blackwell, 2017).
–/Yoo, Y. (ed.), *Books As Sacred Beings* (Sheffield: Equinox, forthcoming).

Wogaman, P.J., *Christian Ethics: A Historical Introduction* (Louisville: Westminster John Knox, 1993).
Würthwein, E./Fischer, A.A., *The Text of the Old Testament: An Introduction to the Biblia Hebraica* (Tr. E.F. Rhodes; Grand Rapids: Eerdmans, [3]2014).
Zyl, D.C. van, "In Africa, Theology is Not Thought Out but Danced Out: On the Theological Significance of Old Testament Symbolism and Rituals in African Zionist Churches," *OTE* 8 (1995) 425–38.

News Articles and Websites

"Anti-Semitism Worldwide 2017," Kantor Center for the Study of Contemporary European Jewry, Tel Aviv University; http://kantorcenter.tau.ac.il/sites/default/files/Doch_full_2018_110418.pdf (accessed May 14, 2018).
Cohen, N., "Crossing Out, for Emphasis," *New York Times*, July 23, 2007 (https://www.nytimes.com/2007/07/23/business/media/23link.html; accessed April 8, 2018).
Gettlemanjan, J., "Americans' Role Seen in Uganda Anti-Gay Push," *New York Times*, January 3, 2010 (https://www.nytimes.com/2010/01/04/world/africa/04uganda.html; accessed April 17, 2018).
Henry, D., "West Auckland pastor preaches gay people should be shot," *The New Zealand Herald*, August 15, 2017 (https://www.nzherald.co.nz/nz/news/article.cfm?c_id=1&objectid=11904818; accessed May 28, 2018).
Just, F., "Lectionary Statistics" on the Roman Catholic Lectionary for Mass (2009) (http://catholic-resources.org/Lectionary/Statistics.htm, accessed April 17, 2018).
"Manifeste 'contre le nouvel antisémitisme,'" *Le Parisien*, April 21, 2018 (http://www.leparisien.fr/societe/manifeste-contre-le-nouvel-antisemitisme-21-04-2018-7676787.php; accessed May 5, 2018).
Humane Society Legislative Fund, "U.S. Senate unanimously passes bill to prohibit animal cruelty, bestiality," December 14, 2017 (http://www.humanesociety.org/news/press_releases/2017/12/PACT-passes-Senate-12142017.html; accessed May 28, 2018).
Karol, G., "Baptist pastor stands by anti-gay Orlando shooting sermon," *ABC 10*, June 15, 2016 (https://www.abc10.com/article/news/local/sacramento/baptist-pastor-stands-by-anti-gay-orlando-shooting-sermon/243921283 (accessed May 28, 2018).
Keene, B.C., "Medieval Copyediting," *The Iris: Behind the Scenes at the Getty*, April 8, 2014 (http://blogs.getty.edu/iris/medieval-copyediting/; accessed April 18, 2018).
Moyo, J., "Living with HIV and AIDS, and unwelcome in Zimbabwe's churches," *Religion News Service*, November 15, 2017 (https://religionnews.com/2017/11/15/living-with-hiv-and-aids-and-unwelcome-in-zimbabwes-churches/; accessed May 28, 2018).
Ticak, M., "Strikethrough and Why It's so Popular," *Grammerly Blog* (https://www.grammarly.com/blog/strikethrough-formatting-popularity/; accessed January 2, 2018).

List of Contributors

Christian A. Eberhart (ceberhart@uh.edu) is Professor and Program Director of Religious Studies at the University of Houston, USA. He is the founder and former chair of the Annual Conference SBL Section "Sacrifice, Cult, and Atonement."

Roy E. Gane (gane@andrews.edu) is Professor of Hebrew Bible and Ancient Near Eastern Languages at the Seventh-day Adventist Theological Seminary, Andrews University, in Berrien Springs, Michigan, USA. He published his commentary *Leviticus, Numbers* in the *NIV Application Commentary* series (by Zondervan) in 2004 and is currently completing another commentary on Leviticus for the new *Seventh-day Adventist International Bible Commentary* (SDAIBC) series.

William K. Gilders (wgilder@emory.edu) is Associate Professor of Religion and Jewish Studies at Emory University, Atlanta, USA. He is preparing his commentary on Leviticus for the *Old Testament Library* series published by Westminster John Knox Press.

Hannah K. Harrington (hharrington@patten.edu) is Professor of Old Testament at Patten University, Oakland, CA, USA. She has written the contribution about "Leviticus" in the *Women's Bible Commentary* (Louisville: Westminster John Know, 2012).

Thomas Hieke (thieke@uni-mainz.de) is Professor for Old Testament Studies at the Johannes Gutenberg University of Mainz, Germany. He published his commentary on Leviticus in the series *Herders Theologischer Kommentar zum Alten Testament* (HThKAT) in 2014.

Naphtali S. Meshel (nmeshel@mail.huji.ac.il) is Assistant Professor in the Department of Bible and in the Department of Comparative Religion at the Hebrew University of Jerusalem, Israel. He is writing a commentary on Leviticus in the series *International Exegetical Commentary on the Old Testament* (IECOT)/*Internationaler Exegetischer Kommentar zum Alten Testament* (IEKAT), published by Kohlhammer, Stuttgart.

Nicole J. Ruane (Nicole.Ruane@unh.edu) is Lecturer in the Humanities Program in the Department of Classics, Humanities and Italian Studies at the University of New Hampshire, USA. She is planning to write a volume on the reception history of Leviticus in the *Blackwell commentary* series.

James W. Watts (jwwatts@syr.edu) is Professor in the Department of Religion at Syracuse University, NY, USA. He is writing the second and third volumes of his commentary on Leviticus in the *Historical Commentary on the Old Testament* series from Peeters.

David P. Wright (wright@brandeis.edu) is Professor of Hebrew Bible and Ancient Near East at Brandeis University, Watham, MA, USA. His most recent book is *Inventing God's Law: How the Covenant Code of the Bible Used and Revised the Laws of Hammurabi* (Oxford University Press, 2009). He is currently working on the commentary on Leviticus for the *Hermeneia* commentary series.

Contributors' Publications about Leviticus

Christian A. Eberhart

"Opfer, Sühne und Stellvertretung im Alten Testament," in M. Hüttenhoff/W. Kraus/K. Meyer (ed.), "... *mein Blut für Euch": Theologische Perspektiven zum Verständnis des Todes Jesu heute* (BThS 38; Göttingen: Vandenhoeck & Ruprecht, 2018) 40–55.

Sacrifice, Cult, and Atonement in Early Judaism and Christianity: Constituents and Critique, ed. C. A. Eberhart/H. L. Wiley (SBLRBS 85; Atlanta: SBL Press, 2017).

"Introduction: Constituents and Critique of Sacrifice, Cult, and Atonement in Early Judaism and Christianity," in C. A. Eberhart/H. L. Wiley (ed.), *Sacrifice, Cult, and Atonement in Early Judaism and Christianity: Constituents and Critique* (SBLRBS 85; Atlanta: SBL Press, 2017) 1–29.

"To Atone or Not to Atone: Remarks on the Day of Atonement Rituals According to Leviticus 16 and the Meaning of Atonement," in C. A. Eberhart/H. L. Wiley (ed.), *Sacrifice, Cult, and Atonement in Early Judaism and Christianity: Constituents and Critique* (SBLRBS 85; Atlanta: SBL Press, 2017) 197–231.

"Was ist ein Opfer?," in W. Kraus/M. Rösel (ed.), *Update-Exegese 2.1: Ergebnisse gegenwärtiger Bibelwissenschaft* (Leipzig: Evangelische Verlagsanstalt, 2015) 42–50.

"Beobachtungen zu Opfer, Kult und Sühne in der Septuaginta," in W. Kraus/S. Kreutzer (ed.), *Die Septuaginta—Text, Wirkung, Rezeption: 4. Internationale Fachtagung veranstaltet von Septuaginta Deutsch (LXX.D), Wuppertal 19.-22.7.2012* (WUNT 325; Tübingen: Mohr Siebeck, 2014) 297–314.

"Blut des Bundes: Das Opferverständnis im Buch Levitikus und in der Eucharistie," *BiKi* 2 (2014) 69–73.

Kultmetaphorik und Christologie: Opfer- und Sühneterminologie im Neuen Testament (WUNT 306; Tübingen: Mohr Siebeck, 2013).

"Das Opfer als Gabe: Perspektiven des Alten Testaments," *JBTh* 27 (2012) (*Geben und Nehmen*, ed. M. Ebner et al.) 93–120.

"Blood. I. Ancient Near East and Hebrew Bible/Old Testament," *EBR* 4 (2012) 201–12.

Ritual and Metaphor: Sacrifice in the Bible, ed. C. A. Eberhart (SBLRBS 68; Atlanta: SBL, 2011).

"Opfer und Kult in kulturanthropologischer Perspektive," *Verkündigung und Forschung* 56/2 (2011) 4–16.

"Sacrifice? Holy Smokes! Reflections on Cult Terminology for Understanding Sacrifice in the Hebrew Bible," in C. A. Eberhart (ed.), *Ritual and Metaphor: Sacrifice in the Bible* (SBLRBS 68; Atlanta: SBL, 2011) 17–32, reprinted in this volume, pp. 77–99.

"Atonement. I. Hebrew Bible/Old Testament," *EBR* 3 (2011) 24–32.

"Qorban," *Wissenschaftliches Bibellexikon im Internet (WiBiLex)* (Stuttgart: Deutsche Bibelgesellschaft [http://www.wibilex.de], 2010).

"Sühne: Altes Testament," *Wissenschaftliches Bibellexikon im Internet (WiBiLex)* (Stuttgart: Deutsche Bibelgesellschaft [http://www.wibilex.de], 2007).

"Schlachtung/Schächtung," *Wissenschaftliches Bibellexikon im Internet (WiBiLex)* (Stuttgart: Deutsche Bibelgesellschaft [http://www.wibilex.de], 2006).

"A Neglected Feature of Sacrifice in the Hebrew Bible: Remarks on the Burning Rite on the Altar," *Harvard Theological Review* 97/4 (2004) 485–93.

Studien zur Bedeutung der Opfer im Alten Testament: Die Signifikanz von Blut- und Verbrennungsriten im kultischen Rahmen (WMANT 94; Neukirchen-Vluyn: Neukirchener, 2002).

"Beobachtungen zum Verbrennungsritus bei Schlachtopfer und Gemeinschafts-Schlachtopfer," *Biblica* 83 (2002) 88–96.

Roy E. Gane

Old Testament Law for Christians: Original Context and Enduring Application (Grand Rapids: Baker Academic, 2017).

"Didactic Logic and the Authorship of Leviticus," in R.E. Gane/A. Taggar-Cohen et al. (ed.), *Current Issues in Priestly and Related Literature: The Legacy of Jacob Milgrom and Beyond* (SBLRBS; Atlanta: SBL, 2015) 197–221.

"The Nature of the Human Being in Leviticus," in C. Wahlen (ed.), *"What Are Human Beings That You Remember Them?" Proceedings of the Third International Bible Conference, Nof Ginosar and Jerusalem, June 11–21, 2012* (Silver Spring, MD: Biblical Research Institute, 2015) 43–57.

"Leviticus," in G.M. Burge/A.E. Hill (ed.), *The Baker Illustrated Bible Commentary* (Grand Rapids: Baker, 2012) 87–115.

"Some Attempted Alternatives to Timeless Biblical Condemnation of Homosexual Acts," in R.E. Gane/N.P. Miller/H.P. Swanson (ed.), *Homosexuality, Marriage, and the Church: Biblical, Counseling, and Religious Liberty Issues* (Berrien Springs, MI: Andrews University Press, 2012) 163–174.

"Leviticus," primary translator, in *Common English Bible: A Fresh Translation to Touch the Heart and Mind* (Nashville: Common English Bible, 2011) 93–123.

"The Unifying Logic of Israelite Purification Offerings Within Their Ancient Near Eastern Context," *Journal of the Adventist Theological Society* 21 (2010) 85–98.

"Leviticus," in J.H. Walton (ed.), *Zondervan Illustrated Bible Backgrounds Commentary* (Grand Rapids: Zondervan, 2009) 1.284–337.

"Ablutions," in H.-J. Klauck et al. (ed.), *Encyclopedia of the Bible and its Reception* (Berlin: Walter De Gruyter, 2009) 1.108–12.

"Privative Preposition *min* in Purification Offering Pericopes and the Changing Face of 'Dorian Gray,'" *JBL* 127 (2008) 209–22.

"The Function of the Nazirite's Concluding Purification Offering," in B.J. Schwartz/D.P. Wright/J. Stackert/N.S. Meshel (ed.), *Perspectives on Purity and Purification in the Bible* (New York: T&T Clark, 2008) 9–17.

Cult and Character: Purification Offerings, Day of Atonement, and Theodicy (Winona Lake, IN: Eisenbrauns, 2005).

Ritual Dynamic Structure (Gorgias Dissertations 14, Religion 2; Piscataway, NJ: Gorgias Press, 2004).

Leviticus, Numbers (NIV Application Commentary; Grand Rapids: Zondervan, 2004).

"qarab," co-authored with Jacob Milgrom, in G.J. Botterweck/H. Ringgren/H.-J. Fabry (ed.), *Theological Dictionary of the Old Testament* (Grand Rapids: Eerdmans, 2004) 13.135–48.

"paroket," co-authored with J. Milgrom, in G.J. Botterweck/H. Ringgren/H.-J. Fabry (ed.), *Theological Dictionary of the Old Testament* (Grand Rapids: Eerdmans, 2003) 12.95–7.

"Leviticus, Book of," in J.H. Hayes (ed.), *Dictionary of Biblical Interpretation* (Nashville: Abingdon, 1999) 2.54–9.

"Schedules for Deities: Macrostructure of Israelite, Babylonian, and Hittite Sancta Purification Days," *AUSS* 36 (1998) 231–44.

"'Bread of the Presence' and Creator-in-Residence," *VT* 42 (1992) 179–203.

William K. Gilders

"Leviticus," in E. Orlin (ed.), *The Routledge Encyclopedia of Ancient Mediterranean Religions* (London/New York: Routledge, 2016) 538–39.
"Priestly Law," in B. A. Strawn (ed.), *The Oxford Encyclopedia of the Bible and Law* (Oxford/New York: Oxford University Press, 2015) 2.166–75.
"Purity," in B. A. Strawn (ed.), *The Oxford Encyclopedia of the Bible and Law* (Oxford/New York: Oxford University Press, 2015) 2.193–204.
"חטאת as 'Sin Offering': A Reconsideration," in C. Johnson Hodge/S. M. Olyan/D. Ullucci/E. Wasserman (ed.), *"The One Who Sows Bountifully": Essays in Honor of Stanley K. Stowers* (BJS 356; Providence, R. I.: Brown Judaic Studies, 2013) 119–28.
"Ancient Israelite Sacrifice as Symbolic Action: Theoretical Reflections," *Svensk exegetisk årsbok* 78 (2013) 1–22.
"The Day of Atonement in the Dead Sea Scrolls," in T. Hieke/T. Nicklas (ed.), *The Day of Atonement: Its Interpretation in Early Jewish and Christian Traditions* (Themes in Biblical Narrative 15, Leiden: Brill, 2012) 63–73.
"Jewish Sacrifice: Its Nature and Function (According to Philo)," in J. Wright Knust/Z. Várhelyi (ed.), *Ancient Mediterranean Sacrifice* (New York: Oxford University Press, 2011) 94–105.
"Sacrifice before Sinai and the Priestly Narratives," in S Shectman/J. S. Baden (ed.), *The Strata of the Priestly Writings: Contemporary Debate and Future Directions* (AThANT 95; Zürich: Theologischer Verlag, 2009) 57–72.
"Anthropological Approaches: Ritual in Leviticus 8, Real or Rhetorical?," in J. M. Lemon/K. H. Richards (ed.), *Method Matters: Essays on the Interpretation of the Hebrew Bible in Honor of David L. Petersen* (Leiden: Brill, 2009) 233–50.
"Blood as Purificant in Priestly Torah: What Do We Know and How Do We Know It?," in B. J. Schwartz/D. P. Wright/J. Stackert/N. S. Meshel (ed.), *Perspectives on Purity and Purification in the Bible* (New York: T&T Clark, 2008) 77–83.
"Blut, 'Leben' und Opferritual in der hebräischen Bibel," in C. von Braun/C. Wulf (ed.), *Mythen des Blutes* (Frankfurt/New York: Campus, 2007) 31–42.

Hannah K. Harrington

"Accessing Holiness via Ritual Ablutions in the Dead Sea Scrolls and Related Literature," in C. A. Eberhart/H. L. Wiley (ed.), *Sacrifice, Cult, and Atonement in Early Judaism and Christianity: Constituents and Critique* (SBLRBS 85; Atlanta: SBL Press, 2017), 71–95.
"The Use of Leviticus in Ezra-Nehemiah," *JHS* 13 (2013) 1–20.
The Purity Texts (Companion to the Qumran Scrolls 5; London: T&T Clark, 2005).
Holiness: Rabbinic Judaism and the Graeco-Roman World (London: Routledge, 2001).

Thomas Hieke

"Priestly Leadership in the Book of Leviticus: A Hidden Agenda," in K. Pyschny/S. Schulz (ed.), *Debating Authority. Concepts of Leadership in the Pentateuch and the Former Prophets* (BZAW 507; Berlin/New York: De Gruyter, 2018) 68–8.
"Opfer und Liebe Gottes im Buch Levitikus," in M. Oeming (ed.), *AHAVA—Die Liebe Gottes im Alten Testament* (ABG 55; Leipzig: Evangelische Verlagsanstalt, 2018) 133–42.

"The Covenant in Leviticus 26: A Concept of Admonition and Redemption," in R. J. Bautch/G. N. Knoppers (ed.), *Covenant in the Persian Period. From Genesis to Chronicles* (Winona Lake, IN: Eisenbrauns, 2015) 75–89.

"Die Heiligkeit Gottes als Beweggrund für ethisches Verhalten. Das ethische Konzept des Heiligkeitsgesetzes nach Levitikus 19," in C. Frevel (ed.), *Mehr als Zehn Worte? Zur Bedeutung des Alten Testaments in ethischen Fragen* (QD 273; Freiburg i. Br.: Herder, 2015) 187–206.

"Kennt und verurteilt das Alte Testament Homosexualität?," in S. Goertz (ed.), *"Wer bin ich, ihn zu verurteilen?" Homosexualität und katholische Kirche* (Katholizismus im Umbruch 3; Freiburg i. Br.: Herder, 2015) 19–52.

"Menstruation and Impurity. Regular Abstention from the Cult According to Leviticus 15:19–24 and Some Examples for the Reception of the Biblical Text in Early Judaism," in G. G. Xeravits (ed.), *Religion and Female Body in Ancient Judaism and Its Environments* (DCLS 28; Berlin/Boston: De Gruyter, 2015) 54–70.

"Tenufa—Emporhebungsgabe statt Schwingopfer," in: S. J. Wimmer/G. Gafus (ed.), *"Vom Leben umfangen." Ägypten, das Alte Testament und das Gespräch der Religionen. Gedenkschrift für Manfred Görg* (ÄAT 80; Münster: Ugarit-Verlag, 2014) 83–9.

"Das Gebot der Nächstenliebe als Angebot. Lev 19 als Ausdruck und Summe der Theologie des Levitikusbuches," *BiKi* 69/2 (2014) 74–9.

Levitikus 1–15, Levitikus 16–27 (HThKAT; Freiburg i. Br.: Herder, 2014) (Website: http://lev.thomashieke.de).

"'Ihr sollt meine Satzungen und meine Vorschriften befolgen: durch sie wird der Mensch, der nach ihnen handelt, leben' (Lev 18,5). Bedeutung und Hermeneutik der Bibel in der Kirche," *RU heute* 2 (2013) 12–17.

"Warum Christen etwas vom Buch Levitikus wissen sollten ...," *BiLi* 86 (2013) 19–30.

"Die Eignung der Priester für ihren Dienst nach Lev 21,16–24. *Mūm*, körperlicher Schaden, als Kriterium des Ausschlusses vom Priesterdienst," in W. Grünstäudl/M. Schiefer Ferrari (ed.), *Gestörte Lektüre. Disability als hermeneutische Leitkategorie biblischer Exegese* (Behinderung—Theologie—Kirche. Beiträge zu diakonisch-caritativen Disability Studies 4; Stuttgart: Kohlhammer, 2012) 48–66.

T. Hieke/T. Nicklas (ed.), *The Day of Atonement. Its Interpretations in Early Jewish and Christian Traditions* (Themes in Biblical Narrative 15; Leiden/Boston: Brill, 2012).

"Das Verbot der Übergabe von Nachkommen an den 'Molech' in Lev 18 und 20. Ein neuer Deutungsversuch," *WO* 41 (2011) 147–67, English translation in this volume, pp. 171–199.

"Die Unreinheit der Leiche nach der Tora," in T. Nicklas/F. V. Reiterer/J. Verheyden (ed.), *Deuterocanonical and Cognate Literature Yearbook 2009: The Human Body in Death and Resurrection* (Berlin/New York: De Gruyter, 2009) 43–65.

"Der Kult ist für den Menschen da. Auf Spurensuche in Levitikus 1–10," *BiKi* 64 (2009) 141–7.

Naphtali S. Meshel

"Hermeneutics and the Logic of Ritual," *Journal of the Hebrew Bible and Ancient Israel* 8 (2019), forthcoming.

"To Be Taken with a Grain of Salt: Between a 'Grammar' and a GRAMMUR of a Sacrificial Ritual System" in R. A. Yelle/C. I. Lehrich/C. Handman (ed.), *Language and Religion* (Language Intersections; Berlin: De Gruyter, 2018).

"Sacrifice and the Temple," in A.-J. Levine/M. Zvi Brettler, *The Jewish Annotated New Testament* (Oxford/New York: Oxford University Press, [2]2017) 658–62.

"What is a Zoeme? The Priestly Inventory of Sacrificial Animals," in R. E. Gane/A. Taggar-Cohen (ed.), *Current Issues in Priestly and Related Literature: The Legacy of Jacob Milgrom and Beyond* (SBLRBS; Atlanta: SBL, 2015) 19–45.

The "Grammar" of Sacrifice: A Generativist Study of the Ancient Israelite Sacrificial System in the Priestly Writings with A "Grammar" of Σ (Oxford: Oxford University Press, 2014).
"The Form and Function of a Biblical Blood Ritual," *VT* 63 (2013) 276–89, reprinted in this volume, pp. 101–114.
"Towards a 'Grammar' of Sacrifice: Hierarchic Patterns in the Israelite Sacrificial System," *JBL* (2013) 543–67.
"P1, P2, P3, and H: Purity, Prohibition, and the Puzzling History of Leviticus 11," *Hebrew Union College Annual* 81 (2010) 1–15.
B. J. Schwartz/D. P. Wright/J. Stackert/N. S. Meshel (ed.), *Perspectives on Purity and Purification in the Bible: Papers Read in the Pentateuch Section at the 125th Annual Meeting of the Society of Biblical Literature* (New York, London: T&T Clark, Continuum Books, 2008).
"Pure, Impure, Prohibited, Permitted," in B. J. Schwartz/D. P. Wright/J. Stackert/N. S. Meshel (ed.), *Perspectives on Purity and Purification in the Bible: Papers Read in the Pentateuch Section at the 125th Annual Meeting of the Society of Biblical Literature* (New York, London: T&T Clark, Continuum Books, 2008) 32–42.
"Food for Thought: Systems of Categorization in Leviticus 11," *HTR* 101 (2008) 203–29.

Nicole J. Ruane

"Pigs, Purity and Patrilineality: The Multiparity of Swine and Its Problems for Biblical Ritual and Gender Construction," *JBL* 134 (2015) 489–504.
Sacrifice and Gender in Biblical Law (Cambridge: Cambridge University Press, 2013).
"Bathing, Status, and Gender in Priestly Ritual," in D. W. Rooke (ed.), *"A Question of Sex?" Gender and Difference in the Hebrew Bible and Beyond* (HBM 14; Sheffield: Sheffield Phoenix Press, 2007) 66–81.

James W. Watts

"Text Are Not Rituals and Rituals Are Not Texts, with an Example from Leviticus 12," in C. Nihan/J. Rhyder (ed.), *Text and Ritual in the Pentateuch* (Winona Lake, IN: Eisenbrauns, forthcoming).
"Incense in the Rhetoric and Political Economy of the Aaronide Dynasties," in C. Frevel/K. Pyschny (ed.), *Contact and Exchange in Incense Practices of the Southern Levant* (Tübingen: Mohr Siebeck, forthcoming).
"Leviticus, Book of—Visual Arts," *Encyclopedia of the Bible and its Reception* (Berlin: De Gruyter, forthcoming).
"The Unstated Premise of the Prose Pentateuch: YHWH is King," *JHS* 18/2 (2018) (online at http://dx.doi.org/10.5508/jhs.2018.v18.a2).
Understanding the Pentateuch as a Scripture (Oxford: Wiley Blackwell, 2017).
"Narrative, Lists, Rhetoric, Ritual and the Pentateuch as a Scripture," in J. Geertz et al. (ed.), *The Formation of the Pentateuch: Bridging the Academic Cultures of Europe, Israel, and North America* (Tübingen: Mohr Siebeck, 2016) 1135–45.
"Writing Commentary as Ritual and as Discovery," in W. Yarchin/T. Finlay (ed.), *The Genre of Biblical Commentary: Essays in Honor of John E. Hartley* (Eugene: Wipf & Stock, 2015) 40–53.
Leviticus 1–10 (Historical Commentary on the Old Testament; Louvain: Peeters, 2013).
"Scripturalization and the Aaronide Dynasties," *JHS* 13 (2013) (online at http://www.jhsonline.org/Articles/article_186.pdf).
"Illustrating Leviticus: Art, Ritual and Politics," *Biblical Reception* 2 (2013) 3–15.

"The Historical and Literary Contexts of the Sin and Guilt Offerings," in F. Landy/L.M. Trevaskis/B. Bibb (ed.), *Text, Time, and Temple: Literary, Historical and Ritual Studies in Leviticus* (Sheffield: Phoenix, 2015) 85–93. Reprinted from Watts, *Leviticus 1–10* (Leuven: Peeters, 2013) 309–16.
"The Political and Legal Uses of Scripture," in J. Schaper/J.C. Paget (ed.), *The New Cambridge History of the Bible* (Cambridge: Cambridge University Press, 2013) 1.345–64.
"Aaron and the Golden Calf in the Rhetoric of the Pentateuch," *JBL* 130 (2011) 417–30.
"Using Ezra's Time as a Methodological Pivot for Understanding the Rhetoric and Functions of the Pentateuch," in T.B. Dozeman/K. Schmid/B.J. Schwarz (ed.), *The Pentateuch: International Perspectives on Current Research* (Tübingen: Mohr Siebeck, 2011) 489–506.
"The Rhetoric of Sacrifice," in C.A. Eberhart (ed.), *Ritual and Metaphor: Sacrifice in the Bible* (Atlanta: SBL, 2011) 3–16 = Watts, *Ritual and Rhetoric in Leviticus* (2007) 173–92.
"Legal Literature," in *The New Interpreter's One-Volume Commentary on the Bible* (Nashville: Abingdon, 2010) 953–55.
"Torah," in *The New Interpreter's Dictionary of the Bible* (Nashville: Abingdon, 2009) 5.629–30.
"Ritual Rhetoric in Ancient Near Eastern Texts," in C. Lipson/R. Binckley (ed.), *Ancient Non-Greek Rhetorics* (West Lafayette, IN: Parlor Press, 2009) 39–66.
"Ritual Rhetoric in the Pentateuch: The Case of Leviticus 1–16," in T. Römer (ed.), *The Books of Leviticus and Numbers* (BETL; Leuven: Peeters, 2008) 305–18.
Ritual and Rhetoric in Leviticus: From Sacrifice to Scripture (New York: Cambridge University Press, 2007).
"The Torah as the Rhetoric of Priesthood," in G. Knoppers/B.M. Levinson (ed.), *The Pentateuch as Torah: New Models for Understanding Its Promulgation and Acceptance* (Winona Lake: Eisenbrauns, 2007) 319–32.
"'Olah: The Rhetoric of Burnt Offerings," *VT* 66/1 (2006) 125–37.
"Ritual Legitimacy and Scriptural Authority," *JBL* 124/3 (2005) 401–17.
"Story, List, Sanction: A Cross-Cultural Strategy of Ancient Persuasion," in C. Lipson/R. Binkley (ed.), *Rhetoric Before and Beyond the Greeks* (Albany: SUNY Press, 2004) 197–212.
"The Rhetoric of Ritual Instruction in Leviticus 1–7," in R. Rendtorff/R. Kugler, *The Book of Leviticus: Composition and Reception* (VTSup 93; Leiden: Brill, 2003) 79–100.
Reading Law: The Rhetorical Shaping of the Pentateuch (The Biblical Seminar 59; Sheffield: Sheffield Academic Press, 1999).
"Reader Identification and Alienation in the Legal Rhetoric of the Pentateuch," *BibInt* 7/1 (1999) 101–12.
"The Legal Characterization of Moses in the Rhetoric of the Pentateuch," *JBL* 117 (1998) 415–26.
"The Legal Characterization of God in the Pentateuch," *Hebrew Union College Annual* 67 (1996) 1–14.
"Public Readings and Pentateuchal Law," *VT* 45/4 (1995), 540–57.
"Rhetorical Strategy in the Composition of the Pentateuch," *JSOT* 68 (1995) 3–22.

David P. Wright

"Law and Creation in the Priestly-Holiness Writings of the Pentateuch," in K. Schmid/C. Uehlinger (ed.), *Laws of Heaven—Laws of Nature: Legal Interpretations of Cosmic Phenomena in the Ancient World* (OBO 276; Fribourg: Academic Press; Göttingen: Vandenhoeck & Ruprecht, 2016) 71–101, reprinted in this volume, pp. 201-233.
"Source Dependence and the Development of the Pentateuch: The Case of Leviticus 24," in J. Gertz et al. (ed.), *The Formation of the Pentateuch: Bridging the Academic Cultures of Europe, Israel, and North America* (Tübingen: Mohr Siebeck, 2016) 651–82.

"Profane Versus Sacrificial Slaughter: The Priestly Recasting of the Yahwist Flood Story," in R. Gane/A. Taggar-Cohen (ed.), *Current Issues in Priestly and Related Literature: The Legacy of Jacob Milgrom and Beyond* (SBLRBS; Atlanta: SBL, 2015) 125–54.
"Ritual Speech in the Priestly-Holiness Prescriptions of the Pentateuch and its Near Eastern Context," in R. Rollinger/E. van Dongen (ed.), *Mesopotamia in the Ancient World: Impact, Continuities, Parallels: Proceedings of the Melammu Symposium, Obergurgl, Austria, November 2013* (Münster: Ugarit-Verlag, 2015) 107–23.
"Methods of Studying Ancient Law: Ancient Near East/Hebrew Bible," in B. Strawn et al. (ed.), *Oxford Encyclopedia of the Bible and Law* (New York: Oxford University Press, 2015) 2.27–38.
"Ritual Theory, Ritual Texts, and the Priestly-Holiness Writings of the Pentateuch," in S. Olyan (ed.), *Social Theory and the Study of the Israelite Religion: Essays in Retrospect and Prospect* (Atlanta: SBL, 2012) 195–216.
"Leviticus (Translation and Commentary)," in Confraternity of Christian Doctrine/United States Conference of Catholic Bishops (ed.), *The New American Bible Revised Edition.* Various editions: e.g., Charlotte, NC: Saint Benedict Press, 2011, 120–56.
"'She Shall Not Go Free as Male Slaves Do': Developing Views About Slavery and Gender in the Laws of the Hebrew Bible," in B.J. Brooten et al. (ed.), *Beyond Slavery: Overcoming Its Religious and Sexual Legacy* (New York: Palgrave Macmillan, 2010, 125–42.
Inventing God's Law: How the Covenant Code of the Bible Used and Revised the Laws of Hammurabi (Oxford/New York: Oxford University Press, 2009).
"The Study of Ritual in the Hebrew Bible," in F.E. Greenspahn (ed.), *Jewish Studies in the 21st Century* (New York University Press, 2008) 120–38.
"Holiness in Leviticus and Beyond: Differing Perspectives," *Interp.* 53 (1999) 351–64.
"Holiness, Sex, and Death in the Garden of Eden," *Bib.* 77 (1996) 305–29.
"Analogy in Biblical and Hittite Ritual," in K. Koch/B. Janowski/G. Wilhelm (ed.), *Internationales Symposion: Religionsgeschichtliche Beziehungen zwischen Kleinasien, Nord-Syrien und dem Alten Testament im 2. und 1. vorchristlichen Jahrtausend* (OBO 129; Freiburg/Göttingen: Vandenhoeck & Ruprecht, 1993) 473–506.
"Holiness, OT," in D.N. Freedman et al. (ed.), *Anchor Bible Dictionary* (New York: Doubleday, 1992) 3.237–49.
"Unclean/Clean, OT," in D.N. Freedman et al. (ed.), *Anchor Bible Dictionary* (New York: Doubleday, 1992) 6.729–41.
"The Spectrum of Priestly Impurity," in S. Olyan/G. Anderson (ed.), *Priesthood and Cult in Ancient Israel* (JSOTSup 125; Sheffield, England: JSOT Press, 1991) 150–81.
The Disposal of Impurity: Elimination Rites in the Bible and in Hittite and Mesopotamian Literature (SBLDS 101; Atlanta: Scholars Press, 1987).
"The Gesture of Hand Placement in the Hebrew Bible and in Hittite Literature," *JAOS* 106 (1986) 433–46.
"Purification from Corpse Contamination in Num XXXI," *VT* 35 (1985) 213–23.

Index

Hebrew Bible

Qumran and Early Jewish Literature

Other Ancient Sources

New Testament

Rabbinic Works

Subject Index

Select Greek and Hebrew Terms